Coherency Management

Coherency Management

Architecting the Enterprise for Alignment, Agility and Assurance

Gary Doucet
John Gøtze
Pallab Saha
Scott Bernard

IEAi

International Enterprise Architecture Institute

2009

AuthorHouse™
1663 Liberty Drive
Bloomington, IN 47403
www.authorhouse.com
Phone: 1-800-839-8640

First published by AuthorHouse 01/13/2011

ISBN: 978-1-4389-9606-6 (sc)
ISBN: 978-1-4389-9607-3 (hc)
ISBN: 978-1-4567-1626-4 (e)

Library of Congress Control Number: 2009906890

Printed in the United States of America
Bloomington, Indiana

This book is printed on acid-free paper.

authorHOUSE®

ACKNOWLEDGEMENTS

We would collectively like to acknowledge the effort, contribution and support of all of our contributing authors and those that participated in the solicitation for material. It gives us great inspiration to see such intelligence, effort, and sense of common purpose in our EA community. We might have different ideas about the course to take, but we share a common target.

- Gary, John, Pallab, Scott

When I began with the Government of Canada, I was steeped in the "Business Transformation Enablement Program" and as a result, I became extremely business-oriented in my way of thinking about Enterprise Architecture. So, I would like to thank the people responsible for shaping this EA effort. With this as a foundation I was able to enter an exchange of ideas and EA leadership with many around the world and most recently with John, Scott and Pallab in a way many professionals can only hope for. To them, I am most grateful for their support, insights, candor, patience and a shared belief in an idea that EA should now come of age. Thanks ever so much to John Zachman, upon whose shoulders an entire profession seeks to stand. It is only upon considering his words that I can begin to form my own, all the while, hoping I keep to the course he has set for us. I would like to thank the many authors participating with us on this endeavor, for their insights, their support and their patience. While collaborating on the first and last chapters, I drew upon material I've delivered in my role with the Government of Canada, so I would like to acknowledge the Government of Canada and all those that helped with this material. From subject matter experts to managers to reviewers and approvers, it was a group effort. Finally, I am most grateful to my wife Margaret and my children Sheldon, Tyler and Jacqueline who, as always, provided me with the greatest of support during this undertaking.

- Gary Doucet

It has been a privilege and a pleasure to work with my co-editors Gary, Pallab and Scott, on making this book happen. I am grateful to them, and to all the contributing authors, for sharing what must be several hundreds of years of experience with enterprise architecture, and for embracing the coherency management concept. I would like to thank the members and friends of the Association of Enterprise Architects, who have provided a lot of good feedback. I would also like to thank my co-partners in EA Fellows, Allan Bo Rasmussen, Bo Møller, and Torben Deleuran, for stimulating EA-dialogues over the years, and all my students at the IT University of Copenhagen and at the Copenhagen Business School for their encouragement and challenges. Last, but not least, I would also like to thank my parents, Ilse and Mogens Gøtze, for their love and support.

- John Gøtze

So many people deserve thanks that it's hard to know where to start. This book is a culmination of ideas and contributions of many individuals. In particular, I am indebted to my co-editors Gary, Scott and John, who helped bring to life the stories about EA. Personally, I am a 'practicing-academic' and always striving to balance academic rigor with practical relevance. I have been privileged to be involved as a lead author to the Singapore Government's Methodology for Agency Enterprise Architecture (MAGENTA). In many places, ideas that I have learned through various engagements are reflected in this book. I thank all those numerous people who helped shape my own philosophy and practice in EA. I would like to thank my parents, Anima and the Late Jagatbandhu Saha; and my wife, Neeta for their love and patience. This is my third book in four years. My first book was released at the same time when our adorable daughter, Anushka was born. Her journey from being an infant to now being a preschooler has been a great learning experience for me both personally and professionally for which I am grateful to God.

- Pallab Saha

I would like to thank my co-editors; John Gøtze, Gary Doucet, and Pallab Saha for making this book possible and for expanding the concept of what Enterprise Architecture is to now include a focus on Coherency Management as a major outcome objective. Creating formalized architectures for many types of enterprises is increasingly important for them to be able to survive and thrive in highly dynamic operating environments, and this book brings a number of leading-edge views from the editors and contributing authors on how to do this, which hopefully will make it a valuable reference. I would like to thank John Zachman for writing the Foreword to this book, and for being a wonderful mentor and inspiration to me and for 'getting it right' over twenty years ago - in writing the seminal articles that became the foundation for the practice of Enterprise Architecture. I would like to thank John Grasso at Carnegie Mellon University for collaborating on our chapter about the new EA Audit Model and for helping to move the profession of Enterprise Architecture forward by sponsoring a training and certification curriculum, supporting the Journal of Enterprise Architecture, and arranging for speaking opportunities with groups around the world. I would also like to thank my wife Joyce and my children; Bill, Kristen, and Katie who provided great support and understanding during the time it took to help produce this book. Last, but definitely not least, I would like to thank the authors from many different countries who contributed a chapter to this book and the many colleagues from around the world that I have met in the ten years that I have practiced and written on Enterprise Architecture-related concepts and practices. This is still a young profession, and it is growing in importance and acceptance as a meta-approach to integrate strategic, business, and technology planning and decision-making.

- Scott Bernard

CONTENTS

SECTION II
COHERENCY MANAGEMENT IN ACTION:
INSIGHTS FROM ENTERPRISE ARCHITECTURE IMPLEMENTATIONS

FOREWORD

John A. Zachman

This is only 2009 ... we have a lot, *a lot* more to learn about Enterprise Architecture.

It is like any other discipline. At any point in time, the body of knowledge is only so big ... and the bigger the body of knowledge becomes ... the more you know ... the more you don't know!

In 2009 we are only beginning to see some structure in this very important domain of Enterprise Architecture. In fact, I typically argue the case that Enterprise Architecture can no longer be treated as optional. It is mandatory. In 1998, the turn of the new Century, I wrote an article for Database Programming and Design Magazine entitled, "Enterprise Architecture: The Issue of the Century" in which I argued the case that I do not believe that any Enterprise of any substance is going to be viable in the kind of environment in which it has to exist without accommodating the concepts of architecture. Enterprise Architecture may well be the gate the Enterprise has to go through if it intends to stay in the game. I know I am making a somewhat radical assertion but I actually believe this and the logic that supports this assertion is very strong.

The argument centers around the issues of complexity and change. The question boils down to, how do you intend to "assure" that the Enterprise as implemented is "aligned" with the intent of the Executive Leadership and "agile" to accommodate the dynamics of the external environment in the face of extremely escalating complexity and change? Alignment, agility and assurance are not achieved through building and running systems ... they are engineering derived characteristics ... Enterprise engineering derived characteristics. The "raw material" for doing engineering is a set of engineering design artifacts that constitute the descriptive representations of the object being engineered, in this case that constitute Enterprise Architecture.

If you do a survey of 7,000 years of known history to determine how humanity has accommodated two things, complexity and change, you will find that there is only one game in town … architecture. If the object you are trying to create is so complex you cannot see the entire thing at one time at a level of definition required to actually create the object, you have to be able to describe the object … *architecture*. If you can't describe it, you can't create it.

And, after you get the object created and you want to change it, the basis for changing it is *architecture*. If you want to change an object you have already created for which you have no architectural representations, you only have three options … you can change the object by trial and error and see what happens … that is just as high risk because you could make some small changes and possibly lose the whole thing. Or, you can reverse engineer the architectural characteristics from the existing instantiation … that takes time and money. Or, you can scrap the whole thing and start over again.

In short, the key to complexity and change of anything is *architecture*.

It has only been in the last hundred years or so of the Industrial Age that we have seen the development of extremely complex industrial products, hundred story buildings, Boeing 747's, super computers, oceanic cruise ships, etc. This is probably because the older disciplines of Architecture and Construction, Engineering and Manufacturing stopped arguing about what architecture was, accepted standard descriptive representations and started concentrating on how to use the standard engineering design artifacts to actually get creative in building complex industrial products. In the Industrial Age, it was the industrial products that were increasing in complexity and changing. Probably the key to the Industrial Age was architecture … industrial product architecture.

I would suggest that in the Information Age, it is the Enterprise that is increasing in complexity and the Enterprise that is changing and the key to the Information Age is therefore, Enterprise Architecture. I spent most of my professional life trying to define what Enterprise Architecture is and if I did anything of any value, my contribution has been in the form of a Framework, a Framework for Enterprise Architecture. My Framework doesn't do anything … it simply defines what architecture is ... specifically what Enterprise Architecture is. I recently wrote an article for a new electronic newsletter, the Enterprise Information Management Institute (EIMI) newsletter I entitled, "Architecture Is Architecture Is Architecture", in which I argued that architecture, specifically Enterprise Architecture, is not arbitrary and it is not negotiable.

Airplanes, buildings, computers, locomotives, battleships ... Enterprises ... all have bills of materials. They all have functional specifications. They all have geometry ... etc., etc. They all have requirement concepts. They all have design logic. They all have technology physics ... etc., etc. Architecture is architecture is architecture. I think what enables a discipline to accommodate extreme complexity and extreme rates of change is the acceptance of an ontological structure that constitutes the basis for a science in which things become repeatable and predictable. This ontological structure releases the practitioners of the discipline to become creative in addressing extreme complexity and extreme change.

Clearly, my assertion is that there is an ontological structure that constitutes the basis for making Enterprise Architecture a science where methodological practices become repeatable and predictable. It would release the practitioners to focus on escalating complexity and escalating change ... survival characteristics of the Information Age. They could stop arguing about what architecture is and start focusing on how to do it!

The contributors to this work on "Coherency Management" may or may not be familiar with my ontological proposition, the Framework for Enterprise Architecture ... however, in this book there is a very impressive concentration on the practice of Enterprise Architecture. Clearly, the issues of Alignment, Agility and Assurance are engineering derived and I think you will find this piece of work a valuable addition to your professional library for Enterprise survival in the Information Age.

Thank you Scott, Gary, John and Pallab for this very ambitious piece of work.

John A. Zachman
Glendale, California 2009

FOREWORD

John Herhalt

This book opens the door on an exciting new era in the evolution of Enterprise Architecture (EA). For the past three decades Enterprise Architecture has concerned itself with ensuring that well-structured and well-implemented information technology serves business. But now Enterprise Architecture is evolving so that it will assist in the design of successful enterprises.

The paradox of the Information Age is that while information has never been more readily created and distributed, its sheer volume - often distributed in fragmented or incomplete messages - has caused us to lose sight of the overall picture of what we do. EA is evolving into a discipline whereby the enterprise can enhance information so it can provide a coherent vision of where it is going and how it can get there. It can, for the first time since the Information Age began, give managers the insights to prepare not just for transformational change, but also for the ongoing needs of enterprise evolution, even crisis management. It is best described as Coherency Management.

In the coherent enterprise, information is focused and complete, enabling managers to take real, swift, and certain action. They have a magic arrow that pierces only the precise pieces of knowledge required and delivers it to them in a coherent vision. It is much more than technology; it is procedures and practices that evolve with an enterprise's needs. Yet achieving a coherent enterprise is far from easy. How can you tell which services or products will be the most useful? How services should be expanded, where can costs be trimmed, and, in times of crisis, how can results be continuously delivered?

Key methodologies have assisted in the rapid evolution of Coherency Management. A significant contribution was made by Chartwell IRM Inc., a firm that is a leader in helping public sector organizations embrace Enterprise Architecture. Chartwell created reference models with governments and for governments, morphing the science of Enterprise Architecture into a discipline that better informs business decisions, enabling users to answer the above questions. Chartwell developed these reference models to serve as toolkits that underpin Enterprise Architecture practices. In so doing, they have evolved Enterprise Architecture beyond methods of planning technology and its role in business strategy toward a more holistic organizational strategy and planning.

Since then, these models have been embraced and adopted early on by many governments in Canada, providing them with a common language and a highly effective common set of strategic management tools that help with the creation of government business and systems. KPMG's acquisition of Chartwell in early 2009 is a clear signal of its commitment to the betterment of government operations, both nationally and around the world through the use of these advances in Enterprise Architecture.

In keeping with this international perspective, this book draws on the knowledge of authors who are international authorities in Enterprise Architecture. They have come together to share their experiences and insights on the fundamental architecture of Coherency Management and where they believe it is heading. The enterprise of the future will need to respond to complex and rapidly changing environments, and this book provides a glimpse of how that can be accomplished.

The complex evolution of Coherency Management within Enterprise Architecture will be challenging in the years to come, but as this book ably indicates, the potential is truly exciting. Out of the complexity of the Information Age will emerge the kinds of clear and potent insights that can help enable businesses and governments around the world to prepare for change and thrive in a fast-evolving world.

John Herhalt
Canadian Managing Partner
Advisory Services, KPMG LLP

PROLOGUE

Gary Doucet, John Gøtze, Pallab Saha & Scott Bernard

Change is hard; not changing is easier…it just hurts more!

That is to say, we agree with the idea that you must change to survive. It is a law of nature. And right now there are major changes happening, and everybody (people and enterprises) must deal with them. Whether it is the economic crisis of 2009, environmental awareness, globalization, or the information age … things are changing. New ideas are needed in such times. Maybe it is idea of co-creation through globalization as a strategy for continued value creation that C.K. Prahalad talks about, or maybe it's dealing with the 'flat world' as described by Thomas L. Friedman.

Let's look at the "Information Age". We might differ on the exact definition or interpretation, but there can be no doubt that the global economy is moving from and expanding beyond the production of physical goods to the production and trade of information. The growth of Information and Communications Technology over the past 50 years has been evident in all aspects of daily living in developed countries, and is gradually becoming so in the developing world too.

The explosion of information has been unbridled, but it is our contention that the information being created and exchanged lacks the inherent coherency for it to sufficiently support decision-making. In any large organization, numerous reports, designs, descriptions and artifacts describing the activities of the organization can be found, but they are held in different formats, different medium, following different rules for describing and using the same words with different meanings. For example, it recently took several months for a national level government to answer the question: What services do we have that benefit a certain target group? It did not take this long because the information was missing; it was mostly there, but in thousands upon thousands of documents in hundreds of forms and formats. This government is very well run but the example illustrates that a mountain of information (or data) does not actually guarantee knowledge. And it certainly does not provide assurance that things are operating coherently.

It is certainly paradoxical that in the information age, we can collect, process, and exchange mountains of data (documents, pictures, messages, mails, etc) almost instantaneously across vast distances, but at the same time, we suffer from a knowledge deficit or, as Chris Pollitt and others have called it, "Institutional Amnesia".

One could say we are in a period of incoherency within the Information Age. It started a few years ago but it may take some decades to resolve enough for us to say it is no longer a significant issue. This period of incoherency starts with the recognition that we simply have too much information to process. One might say that the unintended plague of the information age is ...information. Not information in and of itself, but rather, incoherent information.

Communication Etiquette

Many people are inundated with information of every sort in their personal and professional lives on a daily basis. We may think it's all too much but we willingly participate in the creation and consumption of huge amounts of information and we set ourselves up for the collapse of "communication etiquette". Communication etiquette used to happen when it was hard to create and distribute knowledge. Back in the days before e-mails and the internet we would ensure our non-verbal communications were complete, in and of themselves. We would check things over and be certain that our requests (and our replies) were correct and complete. Communications would be clearly addressed, provide the necessary context, and usually provide some clear instruction on follow up. Today, you are lucky to know who sent the note, let alone to have sufficient context to allow the note to stand on its own.

With this sort of explosion of information and a lack of care around its management, we easily end up in the state of 'information indecision'. We have all the information we need (e.g. annual plans, contracts, process flows, sales agreements, client research databases, etc), but no information we can use. It simply takes too long to knit it together into a coherent story for decision-making purposes.

We are good at producing and communicating information but it is not easily consumed. It is likely that the information about the collapse of Enron, WorldCom and Lehman Brothers existed well before anyone heard of them; we just never saw the information coherently enough to understand the full picture. It is quite likely that if you had added all the business plans together at the height of the Dot Com boom you would have had clear knowledge of the impending collapse. Maybe we would have seen that, for a reasonable number of the businesses to be successful, the average household would have to have a dozen fully busy high speed internet connections with a total on-line spending of $10 Million a year.

A thousand facts and no information, such is the case as we sit in this period of incoherency. Incoherency makes enterprises less manageable. As Gary Hamel said in *The Future of Management*, "Management is out of date. Like the combustion engine, it's a technology that has largely stopped evolving, and that's not good." We believe that Coherency Management, as a practice within the overall metaframework of Enterprise Architecture, is the next frontier in management innovation that is bound to become a pervasive management practice.

However, the EA profession is mired in a technology paradigm that grossly undersells its capability to bring coherence to the entire business. Infosys recently published a survey in which the major finding is that "Alignment of business and IT organization is the #1 objective of enterprise architecture ..." That is certainly goodness, but how about assuring that all parts of the business are aligned with each other? How about ensuring all the oars are pulling together? According to the same survey, some business-oriented indicators are starting to gain traction. We are here to promote that evolution, something that started years ago with John Zachman.

Competitive Advantage?

John Zachman, the originator of the "Framework for Enterprise Architecture" which has received broad acceptance around the world as an integrative framework, or "periodic table" of descriptive representations for enterprises, tells us we are in the transformation to the Information Age, and that we should leverage something called

Enterprise Architecture (EA). In a recent interview with Roger Sessions, Zachman said, "My opinion is that in the Information Age, it is the Enterprise that is increasing in complexity and changing dramatically and that whoever figures out how to accommodate and exploit Enterprise Architecture concepts and formalism, and therefore can accommodate extreme complexity and extreme change of Enterprise, is likely to dominate the Information Age".

From the perspective of coherency, we would say that managers need a coherent view of things to be successful. Those who do that best will dominate in the information age. You may be familiar with the idea that:

> *You can't manage what you can't see.*

In this Information Age, the phrase needs to go a little further. For thousands of companies and governments around the world that need to survive and thrive the better phrase might be:

> *You can't manage well what you can't see coherently.*

We, too, believe that those that are good with Enterprise Architecture will best address the coherency challenge. There are other disciplines to involve in Coherency Management but Enterprise Architecture provides the key structures, design rigor, techniques and 'science' to make it the cornerstone discipline.

Quite often EA only gets considered as part of a major effort of change. However laudable that might be, this also falls well short of EA's full potential. If we only ever do EA as part of a transformation project, how can EA ever tell us what transformation to make? EA must become pervasive and regularized.

When we talk of coherency for large enterprises it may seem a bit like boiling the ocean or tilting at windmills but, ironically, Coherency Management, in the way we talk about it, is exactly the opposite. It is the practical, stepwise approach to getting superior results and the best possible return on assets. With Coherency Management, managers will understand and design the business better than ever. The oceans of information will continue to be created in ways we can't predict and our need to know things will also change in ways we can't predict. The only thing we know for certain is that the change will be constant and growth will be unrelenting on the demand and supply side of information. The solution is to set up the enterprise such that it continually improves its coherency. A coherent enterprise deals with complexity and change better, and hence is more manageable. For instance, a coherent enterprise is better able to plan and react appropriately in situations of crises. A good example is the difference between the handling of Hurricanes Katrina in 2005 and Gustav in 2008. In 2008, the concerned authorities had open communication lines; information was being processed into actionable knowledge. In short, things were a lot more coherent.

Coherency Applied

As you read on it is important to know some context of application. We are not proposing that enterprises do a 'Coherency' project, and then everything will be better. In considering an improvement to a functioning organization, one approach might be to perform the change (or transformation) as an external influence on an operating organization/system. That is, you might launch a project to make a change. Once that project completes, the functioning organization returns to operating without that external influence.

For example, if a company has too many and incoherent procedures, you could launch a project to change them all in one fell swoop. Once completed, the well-formed set of procedures would likely operate very well, but in a few short months new procedures and changes would creep in to the system, and years later you would be no farther ahead.

Coherency Management proposes that in addition to (or instead of) the conventional approach you consider the system as the target of the change, not the procedures themselves. In this example, you would adjust processes and services in the organization to spot and correct incoherency. This could be in the procedure writing or approval process or maybe in annual assessment models. After making the changes you would observe and determine if the procedures started to rationalize and become more coherent. If not, you would make more adjustments until the system started to self-correct. In this way, the system would continually improve and would not return to incoherent tendencies, at least in regard to procedures.

This then brings us to the role of the Enterprise Architect. Moving forward, we see this role expanding to include a large 'coaching' and/or 'mentoring' aspect. A bulk of the architecting work will actually be done by line managers and their team themselves. This is a massive shift as compared to what we are used to now. Our assertion is that such a shift would eventually (and literally) make EA the mastery of the 'architecture of the enterprise'.

Call to Action

Ten years ago, in *The Next Common Sense*, Lissack & Roos wrote that:

> *"The mastery we are alluding to is that of the craftsman, not that of the M in MBA. The ability to act coherently in the face of complexity, and to do so on an ongoing basis, is the hallmark of a true master. ... Coherence is the key to mastering complexity because it is the enabling force that allows conscious intention to replace inertia, overload, and unconscious flailing about. It is all too easy to let complexity get the better of you. Coherence offers you the alternative of mastery - but the choice is yours."*

This book is for those who choose mastery.

Although Enterprise Architecture is a few decades old, evolving it to include Coherency Management is a new idea. As such, this book seeks to present ideas, start dialogues, and launch the evolutionary development process.

We invite you to contribute to the conversation and evolution via our website at www.coherencymanagement.org. As we gradually extend and expand the ideas and application of Coherency Management, we will break through this period of incoherency and maximize the full potential of the Information Age.

With a coherent enterprise, knowledge will be complete, understanding will be real, and action can therefore be swift and certain. This will certainly help private sector organizations compete well in the global economy, but the altruistic value should not be forgotten. With Coherency Management, public sector organizations will dramatically improve effectiveness and efficiency. When all orders of government start saving time and money, they will be able to invest in new outcomes for their constituents.

In our first step to formalize Coherency Management within Enterprise Architecture, we published a paper "Coherency Management - Using Enterprise Architecture for Alignment, Agility and Assurance" in the May 2008 issue of the Journal of Enterprise Architecture. We received excellent comments to that paper.

Continuing our journey, we now take the next step in this nascent practice. In the spirit of co-creation and globalization, we invited co-authors from around the world. Hence, the book is a compilation of chapters that have been carefully selected. Each chapter discusses a different facet of enterprise architecture and/or coherency management. As editors, we wanted the readers to know why these chapters were selected and included in the book. We have, thus, provided brief introductions to every chapter summarizing our rationale for their inclusion.

If you:

-   feel stifled by indecisiveness and consequent inaction,
-   are tired of duplicate or wasted effort,
-   feel you manage in a knowledge vacuum whilst being surrounded by information,
-   can't get your organization to respond to challenges quick enough,
-   haven't got enough time to process all your information, or
-   would like to know you if are doing the right things and doing things right ...

... then this book is for you because incoherency may be the root cause of your problems. With Coherency Management we are beginning to understand that now, and we believe this is just the commencement.

Welcome aboard!!

Chapter 1

INTRODUCTION TO COHERENCY MANAGEMENT: THE TRANSFORMATION OF ENTERPRISE ARCHITECTURE

Gary Doucet, John Gøtze, Pallab Saha & Scott Bernard

Editors' Preface

An earlier version of this chapter originally appeared in the Journal of Enterprise Architecture in May 2008 (www.aeajournal.org). The article was written because the four editors of this book recognized the need to talk about a change that was happening to enterprise architecture. More and more often, it is being used as the overarching framework for business design, not just as a form of capturing business requirements, but in a way that allows business owners to exchange their services, processes and strategies with a scientific-like approach. More recent development saw EA tools getting used by process owners quite far apart from the traditional CIO circles and allowing enterprises to better plan and report every aspect of their business.

This chapter formed the basis of the solicitation that went out to EA leaders throughout the world as we looked for others to contribute to this book. It also formed the starting point for the last chapter which acted as a catalyst for many conversations and evolutionary thought among the invited authors. We hope this book acts the same way for you.

Introduction

More information does not mean better knowledge. In fact, Hebert Spencer is known to have said "When a man's knowledge is not in order, the more of it he has the greater will be his confusion." He was a British social philosopher and he lived up until 1903. This was a half-century before the birth of information technology, before we developed the ability to store billions of pages of information, access it in milliseconds and send it around the world on a whim. Before all of this, he knew that lack of 'order' causes confusion and *more* does not mean *better* unless it comes in order.

This is a book dedicated to bringing order to our knowledge and our communications. It is about managing your business, government, or enterprise in a way that enables you to answer familiar questions like:

"Are we doing the right things?" and "Are we doing things right?"

This book, like many on the subject, will discuss technology and that will be of interest to technology managers, but the subject of this book goes well beyond technology. Great technology built on a foundation of poor knowledge will simply expose our disorder faster and in ways that Herbert Spencer could never have imagined. Coherency Management is not a technology story per se. It is a story about solving confusion and delivering coherence regardless of the media or medium.

CEO's need to know how well things are working; they want to maximize ROI, reduce profit leakage and they want the information simply! They and every stakeholder need to know:

- How effective and efficient is the organization?

- How is this measured and how does this relate to real loss?

- Do I have gaps and overlaps in my plans, services, policies, processes, or technology?

- What do I need to fix? How do I do it?

To answer any of these questions holistically (and we would argue that is the only way to answer these) you first need to see things in a structured way. You need to see apples for apples. To do this, you need to have a disciplined and structured approach that helps you to understand and to plan things in a holistic sense. For this, the field of **Enterprise Architecture** is ideally suited.

COHERENCY MANAGEMENT

Understanding Enterprise Architecture[1]

The field of Enterprise Architecture is quite scientific in nature with highly specialized words, models and concepts and, as such, it can seem unconnected to the average person. This is a major problem for something that should inform and influence the work of so many. To help get past this hurdle we have a "lay speak" way of looking at Enterprise Architecture.

First: What is Architecture?

Almost everything that humans create or build requires some sort of description so that those doing the building know what to build. For our purposes, we call these descriptions 'Architecture'. Descriptions can be in textual and/or graphical format; words and/or pictures to describe how to build whatever is being built, be it a bridge, a house, a plane, etc. It explains the parts and how they fit together to form a coherent whole. If it is a simple birdhouse, it may be acceptable to hold the architecture in your head, which makes it implicit architecture. Once it gets a little more complex, then you might want to write it down which makes it explicit architecture. If the house needs a change (e.g. a modification to stop the squirrels) then the architecture will need to be adjusted. Hence, it is important to have a current version of the architecture if you are planning any changes.

Second: What is Enterprise Architecture?

An Enterprise Architecture is the architecture (words and pictures) that describes a functioning organization (company, government, business line, department ...). In order for the architecture to allow us to build or change the functioning organizations it would have to

---

[1] The "lay speak" definition of EA is based on Doucet (2008).

include all the key descriptions such as the mission statement, organization design, business plan, job descriptions, process models, workflows, system specifications, information models, etc. **Note that this is far more than technology descriptions!**

For instance, in the case of setting up a franchise business, the 'architecture' for the enterprise would be all the words and pictures in sufficient detail for the entrepreneur to build (or have built) the business and to start selling to customers. This is different than the architecture for a house because of the dynamic nature of the resources involved. Buildings are comprised of wood, steel and concrete whereas people are a big part of any functioning enterprise. People are much more dynamic than wood or steel so things constantly change. That is why Enterprise Architecture can be more difficult to keep current than other forms of architecture (e.g. House, Bridge…).

It then follows that if the Enterprise Architecture is really all those things, then the practitioners of Enterprise Architecture have a huge task before them. That is, bringing structure and coherence to all these descriptive and planning processes and then helping the leaders of the Enterprise make the right decisions for evolution, growth and sustainability.

This leads us to establishing the following definition of Enterprise Architecture:

> *Enterprise Architecture is the inherent design and management approach essential for organizational coherence leading to alignment, agility and assurance.*

The following are the key ideas/words in the definition:

Inherent: The structured way of designing and managing the organization should be intrinsic and essential (and not something extrinsic or additional) to the organization's activities. This leads to the idea of 'embeddedness'.

Design and Management Approach: The intent here is to capture the idea that EA is to be used for broader design and management of enterprises (not just IS/IT). Approach is used as a generic term. In realizing the 'approach', organizations can manifest it as frameworks, models, blueprints, strategies, policies, principles, structures and practices as may be most effec-

COHERENCY MANAGEMENT

tive. A possible realization of the design and management approach could be the Zachman Framework, which is an ontology for describing the enterprise.

Organizational Coherence: The logical, orderly and consistent relation of the parts to the whole represents the primary goal of the EA. Again, referring to the Zachman Framework as an ontology, provides a mechanism to link the various parts of the enterprise, interconnecting concerns (columns) and stakeholders (rows).

Alignment: This refers to the ability of the organization to operate as ONE by working towards a common shared vision supported by a well orchestrated set of strategies and actions.

Agility: This refers to the ability of the organization to respond to and manage change.

Assurance: This refers to the ability of the organization to establish and institutionalize (internalize) practices that ensure fulfillment of organizational goals and achievement of outcomes.

Current literature in EA lists several other benefits like business-IT alignment, standardized business processes, business and process flexibility, business transformation, IT cost reduction, operating cost reduction, application maintenance cost reduction, business risk management, senior management satisfaction, and quality of service improvements, among many others. These, in our view, are intermediate benefits contributing towards the primary benefits and outcomes briefly described above.

Evolution of Enterprise Architecture

Enterprise Architecture, as a named discipline, has only been around for 30 years and despite its tremendous promise, few would argue that it is a promise unfulfilled as of yet. This book introduces the concept of Coherency Management as a practice within Enterprise Architecture (EA), to help manage confusion out of the enterprise, to help business owners make the right decisions, and to allow organizations to transform with confidence.

There are thousands of books on improving business management as well as many on the subject of Enterprise Architecture. These all speak to business design, strategy, alignment, structure, order, etc. Why is this different? This is different because:

- It introduces science to a traditionally non-scientific part of corporations and governments.

- A major tenant of this book is that we recognize that EA is NOT really new. It was always there. It needs to be better (structured, consistent, and clear) and should be led by Enterprise Architects but it, in fact, involves many people actually doing the EA.

- Enterprise Architecture is now being viewed as a part of other processes for the sake of their benefit, not only because it helps with the Technologist's need to understand someone else's need (e.g. Systems Developers).

- The people involved in making the enterprise coherent (i.e. doing and improving the architecture) will be numerous. It won't only be done by a small elite group of specialists.

- Coherency Management will, when mature, reduce its own footprint.

The questions like 'What should we do?" and "How does this fit?" will be answerable, on a scientific basis.

Coherency Management represents a significant point of evolution in the design and management of all enterprises. This includes, and is especially beneficial for, highly dynamic organizations that sometimes have chaotic operating environments. The concept of Coherency Management is about using Enterprise Architecture (EA) to advance alignment, agility, and assurance in large, complex organizations. The essence of this concept is that the architecture (words and pictures) of enterprises should become consistently structured, formalized, and used to attain coherency. The best way to do this is to adopt EA as the ongoing, overarching method for describing, abstracting, analyzing, designing, and re-engineering new and existing enterprises - regardless of the market, industry, or government sector. Most importantly, it is about EA becoming pervasive.

We see EA as the primary capability for Coherency Management. Enterprise Architecture was originally viewed as a discipline related to technology because technologists need to understand the business in structured ways before they can automate it. Computer programs cannot deal with abstract concepts, they need clear and precise explanations of the business and EA has always held that promise. However, this has meant that business people have viewed EA as a tool that the CIO uses to do his/her work. This is changing; it is becoming clear to some progressive leaders that a clear and well-structured understanding of the business, services, processes etc is useful for business people too. Not only for the development of systems, but to help manage change in the business, to help with mergers and acquisitions, to help with downsizing, right-sizing, growth planning, and economic troubles. No longer is it only the CIO that cares about a good business design, it is now a concern of the CEO and everyone that sits at the CEO table.

EA is about much more than technology! It has strategic and business dimensions, all of which must align to create agility and assurance in promoting transformation and delivering value. EA is still a young and evolving management discipline and therefore is uniquely able to serve as the "meta"-approach for designing and/or redesigning enterprises to successfully compete in highly dynamic public and private sector environments.

The term "enterprise" encompasses any area of systematic and purposeful human activity. The term "architecture", when used in the context of abstracting the enterprise to identify scope, function and relationships, includes the frameworks, methods and artifacts that describe the design and function of enterprises in current and future states. Architecture is often implemented at the enterprise, business unit, service, and system levels in a consistent manner, which allows for decomposition and aggregation.

EA has the potential to facilitate alignment of strategy, business, and technology elements across the entire enterprise, and can provide the context and standards for implementing a number of industry and government best practices including strategic planning, capital planning, service-oriented architecture, information technology infrastructure libraries, knowledge management, program management, security controls, internal controls, quality management and human capital management (Bernard, 2005; Saha, 2007).

We use coherence as a term that speaks to a logical, orderly, and consistent relation of parts to the whole. This the central theme of this book, which is about how to design and operate complex enterprises that must continually adapt to changes in mission and market conditions.

Coherency management has three fundamental outcomes:

- **Alignment** - a term that covers the need for all parts (people, process and technology) of an organization to be working together. An important concept for complex enterprises that are composed of a number of lines of business and business functions with competing priorities and limited resources. It underlines the need for similarity in EA methods at all levels/areas of the architecture.

- **Agility** - a term that addresses an enterprise's ability to manage change, and a concept that is essential for the survival of enterprises operating in dynamic environments where change is constant and windows for important opportunities now open and close in weeks, days, and even hours, where customer expectations are driven by increasing choices in providers and access to best-of-breed service delivery as well as new technologies that improve many facets of everyday life.

- **Assurance** - a term that addresses control, and a concept that speaks to confidence and fidelity in the sources and use of enterprise products and services, as well as the resources that create them. This fits well with the need for transparency and accountability as well, which is increasingly a concern for public sector and more recently private sector organizations.

While alignment, agility, and assurance are the outcomes of managing coherence, the means for achieving this is the use of EA as a methodology. Figure 1 below shows these relationships.

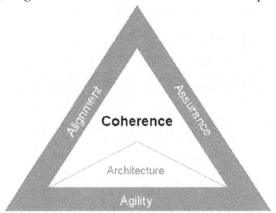

Figure 1. Coherency Management

In the final section of their book *Enterprise Architecture as Strategy*, authors Ross, Weill and Robertson state that "Enterprise Architecture (EA) in many companies refers to a detailed blueprint of systems, data and technology (Ross et al., 2006). It is now clear that EA is instead a business vision. EA begins at the top – with a statement of how an enterprise operates – and results in a foundation of IT and business process capabilities on which it builds its competitiveness." EA continues to evolve and mature as an area of theory and practice. It continues to influence a number of management and technology areas and disciplines, directly and indirectly.

Metaphorically, an EA is to an organization's operations and systems as a set of blueprints is to a building. As IT departments build systems, they create legacies based on business assumptions that might no longer hold true. By following an architecture-based approach to systems development, organizations strive to address several IT issues. Though EA is often assumed to follow business strategy, to align IT with business's strategic objectives, increasingly evidence of business strategies depending on IT capabilities are also surfacing. Defining, describing and deploying EA is a large and complex undertaking that allows enterprises to:

1. Understand business operations and uncover deeply embedded business rules,

2. Elevate the role of information within the organization and treat it as a core asset,

3. Understand gaps between the information needs of the business and the information provided by processes and systems,

4. Create synergies between available and stable technologies and emerging technologies, and

5. Leverage technologies to discover and take advantage of new business opportunities.

These in turn allow organizations to be more agile when need arises.

Enterprise Architecture provides significant business benefits to many types of enterprises, many of which demonstrate a high degree of capability and discipline in areas such as strategic planning, policy design and execution, technology planning and standardization, knowledge and data management, enterprise integration, program management, service management, portfolio management, and system development life cycle management. Many of these best practices also embody and contain a number of critical success factors for the enterprise (Gøtze & Östberg, 2007). Despite incorporating best practices, many enterprises still allow key business units to define their own priorities, workflow, standards, and budgets, which often lead to 'silo' or 'stovepipe' programs, services, and systems within and between the business units. It is clearly evident that this approach leads to sub-optimization in the enterprise as the full benefit of common standards and collaboration opportunities are not realized across the enterprise. Advancing the current EA body of knowledge and state of practice is imperative because:

- Many current EA programs are primarily driven by the IT/IS-department.

- EA is often reduced to IT centric architecture and hence relegated as 'yet another technology initiative'.

- Organizational levers lead to higher degree of management attention and as a consequence greater sustainability of the EA program, and

- Active participation by individual functions and departments and contribution to overall enterprise-wide architecture is critical to the success of the EA program.

EA is not just about creating good documentation (aka artifacts). Good artifacts serve no purpose if not utilized. That is, in fact, the bane of many EA efforts. EA is about good governance and a disciplined approach. As far as artifacts are concerned, our take is that you should leverage on what you already do or produce. What enterprises need to ensure is that the artifacts serve the objectives (with minimal adaptation). Hence any structure/format/rules in creating artifacts should be used as soft guidelines, not prescriptions. What EA provides is a unifying and alignment mechanism focused towards a common vision for the enterprise.

We see that today EA is highly isolated, detached, and disconnected from the rest of the enterprise (with the exception of the IT department). The primary reason for the disconnectedness is that most (if not all) EA programs are still driven by the CIO/IT Department (Gøtze & Christiansen, 2007). In such situations, the credibility of the IT department (and its perceived role in the enterprise) is a critical factor in characterizing the EA program. As a result, current EA tends to eventually reduce itself to Enterprise IT Architecture, at times with a strong business focus. We envisage EA being much more than that.

A plethora of practices and programs often leads to confusion, resentment and cynicism towards anything new, EA included. Typical response in such scenarios includes furious efforts to measure and demonstrate the value of EA programs. It is also typical for EA programs not to be tightly coupled to other relevant management practices. The positioning of and linkages to and from EA vis-à-vis other relevant upstream and downstream management practices need to be accomplished following careful analyses of current and future practices. For example; Human Resource Management and EA are rarely tightly coupled but HR produces very important parts of the EA on a regular basis (job descriptions, org designs, resource profiles, etc). Perhaps we'll know EA is reaching its audience when it is the keynote address at an HR practitioners meeting.

The EA process is not restricted to "transformation". If EA is done only when something else says that the enterprise needs to change then EA will never say when the enterprise needs to change. EA is inherently designed as a strategic management tool that allows organizations to realize the Integrated Enterprise Life Cycle. The approach taken is to weave in EA and position it within existing management practices and leverage upon them instead of designing the EA program as a separate line of activity. This approach allows enterprises to maintain linkages between their respective functional strategies and plans. However, as an enhancement, the EA layer between corporate strategy and implementation facilitates common standards, requirements, principles and effective governance and control (not limited to IT alone). EA is intended to allow enterprises to move towards shallower 'silos' and seek greater collaboration opportunities. Within an enterprise, leveraging on other management practices ensures continuity and sustainability in the EA program, and tighter vertical and horizontal alignment.

The authors advocate the use of EA to promote the coherent management of enterprises. Since the introduction of early EA concepts by John Zachman in the late 1980's (Zachman, 1989), this discipline has evolved into three primary modes of being practiced: Foundation Architecture; Extended Architecture, and Embedded Architecture. Balanced Architecture is a term that is used in this paper to describe when an enterprise utilizes the best and the most appropriate characteristics of each of the three modes of EA. The authors believe that is unlikely that any organization has yet reached a level of maturity in their EA program so as to have a truly balanced architecture state.

The Three Modes of Enterprise Architecture

To illustrate the three modes, let us first consider an enterprise that is new to EA. This scenario is depicted in Figure 2 below.

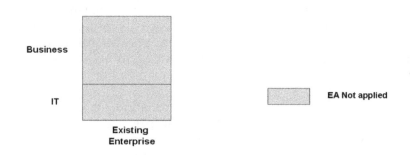

Figure 2. Enterprise Architecture Not Applied to an Enterprise

Even without EA as a named discipline, the enterprise exists, and is operational. It does business, and it probably has some Information Technology. However, it does not manage enterprise-wide coherency. It performs poorly (or at best it is unsure of its performance) when it comes to alignment, agility and assurance.

Then there was a very interesting paper on something called Enterprise Architecture and because it made a lot of sense, people added EA to their functioning enterprise. At this point the Foundation Mode of Enterprise Architecture commenced.

Foundation Architecture

The most common and classical form of EA is what we call Foundation Architecture. The EA is most often done to align IT to the business. The Foundation Architecture can be seen in the most widely accepted definition of EA provided by Ross, Weill and Robertson where "EA is defined as the organizing logic for an organization's core business processes and IT capabilities captured in a set of policies and technical choices, to achieve business standardization and integration requirements of the firm's operating model". Figure 3 depicts the Foundation Architecture graphically along with its primary purpose.

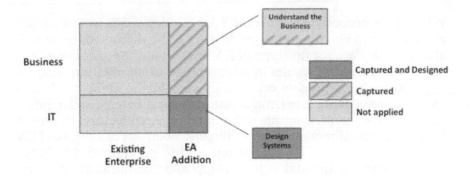

**Figure 3. Foundation Architecture
- Aligning Business and IT**

Within Foundation Architecture there are two levels of maturity. The first level is where the organization's IT architecture is documented for the entire enterprise in its current and future states. The focus is on well-architected, well-designed IT systems with enterprise-level alignment, interoperability, and efficiency. Accordingly, this level of Foundation Architecture is very IT-centric, and for many enterprises EA is still viewed as this type of data and technology architecture, just that it is being implemented at the enterprise level. This is very beneficial in many ways and should be a priority for firms with any sort of an IT investment. It helps save money, improves services and streamlines the business itself with the use of concepts such as federated patterns, standards for interoperability and common solutions. However, an enterprise-wide view of information and information technology, by definition, does not address enterprise-wide concerns from a business, service and strategy perspective.

At the second level of maturity, in addition to providing descriptions of IT systems across the enterprise, the business of the enterprise is captured in a standardized and consistent manner. This well understood business description then forms the input and provides the context for well designed IT systems and applications. The value of EA is measured according to the success of investments in IT and their alignment to business requirements. Figure 3 illustrates this concept of capturing the business for the sake of IT – Business Alignment. A mature Foundation practice will have a well-documented Enterprise Business Architecture. It will, usually, be managed by the CIO as a basis for understanding requirements.

When done properly 'Foundation' EA provides excellent value to an enterprise and even with the other ways to be discussed, there will always be a place for this type of EA. Ross et al (2006) said that "Enterprise architecture results in a foundation of information technology and business process capabilities on which a company builds its competitiveness." The United States' Federal Enterprise Architecture (FEA) is a good example of Foundation Architecture. Designed to fulfill the requirements of the Clinger-Cohen Act of 1996, the FEA is primarily a CIO / IT department centric program (Saha, 2008). The agencies are mandated to develop and communicate their respective EAs to the Office of Management and Budget for the purposes of justifying IT budgets. This represents the control mechanism built within the EA program to realize architecture governance.

Extended Architecture

The concepts of Extended Architecture came about in the late 1990's and focused on engineering an entire enterprise from an integrated strategy, business, and technology perspective. It is an expanded view to the earlier described Foundation Architecture. To support this expanded view of EA, a number of approaches and tools were developed to provide standardized, repeatable methods for describing an enterprise in all dimensions - beyond just the IT perspective. Whereas Foundation Architecture used architecture methods and tools to capture business requirements in order to design better IT systems, in the Extended approach, architecture methods and tools capture strategic goals and related business requirements in order to design the enterprise. Figure 4 depicts the Extended Architecture.

It should be noted that the only difference between Foundation and Extended is the purpose and utility of the Enterprise Business Architecture (EBA). Whereas, Foundation's EBA was used by the CIO to understand requirements, the Extended's EBA is done by business managers wanting to redesign their business. When done, the EBA will certainly be used by the CIO but that is only after the business people have used it to redesign their business.

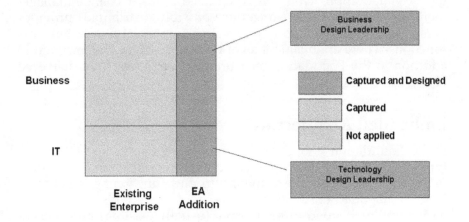

**Figure 4. Extended Architecture
- Driving Business Transformation**

The following represents illustrations of how Extended Architecture uses architecture methods and tools to capture strategic goals and related business requirements in order to design the enterprise.

- Line of business and program owners use the Extended Architecture concepts to transform business units and services.

- Executives use Extended Architecture to ensure consistency between policy instruments and to measure alignment between strategy, business, and technology initiatives.

- Senior management and audit use Extended Architecture to review the effectiveness of business lines and programs.

- Human Resource managers use Extended Architecture to ensure that processes and products for managing human capital are consistent, effective, and aligned.

- IT managers use Extended Architecture to ensure that their systems and investments are properly aligned to business goals and strategic direction.

An interesting example of Extended Architecture is the Canadian Government's Business Transformation Enablement Program which, by its very name, can be seen as a tool to help program owners transform their business (Treasury Board of Canada, 2004). With the Extended approach, EA is recognized as a key change management tool and the EA organization (possibly distributed) provides greater and greater value to a growing number of non-IT business functions. There are business level valuations of the EA program in addition to the Foundation measurement of successfully delivered IT.

Embedded Architecture

In the Foundation and Extended modes of EA, artifacts (various types of documentation) are created as the result of an EA process or method, somewhat extraneous to the functioning enterprise. With Embedded EA, architecture tools, methods, and models become embedded in the normal (usually existing) processes of the day. Rather than relying on processes and people extraneous to the business programs (and their processes), the architecture is produced by the processes themselves. In this way, the architecture is organic and ever greened naturally. Shown in Figure 5, the existing enterprise produces well architected artifacts (illustrated by the grid pattern) which then allows the EA addition to shrink to a steady state where the predominate activities are:

Design leadership

Given that so many process owners will be creating parts of the Enterprise Architecture, it is critical for the EA leader(s) to have framed the overall architecture and to have all the rules established which allows the process owners to easily create artifacts that follow the standard and fit the overall vision.

Alignment

As process owners create descriptions and designs, the EA Leader(s) will continually assess the alignment of the artifacts to the standards, the overall vision/framework and other artifacts being created concurrently.

Examples of Embedded Architecture are:

- Annual planning artifacts that employ architecturally aligned rules for how annual plans are expressed. That is, they follow the normative models (e.g. Reference models) for expressing what the business is about, their clients, goals, objectives, etc.

- All human resource artifacts are created according to EA rules. This means that organization charts get refreshed regularly, and when they do, they are expressed in a way that supports enterprise wide views of roles and responsibilities.

- Artifacts from different processes are interoperable to support cross-functional decision support and business design. For example, process maps leverage EA standards which allow them to be linked to job descriptions which, in turn, link to organizational design artifacts and business plans. With these types of linkages, an analysis to determine the security implications of using an externally delivered service can be made much more efficiently.

- Web service catalogues get updated with every release of online services and are categorized according to the same models which define the annual budget. In this way a user can come to the web pages and be profiled according to the same way services are profiled and the services can be dynamically combined based on their fit. And just in case the users are curious, they can see how much this service and/or all services for their community costs on an annual basis.

- Strategic planning uses methods and common language to ensure a holistic plan which aligns to all other key players in the planning arena. (e.g., the strategic plan uses outcome logic models which every division leader / functional head can link into).

- Public reporting uses terms and language which is consistent throughout the enterprise. (e.g., services for youth can be identified as such, costed consistently, and results determined consistently - whereas all process owners currently use their own categorization for their customers making aggregate analysis impossible).

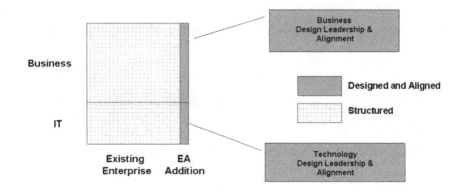

Figure 5. Embedded Architecture
For Designing and Managing the Enterprise

With Embedded Architecture, evaluation of the EA program becomes a matter of assessing how well all parts of the enterprise are working with each other. Embedded Architecture enables the greatest degree of enterprise coherence but is admittedly a longer road to travel, although it is ultimately more comprehensive and holistic. It does not mean enterprises cannot start, because every single process brought into alignment brings a degree of more coherence. To be truly on top of the game enterprises, however, all three modes of EA need to be going on simultaneously.

A project or a program should not be the reason to develop EA. The architecture should already be there and be usable by the project and an organization's EA should be context neutral. Embedded Architecture demands that CFOs, CTOs, Chief Planners, Chief Strategists, and HR Managers embed the EA discipline so that they produce well architected artifacts as a product from their normal routine, not only for the sake of the project or the EA effort in and of itself. There are many regulations, acts, policies, and procedures causing organization and departments within those organizations to file artifacts of every stripe but they do not have the necessary rules/constructs to be useful for generalized purposes. Rather than developing a new report, the embedded approach expects enterprises to get the existing reports to be more multi-purpose. EA can be used to ensure artifacts achieve higher degrees of reusability. The unintended benefit of coherent artifacts is the reduction of the reporting burden which plagues many large enterprises today. This mode of EA needs minimal additional engagement mechanisms and the program is able to sustain itself.

In the embedded approach, the strategic goals drive business requirements, which drive technology solutions. Here, not only is the level of EA elevated to include strategy, but the ubiquitous (organic) nature of the architecture is acknowledged as well. The architecture of an enterprise exists in all dimensions, whether it is acknowledged as such or not, and EA makes all aspects of the organic architecture explicit by formalizing the relationships between strategic, business, and technology views across all operating units with the ultimate intent of making better enterprises.

Summary

One interesting aspect of the progression of EA thought and practice is that it has largely been a process of accumulation, not replacement. This means that the concepts about how to improve the planning and implementation of IT systems that grew out of the first way to do EA are still applicable and work well with the business design and integration concepts of the "Extended" mode. These are also critical activities to advance the coherence needed in the Embedded Architecture. Hence, EA thought and practice is an accumulation of ideas and methods that have come together to form a body of knowledge that can be used to holistically understand, optimize and create enterprises of many types. The ideas captured in each of the modes of EA can be viewed as independent, and are applicable to enterprises either alone or in combination. In other words, they are not mutually exclusive. Such advancement in EA thinking takes it to the next level of maturity. In some cases, an attempt to rapidly implement this multi-modal approach to EA programs can be disruptive to enterprises. Indeed EA only has its tremendous value when done properly. It is the opinion of the authors that EA researchers and practitioners must do to themselves that which they seek to do to others; that is, manage their change and the change they introduce to the enterprise with EA. Figure 6 below summarizes the modes of EA described above. The key distinguishing characteristics are also depicted.

	Foundation Architecture	Extended Architecture	Embedded Architecture
Strategic Drivers (Why do we do it?)	→ Technology and business standardization → Systems engineering → IT asset utilization	→ Business transformation → Product / service leadership → Business agility → Enterprise engineering	→ Enterprise design & management → Enabled agility → Service oriented enterprise → Ubiquity
Locus of Control (Who leads the programme?)	→ CIO / IT Organization	→ CXO involved during change → Business architects / process owners	→ CXO involved all the time
Critical Management Innovation (How is it accomplished?)	→ Architecture by compliance → Replacement approach → Flexible program intensity and cope → Project oriented	→ Enterprise business architecture → Organizational improvements → Architecture by push with extraneous processes → Actionable architecture	→ Organic design → Architecture by pull with intrinsic processes → Architecture is everyone's job → Management DNA → Outcome driven
Key Governance Mechanisms (What is used to accomplish?)	→ Specialized EA team → Project business cases → Architecture review board → Led by CIO	→ Cross-institutional governance → Value based tracking → Business leadership in IT projects → Led by CXO	→ Diffused architecture team → Enterprise architecture by stealth → Context neutrality → Led by CXO, but not separately
Programme Metrics (How is it measured?)	→ Cost efficiency → IT responsiveness → IT risk management → Business-IT alignment	→ Time to market → Business responsiveness → Strategic alignment → Coherency in IT and non-IT space	→ Aligned organization → Decision capability → Shared delivery → Comprehensive service excellence
Benefits & Outcomes (What do we get?)	→ Shared technology platforms → Economies of scale → Better systems design	→ Shared business platforms → Business value of IT → Better information governance	→ Better corporate governance → Deeper engagement → Coherent enterprise → Unnoticeable EA effort

■ ■ ■ Balanced ■ ■ ■
(Alignment, Agility, Assurance)

Figure 6. Characteristics for the Three Modes of Enterprise Architecture

Conclusion

This chapter introduced the idea of Coherency Management but the primary discussion was Enterprise Architecture and the three modes of EA. The last chapter will present what else might be done in addition to the three modes of EA to achieve coherency and it will move Coherency Management to the center of the conversation. It will introduce a proposal for a Coherency Management Framework and other aspects of this practice within the EA program. The intervening chapters are written by EA leaders from around the world discussing successes and ideas they have in regards to EA. Some chapters will be narrowly focused on a particular business problem whereas other chapters will present where EA is going and in some cases this is discussed in relation to the three modes of EA.

Coherency Management proposes that existing and new EA practices in the foundation, extended, and embedded areas should be used synergistically to achieve coherence in complex organizations. The focus on coherence requires that an EA extend beyond technology solutions and business requirements, to include the strategic goals that drive the enterprise. Like Occam's razor, the value proposition of coherence management is that it is helpful to stakeholders when complex entities are made simpler and therefore are more understandable. Managing coherence through EA promotes alignment, agility, and assurance which make the enterprise more capable and competitive.

We foresee the evolution of Coherency Management into a critical function of corporate and public sector management. There will be clear, measurable, and obtainable targets. There will be a program of continuous improvement for coherency and Enterprise Architecture will be the cornerstone of the coherent enterprise.

References

Bernard, S. (2005). An Introduction to Enterprise Architecture. Second Edition. AuthorHouse: Bloomington, IL.

Bernard, S. (2006). Using Enterprise Architecture to Integrate Strategy, Business, and Technology Planning. Journal of Enterprise Architecture. Volume 2, Number 4.

Gøtze, J. and Christiansen, E. (2007). Trends in Government Enterprise Architecture - Part 1. Journal of Enterprise Architecture. Volume 3, Number 1.

Gøtze, J. and Östberg, O. (2007). Interoperability, Change, and Architecture. ICA Study Group Report. International Council for Information Technology in Government Administration.

IFIP-IFAC Task Force (1999). GERAM: Generalized Enterprise Reference Architecture and Methodology, IFIP-IFAC Task Force on Architectures for Enterprise Integration, Version 1.6.3, (March).

Morabito, J., Sack, I. and Bhate, A. (1999). Organization Modeling: Innovative Architectures for the 21st Century. Prentice Hall PTR: Upper Saddle River, NJ.

Ross, J., Weill, P., and Robertson, D. (2006). Enterprise Architecture as Strategy. Harvard Business School Press: Boston, MA.

Saha, P. (2006). A Real Options Perspective to Enterprise Architecture as an Investment Activity. Journal of Enterprise Architecture. Volume 2, Number 3.

Saha, P. (2007). Handbook of Enterprise Systems Architecture in Practice. IGI Global Information Science Reference: Hershey, PA.

Saha, P. (2008). Advances in Government Enterprise Architecture. IGI Global Information Science Reference: Hershey, PA.

Treasury Board of Canada (2004). Business Transformation Enablement Program. http://tinyurl.com/asrckh.

Treasury Board of Canada (2008). EA@GC: Enterprise Architecture at the Government of Canada. Gary Doucet, Chief Architect. Presentation at World Bank conference "Government Enterprise Architecture as Enabler of Public Sector Reform" Washington D.C., U.S.A., 17 April 2008.

United States Congress (1996). The Information Technology Management Reform Act of 1996 (renamed the Clinger-Cohen Act). Public Law 104-106, Division E.

United States Federal Enterprise Architecture Program Management Office (2006). FEA Consolidated Reference Model, Version 2.0. Federal CIO Council.

Zachman, J. (1989). A Framework for Information Systems Architecture. IBM Systems Journal. Volume 26, Number 3

About the Authors

Gary Doucet is the Chief Architect of the Federal Government in Canada. He is serving a two-year term as Vice President of a l EA International and is the past president of the Canadian Chapter. Gary came to EA after nearly twenty years with ICT, doing everything from programming to project management. He got serious about EA when he came to the federal government in 2003 to revitalize the architecture program, which had directed most of its energy supporting Canada's very successful GOL (Government On Line) program. He reports directly to the Federal CIO in the Treasury Board Secretariat (TBS), which for those of you that don't know is quite similar to the U.S. Office of Management and Budget. Gary can be contacted at Gary.Doucet@rogers.com.

Dr. John Gøtze is a founding partner in the Danish think-tank EA Fellows. He also serves as the International President of the Association of Enterprise Architects (a l EA). He certifies enterprise architects via Carnegie Mellon University's Certified Enterprise Architect program, and also teaches EA at the Copenhagen Business School and the IT University of Copenhagen. For almost 10 years, he was a civil servant. As chief consultant in the National IT and Telecom Agency he initiated the first government-wide EA program in Denmark. Previously he worked for the Swedish Agency for Public Management, and co-created the national e-government strategy. He holds a M.Sc. in Engineering and a Ph.D. in participatory urban design, both from the Technical University of Denmark. He can be reached at john@gotzespace.dk.

Dr. Pallab Saha is currently a member of the faculty with the National University of Singapore (NUS). His current research and consulting interests include Enterprise Architecture, IT Governance, and Business Process Management. Pallab has published several books, including "Handbook of Enterprise Systems Architecture in Practice" (2007 and "Advances in Government Enterprise Architecture" (2008). Dr. Saha leads the Information Systems Management research group within NUS–Institute of Systems Science. He has worked on engagements in several Fortune 100 organizations in various capacities. Pallab received his Ph.D in 1999 from the Indian Institute of Science, Bangalore. He can be contacted at pallab@nus.edu.sg.

Dr. Scott Bernard is the founding editor of the *Journal of Enterprise Architecture* and teaches at Syracuse University and Carnegie Mellon University. In 2004 he wrote the book *An Introduction to Enterprise Architecture* that presented the 'EA^3 Cube' architecture framework, the 'Living Enterprise' repository design and an associated implementation approach. Dr. Bernard has over 20 years of experience in IT management, including work in the academic, government, military, and private sectors. Dr. Bernard has developed enterprise architectures for public, private, and military organizations, started an EA practice for an IT management consulting firm, developed his own consulting practice, and taught EA at a number of universities, businesses, and agencies. He holds a Ph.D. in Public Administration from Virginia Tech (2001); a M.S. in IT Management from Syracuse University (1998); a M.A. in Business Management from Central Michigan University (1984); a B.S. in Psychology from the University of Southern California (1977), and a CIO Certificate from the U.S. National Defense University (2000). Dr Bernard can be reached at sabernar@syr.edu.

Section I

INNOVATIONS IN ENTERPRISE ARCHITECTURE: THE ENABLERS OF COHERENCY MANAGEMENT

Chapter 2

THE FOUR DESIGN MODELS OF ENTERPRISE ARCHITECTURE

Pallab Saha

Editors' Preface

Organizations embark on a formal EA journey for several reasons. In the current scenario there are several frameworks available for organizations to adopt and adapt. These frameworks come with their own body of knowledge that includes reference models, standards, guidance documents, toolkits, methodologies and illustrations. On discussion, it is clearly evident from several adoptions of available EA frameworks, models, standards and methodologies that a 'one-size-fits-all' approach to EA development is neither feasible nor desirable. Though the frameworks themselves are holistic and generic to encourage widespread adoption, organizations have the discretion to design and tailor their EA programs to suit their business and technology objectives. This kind of flexibility to program design encourages autonomy and supports the federated governance structure at the whole-of-enterprise level, thereby enhancing the overall effectiveness of EA and EA programs. The need for good EA design is further exacerbated as EA is viewed as a strategy execution mechanism.

This chapter proposes and elaborately discusses the four potential design models. These design models present an approach to capture organizational EA programs via their various distinct characteristics. These design models allow organizations to select the 'right reasons' for doing EA and adapting the program to fulfill the real objectives.

As part of design model selection, the Chapter presents the consequences of abdicating the decision or making the incorrect decision. This, we believe, is a very effective way to get senior management actively involved. Each design model discussed in the Chapter is further linked to a typical set of architecture concerns that are addressed by the associated design model. Such information, in our view, is extremely useful to organizations as it allows the organization to ascertain why they are doing EA and how it will impact the organization. In the final section, the Chapter shows how each design model enables the realization of organizational coherence.

Introduction and Background

Ever since Zachman's seminal paper on Information Systems Architecture was first published in 1987, organizations around the world have been challenged, intrigued and even intimidated by the very scope and complexity of Enterprise Architecture (EA). The realization and acceptance that EA is a critical success factor for any organization is beyond doubt. This is made further perceptible by the fact that several Governments around the world have actually crafted legislation that makes it mandatory for Government agencies to develop and demonstrate their EA. A case example is the Clinger-Cohen Act of 1996, enacted by the US Federal Government and applicable to all Federal Agencies in United States (United States Congress, 1996). There is also a similar law in South Korea. However, current EA programs are overly skewed towards the development of frameworks, reference models, architectural artifacts, establishment of EA practice, maturity models and technology. This may have been sufficient given the newness of EA and its concepts. Going forward, it is imperative for organizations to sustain their EA programs and use EA as an approach to extend and enhance their business competitiveness.

To understand how organizations consistently succeed in their EA programs and, going forward, how they intend to sustain it, a series of telephone interviews with several CxO level executives were conducted. The executives included CIOs, CFOs and COOs. The discussions were based on uncovering and gaining insights into how next generation EA programs might look over the next three to five years. As executives commented on the nature of changes confronting organizations and the resulting progression of the EA program, several underlying commonalities emerged. An outcome of the research was to define four fundamental models of EA design and to identify factors guiding when each model should be selected and adopted. This framework of next generation EA is intended to help organizations avoid costly trial-and-error mistakes when selecting and designing the most appropriate EA programs for their objectives.

What is Enterprise Architecture?

MIT's Sloan Center Information Systems Research defines EA as "the organizing logic for a firm's core business processes and IT capabilities captured in a set of policies and technical choices, to achieve business standardization and integration requirements of the firm's operating model". From a scoping perspective, it is absolutely essential for organizations to focus on their core business processes and address the issue of how EA can facilitate business standardization and integration. In other words, EA is the enabling framework that explicitly connects strategy, business models, business processes and the underlying technical infrastructure.

The chain of connections brings about two keys outcomes: (1) business results; and (2) clarity to business strategy (Kaplan and Norton, 2008; Prahalad and Krishnan, 2008). As digitization permeates every aspect of business, the effective EA gains predominance. Typical components of EA include four architecture views or domains. The most commonly accepted ones are: business, information, application and technology architectures. Traditionally, the architecting process includes defining the current (as-is) architecture, defining the target (to-be) architecture for the each of the four domains, followed by constructing a transition plan consisting of a series of initiatives that enable the migration from the current to the target architecture (Bernard, 2005). The current state of EA programs are characterized by the following (all of which resonate with the earlier definition of EA):

- EA is still largely a CIO / IT organization led initiative,

- More often than not, the primary purpose of EA still remains to be building better IT systems,

- The footprint of the EA program is variable,

- Usually EA is disconnected and disengaged from the rest of the organization, and

- EA and their recommended artifacts and models often tend to become the end leading to legislations and compliance requirements.

Aside from the architecting process, another critical success factor in all EA programs is architecture governance and management. Analyzing the definition above, it becomes very clear that at this point of evolution most EA efforts are still primarily to build better IT systems and applications that are very closely aligned to business needs. There have been very few instances where EA was used to build better enterprises. This transformation from using EA to build better systems to using EA to build better enterprises is new and adds another dimension to the whole discipline of EA. This emerging phenomenon is discussed in Chapter 1 of this book.

In the past, organizations have overly focused on driving their EA programs by selecting one of the several available EA frameworks and adopting the guidelines in the framework. Thus, current generation EA programs do not generally follow a differentiated design approach and tend to be very IT-centric and largely take a one-size-fits-all approach. Unfortunately, this approach also constrains what the EA program can do for the organization as a whole. Indeed, the failure to recognize the differences that organizations might have in their strategy and operations that require significantly different design models often leads to missed opportunities. Given that EA is the 'architecture of the enterprise' and in scope much larger and complex than simply the IT architecture, hence the need for EA design models (Bernard, 2006; Saha, 2007).

About the Research

Since the 1990s, organizations both in the government and in the corporate sectors have adopted Enterprise Architecture. The real push for EA came after the enactment of the Clinger-Cohen Act of 1996 which mandated United States Federal Agencies to have their architectures documented and deployed. Following the Zachman Framework in 1987, there have been several programs to develop an EA body of knowledge comprised of methodologies, practice guidance, reference models, maturity approaches and development languages. To make sense of a plethora of such programs and practices, nearly thirty (30) companies were analyzed on their architecture programs. The dimensions examined included – trigger, management support, approach, design, governance, frameworks, and metrics, among others, consistent and derived from the current state of practice. The objective was to design a framework useful for managers and practitioners. This chapter describes the framework.

Design Models of Enterprise Architecture

Currently, there are several EA frameworks available for organizations to adapt and adopt. These include the Federal Enterprise Architecture Framework (FEAF), the Department of Defense Architecture Framework (DODAF), The Open Group Architecture Framework (TOGAF), and the Gartner Enterprise Architecture Framework, among others. Each framework comes with its own body of knowledge that includes reference models, standards, guidance documents, toolkits, methodologies and illustrations. An example of a standard methodology is the Federal Segment Architecture Methodology (FSAM) recently released by the U.S. Office of Management and Budget (Office of Management and Budget, 2008). On discussion, it is clearly evident, from several adoptions of available EA frameworks, models, standards and methodologies, that a 'one-size-fits-all' approach to EA development is neither feasible nor desirable (Saha, 2008). Though the frameworks themselves are holistic and generic to encourage widespread adoption, organizations have the discretion to design and tailor their EA programs to suit their business and technology objectives. This kind of flexibility to program design encourages autonomy and supports the federated governance structure at the whole-of-enterprise level, thereby enhancing the overall effectiveness of EA and EA programs.

The need for good EA design is further exacerbated as EA is viewed as a strategy execution mechanism (Saha, 2008). In their book The Execution Premium, the authors identify the Architect role as a key role needed for strategy execution (Kaplan and Norton, 2008). The five activities recommended for effective strategy execution include: (1) building a platform for enterprise processes, (2) developing metrics for ensuring performance of core business processes, (3) balancing enterprise and business objectives, (4) driving value from data, and (5) involvement in IT governance processes (Ross and Weill, 2007). It is clearly evident that EA (and its design) has a great deal of influence and impact on each of the strategy execution activities.

To build the EA design model, questions pertaining to the characteristics of EA programs were used to conduct a survey in a series of telephone interviews. The organizations represented both the corporate and the government sectors. Furthermore, interviews were conducted both with senior business and IT executives. The central focus of the survey was to uncover and understand characteristics of typical EA programs and how EA is expected to evolve over the next three to five years. As respondents commented on the nature of changes confronting organizations and the resulting transformation of the EA programs, both common underlying characteristics and contradictory scenarios emerged. It was clear, what works for one organization, need not, necessarily, work for another. Through the research conducted (that included the survey), two dimensions under the direct control of organization's management that consistently differentiate how organizations approach EA were identified. The dimensions are:

1. **EA Value Proposition:** The primary benefit derived out of the EA program captured in a statement of the way an organization proposes to use its resources to deliver superior value to its EA stakeholders. Within the value proposition continuum, organizations look to build their EA either to achieve **standardization** or **differentiation**.

2. **EA Emphasis**: The area of special importance that is significant enough to be highlighted. Within the emphasis continuum, organizations look to focus their EA either on **technology** or **business**.

Together the two dimensions generate a matrix of four dominant models, called the EA Design Models and each design model represents the intersection of an agency's **EA Value Proposition** and **EA Emphasis**. The four quadrants, each representing an EA design model, are: **Technology Standardization Model, Technology Differentiation Model, Business Standardization Model** and **Business Differentiation Model** (Saha, 2008). The EA Design Models are depicted in Figure 1 below.

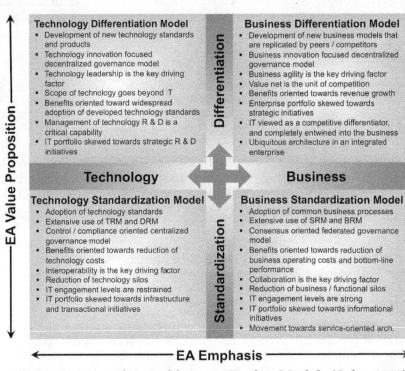

Technology Differentiation Model
- Development of new technology standards and products
- Technology innovation focused decentralized governance model
- Technology leadership is the key driving factor
- Scope of technology goes beyond IT
- Benefits oriented toward widespread adoption of developed technology standards
- Management of technology R & D is a critical capability
- IT portfolio skewed towards strategic R & D initiatives

Business Differentiation Model
- Development of new business models that are replicated by peers / competitors
- Business innovation focused decentralized governance model
- Business agility is the key driving factor
- Value net is the unit of competition
- Benefits oriented towards revenue growth
- Enterprise portfolio skewed towards strategic initiatives
- IT viewed as a competitive differentiator, and completely entwined into the business
- Ubiquitous architecture in an integrated enterprise

Technology ⬌ **Business**

Technology Standardization Model
- Adoption of technology standards
- Extensive use of TRM and DRM
- Control / compliance oriented centralized governance model
- Benefits oriented towards reduction of technology costs
- Interoperability is the key driving factor
- Reduction of technology silos
- IT engagement levels are restrained
- IT portfolio skewed towards infrastructure and transactional initiatives

Business Standardization Model
- Adoption of common business processes
- Extensive use of SRM and BRM
- Consensus oriented federated governance model
- Benefits oriented towards reduction of business operating costs and bottom-line performance
- Collaboration is the key driving factor
- Reduction of business / functional silos
- IT engagement levels are strong
- IT portfolio skewed towards informational initiatives
- Movement towards service-oriented arch.

EA Value Proposition (vertical axis)
Differentiation / *Standardization* (center vertical labels)
← **EA Emphasis** →

Figure 1. Enterprise Architecture Design Models (Saha, 2008)

The design models, influenced by design priorities of the IT department (Ross, 2006), represent the common underlying characteristics and contradictory scenarios of the EA programs. The following descriptions highlight the differences in the four emerging design models for EA.

Technology Standardization Model

Most organizations begin with the Technology Standardization Model. Evidenced by the fact that almost all EA programs have significant involvement from the IT departments and are typically CIO driven, organizations view this approach to their EA program as a facilitator to achieve quick wins. This serves to improve the credibility of the EA program by showing early benefits and aids continued management and organization interest. In this model, organizations look to adopt common technology standards (largely focused on common technology infrastructure and common data). These common standards are shared across the organization thereby deriving benefits through economies of scale and reduction of replicated technologies. Adoption of common standards necessitates extensive use of industry standard Technology Reference Models (TRM) and Data Reference Models (DRM).

To make this model work, a strong, compliance oriented, centralized governance mode works best, as this ensures every part of the organization follows and complies with the same common standards. A note of caution here is that the governance approach adopted for this design model must be in synergy with the overall corporate governance approach of the organization. For instance, if at the corporate level, the governance mode is very decentralized in nature, organizations have difficulty adopting this design model, as it is in conflict with the very ethos of the organization. The benefits derived out of this design model tend to be cost reductions and other associated business efficiencies. These benefits are usually very short-term oriented, operational in nature, more easily quantifiable and demonstrable. Hence, organizations use this design model to garner management interest into a very technology centric EA program.

Clearly, the benefits derived increase as the technology standards are more widely and intensely adopted. The higher the adoption, the greater are the benefits. All the benefits aside, the key driving factor for organizations to adopt this design model is to achieve interoperability between their IT applications and systems. This design model leads to the identification and removal of replicated / redundant technologies resulting in shallower technology silos and IT consolidation. However, the caveat here is that the interoperability accomplished is very much at the data and technology infrastructure level.

A good example of the Technology Standardization Model is the Singapore Government's Standard Operating Environment (SOE) initiative. According to Infocomm Development Authority of Singapore (IDA), SOE is the implementation of a standard ICT operating environment that allows the public service to reap substantial cost savings, reduce ICT manpower costs, increase agility and robustness of ICT infrastructure, and enhance user convenience. With a common ICT environment, service-wide systems can also be deployed centrally, swiftly and at lower cost, as there is no need to duplicate testing effort of the common environment across multiple agencies. The SOE comprises: (1) a standard desktop operating environment, (2) a standard messaging & collaboration environment, and (3) a standard network environment (Infocomm Development Authority of Singapore, 2005). With SOE, the Singapore Government aims to: (1) reduce the time to deploy new ICT services, (2) improve responsiveness, and (3) simplify operations and maintenance. Key drivers for the SOE program include: (1) cost savings, (2) reduction of complexity of IT infrastructure, and (3) enhancement of IT agility. One caveat exists however, as SOE in its current form does not include data.

Standardization of technology into services eventually leads to its commoditization. The Technology Standardization Model is the most traditional of the four alternative design models and it is relatively easy to demonstrate business value for it. This stems from the fact that decisions pertaining to Technology Standards usually do not require very deep and intense involvement from the business side. Most of the progress can be accomplished by the IT department with the CIO / CTO at the helm.

Technology Differentiation Model

Innovation provides the single largest opportunity for organizations to differentiate their businesses. Technology innovation faces the same challenges as traditional solution delivery, in addition to being plagued by antiquated enterprise management models that further prevent agile IT delivery (Chow et. Al., 2007). There is substantial empirical evidence that increasing innovation does lead to higher growth and an opportunity for organizations to differentiate themselves (Linder, 2006).

Given such a scenario, a small group of organizations aim for the Technology Differentiation Model. It works very well for organizations intending to utilize technology to gain competitive differentiation. Typically, for organizations adopting this design model, technology (especially information and communication technology) is their core business. As one of the key criteria in this model is to achieve technology differentiation, organizations in this quadrant rely on technology as a driver of research and innovation. These organizations expend a lot of resources and senior management bandwidth in developing new technology standards. Of course, the attempt does not stop just at developing new standards but also ensures that such technologies are widely adopted and that they eventually become de-facto or official standards for the industry.

Organizations with this design model have excellent technical capabilities, are often at the leading edge, and do not derive significant benefits from the use of existing reference models. EA in organizations adopting this design model are often used to gain competitive advantages and speed to market is a critical success metric. Cost reduction, although important, is not the critical factor as these organizations are easily able to charge a premium on technologies that are first to the market. Typical innovation categories based on 'Innovation Goal' and 'Locus of Control' are Traditional Improvements, Directed Experimentation, Local Exploration and Edge Enhancements (Westerman, 2007).

Critical success factors in this design model are not limited to the innovations themselves, but also to the organizations' ability to manage the innovations. To make this model work, a strong innovation- focused, decentralized governance model works best. An excellent pipeline of new technology ideas to realization is a key characteristic and this is aimed at avoiding product line gaps due to technology obsolescence. The benefits derived out of this design model tend to be revenue and profitability growth resulting from technology leadership. These benefits tend to be long-term oriented, strategic in nature, and subject to several risks and uncertainties.

The key driving factor for organizations in this quadrant is the development and release of the new technologies that have the potential to be adopted as standards. Management of technology research and development is also an important capability. Organizations with this model demonstrate very high risk appetite and long-term perspective to EA and EA derived initiatives.

A good example of the Technology Differentiation Model is Cisco's Service Oriented Network Architecture (SONA) (Cisco, 2007). The SONA framework summarizes how organizations evolve their IT infrastructure into an Intelligent Information Network that accelerates applications, business processes and resources, and enables IT to have a greater impact on business. The three layers of SONA include: (1) the networked infrastructure layer, (2) the interactive services layer, and (3) the applications layer. Providing a detailed description of SONA framework is not within the scope of this chapter; it is very clear that CISCO certainly hopes that the SONA framework would be a de-facto or an official standard that is then adopted by organizations with the other three design models as part of their EA programs.

The IBM Technology Adoption Program (TAP) presents a good example of a successful, organization-wide innovation management program. It was created to address the challenges IBM innovators face in developing their work from the design phase to the point at which it can influence products, services and solutions (Chow et. Al., 2007). TAP changes the primary role of the CIO, from operations manager, to that of innovation manager. TAP is based on shifting the power of IT decision-making to early adopters and innovators. In this way, TAP radically shifts how technology is identified, developed, evaluated and transitioned (Orlov, 2005).

The design model itself can span all the four innovation categories. However, the business leaders and organizations would have to tweak their architecture and governance processes to accept the differences among the four innovation categories. The Technology Differentiation Model is the most specialized of the design models and is adopted by 'technology companies'. It is adopted to drive innovation and growth, at times at the cost of potential economies of scale. Organizations with this design model have higher risk appetite and generate benefits often after a great deal of experimentation.

Business Standardization Model

Some forward thinking organizations use EA as a management approach to improve business efficiencies. The focus here is more on business and business process expertise, rather than mere technical capability. Typically, organizations adopting this design model view technology as a resource to be exploited for business gains. For these organizations, the greatest contribution of IT is in providing enablement to business needs. In this model, organizations look to adopt common business processes which are shared across the organization, thereby deriving benefits through economies of scale and reduction of replicated processes and activities. Adoption of common process standards necessitates extensive use of Business Reference Models (BRM) and to some extent Solutions Reference Models (SRM).

To make this model work, a strong, consensus-oriented, federated governance mode works best. This ensures every part of the organization: (1) is party to common vision, definition, understanding and outcome of the shared business processes, and (2) complies with such agreed upon processes. The benefits derived out of this design model tend to be reduction of business operating costs and bottom-line performance, primarily due to the increased digitization of business processes. These benefits are usually medium to long term oriented, operational in nature, reasonably quantifiable and demonstrable.

The business standardization model, at times, leads to the establishment of shared services, either within or outside the organization. Over time, this model tends to favor commoditization of certain non-core processes. Another key driving factor for organizations to adopt this design model is to accomplish greater collaboration and seamless partnership between their business units and functions. This design model leads to the identification and removal of replicated/ redundant processes and activities, resulting in shallower business and functional silos.

Similar to the Technology Standardization Model, this design model has the potential to commoditize business services. As a result, the business becomes more agile because business services are loosely coupled and inter-changeable. The United States Federal Enterprise Architecture (FEA) is a good example of business standardization model. According to the FEA Program Management Office, the FEA is a business and performance based framework to support cross-agency collaboration, transformation and government-wide improvement (Federal CIO Council, 2006).

Mandated by the Clinger-Cohen Act of 1996, the Office of Management and Budget (OMB) along with the Federal CIO Council developed the Federal Enterprise Architecture Framework (FEAF), which is a business-based framework for government wide improvement envisioned to facilitate efforts in transforming the US Federal Government to one that is citizen-centered, results oriented and market-based (Federal CIO Council, 2006). The framework provides an approach to identify, develop and specify architecture descriptions of high priority areas that are built on common business areas and designs spanning multiple organizations not limited by organizational boundaries (Federal CIO Council, 2006). The FEAF provides a structured approach to federal organizations to integrate their respective architectures into the FEA. The FEA was commissioned in 2002. According to the CIO Council, the primary objectives of developing the FEAF were to organize federal information on a government wide scale; to promote information sharing among federal organizations; to facilitate federal organizations developing their respective architectures; to facilitate federal organizations developing their IT investment processes; and to serve customer needs better, faster and cost effectively.

COHERENCY MANAGEMENT

In designing the FEAF, eight core components were taken into consideration and elaborated. These components, deemed essential to develop and maintain the FEA, were: architecture drivers, strategic direction, current architecture, target architecture, transitional processes, architectural segments, architectural models and standards. The FEA consists of a collection of interrelated "reference models" designed to facilitate cross-agency analysis and the identification of duplicative investments, gaps, and opportunities for collaboration within and across Federal Agencies. Collectively, the reference models comprise a framework for describing important elements of the FEA in a common and consistent way. Though the FEA includes five inter-related reference models, the business reference model is viewed as the driver for the remaining four. The FEA BRM facilitates an end-to-end process (rather than organizational) view of the federal government's lines of business. The BRM describes the federal government around common business areas instead of a siloed, agency-by-agency view. It thus promotes agency collaboration (Gøtze and Christiansen, 2007).

The Business Standardization Model seeks to help organizations transform into process centric entities. The management of such organizations includes continuous discovery, analysis, design, deployment and operation of core business processes, and as a result, needs very deep and intense involvement from the business side. In this model, the IT department plays a supporting role.

Business Differentiation Model

This is the design model of choice for organizations with extremely mature EA programs. It works well for organizations intending to utilize EA for gaining competitive differentiation. This is realized through the development of highly acclaimed business processes and capabilities that can then be replicated / imitated by others in the industry. In other words, these organizations are in a position to establish industry-wide benchmarks, thereby always keeping ahead of the competition. These organizations view their value chains as the unit of competition and, at times, it culminates into innovative products. The role of EA is seen as a management approach to uncover opportunities for differentiated business models and processes.

The key message of this design model is to highlight different and better business models and processes that the organization is able to deliver vis-à-vis its competition. As one of the key criteria in this model is to achieve business differentiation, organizations in this quadrant expend a lot of resources and senior management bandwidth towards business innovations. These innovations are of three types: (1) innovations in industry models, (2) innovations in revenue models, and (3) innovations in enterprise models (Giesen et. Al., 2006). This is shown in Figure 2. Through EA, these organizations identify core and non-core business processes, and eventually outsource their non-core processes to service providers and business partners. Within the core business processes, such organizations seem to have the ability to create new and customer centric processes through plug and play capabilities. Although organizations in this quadrant find value in a low-cost infrastructure, their key concern is enablement of process innovation. The benefits derived out of this design model tend to be revenue growth resulting from innovative and differentiated business processes and being perceived as a leader.

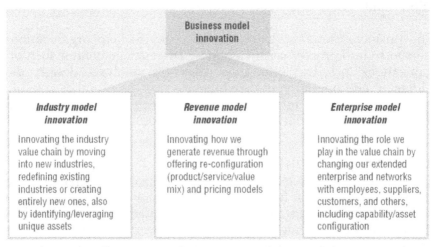

Figure 2. Business Innovation Models
(Reprint Courtesy of International Business Machines Corporation copyright © (2007) International Business Machines Corporation)

IBM's Global CEO Study in 2006 affirmed the importance of business innovation (and differentiation) to financial growth. Organizations that implemented new or changed business models saw significant operating margin growth over a five-year period when compared with their peers (IBM Global Business Services, 2006). However, these benefits are usually long term oriented, strategic in nature, and subject to several risks and uncertainties.

The key driving factor for organizations in this quadrant is the development and release of the process innovations that have the potential to be adopted as standards. Management of business research and development is an important capability. Organizations with this model demonstrate a very high risk appetite and long-term perspective to EA and EA derived initiatives.

A good example of the Business Differentiation Model is IBM's Globally Integrated Enterprise (GIE) approach. A GIE is defined as an organization that designs its strategy, management and operations in pursuit of global integration of production and value (Palmisano, 2006). A GIE seeks to use the best resources from the best locations at the optimum time to gain competitive advantage, so as to transform the way organizations address the 'how' and 'where' of the business and not so much the 'what'.

Organizations in this quadrant are more interested in business and process innovation than in pure technology innovation. EA in organizations with the Business Differentiation Model tend to have a completely ubiquitous architecture with such innovations having significant impact on their strategies. Interestingly, the research revealed that organizations in this quadrant are the most likely to achieve Prahalad and Krishnan's (2008) [N = 1 and R = G] paradigm.

In the Business Differentiation Model, the focus of the differentiation is on the centrality of the individual (providing unique personalized experiences) and access to resources (not ownership of resources). In such organizations, for instance, the outsourcing decisions tend to be more strategic in nature (Ross, Weill and Robertson, 2006). Figure 3 provides comparison between decision criteria for traditional outsourcing vis-à-vis for a GIE (IBM, 2008).

Decision criteria	For traditional outsourcing	For the globally integrated enterprise
Primary driver	Cost reduction driven by economies of scale	Cost reduction driven by value creation
Measures of success	Performance results, predictablity, service level agreements (SLAs)	Business transformation, innovation
Client-provider relationship	Technology-based relationship	Business-based strategic partnership
Risk/reward model	Risks predominantly borne by client; rewards shared by client and provider	Risks and rewards shared by client and provider
Service delivery model	Local resources and partners	Globally diverse resources and partners
Outsourced processes	Non-core, back-office and customer support functions	Core and non-core business functions
Skill access	Access to a broad array of skills and services from a single or few providers	Access to specialized skills and services from multiple providers
Contract	Long duration; rigid terms	Shorter duration; flexible terms with option to renegotiate
Pricing	Fixed cost structures tied to IT performance	Variable cost structures aligned to business outcomes

Figure 3. Outsourcing Decision Criteria Comparison
(Reprint Courtesy of International Business Machines Corporation copyright ©
(2008) International Business Machines Corporation)

Selecting the Right Model

Organizations might argue that their EA programs must operate in all four quadrants. The choice of an EA design model is a critical decision for an organization. The design model decision (or the lack of) has a profound impact on the rest of the EA program. Each model places different demands on the agency's EA program with respect to its objectives, metrics, scope, intensity, resources, senior management involvement, outcomes and benefits – to name a few. Inability to select the right model or selecting multiple models potentially makes the EA program more complex, less focused and expensive.

Based on the research findings, Figure 4 provides a set of six assessment questions developed for organizations intending to embark on their EA programs or fine-tuning their existing programs. The role of the organization's senior management and the consequences of abdicating the decision or making an incorrect decision are also elaborated. The questions are meant for organizations to pinpoint their strengths, shortcomings and options for architecture designs, resulting in critical inputs for developing a roadmap to an effective EA program.

Decision Criteria	Technology Standardization Model	Technology Differentiation Model	Business Standardization Model	Business Differentiation Model
Strategic Goal	Achieve reduction in IT costs through economies of scale and reduced duplication.	Build and maintain technology leadership to gain competitive differentiation.	Achieve reduction in business costs through economies of scale and reduced duplication.	Build and maintain business innovation leadership.
Essential Function	Interoperability and consolidation among deployed technologies.	Evangelize, coach and facilitate business units in pursuing new IT opportunities.	Common and uniform business processes that are shared across business units with a common vision.	Value network as unit of competition; evangelize, coach and facilitate business units in pursuing innovation.
Inputs	Technical and Data Reference Models; standards; guidelines and best practices.	New opportunities; senior management bandwidth and technical capabilities.	Business Reference Models; business standards; guidelines and best practices.	New opportunities; senior management bandwidth and business innovation capabilities.
Outputs	Strong technical and data architectures; IT responsiveness and compliance based governance.	Potential technical standards; innovative products and high performing IT with decentralized governance.	Business agility; shared business platforms and consensus oriented federated governance.	Integrated enterprise; long term competitive advantage; high performance business with decentralized governance.
Success Factors	Strong governance; appreciation for uniformity and availability of acceptable standards.	Respected and credible CIO / CTO; innovation culture; appetite to accept failures and time to market.	CIO as a business manager; deep business involvement; effectiveness governance.	Senior business managers' active involvement in EA; organic design and context neutrality.
Typical Challenges	Senior management attention; limited IT engagement levels and short term benefits.	Limited adoption of standards; and retaining and building technical capabilities.	Gaining consensus; shared business process ownership and credence in long term benefits.	Risky, hence difficult to gain conviction; and failures in innovation models.

Figure 4. Six Key Questions in Selecting the Right Design Model

Based on the six key questions in Figure 4, Figure 5 summarizes the key distinguishing characteristics of the four EA Design Models discussed earlier.

EA Design Decision	Senior Management's Role	Consequences of Abdicating the Decision or Making the Incorrect Decision
Why are you embarking on the EA program?	Define and communicate the strategic role that EA will play in the organization, including its focus area, objectives, orientation metrics and rationale.	The organization could be doing EA for the wrong reasons, opening itself up for rumors, cynicism and resentment.
How and where do you intend to utilize the EA?	Establish ways and approaches needed to institutionalize the EA and ensure that the interest is sustained, including governance strategies.	Lack of clarity in this area can lead to EA being unutilized or underutilized leading to less than optimum benefits derived out of the program.
What can you make available to design and sustain and effective EA program?	Decide which organizational capabilities and resources can be made available to the development and institutionalization of EA.	Ambiguity in available inputs can lead to wrong assumptions and laid back approach to EA commitments.
What will be produced or delivered as a result of EA program?	Ascertain the expected deliverables from the program, and provide management oversight in ensuring they are produced.	Vague deliverables lead to questionable quality, lack of commitment to adopt and also limited derivation of the program benefits.
What are the key areas that you have to do well in order for the EA program to succeed?	Lead the decision on identification of critical success factors, and decide on appropriate trade-offs, should there be any.	Uncertainty in the critical success factors will lead the organization to focus on the less important areas and has the potential to lead to program failure.
What are some of the challenges that you expect to confront in your EA journey?	Identify expected areas of difficulty in development and adoption of EA, along with alternative plans (as scenarios) should something pop-up.	The organization could be ill prepared for any eventual and unexpected event that could stall or hold back the program.

Figure 5. Decision Criteria for Selecting the Right EA Design Model

The profound differences between the different design models are clearly evident when the design models are mapped to the architecture concerns that the EA helps address.

Figure 6 maps the four design models to architecture concerns. The Enterprise Architecture Management Patterns have been used as a basis for the architecture concerns (Buckl et. Al., 2008). Furthermore, Figure 6 can be used to identify the architecture patterns (M-Patterns; V-Patterns; and I-Patterns) (Buckl et. Al., 2008) that could plausibly be used to address the concerns associated to the respective design models, leading to more effective EA management.

Note that Figure 6 largely highlights the distinguishing and unique concerns. There could be other concerns that are common to more than one design model. This is likely, given the underlying nature of EA programs in general.

	Typical Set of Architecture Concerns That Get Addressed		
Business Differentiation Model	Technology Differentiation Model	Business Standardization Model	Technology Standardization Model
Which business processes constitute core competencies of the organization? Which business processes are suitable for being outsourced?	Which are the core technology capabilities? In what areas can we be leaders? Where must we innovate?	What activities have to be performed in order to increase conformance to standards? What has to be done to modify current business applications to increase their conformance and reduce heterogeneity?	Where are the technology standards used and are there areas where these standards are not complied?
Are the core business processes a source of competitive advantage? Are some of these processes being replicated by competitors?	Do our governance and leadership encourage technology innovation? Do we have an organization-wide approach to adopt technologies?	Which are the department / business function specific applications that can be moved out and made available as common business services (as an organization standard)?	Which technologies used in the applications / solutions landscape should be replaced, which ones should be retained?
Which business processes extend beyond the continues of our enterprise and integrate to the processes of our partners and external stakeholders?	What kinds of risks are we required taking in order for us to be successful innovators?	Which business applications currently conform to architecture blueprints and architectural standards? Are there strategic reasons to support a non-conformance?	What activities have to be performed in order to increase conformance to standards?
Which business objects are used or exchanged by which business applications / services? What are the dependencies between the business objects? Which business objects are exchanged over which interfaces?	How can the architecture be utilized as a governance mechanism to prioritize projects and initiatives?	How can the architecture be utilized as a governance mechanism to prioritize projects and initiatives?	Where are areas improvement with respect to reduction of overall cost of technology ownership and usage?
Do business processes adequately factor in the organization environment and conditions?	How does our R & D cycle look like? How well do we manage our innovations? Have we successful in commercializing our innovations?	What dependencies exist between business applications and are impacted by current and target architecture?	How can the architecture be utilized as a governance mechanism to prioritize projects and initiatives?
How can the architecture be utilized as a governance mechanism to prioritize projects and initiatives?	Are our technologies a source of competitive advantage? Are some of these technologies being replicated by competitors?	How can operating expenses and maintenance costs be reduced by identification of business applications providing the same functionality?	What infrastructure software is used by business applications?
How to discover business services within the development process of the application landscape? Which services are offered by which business applications? Which business processes are supported by which business services? How does the lifecycle of a business service look like?		Which business applications / services? What are the dependencies between the business objects? Which business objects are exchanged over which interfaces?	What is the impact of a shutdown of an infrastructure element?
Which interfaces are offered / used by which business applications? What is the type of a specific interface? How is the interface implemented? What are its capabilities?		What are the domains of the application landscape? How will they evolve?	How often do we intend to revisit and (if needed) update our technology standards?
To what extent are business processes supported by business applications? Which business processes are manual? Can the extent of business process digitization be increased? How can un-interrupted IT support for business processes be realized?		How to discover business services within the development process of the application landscape? Which services are offered by which business applications? Which business processes are supported by which business services? How does the lifecycle of a business service look like?	What is the level of technology diversity and how does it impact overall IT risks?
To what extent does IT support business flexibility? Where is the flexibility put at risk?		Which interfaces are offered / used by which business applications? What is the type of a specific interface? How is the interface implemented? What are its capabilities?	What proportion of the IT budget is spent on projects that are purely infrastructure and transaction oriented?
Which business processes are hosted by which organization unit? Which business processes are supported by which business applications?		To what extent are business processes supported by business applications? Which business processes are manual? Can the extent of business process digitization be increased? How can un-interrupted IT support for business processes be realized?	
		Which business processes are hosted by which organization unit? Which business processes are supported by which business applications? Which applications are used by which organizational units?	

Figure 6. Architecture Concerns and Design Models

COHERENCY MANAGEMENT

Deploying Different Design Models at Different Organizational Levels

The four design models discussed earlier represent the key factors that organizations need to take into consideration while designing their EA programs. However, it is entirely possible that organizations can actually identify characteristics that fit multiple design models. It is recommended that such organizations select one design model to guide management thought and organizational preparation to developing EA and as a mechanism to drive strategy execution.

It is clearly evident from Figure 6 that deploying different design models at different organizational levels could cause confusion in the way concerns get addressed. Too many concerns, often, are a source of disadvantage, as limited organizational resources get spread too thinly to make any real impact to the organization. Selecting a single design model provides focus and can be used to respond to contradictory demands to the EA program.

Larger organizations may choose to adopt different design models at different organizational levels. Such scenarios then need to be supported by relevant decentralized governance modes. Conglomerates consisting of loosely coupled organizations are natural candidates for multiple design models. This stems from the fact that, in such a scenario, individual organizations within the conglomerate function largely independent of each other. This needs to be supported by a decentralized approach of governance. However, a decentralized approach to governance further needs to be in synergy with the organization culture and ethos.

With respect to resources, the 'standardization' based design models can generally be maintained in a much leaner fashion. Furthermore, a single design model across the organization demands less organizational bandwidth and management attention.

Transforming to a New Design Model

The research revealed instances where organizations have included transitioning to a new design model as part of their overall EA program migration plan. Such transitions are transformational as they entail new ways of thinking and behaving, and are disruptive in nature. Organizations with successful and effective EA programs tend to start with a small, credible team and with a mandate from the senior management group. Each model demands different forms of leadership, management attention, processes and skill sets. Whichever model is selected, a set of 'quick wins' has tremendous potential to earn management support, organizational attention and credibility beyond the initial mandate. This is absolutely critical given the general state of EA programs discussed earlier.

Realizing Organizational Coherence with Design Models

Coherence is defined "*as the logical, orderly and consistent relation of parts*". The United States General Accounting Office affirms that EA provides a clear and comprehensive picture of an organization (United States General Accounting Office, 2002). Developed and managed properly, architectures can clarify and help optimize the interdependencies and interrelationships among related enterprise operations. In short, architectures allow organizations to manage complexity and provide coherence.

As has been presented in Chapter 1 of this book, Coherence is the primary outcome of EA. The architecture of the enterprise needs to be formalized and should further coherency (Doucet et. Al., 2008). There is a definitive and preferred influence exerted by the architecture mode to the enterprise's architecture design model. Hence, it is important to understand the role of design models in supporting / enabling organizational coherence. Deriving expected benefits from EA is not just a factor of selecting the right design model (see Figure 5), but also ensuring that the relevant management practices and mechanisms are adopted and institutionalized. As mentioned in Chapter 1, organizations could very well be doing all three modes of EA simultaneously, but due to practical consideration, certain design models work naturally well with specific modes. This is depicted in Figure 7.

COHERENCY MANAGEMENT

	Typical Management Practices for Realizing Organizational Coherence
Technology Standardization Model	• Centralized IT standards group • Centralized and structured IT governance • Technology acquisition and deployment process • Focus on low risk / low return infrastructure and transactional IT initiatives • **Foundation Architecture** as the preferred mode
Business Standardization Model	• Office of business processes • Centralized and structured business governance • Shared and collaborative business processes with clear process owners • Focus on reducing duplicative and redundant business investments • **Extended Architecture** as the preferred mode
Technology Differentiation Model	• Technology innovation factories and incubation mechanisms • Research and development portfolio management • Decentralized and distributed IT governance • Focus on high risk / high return strategic IT initiatives • **Embedded Architecture** as the preferred mode
Business Differentiation Model	• Business innovation factories and incubation mechanisms • Strong process discovery and design teams • Synchronization and integration groups • Decentralized and distributed business governance with clear accountability • **Balanced Architecture** as the preferred mode

**Figure 7. Realizing Organizational Coherence
with Design Models**

Further Research and Conclusions

Enterprise Architecture is a complex and resource intensive undertaking. Successful EA programs usually require dedicated teams and a mandate from senior management. It is imperative to have a clear understanding and secure consensus from senior management on the key objectives of the EA program (the 'why' of the EA program). From a point of view of positioning EA vis-à-vis other management practices in the organization, the probability of success of the EA has been higher when it is 'designed' as an integral part between strategy management upstream and operational management downstream (Saha, 2008).

Each of the design models requires different forms of management structure, capabilities, processes and skill sets, and addresses different architectural concerns. While the selection of the design model itself depends on numerous factors described in this chapter, identifying 'quick wins' is always recommended, as it helps secure senior management attention and credibility. It is up to the organizations to understand and appreciate that EA is not limited to the traditional goal of building good systems; EA is needed to build good enterprises and facilitate management innovation (Hamel, 2007). The design models derived out of research are meant for guidance. The idea is to provide a framework for organizations to study and to tailor their EA programs in accordance with their goals and objectives and to provide an approach for organizations to define their long term architecture vision. Nonetheless, more research is needed. Some of the plausible areas for further research could include (but are not limited to):

1. Impact of Design Models on Effectiveness of EA / EA Management.

2. Integration of Design Models to Existing EA Methodologies (like TOGAF ADM) and EA Audit practices.

3. Role of Design Models In Improving Organization's Coherency Quotient and Management Architecture.

Kaplan and Norton (2008) advocate the Office of Strategy Management. Furthermore, Ross, Weill and Robertson's (2006) approach to make EA an integral part of strategy has gained widespread acceptance. The research conducted for the purposes of this chapter reveals that companies with successful and effective EA programs have been able to integrate EA with strategy and use it to innovate management. This is in line with the need for seamless integration of strategy, business processes, technology and people (Prahalad and Krishnan, 2008). The design models in this chapter provide the broad framework. The objective of this chapter was not to prescribe the design model that organizations must use, but to help organizations design their EA. It is a continuous process of learning and management innovation to improve organizational coherence.

COHERENCY MANAGEMENT

References

Bernard, S.A. (2005). An Introduction to Enterprise Architecture– 2nd Edition. AuthorHouse: Bloomington, IL.

Bernard, S.A. (2006). Using Enterprise Architecture to Integrate Strategy, Business and Technology Planning. Journal of Enterprise Architecture. Volume 2, Number 4. pp. 11 – 28.

Buckl, S., Ernst, A.M., Lankes, J., and Matthes, F. (2008). Enterprise Architecture Management Pattern Catalog Version 1.0. Technical University of Munich Technical Report TB 0801. (Available online at http://tinyurl.com/chzu28).

Chow, A.W., Goodman, B.D., Rooney, J.W., and Wyble, C.D. (2007). Engaging a corporate community to manage technology and embrace innovation. IBM Systems Journal. Volume 46, Number 4. pp. 639 – 650.

Cisco. (2007). The Role of SONA in Enterprise Architecture Frameworks and Strategies. Cisco White Paper, (Available online at http://tinyurl.com/cjq6z6).

Doucet, G., Gøtze, J., Saha, P., and Bernard, S.A. (2008). Coherency Management: Using Enterprise Architecture for Alignment, Agility and Assurance. Journal of Enterprise Architecture. Volume 4, Number 2. pp. 27 – 38.

Federal CIO Council. (2006). Federal Enterprise Architecture Consolidated Reference Model Version 2.0. United States Federal Enterprise Architecture Programme Office. (Available online at http://tinyurl.com/2qoaff).

Giesen, E., Berman, S.J., Bell, R., and Blitz, A. (2007). Paths to Success: Three ways to innovate your business model. IBM Institute for Business Value http://tinyurl.com/dx75wp.

Gøtze, J. and Christiansen, E. (2007). Trends in Government Enterprise Architecture: Reviewing National Enterprise Architecture Programmes. Journal of Enterprise Architecture. Volume 3, Number 1. pp. 8 – 18.

Hamel, G., (2007). The Future of Management. Harvard Business School Press: Boston, MA.

Infocomm Development Authority of Singapore. (2005). Standard ICT Operating Environment for the Singapore Government. IDA: SiTF Briefing. (Available online at http://tinyurl.com/bsgz54).

International Business Machines Corporation. (2008). The outsourcing decision for a globally integrated enterprise: from commodity outsourcing to value creation. IBM Center for CIO Leadership. (Available online at http://tinyurl.com/cmqe26).

Kaplan, R.S., and Norton, D.P. (2008). The Execution Premium: Linking Strategy to Operations for Competitive Advantage. Harvard Business School Press: Boston, MA.

Linder, J.C. (2006). Measuring Profitable Growth and Innovation. Accenture Research Note. Institute for High Performance Business. (Available online at http://tinyurl.com/ch2yda).

Orlov, L.M. (2005). IBM's Technology Adoption Program Taps Ideas. Forrester Research Inc. (Available online at http://tinyurl.com/cennoz).

Palmisano, S.J. (2006). The Globally Integrated Enterprise. Foreign Affairs. Volume 85, Number 3. pp. 127 – 136.

Prahalad, C.K., and Krishnan, M.S. (2008). The New Age of Innovation: Driving Co-Created Value Through Global Networks. McGraw-Hill Professional: New York, NY.

Ross, J., and Weill, P. (2007). Who Owns Strategy Execution in Your Company. MIT Sloan Center for Information Systems Research: Research Briefing. Volume VII, Number 2C. (Available at http://tinyurl.com/c33ov9).

Ross, J., Weill, P., and Robertson, D. (2006). Enterprise Architecture as Strategy: Creating a Foundation for Business Execution. Harvard Business School Press: Boston, MA.

Ross, J.W. (2006). Design Priorities for the IT Unit of the Future. MIT Sloan Center for Information Systems Research: Research Briefing. Volume VI, Number 3D. (Available at http://tinyurl.com/ddr8ab).

Saha, P. (2007). Handbook of Enterprise Systems Architecture in Practice. IGI Global Information Science Reference: Hershey, PA.

Saha, P. (2008). Advances in Government Enterprise Architecture. IGI Global Information Science Reference: Hershey, PA.

United States Congress. (1996). The Information Technology Management Reform Act of 1996 (Clinger-Cohen Act). Public Law 104-106, Division E.

United States General Accounting Office. (2002). Enterprise Architecture Use Across Federal Government Can Be Improved. Report to Congressional Committees GAO-02-6. (Available online at http://tinyurl.com/d6n5cs).

United States Office of Management and Budget. (2008). Federal Segment Architecture Methodology Version 1.0. Federal Segment Architecture Working Group. (Available at http://www.fsam.gov).

Westerman, G. (2007). Managing the IT-Enabled Innovation Portfolio. MIT Sloan Center for Information Systems Research: Research Briefing. Volume VII, Number 3E. (Available at http://tinyurl.com/c33ov9).

Zachman, J. (1987). A Framework for Information Systems Architecture. IBM Systems Journal. Volume 26, Number 3. pp. 276 – 292.

About the Author

Dr. Saha is currently a member of the faculty with the National University of Singapore (NUS). His current research and consulting interests include Enterprise Architecture, IT Governance, and Business Process Management. He has published several research papers in these areas. Pallab is an active researcher in the area of Enterprise Architecture and published his first book titled "Handbook of Enterprise Systems Architecture in Practice" in March 2007. He has completed his second book titled "Advances in Government Enterprise Architecture", published in October 2008. Dr. Saha leads the Information Systems Management research group within the NUS–Institute of Systems Science. He teaches courses in Enterprise Architecture and IT Governance at the post-graduate and senior executive levels. Dr. Saha is the primary author of the Enterprise Architecture Methodology and Toolkit for the Government of Singapore. His current consulting engagements are in Enterprise Architecture for Singapore Government agencies. He has provided consulting and advisory services to Infocomm Development Authority of Singapore, Intellectual Property Office of Singapore, CPF Board, Singapore Healthcare Services and Great Eastern Life Assurance among others. He has been invited as a speaker to the World Bank, SAP Labs Lecture Series and Korea Institute for Information Technology Architecture. His books, papers and presentations have been posted by the United Nations, cited by the World Health Organization, United States Department of Defense and The Open Group. He has been an external examiner to doctoral research thesis at the University of New South Wales (UNSW@ADFA). Prior to academia, he was instrumental in managing Baxter's environmental health and safety offshore development centre in Bangalore as Head of Projects and Development. He has worked on engagements in several Fortune 100 organizations in various capacities. Pallab received his Ph.D in 1999 from the Indian Institute of Science, Bangalore. His Ph.D dissertation was awarded the best thesis.

Pallab Saha
National University of Singapore
Institute of Systems Science
25 Heng Mui Keng Terrace, Singapore 119615
pallab@nus.edu.sg

Chapter 3

BUSINESS ENGINEERING NAVIGATOR: A BUSINESS-TO-IT APPROACH TO ENTERPRISE ARCHITECTURE MANAGEMENT

Stephan Aier, Stephan Kurpjuweit, Jan Saat & Robert Winter

Editors' Preface

"Business Engineering Navigator" is an overview of how Enterprise Architecture and its management can provide value to a variety of stakeholders. The authors are leading the research with the intent to ensure structured engineering for 'business-to-IT', integration management, IT/Business Alignment, and more. The concept is not necessarily new but Aier et al introduce a heuristic to accomplish this as well as to have some tools in development based on their work. The precise tool is not what is being sold to the reader; rather it is the idea and heuristic approach that is the target of our interest.

In Coherency Management, there is recognition that the Architecture for the enterprise is being created and maintained by many people not necessarily associated with IT, IM or the word 'Architecture'. BEN reaffirms that EA must help others by using structured approaches towards their work.

In the editors' opinion there is a capability being developed which has the potential to be widespread throughout the business. Structured (engineering based) approaches to managing the Enterprise Architecture and recognition that architecture is widespread leads us to the idea that the EA Tool and EA Processes will also be widespread. For example, the annual budget exercise creates documents that could be said to update elements of the 'enterprise architecture' every year. Rather than rewrite or reenter the information created in that process, for the purpose of EA, we see a time when the budget office uses an EA compliant tool. They will still create the budget but the structure, conventions, engineering approaches, standards, and common language used in the process will allow the budget to influence EA instead of being considered a separate process. The more processes that align in this fashion, the more the enterprise will enable itself to become coherent.

Introduction

Organizations are subject to constant evolution. Organizational change can be distinguished into incremental change (optimization) and fundamental change according to its impact. While most functional methods of business administration, such as marketing, finance and human resources provide support for optimization (e.g. six sigma[2] (Harry 1988)), the structured design of innovative and fundamental change requires a holistic engineering approach. Business engineering is a discipline supporting organizational transformation by providing integrated model- and method-based guidance for change projects (Winter, 2008).

Innovative and fundamental change most often affects not only IT or business artifacts, but requires consistent evolution "business-to-IT". The business engineering framework distinguishes artifacts and models on a strategy, organization, integration, software/data, and IT infrastructure layer (Figure 1).

---

[2] Six Sigma is a set of methods to improve the quality of business processes by using defined means of statistical analysis, defined optimization processes, and specially trained personnel.

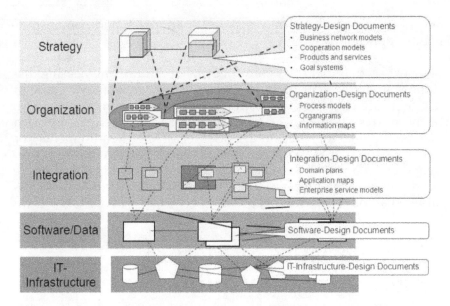

Figure 1. Architectural Layers and Model Types in Business Engineering (Winter and Fischer 2007).

Since it comprises all relevant artifacts and relationships "business-to-IT", the business engineering framework is considered as a suitable foundation for enterprise architecture management (EAM). Compared to other EA frameworks, the business engineering framework is intended to deliver a high level picture of the entire organization to achieve transparency of structures and interdependencies. Therefore, EA coherency can be achieved by providing a logical, orderly, and consistent relation of parts to the whole. The business engineering navigator (BEN) concept provides construction, navigation and analysis functionalities for business engineering artifacts and relationships. We, therefore, propose its application to EAM in this article. In addition to most existing approaches to EA, that mostly evolved from the IT architecture topic, BEN focuses on scenarios in transformation projects with impact on the entire enterprise. As a consequence of IT-centric EAM history, most models and methods are fairly mature on the IT side but lack sufficient structure on business focused architectural layers. To support the management of systematic and complex change and to avoid ad hoc decisions and untraceable results, BEN is based on core ideas of engineering, such as a structured design process, clear and defined documentation, and the division of labor, which is essential to complex design challenges. The approach presented seeks to contribute to the scientific discussion on organizational engineering and EAM by presenting a holistic "business-to-IT" approach and demonstrating its applicability.

The next section identifies core concepts of mature engineering disciplines and transfers them to EAM. Thereafter, major EA design decisions are characterized from a business engineering viewpoint. In the next section BEN is presented as an engineering approach that is suitable for stakeholder-oriented EAM. Requirements for "business-to-IT" EAM tool support are derived and ADOben is presented as an appropriate solution and lessons from practical usage are discussed. The findings are summarized, and future research is outlined at the end of this chapter.

Characteristics of Mature Engineering Disciplines

Mary Shaw (Shaw, 1990) analyzed the development of classical engineering disciplines. She found that engineering disciplines produce cost efficient solutions for relevant problems by using scientific knowledge in the artifact design process in service to society. These aspects are now further characterized:

1. "Cost efficient solutions": Engineering does not only imply the construction of suitable solutions, but also emphasizes reasonable handling of given resources and conditions.

2. "For relevant problems": The constructed solution addresses practically relevant problems.

3. "By using scientific knowledge": The construction process is comprehensible and traceable based on scientific construction languages, methods, and frameworks so that the solutions will most likely fit the requirements.

4. "In service to society": The engineer acts in a responsible way by providing useful innovations to society and to the environment.

The following subsection gives an idea of addressing these aspects by analyzing classical engineering.

Reusability of Engineering Knowledge

Classical engineering disciplines distinguish between innovative construction and construction routine. Innovative constructions have to address new solutions while construction routine involves reusing existing solution patterns for known problems (Zwicky 1948).

Construction routine is the usual design form in classical engineering disciplines, while innovation is rather rare. To make the construction process as efficient as possible, the collection, organization, and conditioning of knowledge is necessary to make this knowledge available to less experienced engineers. All disciplines found appropriate media for this knowledge transfer, e.g. engineering handbooks (Avallone, et al. 2007; Dubbel, et al. 1994) and tool support for collaborative engineering (McGuire, et al. 1993).

Both construction routine and innovative construction are relevant in business engineering. To develop new innovative business models, thorough industry knowledge and creativity is needed, which prevents the application of a standardized design process. A major part of construction tasks in business engineering relies on routine processes, e. g. improving efficiency of a production process, standard software deployment or consolidation of business units. Business engineering principles, methods, techniques and tools have been designed and tested for these kinds of purposes.

Central Construction Plan and Standardized Construction Language

Mature engineering disciplines use a high level documentation (architecture) of the design artifact.[3] This plan depicts the main components and their relationships to each other that are needed in order to achieve the desired behavior. All mature engineering disciplines have developed standardized construction languages for architectural description. In mechanical engineering, for example, a dozen standards exist on how to design construction plans (Giesecke, et al. 2008). These standards are subject to early stages of mechanical engineering education since they are an essential means of

---

[3] Some engineering disciplines, including civil engineering and software engineering, use the "architectural blueprint" or "architectural design" (short architecture) as a central construction plan. In the following the term "architecture" is used as synonym for the central construction plan of all engineering disciplines.

communication. As an implicit part of corporate culture, every organization uses its own vocabulary for certain artifacts. Therefore a common language, which is not subject to standardization, but well understood within the individual organizational context, is often used.

Division of Labor

Besides structuring the system to be designed, the construction plan is used to structure the design process: the components of a system are constructed in teams and then assembled in order to become a whole according to the architecture. The division of labor during the construction process is a core feature of classical engineering disciplines, since it is the only way to construct complex systems in large teams.

Systematic Construction and Blueprint Analysis

Designing the architecture is the supreme discipline in engineering, which involves the transformation of requirements (problem space) into a high level blueprint of the system to be designed (solution space). Designing the architecture involves fundamental design decisions which have an impact on the whole design process. An example can be found in the definition of quality characteristics that the system to be constructed must address (e. g. Which changes to the system can be made easily, which not? What is the system's performance? What is the capacity of the system? How scalable is the system?).

Due to the mentioned responsibilities, great attention is paid to architecture and only experienced and highly qualified engineers are involved in the architectural design. By involving internal and external experts as well as complex analysis frameworks, engineers seek to ensure the quality of the architectural blueprint so that the architecture addresses all the required characteristics of the system to be designed.

In business engineering, enterprise architecture is the central construction plan to support documentation of the as-is architecture and to design the desired to-be state of the whole organization. This goes beyond most existing – mainly IT focused – approaches.

EA Management Based on the Business Engineering Approach

The enterprise architecture (EA) can be regarded as the central construction plan in business engineering. EA describes the main business and IT components as well as their relationships. EA is the result of important design decisions and determines fundamental characteristics of the organization, such as strategic positioning, business process efficiency and effectiveness, business/IT alignment, and information systems' capabilities. Indirectly, EA therefore implies e.g. an organization's capability to rapidly launch new products, to adapt to new regulations, or to exploit business potentials of IT innovations.

Following engineering principles, concrete requirements of internal and external stakeholders build the starting point for EA design. Not all of these requirements have effects on the fundamental structure of the organization (or EA), but they might still have partial influence as architectural drivers.

There exist different classes of architectural drivers. Two examples are functional and non-functional drivers. One class focuses on the functional development of the organization. Examples can be found in the opening of new markets and sales channels or business process outsourcing. Another class of architectural drivers focuses on optimization of organizational structures, e. g. by the consolidation of redundant structures or the reuse of existing resources to improve flexibility and prepare the organization for possible future changes.

Architectural drivers tend to have tradeoffs which require compromises in the architectural design. Priorities of the architectural drivers are subject to changes which might cause discontinuities in organizational development. A merger, for example, might change any given situation to set the focus on architectural consolidation.

The sketched complexity of the matter often causes difficulties for enterprise architects to choose the appropriate artifacts and relationships for the EA model. From an engineering perspective and taking experiences from EA projects in companies into account, the following heuristics can be derived.

Criterion of Width – Stakeholder Orientation

EA models must address the information demand of their stakeholders. Information demands are implied by management tasks (concerns) of the respective stakeholders. EA can for example deliver crucial data for project portfolio management to support decision-making, concerning investment decisions for business applications.

A successful method for stakeholder involvement turns out to be the collection and analysis of precise questions that stakeholders have, e. g. "Can investments in applications be justified by additional revenue, gained from the product or service which is supported by this application?" Situational fragments of the EA model (viewpoints) can help to answer such questions by representing the desired information on an aggregate level and in a form of representation which is appropriate for the respective stakeholder.

Following the criterion of width, all artifacts and relationships needed for the creation of viewpoints must be reflected in EA. The sum of information demands of all stakeholders therefore determines the maximum EA extent.

Criterion of Depth – Architecture vs. Detail Model

When EA is only designed in respect to the criterion of width, chances are high that a huge number of detailed structures of implementations or detailed inventories of single artifact types are included.

Architecture strategies which are derived from the architectural drivers and the desired characteristics of the whole system should also be included in EA. These architecture strategies need to be expressed and documented, so that their realization is measurable. Architecture strategies focus on the entire system or on groups of similar artifacts[4] such as all core business processes, all data flows across domains, or all products which are distributed over a certain channel. Structures which only focus on implementation details of one artifact, and which are only relevant for this object, should not be a part of EA. Exceptions might be useful in certain situations, e.g. to support concerns of a key stakeholder. The relevance of an arti-

---

[4] This heuristic is based on the locality criterion, initially published by DeRemer & Kron (1976) and then adapted by Eden & Kazman (2003). This criterion is adapted for enterprise architecture and informally described.

fact can be indicated by the impact that a change of this artifact has on others.[5] If a change of an artifact does not influence others at all, it should most likely not be included in EA. Following the idea that EA is the blueprint for change projects, problems can arise from making unnecessary design decisions for the entire architecture which should be better made for individual projects. Therefore, details such as object oriented class structures, detailed data structures, mapping information of network adaptors to servers, structures of teams in individual business units, workflow specifications of business processes, or construction details of products should not be part of EA. Figure 2 illustrates our general "broad and aggregate" understanding of EA.

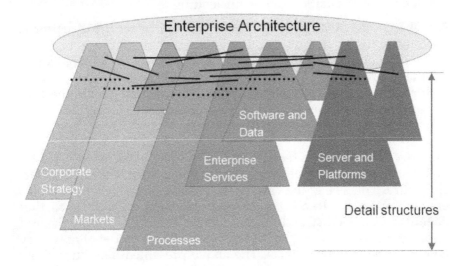

Figure 2. Enterprise Architecture is Broad and Aggregate

In two cases it can be useful to include detailed artifact structures in the EA model. In both cases, changes to the detailed structure cause potential changes to other artifacts, which means that the above mentioned heuristic remains valid:

1. **Relationships to other detailed artifact structures:** Examples can be found when deploying single software components on servers or assigning sub-goals to the responsible business units. A relationship on the detail level (e. g. application component and server) can always be observed on the respective aggre-

---

[5] This heuristic is based on encapsulation and information hiding, which originates in object orientation (cf. e.g. Parnas (1972)).

gated level (e. g. respective application and respective server cluster). Detail structures should only be included in EA when they have an impact on design decisions with effect on the entire system. This is true for the deployment of application components on servers, since the explicit documentation of this relationship might have a considerable impact on the ability of the organization to react in the case of a blacked out computing center. An example for a relationship on the detailed level without significant impact can be found in the assignment of application functions to detailed activities of a business process. In this case, the aggregate relationship between application and business process delivers sufficient information for EA purposes, while detail documentation can be misleading.

2. **Objects on detailed level can be reused in multiple artifacts:** Similar to the case above, the detail level should only be taken into account, if reuse has significant impact on the behavior of the entire system. This is the case in examples such as reuse of product components as part of a platform strategy. On the contrary, it is not the case when reusing libraries in multiple applications.

Moreover, it cannot be recommended to include many objects of a detail structure which all have similar relationships within the architecture. This is e.g. the case when considering all client computers (as inventory). In addition to the presented exceptions, further benefits of detailed structures may occur depending on the desired application scenario of the EA. The optimal level of detail may vary among projects and artifacts. The above presented heuristics allow guidance on a desired level of detail; however, in respect to different context factors no universal statements can be made.

A mature EAM, including organizational manifestation, such as defined maintenance processes and responsibilities and well-established communication of the EA will more easily be capable of providing detailed structures than less experienced green field implementations.

Pragmatic Criterion – Cost / Benefit Considerations

Organizations are subject to constant changes. Therefore EA models need to be updated regularly. Many projects show that continuous maintenance efforts incur high costs. Therefore it needs to be considered if the benefits resulting from covering a stakeholder concern exceed the costs necessary to gather and maintain this information. Not every stakeholder information demand which is claimed by the criterion of width will gain positive revenue. Therefore, the pragmatic criterion proposes to carefully analyze and evaluate the value of artifacts and relationships. No maintenance efforts should be put into artifacts which are not necessary for any concerns (Fischer, et al. 2007). Besides maintenance, initial modeling, establishment of governance structures, and tool support are examples of further cost drivers. Quantifying costs and benefits of information demand is far from trivial (cf. e.g. Schekkerman 2005): Benefit analysis often results in "reverse" considerations (what if we did not have this information?). Costs arise according to type, origin, necessary conditioning efforts, and frequency of usage. Information demands being served from the same pool of data might realize considerable synergies.

The main feature of the architecture is to provide a high level plan to support long term strategic development of an organization. High frequency in changes of detail information incurs high maintenance costs and can be used as an indicator that the level of aggregation is too low. From our experience, in most cases it is sufficient to use and maintain more aggregate structures (as proposed in the criterion of depth). Usually, high level models can be maintained with reasonable efforts manually, i.e. without having to develop and use automated interfaces to detail repositories (such as configuration management database, process model repository, product configuration system).

Business Engineering Navigator

BEN structures the various components of business engineering support for EAM. BEN is based on the above mentioned principles of engineering and addresses the main requirements of EAM. As a conceptualization of engineering support, BEN can also be regarded as the requirements specification for EAM tool support.

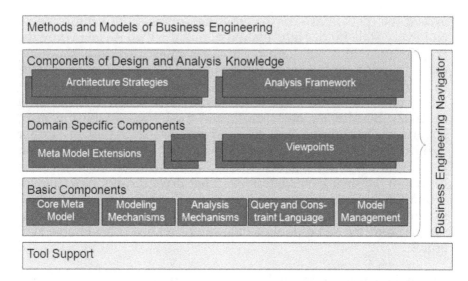

Figure 3. Architecture of the Business Engineering Navigator approach

Figure 3 illustrates the components of BEN and their assignment to abstraction layers. This structure can be used as a framework for practical as well as research projects. The components are sketched in the following.

Basic Components

Basic components include domain independent functionalities which are used to model, analyze and design EA.

- **Core Metamodel:** A common set of vocabulary is a major prerequisite to consistently design the five layers of the business engineering framework. The BEN metamodel is based on generic modeling methods and uses instances of all five layers of the framework. This meta-model serves as a standardized construction language for business engineering.

- **Modeling mechanisms:** A domain independent description language provides basic mechanisms to create EA models. This includes hierarchical refinement of artifacts using "part-of" and "is-in" relationships as well as domain clustering.

- **Analysis mechanisms:** Generic types of analyses and analysis mechanisms are instantiated for each concrete viewpoint (cf. below). Examples for generic types of analyses include matrix analysis, dependency diagrams, list reports, architecture views, and spider web diagrams (Bucher, et al. 2006).

- **Query and constraint language:** A query language is needed to analyze the EA model using predefined and ad-hoc queries. Using the constraint language, the architecture strategy and the architectural principles are specified and verified. Both languages are based on formalized modeling mechanisms, e. g. relational algebra.

- **Model management:** This basic component includes version management functionalities, such variants handling and model history. These aspects are crucial to model lifecycle management

Domain Specific Components

Domain specific components are instances of generic components for the different EA layers.

- **Meta-model extensions:** Specific extensions of the core meta-model allow the application of business engineering in specific contexts (e. g. a certain industry, a certain company size or maturity level) and in specific projects (e. g. business driven changes, IT driven changes, alignment projects).

- **Viewpoints:** A viewpoint catalogue is comprised of generic analysis mechanisms and types of analyses which are suited to given stakeholder information demands on all five architectural layers. Queries needed for each viewpoint can be formulated using the above introduced query language (IEEE, 2000).

Components of Design and Analysis Knowledge

Components of design and analysis knowledge help to keep a record of the EA engineers' knowledge.

- **Architecture strategies:** Generally valid and accepted EA design patterns and architectural strategies (e.g. handling of redundant master data) and principles can be organized as knowledge repositories (Buckl, et al. 2008).

- **Analysis framework:** An analysis framework implements models of quality and metrics for EA (e.g. analysis frameworks which help to refine aggregate targets, such as efficiency, into measurable counts, such as scalability, avoidance of redundancies, capability for multi channel usage (Schelp and Stutz 2007)). Results of the analysis are represented as viewpoints.

The BEN approach proposes to adapt EAM to the respective application scenarios of the respective organization. Therefore, generally valid and accepted components of design and analysis knowledge must be adapted, extended and integrated.

The BEN approach can be understood as the interface between methods of business engineering and the underlying software tools: On one hand, BEN defines requirements for software systems and gives assistance on how to use them in the context of the engineering discipline. On the other hand, BEN is a service layer for different methods, which may give concrete guidance in change and transformation for organizations.

EA Management Tool Support and Lessons from a First Application

BEN can serve as the foundation for the implementation or configuration of existing EAM software tools. Currently, no vendor offers support for the BEN approach in out-of-the-box configurations. The holistic view of the organization and method- and model-based engineering approaches especially are not yet found in commercial products. Therefore we have implemented ADOben as an implementation of BEN requirements based on ADONIS, a commercial modeling tool and flexible metamodeling platform. To support engineering based EAM, ADOben has a built-in reference meta-model that may be tailored to the applying organization and the desired application scenarios.

ADOben implements model types for all five layers of the business engineering framework. Therefore it is possible to design an architecture for the as-is situation. Using the means of architecture analysis and a dedicated architecture strategy, a blueprint for the to-be situation can be designed (Figure 4).

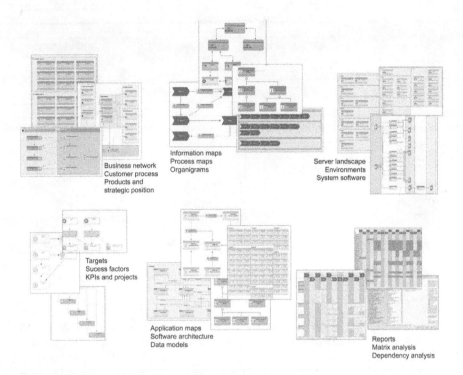

Business network
Customer process
Products and
strategic position

Information maps
Process maps
Organigrams

Server landscape
Environments
System software

Targets
Sucess factors
KPIs and projects

Application maps
Software architecture
Data models

Reports
Matrix analysis
Dependency analysis

Figure 4. Examples for Models and Analysis Types in ADOben

The following examples illustrate some ADOben features by using different scenarios where ADOben can address stakeholders' concerns by delivering adequate analysis results.

1. **Launch of a new product**. Information demands of the respective stakeholders could be: "Do we have adequate application support for the new product?", "Where are potential breaks between applications along the process?" Using the query "Which applications are used in which process for which product?" on the architecture model, a three dimensional matrix report as shown in Figure 5 is created. The matrix shows the products and processes as well as the underlying applications in the matrix cells.

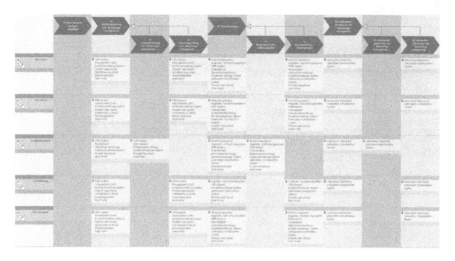

Figure 5. Three Dimensional Matrix Report in ADOben

2. **Business continuity planning.** The stakeholders' concerns in business continuity planning might be "Which applications are affected in case of a hardware failure?" or "Are all critical applications deployed on redundant server clusters?" The ADOben query to answer these questions is "How are the applications distributed across servers/server clusters?", which can also be displayed as a three dimensional matrix report.

3. **Compliance management.** Relevant information demands in this area (e.g. concerning ownership concepts required by Solvency II or Basel II) include "What is the implementation rate of process ownership or data ownership (organization layer)?" and "What is the implementation rate of authorization and reuse (software layer)?" This information demand can be addressed by a report "Show all applications that have not been assigned an owner."

4. **Business development.** Information demands in this field might be "Across which channels are the individual product distributed?" and "Which target groups are addressed by the individual products?" The respective analysis displays the strategic positioning including products, channels and customer segments.

As a first means of feasibility evaluation, the BEN approach has been implemented at a globally operating financial service provider based in Germany using ADOben. The application of the approach verified that EA should be positioned as a planning tool, not as a tool focused on operative tasks (like for example a configurations management database system). To achieve this, the three criteria defining EA scope have proven to be valuable. The criterion of width requires that the EA meta-model and the viewpoints are developed in close collaboration with all stakeholders of the EA. To get the buy-in of the stakeholders, the introduction of EAM should be taken as a chance to revise the planning and documentation processes within the organization in order to ensure that the EAM organization concept is integrated seamlessly and does not cause an overhead work load for the stakeholders. Contrarily, ADOben supported the stakeholders embedded in existing planning processes. The analysis capabilities of ADOben, especially matrix analyses have turned out to be a valuable tool to foster and rationalize the communication between the IT unit and the business units as well as to systematically address alignment questions between business structures and IT structures.

Summary and Outlook

Based on an analysis of the engineering approach in general, this paper presents the business engineering approach to EAM and BEN, a conceptual structure for EAM engineering support. It is shown how EA models can be constructed based on stakeholder requirements in order to create a pragmatic solution representing a "broad and aggregate", business-to-IT architecture – and not a set of enterprise-wide detail models which will never be completed and which will soon be outdated. BEN delivers a foundation for efficient EA design and EAM. BEN can be implemented in software tools and applied using business engineering methods to enable the structured design of solutions.

Business engineering, BEN and ADOben show that the engineering of complex environments involves a complex 'mechanism'. This mechanism can be evaluated according to its applicability and to its connectivity to other approaches, tools, and methods. The development of this mechanism is aimed at a clear structure so that elements can be arranged according to the respective situation as a best-of-breed solution. This means that ADOben is one solution to implement BEN as an EAM support tool. It is, of course, possible to implement BEN using other software tools. At the same time, BEN is not limited for the use in the context of EAM. The core idea is to ensure structured engineering. Further research activities in this area will focus on the methods themselves and their situational character. The ultimate goal is to provide engineering support for the situational development and maintenance of "business-to-IT" solutions – in the context of EAM, but also for integration management, for information logistics management, for IT/business alignment and other complex problem scenarios in information management.

COHERENCY MANAGEMENT

References

Avallone, E. A., Baumeister, T., and Sadegh, A. (2007). Marks' Standard Handbook for Mechanical Engineers, McGraw-Hill Professional.

Bucher, T., Fischer, R., Kurpjuweit, S., and Winter, R. (2006). "Analysis and Application Scenarios of Enterprise Architecture - An Exploratory Study", EDOC Workshop on Trends in Enterprise Architecture Research (TEAR 2006). Tenth IEEE International EDOC Conference (EDOC 2006), Hong Kong.

Buckl, S., Ernst, A. M., Lankes, J.; and Matthes, F. (2008). Enterprise Architecture Management Pattern Catalog. Munich.

DeRemer, F., and Kron, H. H. (1976). Programming-in-the-large versus programming-in-the-small. IEEE Transactions on Software Engineering. Volume 2, Number 2. pp. 80-86.

Dubbel, H., Kuttner, K. H., and Beitz, W. (1994). Handbook of Mechanical Engineering. Springer: Berlin.

Eden, A. H., and Kazman, R. (2003). Architecture, Design, and Implementation. International Conference on Software Engineering (ICSE). Portland, OR. pp. 149-159.

Fischer, R., Aier, S., and Winter, R. (2007). A Federated Approach to Enterprise Architecture Model Maintenance. Enterprise Modelling and Information Systems Architectures. Volume 2, Number 2. pp. 14-22.

Giesecke, F. E., Mitchell, A., Spencer, H. C., Hill, I. L., Dygdon, J. T., Novak, J. E., and Lockhart, S. D. (2008). Technical Drawing. Pearson Education: Denver, CO.

Harry, M. J. (1998). The Nature of Six Sigma Quality. Motorola University Press: Rolling Meadows, IL.

IEEE. (2000). IEEE Recommended Practice for Architectural Description of Software Intensive Systems (IEEE Std 1471-2000). IEEE Computer Society, New York.

McGuire, J. G., Kuokka, D. R., Weber, J. C., Tenenbaum, J. M., Gruber, T. R., and Olsen, G. R. (1993). SHADE: Technology for Knowledge-based Collaborative Engineering. Concurrent Engineering. Volume 1, Number 3. pp. 137-146.

Parnas, D. L. (1972). On the criteria to be used in decomposing systems into modules. Communications of the ACM. Volume 15, Number 12. pp. 1053-1058.

Schekkerman, J. (2005). The Economic Benefits of Enterprise

Architecture: How to Quantify and Manage the Economic Value of Enterprise Architecture. Trafford Publishing: Victoria, British Columbia.

Schelp, J., and Stutz, M. (2007). A Balanced Scorecard Approach to Measure the Value of Enterprise Architecture. Journal of Enterprise Architecture. Volume 3, Number 4. pp. 8-14.

Shaw, M. (1990). Prospects for an Engineering Discipline of Software. IEEE Software. Volume 7, Number 6. pp. 15-24.

Winter, R. (2008). Business Engineering - Betriebswirtschaftliche Konstruktionslehre und ihre Anwendung in der Informationslogistik. In Integrierte Informationslogistik. B. Dinter and R. Winter (Ed.), Springer: Berlin, Heidelberg. pp. 17-38.

Winter, R., and Fischer, R. (2007). Essential Layers, Artifacts, and Dependencies of Enterprise Architecture. Journal of Enterprise Architecture. Volume 3, Number 2. pp. 7-18.

Zwicky, F. (1948). Morphological Astronomy. The Observatory. Volume 68, 1948. pp. 121-143

About the Authors

Dr. Stephan Aier has been Research Project Manager at the Institute of Information Management at the University of St. Gallen since 2006. Stephan studied Industrial Engineering and Management at the Berlin University of Technology, Germany, where he received his Doctoral Degree in 2006. Stephan is a founding member of the competence centers "Enterprise Application Integration" (2002) and "Enterprise Architecture" (2005) at the Berlin University of Technology. Since 2006 he has been head of the Research Group Integration and Architecture at the Institute of Information Management with the "Competence Center Integration Factory". These competence center projects are realized in close collaboration with several companies funding all of the research work. With each of the companies individual research projects are set up, which are coordinated by Stephan. Stephan is a member of the Organizing Committee of the "Trends in Enterprise Architecture Research" (TEAR) workshops. Furthermore he is one of the editors of the "Enterprise Architecture" book series and author of numerous publications in the areas of architecture and integration.

Stephan Kurpjuweit is member of the Business Engineering Navigator (BEN) research team at the Institute of Information Management at the University of St. Gallen (IWI-HSG). After earning a Masters' Degree in Computer Science from the University of Kaiserslautern, Germany, Stephan gained three years of practical project experience in systems development and modeling research. He joined the Institute of Information Management, University of St. Gallen, in September 2005 as Research Assistant and Doctoral Student. His research interests include enterprise architecture management, design and analysis. He has conducted research projects in the area of enterprise architecture modeling and analysis and as a Visiting Scientist at the Software Engineering Institute (SEI), Carnegie Mellon University.

Jan Saat is research assistant at the Competence Center Integration Factory (CCIF) at the Institute of Information Management at the University of St. Gallen (IWI-HSG). After Masters' Studies in Business Administration and Economics at the Technical University of Freiberg (Germany) and Poznan University of Economics (Poland), he joined IWI-HSG in 2006. His research interests include enterprise architecture management, integration management, and service-oriented architectures. Jan is enrolled in the PhD program for Business Innovation at the University of St. Gallen.

Prof. Dr. Robert Winter is tenured Chair of Information Management at the University of St. Gallen (HSG), Director of HSG's research Institute of Information Management and Academic Director of HSG's Executive Master of Business Engineering program. After Masters' studies in Business Administration and Business Education at Goethe University, Frankfurt (Germany), he was Research Assistant in Frankfurt for ten years before joining HSG in 1996. Professor Winter founded HSG's Executive Business Engineering Program in 1998 and is its Academic Director until today. In research, he is responsible for consortia projects ("competence centers") in the areas of information logistics/data warehousing (since 1999), enterprise architecture (since 2000), integration management (since 2002), healthcare (since 2005) and corporate controlling (since 2006). He is a regular speaker at events in Switzerland and abroad, member of the scientific board of several institutions, and has authored and/or edited more than ten books as well as over 100 scientific publications. He is co-editor of "BIT – Banking and Information Technology" as well as Member of the Editorial Boards of "Wirtschaftsinformatik", "Business and Information Systems Engineering", "Information Systems and e-Business Management" and "Enterprise Modelling and Information Systems Architectures".

Stephan Aier, Stephan Kurpjuweit, Jan Saat, Robert Winter
University of St. Gallen
Institute of Information Management
Mueller-Friedberg-Strasse 8
9000 St. Gallen, Switzerland
stephan.aier, stephan.kurpjuweit, jan.saat, robert.winter}@unisg.ch

Chapter 4

FRAMING ENTERPRISE ARCHITECTURE: A META-FRAMEWORK FOR ANALYZING ARCHITECTURAL EFFORTS IN ORGANIZATIONS

Marijn Janssen

Editors' Preface

As part of EA planning, EA programs have the need to estimate the effort needed. Current literature and practice approaches do not offer much help in this regard. EA effort estimations are based on experience of the team involved. There is clearly a lack of scientific / heuristic- based approaches available. There are several reasons for the current state: (A) Most of the EA discipline development, to date, has focused on frameworks, methodologies, notations, tools, toolkits etc. (B) EA is still evolving, as in, the footprint (scope and nature) of the EA programs are currently still left to the specific needs of the organizations, and (C) Emergence (but current lack) of standards in EA.

The chapter presents an architecture meta-framework that views the architectural elements (subsystems) and the dependencies among the elements. These linkages, captured through a series of layers, provide the necessary inputs for coherency.

The meta-framework is comprehensive to the extent that is looks into how it can be useful in the 'extended' and 'embedded' mode. It is important to be mindful of the fact that in the embedded mode, EA happens not because of a special program in the organization, but in the course of regular activities. The EA team / group sets the policies, principles, standards, formats etc. and the organization looks to harvest the usual management artifacts for the purposes of EA.

Even though not mentioned explicitly, the proposed meta-framework is generic enough to be compatible with existing methodologies (like TOGAF ADM) and also provides the capability for further enhancements. Furthermore, the chapter presents scenarios where the framework is expected to perform well and why. This, we believe, is important for understanding the ramifications of adopting the framework for organizations.

Introduction

In the very foundation, Enterprise Architecture (EA) aims to bridge the gap between business and technology. As such it should address the dependencies among a large number of heterogeneous elements (Doucet et al, 2008). Traditionally, the purpose of EA is to effectively align the strategies of enterprises with their business processes and the coordination of their resources (Zachman, 1987). EAs define and inter-relate data, hardware, software, and communication resources, as well as the supporting organization required to maintain the overall physical structure required by the architecture (Richardson et al, 1990). Nowadays, there has been a shift from the foundation architecture, to the extended architecture resulting in the embedded architectures (Doucet et al, 2008).

Enterprise architecture (EA) aims to bridge the gap between business and ICT departments and conceptual and implementation design by defining a systems composition from various viewpoints. Often, it incorporates a blueprint of the existing and desired design and an overall plan regarding the realization of part of it. Enterprise architecture (EA) lacks a universally accepted definition (Ross, 2003). EA has been characterized as a system of systems (Kaisler et al, 2005), as the "master plan" or "city plan" (Rohloff, 2005) detailing policies and standards for the design of infrastructure technologies, databases, and applications (Bernard, 2004; Ross, 2003). EA efforts are often aimed at creating some kind of coherence and structure in a chaotic environment using systematic approaches (Armour et al, 1999; Doucet et al, 2008). Enterprise architecture models provide ways to deal with the complexity including work (who, where), function (how), information (what) and infrastructure (how to) (Ross, 2003). The main idea of enterprise architecture is that it can be used to guide design decisions and to ensure that the dependencies among elements are managed.

The enterprise architecture framework formula specifies how information technology is related to the overall business processes and outcomes of organizations, describing relationships among technical, organizational, and institutional components of the enterprise (Zachman, 1987). While these general frameworks are useful, and there exists some literature comparing the frameworks (e.g. Leist et al, 2006; Schekkerman, 2003), very little is known about how they are adapted and used. Furthermore, the focus of the efforts is dependent on the way the framework is translated to the organization and the allocated resources. The use and effectiveness is determined by the governance of the architecture. As such, there is a need for a framework that supports the evaluation of the use of enterprise architecture in organizations.

Doucet et al. (2008) argue that coherency management is the primarily outcome of EA efforts. Coherence should ensure that the competitive resources and capabilities of the firm should be "complementary" or "synergistic" and that the elements operate in concert. A meta-framework can be used to investigate if the organizational architecture is coherent. In this chapter we will present a framework for analyzing and framing enterprise architecture efforts. The purpose is not to create yet another EA framework. The goal is to help architects and managers to position their EA efforts and to show what elements could be part. As such, the framework remains at a meta-level and can be used to show the focus of the EA and identify elements currently (purposefully) not covered by EA.

Architecture Meta-Framework

Basically, EA is the overview of the enterprise as a whole, from a helicopter point of view, equipped with x-ray vision in which you not only look at the existing state but also at possible future states. In our view, *enterprise architecture* is something abstract that remains at a conceptual level (is an abstract description of reality or an abstract description of wanted realities) and is a frame of reference to guide *design* efforts (design as the creation of an artifact) and, at the same time, serves as a framework for positioning the design projects. The designs are aimed at improving (parts of the) *infrastructure* (the actual reality, i.e. implementations) and take into account the relationships, as depicted by the architecture (or link between strategy and designers). Architecture can be descriptive or prescriptive. Design projects change the infrastructure and therefore the descriptive architecture needs to be updated. The experiences and results of the design projects, and resulting infrastructure, influence the prescriptive architecture, as new standards, architectural principles, reusable building blocks etc., are created in these design projects.

Any functioning enterprise has, either explicitly or implicitly, an 'Architecture'. The progression of EA thought and practice has largely been a process of accumulation, not replacement (Doucet et al, 2008). The foundation architecture is an abstraction of the existing infrastructure and a prescription of the Next Generation of Infrastructures (NGI). Figure 1 schematically depicts this cycle of abstraction, design and implementation and realization of the NGI, which, in turn, results in an update of the descriptive architecture and influences the prescriptive architecture. This view closely resembles problem-solving cycles in which the architecture is the descriptive and prescriptive conceptual model (Mitroff et al, 1974; Sol, 1982). In many organizations the focus might be on architecture in a descriptive, or a prescriptive sense, or in both.

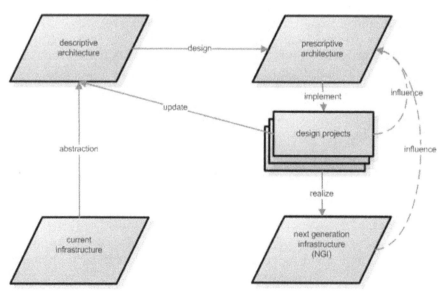

COHERENCY MANAGEMENT

Figure 1. Enterprise Architecture as Abstraction from Reality

Subsystems and the dependencies among subsystems can be viewed to ensure coherency. Malone and Crowston (1994) define *coordination* as "managing dependencies between activities" and a coordinating mechanism as "the way the interdependent activities and decisions are managed". Generically, architecture is the description of the set of elements and the relationships between them (Armour et al, 1999) and architecture is aimed at creating a coherent and consistent set of relationships among (sub)systems (Doucet et al, 2008; Janssen et al, 2005). The common element is that enterprise architecture refers to a set of interdependent elements described at a certain level of abstraction and the blueprint describes the relationships among the elements. We follow Janssen and Verbraeck (2005) and define *enterprise architecture* as the coordination of subsystems at various levels of abstractions for the purpose of developing the NGI. In this definition, enterprise architecture will be used in both a descriptive or prescriptive manner. Furthermore, coordination can occur at various levels of abstraction and a variety of coordination mechanisms are possible. EA looks at the interrelationship between elements and therefore, an essential component of architecture is the description of subsystems and its components.

The subsystems can have a different granularity and be heterogeneous in nature. Often, a layered approach is given to organize these subsystems or components in categories of similar objects... A layered approach is a systems approach aimed at dealing with the complexity. Ideally, a layered model has the following characteristics (e.g. Stallings, 2006):

1.   Each layer performs a cohesive or closely related set of functions

2.   Higher layers use services provided by the lower layers

3.   Layers are sufficiently loosely coupled to allow changes in one layer without affecting other layers

The layered approach is nowadays motivated by Service-Oriented Architectures (SOA). The basic idea of SOAs is to decompose a system into parts that are made accessible by services, to design these services individually and to construct new systems using these single services (Cherbakov et al, 2005). Each component provides a (set of) function(s) accessible by one or more services for use by other components. Service-orientation makes the architecture agile, as companies can easily substitute components without having to change the interface or other components.

Adopting service-orientation offers many benefits to enterprises, making it possible to create services that are modular, accessible, well-described, implementation-independent and interoperable (Fremantle et al, 2002, p. 80). A variety of services can be covered including business services and low-grained software services. The type of services can be divided in layers. In EA, layers can be used to group and structure similar kind of items, including services. Each layer is dependent on other layers and the dependencies within a layer and between layers should be addressed. Furthermore, standards, models and architectural principles can be positioned in each layer. In this way, the EA design process becomes a process of defining layers, as well as the services provided in each of the layers.

The premise of SOA is that it has tremendous potential and can offer improved efficiency, reduce development costs and risks, create agility and flexibility and enable us to reuse existing systems (Khoshafian, 2006; Krafzig et al, 2004; McGovern et al, 2006). Services can occur at various levels of granularity and can be composed of other services. For example, a business service might be the handing of claims which is created by a business process consisting of an application service for identifying the user, and an information service for obtaining customer information. The latter uses, in turn, an infrastructure service for secure communication. In this way, services can occur at various layers including business, business process, information, application and infrastructure, and become the main focus of EA efforts.

Our layered model is especially focused on the characteristic one of Stallings (2006), where layers should describe a set of cohesive or closely related set of elements in order to create structure in a chaotic environment. Characteristics two and three of Stallings can be used as architectural principles guiding the development of a prescriptive architecture, as the current infrastructure might not adhere to these two characteristics. In this way, a complex system can be decomposed in elements categorized using some criterion.

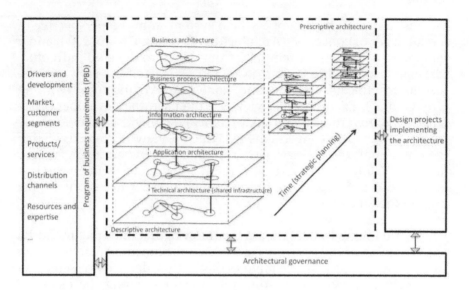

Figure 2. Overview Architectural Meta-Framework

Tapscott and Caston (1993) identified a number of categories of business drivers in which the ICT and business contexts need to be balanced. These categories are adopted as layers in our framework and include the organizational, business process, information, application, and technical architecture layers. EA efforts can be organized using the five layers, depicted in the middle of Figure 2, that constitute the core elements of our meta-framework.

Each layer and even each system can be further decomposed. Functional decomposition is a common approach found in systems theory (Sage et al, 2000). A system can be decomposed into parts, developed and only thereafter integrated with the other systems based on the architecture. Each function has inputs and outputs and the hierarchical decomposition describes the transformation from available inputs to outputs. Layers might be further decomposed in sub layers. For example the information architecture layer might contain the sub layers' product information, management information and operational process information. Furthermore, elements in the layers might be further decomposed into sub-elements. In this way, a more detailed architecture with various levels of abstraction can be created.

The layers provide a coordination view and are aimed at creating coherency; however, they do not include various viewpoints on the system (Architecture Working Group, 2000; Zachman, 1987). A view is "a representation of a whole system from the perspective of a related set of concerns" (Architecture Working Group, 2000) and a viewpoint a "pattern or template from which to develop individual views by establishing the purposes and audience for a view and the techniques for its creation and analysis" (Architecture Working Group, 2000). Examples of a view are the user, the developer or security, the governance and adaptability view, and a viewpoint establishes the rules conventions by which a view is created, visualized and analyzed. These views typically go beyond a single layer and can be added as a vertical column which goes through the layers. We did not add views to the figure, in order to keep it simple and understandable.

EA is often aimed at creating a common operational picture and a shared vision of the enterprise and its environment. An architecture can be descriptive, prescriptive or both. In a descriptive sense, an architecture shows the existing relationships among the elements which can be used to analyze the weaknesses and opportunities. In a prescriptive sense it can be used as a concept of the desired future situation and operationalized as a blueprint that needs to be realized within a certain timeframe. If both descriptive and prescriptive architectures are available, a growth path or strategic roadmap from the current to the envisioned future situation can be realized, as depicted by the time (strategic planning) axis of Figure 2. The need to realize a new situation results in implementation projects, which are shown on the right hand of the figure, which in turn influence the descriptive and prescriptive architecture as already explained using Figure 2.

Figure 2 shows that the enterprise architecture in the middle is closely related to the environment, its governance and to implementation projects. Architectural governance mechanisms are necessary to make the architecture work. It should ensure that the architecture is actually used. The environment, governance and implementation elements can change the enterprise architecture descriptions and in turn, the enterprise architecture can influence these three elements. As such, these other three elements are considered to be part of the meta-framework.

Environment and Strategy

The *business and multi-actor environment* contains the situational factors influencing the architectures. These include elements like the products, market segments, market and technology developments, as well as the resources and capabilities that can be used for realizing the architecture and resulting infrastructure. This element contains all information necessary as input for engineering the EA.

The outcome of this element is a *program of business demands* **(PBD)** that is used as a starting point for defining the desired enterprise architecture (Nijhuis, 2006). The PBD serves as a bridge between the Business environment and strategic objectives, on the one hand, and the enterprise architecture, on the other hand. The PBD has to provide a concrete indication to what requirements the EA has to meet. Thus, the PBD is a guideline for the development of the architectures, and it will be used, in retrospect, to test their quality. Further, the requirements should be consistent and coherent and, as such, contain trade-offs, e.g. preference of low costs over high service levels or proven technology over innovativeness. The PBD focuses completely on the desired situation.

Often the PBD consists of a collection of architectural principles. *Principles* are general rules and guidelines, intended to be enduring and seldom amended, that inform and support the way in which an organization sets about fulfilling its mission (Perks et al, 2002; Richardson et al, 1990). Principles can be described 1) Name, 2) Statement, 3) Rationale and 4) Implications (Perks et al, 2002). These principles provide the basis for decision-making throughout all departments, organizations and projects.

Architecture Layers

The PBD needs to be operationalized in a conceptual architecture. Architecture layers are the core of the meta-framework, as it can be used to analyze the relationship within and between architecture layers and can be used to position systems, standards, architectural guidelines and other architectural methods and tools. Architecture layers are aimed at relating the various systems within and between layers. The highest layers are focused on the business, whereas, the lower layers are more focused on the technical aspects. As such the layers can be used to align the business and IT with each other by analyzing the coherence between business and IT using the layers. The layers can be designed using a top-down approach starting from the strategy or PBD, a bottom-up approach starting with the existing systems, a middle-out approach consisting of a combination of bottom-up and top-down approach or by first creating the vision on the architecture and creating a prescriptive architecture.

Business Architecture

The organizational or business architecture layer is aimed at describing the arrangements of the responsibilities around the most important value-creating activities. This layer describes the decomposition of the enterprise in different responsibilities and the coherence among those responsibilities (Versteeg et al, 2005). This layer deals with who is responsible for a specified organizational part and decouples the business domains from each other. Organizational parts typically provide service to one or more other parts. As such, each organizational part should have clear interfaces and service level agreements with the other parts to ensure coherence and smooth functioning of the complete organization.

The organizational level is related to the business process level, as it should be clear who is responsible for the continuous improvement of the end-to-end process. After all, many business processes will go beyond traditional departmental boundaries. This level is related to the information layer, as accountability for information and information quality should be part of the allocation of responsibilities. Furthermore, in this layer, who is responsible for controlling and maintaining applications in the application layers and ensuring service levels are met should be described.

Business Process Architecture

The business process architecture layer is a collection of business processes and the relationships among them. It describes the functional composition of the business into process flows. Business process architecture can serve to define the scope of design projects by showing the boundaries of the domain of interest and the needed output of a process.

A business process is a collection of interrelated tasks which solve a particular issue. There are at least three types of business processes:

1. Management and control processes: governing the operation of a system;
2. Operational processes: constitute the core business and are aimed at adding customer value;
3. Supporting processes: support the core processes.

A set of business processes begins with a customer's need and ends with that need being fulfilled. A business process can be further decomposed into sub-processes. Sub-processes can be triggered by external or internal events. Usually, these processes are the result of customer interactions, but the business process itself can trigger another one or might start periodically (for example invoicing).

The analysis of business process architecture typically includes the mapping of the main processes triggered by external events. A business process can be further specified into tasks in design and implementation projects. Many reengineering projects start with the business processes and this phenomenon is called Business Process Reengineering (BPR) (Hammer 1990; O'Neill et al, 1999). Each business process can be related to the resources it consumes and the products it produces. Resources include human capacity and information. The products produced by an activity can, themselves, be consumed as resources by other activities.

Information Architecture

The information architecture layer is aimed at describing the information assets aimed at storing, processing, reusing and distribution of information across information resources to fulfill the stakeholder needs. Information architecture is the organization of information to aid information sharing among actors. Information architecture is the pivot between the business processes and applications, business process use and process information and information stored in applications.

Information stewardship is often used as a principle for organizing this layer. Information stewardship is making departments or persons accountable for information and its quality. The steward oversees information throughout its life cycle. If the information steward also owns the information, a vital records registry is created. In such registries information is stored and maintained and all other departments have to make use of this register and are not allowed to store this information in their own systems.

Application Architecture

The application architecture layer contains the conceptualization of the software applications, components and objects, and the relationship between these parts. As such, this layer is typically further decomposed in different types of applications (business process management, document management, office applications etc). In addition this layer should guide application selection and the integration of applications with each other.

Architecture-based application planning should take place at the portfolio level (Hamilton, 2004). "Information technology portfolio management is the management of IT as a portfolio of assets similar to a financial portfolio aimed at improving the performance of the portfolio by balancing risks and returns" (Jeffery et al, 2004). Nowadays, it is sometimes argued that the attention shifts from application to service portfolios, as it can quicken implementation and lower costs, as it enables the rapid composition of service provisioning processes from reusable components (Janssen et al, 2006). As such, the management and development of services become the key focus.

Technical Architecture (or Shared Infrastructure)

The Technical architecture or shared infrastructure is about generic facilities, used by many other systems. It is about functionality that is a common need of many different systems and should not be mixed up with the terms "current or next-generation infrastructure". The shared infrastructure contains the network infrastructure, the operating systems and other generic services and facilities providing functionality that is used by many systems. This layer is the foundation for the creation of the application architecture. Over time more and more systems become part of this layer, as many current efforts are targeted at developing reusable building blocks and assembling new systems using these building blocks.

Implementation, Control and Maintenance

The architecture needs to be implemented by projects and projects change the architecture. In this way, these two parts are mutually dependent on each other. Even sub products, like the realization of a component, might alter the architecture, as a component can be used as a building block in the architecture. Architecture is never the end. Architectures need to be implemented, controlled and maintained in an efficient and effective way. Only in this way, "EA can be considered the ongoing, overarching method for abstracting, analyzing, designing, and re-engineering new and existing enterprises" (Doucet et al, 2008). The projects contribute to the realization of the EA and need to take into account the architecture. For this purpose, architectural governance is needed.

Architectural Governance

Letting an architecture work, depends on people, the creating of commitment and mutual understanding and trust. People should have incentives to adhere to the principles and rules and be motivated to make use of the architecture. Architectural governance is a form of IT governance that can be described as "the structure of processes to direct and control the enterprise in order to achieve the enterprise's goals by adding value while balancing risk versus return over IT and its processes" (Peterson 2004). Governance represents the framework for decision rights and accountabilities to encourage desirable behavior in the use of resources (Weill et al, 2002). Enterprises generally design three kinds of governance mechanisms: (1) decision-making structures, (2) alignment processes and (3) formal communications (Weill et al, 2005). These mechanisms should ensure that the architecture is known and disseminated among the organization and is necessary for embedding architecture in all aspects of the organization, in this way creating an embedded architecture (Doucet et al, 2008).

IT often requires major investments for organizations and can comprise hundreds or even thousands of projects running simultaneously across departments. Therefore, applications or service portfolios can be important government instruments. Furthermore, service portfolios form the bases for planning further development. In this way, a portfolio can help to develop a growth plan determining which services should be developed by whom, when new releases of existing services should be developed, the expected functionality, performance and characteristics of services, who should maintain the services or how the services should be sourced.

Evaluating an Enterprise Architecture

The meta-framework was used to evaluate the architectural efforts of a large organization. This organization consisted of several departments; one department responsible for all front-office activities, several back-office departments, and several supporting departments. In the front office most of the applications were developed in-house, whereas in the back-office applications were bought on the market and provided by proprietary software vendors. The type of research undertaken was action research, as the researchers became involved in the application of the framework. The company wanted to assess its architectural effort and to know how it should be expanded to make architecture an integral part of the organization.

Relation to the environment and strategy

It was found that there were clear strategic objectives; however there was no such thing as a PBD that was used to translate the strategy into a set of requirements on the prescriptive architecture. This resulted in limited coherence among decisions. For example, it was not clear if open source software was favored over vendor developed software and, as a result, both types of software could be found within the company. Another example is that it was unclear if the use of open standards was more important than the cost of buying a software package. As a result, these types of choices were made during the execution of projects. Furthermore, the priority might be different for the front and back office, as the front office applications were primarily developed in-house and the back office applications on the market.

Another example is that the ambition of the board was to integrate with all the systems of all their trading partners. There was no prioritization based on the ease to integrate systems or transaction volumes and it was not clear if it would be feasible to integrate with all systems. It could be easily calculated that integration with all systems would be too expensive and never be profitable. It was concluded that the PBD was necessary to get a better grip on the architecture. In the PBD the front and back office domains should be addressed separately and clear objectives should be stated and prioritized.

Focus on layers

In this company, EA was primarily used to show the dependencies among applications and provide a means for understanding and managing the complex application landscape. Standards for ensuring interoperability were developed, identical and similar systems were identified and rationalized, and reusable software components that could be accessed as web services were identified. The scope of the architectures needs to be balanced, as not everything can be done when having limited resources and capabilities, therefore the focus on the application layer was viewed as the right decision by management. Although the focus on the application layer in the architectural framework is a logical one and can result in large cost savings, the comparison of the relationships with the other architecture layers showed that the responsibilities for developing reusable applications were not allocated. This was left to the projects, which were primarily aimed at developing systems for their own purpose and were not focused on designing reusable systems. The relationship among the application and organizational layer was ignored and a recommendation was to better allocate resources.

Architectural principles were primarily aimed at supporting system design and included principles like the reuse of existing information, defining all data elements and storing it, always allocating ownership of processes and data to a certain owner who is responsible for ensuring the quality. Furthermore, the principles were only stated and the rationale and implications of the principles were not described, as suggested by Perks and Beveridge (2002).

Implementation, control and maintenance

Like in most other organizations, the design of an EA was a balancing act as time as well as resources were limited and circumstances changed continuously. The level of abstraction of the EA needed to be balanced. This included the granularity of the descriptions and prescription of applications. Applications can be spelled out or the EA can only give guidelines at a high level of abstraction. The architects had the tendency to spell out the system in much detail. This did have the advantage that the right kind of granularity was taken for developing reusable components. By having this level of detail, the architecture became less agile and vulnerable to changes, as it provided less freedom to the system developers, required more resources from the architectural department, needed a long time to develop and needed to be changed if new applications would be needed. Instead of making clear decisions concerning the preferred direction and setting the constraints, the architects took over the roles of the designers.

Architectural governance

There were several departments that had their own way of working and defined their own standards; as such the architectural governance was weak. There were no clear decision-making structures and alignment processes. There was formal (and informal) communications to ensure that the architecture was known by the staff and that the staff would understand the role of the architecture. The interviews showed that architecture was primarily viewed as a playing tool for the architectural department, which could be easily ignored. This resulted in a continuation of the interoperability problems and economies of scales could not be accomplished as facilities were not shared and components were not reused.

As a portfolio instrument, a list of applications was created. Every two months an application portfolio team met and decided on the buying of new applications. The primarily focus of the team was on standard software packages like drawing software. Reusable services were not integrated in this portfolio and the portfolio was not used as part of the software development process.

By using the framework it was illustrated that some elements that are typically part of architectural efforts were not addressed in the organization. The framework is not normative in the sense that this would automatically imply that the missing elements should be addressed. Addressing all elements might not be possible given the limited amount of resources or simply not necessary. EA is often focused on solving certain problems and for solving these problems certain elements can be addressed. In this company, management did not mind that the focus of the EA was on the application layer. They viewed EA as being an instrument for getting a grip on the applications, and decided to reconsider this once the other elements were addressed. The managers did mind that there was no PBD, the lack of governance, especially the bypassing of the EA in projects.

The result of this analysis was that elements were included in the year thereafter.

Conclusion

In this chapter a meta-architecture framework was presented aimed at helping architects and managers to position their EA efforts and to show what elements could be part of the EA efforts. The framework remains at a meta-level and can be used to show the focus of the EA and identify elements currently, which could be purposefully, not covered by EA. This was illustrated using a case study.

The core elements of our meta-framework consist of a layered model that can be further decomposed into sub-layers and systems. The layers can group similar elements and the layered models can be used to show the coherence among elements. Components, accessible as services, can be positioned in the layered model. By substituting components, without affecting the service interface, the EA becomes agile. The meta-framework shows that both descriptive and prescriptive architectures can be available, and that a growth path or a strategic roadmap from the current to the envisioned future situation can be determined, as part of the architectural efforts. On each layer, standards, models and architectural principles can be defined and positioned. Another element includes the multi-actor environment and organizational strategy resulting in a program of business demands guiding the decision-making. PBD is crucial as this is the link with the organization strategy and determines the priorities or goals for the architecture. The last elements are the design projects implementing the architecture and architectural governance. Projects update the architecture and governance is necessary to ensure that the architecture will be used and complied with. Architectural governance is necessary for creating an architecture embedded in the business.

The action research showed that the meta-framework can be used to evaluate and position architectural efforts within organizations. For organizations, the design of an EA is a balancing act, as time and resources are limited and circumstances change rapidly. At the least, the level of detail and the focus of the architectural efforts need to be chosen. The case study shows that the meta-framework presented in this chapter is a suitable instrument for evaluating the architectural efforts of an organization and determining if an organization is doing the right things.

References

Architecture Working Group. (2000). IEEE Std 1471-2000 Recommended Practice Architectural Description of Software-Intensive Systems. IEEE Software Engineering Standards Committee.

Armour, F.J., Kaisler, S.H., and Liu, S.Y. (1999). A big-picture look at Enterprise Architecture. IEEE IT Professional. Volume 1, Number 1. pp. 35-42.

Bernard, S.B. (2004). An introduction to Enterprise Architecture. AuthorHouse: Bloomington, IL.

Cherbakov, L., Galambos, G., Harishankar, R., Kalyana, S., and Rackham, G. (2005). Impact of service orientation at the business level. IBM Systems Journal. Volume 44, Number 4. pp. 653-668.

Doucet, G., Gøtze, J., Saha, P., and Bernard, S. (2008). Coherency Management: Using Enterprise Architecture for Alignment, Agility, and Assurance. Journal of Enterprise Architecture. Volume 4, Number 2. pp. 9-20.

Fremantle, P., Weerawarana, S., and Khalaf, R. (2002). Enterprise services. Examine the emerging files of web services and how it is integrated into existing enterprise infrastructures. Communications of the ACM. Volume 45, Number 20. pp. 77-82.

Hamilton, D. (1999). Linking strategic information systems concepts to practice: System integration at the portfolio level. Journal of Information Technology. Volume 14, Number 1. pp. 69-82.

Hammer, M. (1990). Reengineering work: Don't automate, obliterate. Harvard Business Review. Volume 68, Number 4. pp. 104-112.

Janssen, M., and Feenstra, R. (2006). From application to Web service portfolio management: Concepts and practice. European Conference on e-Government (ECEG). Philipps University, Marburg, Germany. pp. 225-234.

Janssen, M., and Verbraeck, A. (2005). Evaluating the Information Architecture of an Electronic Intermediary. Journal of Organizational Computing and Electronic Commerce. Volume 15, Number 1. pp. 35-60.

Jeffery, M., and Leliveld, I. (2004). Best Practices in IT Portfolio Management. MIT Sloan Management Review. Volume 45, Number 3. pp. 41-49.

Kaisler, S.H., Armour, F., and Valivullah, M. (2005). Enterprise

Architecting: Critical problems. Proceedings of the 38th Hawaii International Conference on System sciences, Hawaii, USA.

Khoshafian, S. (2006). Service Oriented Enterprises. Auerbach Publication: New York, NY.

Krafzig, D., Banke, K., and Slama, D. (2004). Enterprise SOA. Service Oriented Architecture Best Practices. Prentice Hall PTR: Indianapolis, Indiana.

Leist, S., and Zellner, G. (2006). Evaluation of Current Architecture Frameworks. Proceedings of the 2006 ACM symposium on applied computing. ACM, Dijon, France.

Malone, T.W., and Crowston, K. (1994). The interdisciplinary study of coordination. ACM Computing Surveys. Volume 26, Number 2. pp. 87-119.

McGovern, J., Sims, O., Jain, A., and Little, M. (2006) Enterprise Service Oriented Architectures: Concepts, Challenges, Recommendations. Springer.

Mitroff, I.I., Betz, F., L.R.Pondy, and Sagasti, F. (1974). On Managing Science in the System Age: Two schemes for the study of science as a whole systems phenomenon. TIMS Interfaces. Volume 4, Number 3. pp. 46-58.

Nijhuis, R. (2006). Enterprise Architectures as a Guideline for the Implementation of Strategy. Realising Sustainable Performance Improvement for Pension Providers and Insurance Companies DCE Holding b.v., Schiphol.

O'Neill, P., and Sohal, A.S. (1999). Business Process Reengineering A review of recent literature. Technovation. Volume 19, Number 9. pp. 571-581

Perks, C., and Beveridge, T. (2002). Guide to Enterprise IT Architecture. Springer: New York, NY.

Peterson, R. (2004). Crafting Information Technology Governance. Information Systems Management. Volume 21, Number 4. pp. 7-22.

Richardson, L., Jackson, B.M., and Dickson, G. (1990). A Principle-Based Enterprise Architecture: Lessons from Texaco and Star Enterprise. MIS Quarterly. Volume 14, Number 4. pp. 385-403.

Rohloff, M. (2005). Enterprise architecture: Framework and methodology for the design of architecture in the large. European Conference on Information Systems.

Ross, J. (2003). Creating a strategic IT architecture competency: Learning in stages. MISQ Executive. Volume 2, Number 1. pp. 31-43.

Sage, A.P., and Armstrong, J.E. (2000). Introduction to Systems Engineering. John Wiley & Sons: New York, NY.

Schekkerman, J. (2003). How to Survive in the Jungle of Enterprise Architecture Framework: Creating or Choosing an Enterprise Architecture Framework Trafford.

Sol, H.G. (1982). Simulation in Information Systems Development. University of Groningen, Groningen.

Stallings, W. (2006). Data and Computer Communications. Prentice Hall PTR: Indianapolis, Indiana.

Tapscott, D., and Caston, A. (1993). Paradigm Shift - The New Promise of Information Technology. McGraw-Hill: New York, NY.

Versteeg, G., and Bouwman, H. (2005). Business architecture: A new paradigm to relate business strategy to ICT. Information Systems Frontiers. Volume 8, Number 2. pp. 91-102.

Weill, P., and Ross, J. (2005). A matrixed approach to designing IT governance. MIT Sloan Management Review. Volume 46, Number 2. pp. 26-34.

Weill, P., and Vitale, M. (2002). What IT Infrastructure Capabilities are Needed to Implement E-Business Models. MISQ Executive. Volume 1. Number 1. pp. 17-34.

Zachman, J.A. (1987). A Framework for Information Systems Architecture. IBM Systems Journal. Volume 26, Number 3. pp. 276-292.

About the Author

Dr. Marijn Janssen is the Director of the interdisciplinary SEPAM (Systems Engineering, Policy Analysis and Management) Master program and an Associate Professor within the Information and Communication Technology section of the Technology, Policy and Management Faculty of Delft University of Technology. He is particularly interested in situations in which multiple public and private organizations want to collaborate, in which information and communication technology (ICT) plays an enabling role and solutions are constrained by organizational realities and political wishes and there are various ways to proceed, all directions having their own implications. His research is published in a large number of conference proceedings, book chapters, and international journals. More information: www.tbm.tudelft.nl/marijnj.

Marijn Janssen
Faculty of Technology, Policy and Management
Delft University of Technology
Jaffalaan 5, 2628 BX Delft
The Netherlands
m.f.w.h.a.janssen@tudelft.nl

Chapter 5

ENTERPRISE ARCHITECTURE, STRATEGIC MANAGEMENT, AND INFORMATION MANAGEMENT

Chris Aitken

Editors' Preface

The idea of integrating EA with other practices like strategic management, information management and others, which is the topic of this chapter, is perhaps not new, but has been poorly practiced by many organizations. More and more organizations have realized the need to integrate these, and are starting to see the multiplier effect provided by one to the rest. This leads to the organization as a whole being more manageable. It is obvious that each of the disciplines presented and discussed in the chapter have a critical role to play in contributing to organizational coherency.

The chapter explicitly states that information is an asset that organizations must learn to manage well if they intend to derive sustainable competitive advantage. Understanding the connections between EA and Information Management is important as they have an influence on coherency. Furthermore, the chapter presents some examples of IM in a non-IT context. Linkages to EA therefore provide the potential to enhance its scope to the extended architecture mode.

The chapter presents and discusses in detail a proposed methodology that neatly integrates the three disciplines of Strategic Planning, EA and

IM. The methodology description consists of steps, key inputs, outputs, intended outcomes, governing policies, rules, primary stakeholders and concerns addressed in each step. Such a level of description, we believe, makes the proposed methodology open to further enhancements and subsequent adoption in organizations. The strength of the methodology is that it has been weaved in, and presented along with, a case study to further enhance its applicability. The methodology also shows how some of the existing organizational artifacts can be leveraged for use within the realms of EA. This is important, as it then gets into the embedded architecture mode.

Introduction

This chapter deals with three key functions that underpin the concept of coherency management in the contemporary enterprise. These functions are; enterprise architecture, strategic planning and information management. All three functions are inter-related and form the basis of any endeavor to leverage market opportunity or competitive advantage. This chapter will make the argument that enterprise architecture provides a foundation which effects greatest enterprise coherency when drawing on the other two functions. In doing so, enterprise architecture in turn enhances the enterprise's capacity for strategic planning and information management.

All three functions are frequently misunderstood and misrepresented. Strategic planning, if done correctly, is much more than the shelf-ware glossy brochures that are so often brandished as the outcome of the latest corporate strategic planning initiative. Enterprise architecture as we will see is also far more than an exercise in enterprise 'archaeology' or a process of enterprise futuring. Likewise, information management has a much wider scope and significance than simply the management of the organization's records and files.

The latter half of this chapter presents a framework and process model which combines features of enterprise architecture, strategic planning and information management to promote enterprise coherency.

Scope and Definition

A colleague once remarked that "when the business wants to talk about aligning resources with purpose it uses the language of strategic planning, and when the IT department wants to discuss the same topic it uses the language of enterprise architecture". Little wonder these types of discussion often end the way they do – with the business not understanding why IT "just doesn't get on with it and deliver something", and IT not understanding why the business "doesn't want to take responsibility for driving ICT as a key enabler of its stated objectives". The frustration is in part due to the difference in language, concepts and paradigm, and can be reduced if the perspectives inherent in each function are better understood.

Enterprise architecture has an engineering heritage and is concerned with the design and construction of all aspects of the enterprise. The scope of concern represented by enterprise architecture is the entire enterprise at all levels from strategic to operational to technology. Strategic planning on the other hand has a performance management heritage and is concerned with directing the enterprise and the measurement and evaluation of performance against identified objectives across the organization. Communication between enterprise architects and strategists is further complicated by the tendency for people to confuse the processes of enterprise architecture and strategic planning with the deliverables of these processes. For example, the publishing of a strategic plan does not constitute strategic planning. Similarly, the various models, associated matrices and frameworks that are produced by an enterprise architecture initiative are not the architecting process itself.

Enterprise Architecture

Enterprise architecture as a discipline is young, and maturing. Although this means that this an exciting time for enterprise architects, it also means that the reader will find that there are a range of views as to what the discipline covers and the methodologies that might be employed (Bernard, 2005; Bernus, Nemes & Schmidt 2003; The Open Group Architecture Framework, 2006; Zachman 2005). Within this chapter the discipline of enterprise architecture will be assumed to have the concept of design as a central theme. It will also be assumed to include a process by which the design of a given enterprise can be transformed into some optimal or preferred design state. In doing this, the process will likely require an understanding of the current enterprise design, the target enterprise objectives, a target enterprise design that demonstrably best supports these objectives, a gap analysis between current and target design states, and a plan which describes transition from one to the other.
Two other terms related to enterprise architecture are 'enterprise archaeology' and 'enterprise futuring'. Enterprise archaeology re-

fers, somewhat tongue-in-cheek, to the detailed documentation of a given enterprise state (typically current state). Enterprise futuring refers to the exercise of describing the predicted future enterprise. Both enterprise archaeology, or baselining, and enterprise futuring are important elements of the overall process of enterprise architecture. Importantly however, the process of enterprise architecture also includes the process of 'enterprise design'.

Enterprise design is the process whereby specific design principles and requirements are identified and applied to define a particular design state. A virtue of the process of enterprise architecture with its engineering heritage is that it makes this process explicit. All too often CxOs make decisions that are essentially enterprise design decisions on the basis of advice, or 'industry accepted practice' or 'experience'. All of which are appropriate factors to draw on, but which typically fail to make underlying design assumptions and principles explicit. As a result it may be difficult to evaluate whether a particular enterprise is successful because of its current configuration of priorities, roles, resources and process or in spite of it. In this respect it is not uncommon to find that senior executives have little appreciation of the actual complexity of the enterprise they are responsible for until presented with the documented output of an initial current state baseline initiative (i.e. documentation of current strategies and objectives, business functions and processes, roles, policies, and, information systems and data stores). For example, a recent baseline exercise within an Australian State Government health agency revealed some 400 separate strategy statements across 10 separate current strategic documents that had been developed across four separate business divisions. Clearly, without purposeful design, a portfolio of this complexity is likely to result in duplication and misalignment between strategies. Moreover, if there is this degree of complexity at the strategic level in an organization, it can only mean further complexity at the operational and technology levels. Obviously, unless enterprise design is explicit from the outset the likelihood of duplicate or even counterproductive effort is high.

The key deliverable of the enterprise architecture process is a set of initiatives within an overall program of work that will move the enterprise closer to its target design state. The program management of these initiatives, although it has an integral relationship with both enterprise architecture and strategic planning, will not be covered in detail in this chapter.

Strategic Planning

Strategic planning is a significant function in most large contemporary companies and government agencies. The strategic planning process is not a 'once only' exercise, but rather an ongoing cycle of goal identification, performance review and adjustment. In the same way that a project plan needs to be established early and maintained throughout the life of a project, so a strategic plan also needs to established and maintained throughout the life of the enterprise. For this reason strategic planning and indeed any planning activity within an organization is a fundamental contributor to the overall architecture of the enterprise.

Kaplan and Norton's (1996) Balanced Score Card and their associated Strategy Maps (Kaplan and Norton, 2004) have become ubiquitous and something of a standard approach. Although there are methodologies such as Balanced Score Card, SWOT (Strengths, Weaknesses, Opportunities and Threats) Analysis (Humphrey, 1970) and PEST (Political, Economic, Social, and Technological) Analysis, or Porter's 5 Forces Analysis (Porter, 1979) that are commonly used, there is not a standardized approach to the process of strategic planning. Furthermore, effective strategic planning is something that many organizations fail to achieve (Kaplan & Norton, 2008).

More recently, in light of the significant proportion of organizations that fail to realize effective strategic planning, Kaplan and Norton (2008) have developed a six point strategy management model that brings together a number of the approaches listed above into a comprehensive approach to developing and executing strategic planning. The authors call this approach an Execution Premium. The six stages outlined in their model are:

- Developing a strategy. This phase involves the organization articulating what it does and what it wants to achieve. This stage might use a range of tools, including Porter's 5 Forces Analysis, to identify how the company is best placed to compete.

- Plan the strategy. This stage of the model requires the organization to put resources into planning how the strategy will be implemented. This phase includes developing a plan together with KPIs, programs of work and funding for initiatives. The Balanced Scorecard might be used to develop such a plan.

- Align the organization. This stage of the model requires the planning within individual business units to be aligned with the corporate strategic plan. A top down succession of Strategy Maps or Balanced Scorecards within the organization might be used to achieve this alignment.

- Plan operations. This stage uses tools such as quality improvement, process management, business process reengineering, process dashboards, activity-based costing, human resource capacity planning, and budgeting to achieve strong links between the day-to-day operations and the strategic goals of the organization.

- Monitor and learn. This stage is concerned with understanding how the organization is tracking against the strategies and goals it has set for itself. Performance information and business intelligence are key inputs.

- Test and adapt. This stage is essentially a review of the strategy to determine whether it is the most appropriate and still reflects competitive advantage for the organization. This stage then commences the next cycle of strategic planning.

Within this chapter strategic planning will be assumed to have the concepts of goal definition and performance monitoring as central themes. The process of strategic planning usually involves environmental scanning, internal review, target or goal definition, a gap analysis and identification of a set of strategies which address the gaps while leveraging the organization's position and current opportunities. The outcome of the strategic planning process is a set of strategies, initiatives or projects, and key performance indicators (KPIs). The KPIs are used to evaluate the extent to which performance is aligned with the organization's stated strategic goals or priorities. The areas or initiatives which report poor performance are candidates for further risk management to improve alignment.

Figure 1 illustrates the strategic planning concepts and their relation to business process management (existing capability) and program management (new capability). An important accountability role is that of the KPI sponsor. The role of the sponsor is to ensure that their KPIs are measured and reported, and to oversee and to be accountable for any remedial actions required as a result of the risk management process.

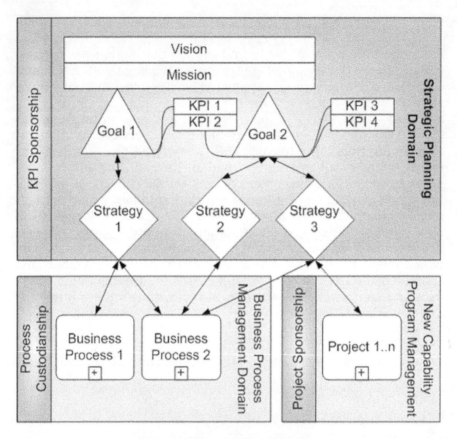

Figure 1. Strategic Planning

Strategic planning within the contemporary enterprise can no longer take the view that technology is something managed by the IT section. IM&ICT strategic planning needs to be as much a part of the corporate strategic planning process as workforce planning and budget planning have become. Although somewhat dated, the framework proposed by Henderson and Venkatraman (1993) still provides a thorough treatment of the perspectives that need to be accounted for in relation to IM&ICT strategic planning. Essentially the perspectives are: IM&ICT asset portfolio management require-ments, the IM&ICT requirements of business strategies, technology opportunities the business wants to leverage, and the configuration and operation of the IT organization. Each perspective will typically generate strategies that should be incorporated within the organiza-tion's corporate strategic plan.

Information Management

For some time now, access to and use of information has increasingly been the dimension of competitive advantage within the market place. Alternatively, government agencies which typically operate from within a public value context rather than for profit (Weill and Ross, 2004) also continue to increasingly rely on timely access to relevant information in order to provide services. Within this chapter information management is considered to encompass the management of all information within, into and out of an enterprise. Information management centers on the concept of information as an asset of the enterprise which, like other assets, requires management across the asset lifecycle. The actual management of information is always achieved via an information system of some description. It is the system that manages the correct context in which data are presented to allow the correct interpretation and communication of intended meaning. It is the combination of both data and context by the system which constitutes the information asset.

Figure 2 below illustrates the information asset lifecycle, and the dependencies between system, data and records management.

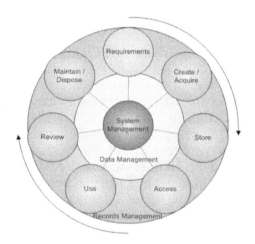

Figure 2. Information Asset Lifecycle

An information system could either be a paper-based file and system, or an electronic and highly distributed system. In either case the scope of concern for information management extends to ensuring the system is adequate to meet the information management requirements across the lifecycle of the information asset. More recently, the term enterprise information management (Newman & Logan 2006) has been coined to convey the essential requirement for contemporary enterprise to effectively maximize the value of its information assets as an enterprise portfolio, bringing together both business intelligence and content management.

Within this chapter information management will be considered to encapsulate the following functions:

Business intelligence

> This function is responsible for the presentation of data from a variety of sources, in a correct context to provide information as input to executive level decision-making. Business intelligence may involve the combining of various data sources to construct new information that would not be available by considering each source in isolation. Business intelligence will source data from enterprise operations systems together with strategic performance data, or data external to the organization.

Records management

> The management of records is a component of information management that typically deals with the management of evidentiary records. These are records that an enterprise requires to meet its legislative and regulatory obligations.

Content management

> Content management is concerned with the controlling, versioning, and publishing of information. This function ensures that the development and publication of information is managed via a workflow of controls and approvals.

Data management

> This function deals with the management of data stores and the data they contain. The role of data management is to ensure that enterprise data are stored and managed in compliance with data standards to promote high data integrity, integration and to maximize data storage performance. Data management also extends to the management of 'static' or reference data such as

meta-data (i.e. data about data) or common vocabularies, ontologies and taxonomies to ensure appropriate levels of semantic interoperability of data items across systems.

System management

The management of the IM & ICT system ensures, together with data management, that the information meets availability, interoperability, business continuity and security requirements. System management also addresses ongoing system maintenance and operation. The processes necessary to undertake effective system management are described in the Information Technology Infrastructure Library (ITIL, Office of Government Commerce 2007).

Organizations use a variety of systems to manage information. Most organizations still own and use a significant amount of information that is paper-based while continuing to increase their usage of information stored and processed using digital and electronic media. This requires most organizations to manage at least two information management systems in parallel; one for paper records and the other for electronic records. The paper-based system will be concerned with management of evidentiary records, libraries of books, periodicals and other publications, and possibly business transactions. The electronic system in most organizations is increasingly concerned with the management of core business information. Key challenges in many organizations include the management of these dual systems, the progressive migration from paper to electronic, the associated changes to business process, and the ongoing need to effectively harvest business intelligence from both systems.

This situation typically means that information management represents a significant risk to an organization in terms of the ongoing possibility of data loss or corruption, costly duplication, limited availability, and breaches of confidentiality and security. Some of these risks are arguably heightened for contemporary organizations as digital environments and systems become increasingly distributed in nature.

Figure3 below illustrates the relationship between the components of information management within a typical distributed digital environment. In a distributed environment data, application services and context need to be managed independently of one another. This approach is designed to maximize data and service re-use while providing information relevant to the context of a given business process. The components that make up the environment are: data stores, some of which may lie outside the organization's sphere of influence or control, a messaging bus to handle the messaging between services and data sources, application services which provide system functionality, and presentation management capability (e.g. web portal technology). The term 'presentation management' is used to mean all the processes that ensure data is presented in the required context to convey the intended meaning and in a way that also meets the business process data accuracy and integrity requirements.

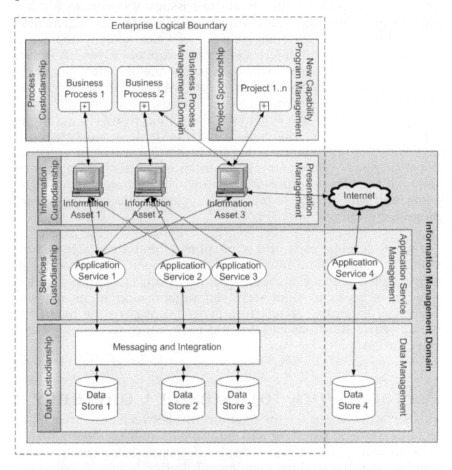

Figure 3. Information Management In A Distributed Environment

In order for data, functionality, information and process to be managed independently of one another, accountability or 'custodianship' must be assigned within the organization across each domain. The effective governance of data, functionality, context and process is another of the key challenges confronting contemporary organizations. The governance roles are highlighted in Figure 3 above. The issue of governance is then a second core theme within the scope of information management, and one which impacts strongly on an organization's ability to achieve coherency.

There are any number of examples of organizations attempting to undertake rapid change to meet the changing requirements of the market economy, but failing to address issues of governance. Governance is no less important when it comes to the management of information. Each information asset of value usually represents significant investment in terms of upfront capital expense as well as employee time and less obvious costs, such as the management of legislative data collection requirements. Without clear lines of accountability and well articulated standards, an organization will quickly find that its investment in information results in a complex mire of incompatible, fragmented, and unreliable systems and holdings which is only compounded by successive waves of organizational change. Without strong governance over its information assets, and the other components upon which they are reliant, an organization will struggle to maximize the use of information to reach its strategic and operational goals.

We have seen that each of the functions of enterprise architecture, strategic planning and information management are related to the concept of coherency management. However, enterprise architecture alone seeks to understand an organization in its entirety. Therefore, enterprise architecture plays a central role in relation to the other two functions and it is this issue which we will now consider further.

A Framework for Greater Coherency

This section will explore the relationships between enterprise architecture, strategic planning and information management with the view to identifying a much needed framework for better understanding the role all three play in contributing to greater enterprise coherency.

Enterprise architecture, as we have seen, is the process of understanding the organization from the level of corporate strategic intent, through to the level of the configuration of technology and other resources required to support the organization both strategically and operationally. For example, most enterprise architecture initiatives will include a description of the organization's current and target business functions. This description will inevitably include a description of strategic planning and information management business functions amongst others. It will also, paradoxically include a description of the organization's enterprise architecture function. Furthermore, it will also include a description of the alignment between these functions and the organization's strategic goals and objectives, as well as the processes, information components and technologies required to support these functions. The same level of description and analysis is likely to be undertaken for business services, processes, roles, organizational structure, policy and logistics.

However, we have also seen that enterprise architecture is much more than simply describing current and future design states. The real value enterprise architecture represents is its design capability. In order to develop a transition plan from the current to the future state, it is crucial to be able to answer the question "Which enterprise design will *best* meet my strategy goals?" It is around the aspect of design that enterprise architecture really distinguishes itself from strategic planning and information management. It is enterprise architecture that is best placed to assist the enterprise in determining which of the many roads it could take to reach its target state, which is the one road that will represent maximum competitive advantage. This is not to suggest that an enterprise architect must have the content expertise to be able to design any aspect of the organization. On the contrary, the enterprise architect will be on the lookout to identify those who are authoritative sources or content experts and able to articulate and plan their ideas. The enterprise architect's contribution will be to use and locate these business artifacts within the broader enterprise context, and assess the degree to which they are aligned with enterprise strategic agenda, design principles and one another (i.e. their coherency). To be effective, any design process is dependent on explicit design principles, design requirements, and requirements management. It is this understanding and perspective that the enterprise architect brings to the issue of coherency management.

Strategic planning is clearly the function within the enterprise which sets the overall direction and priorities. It is also the function responsible for monitoring performance through the use of KPIs and managing risk where performance is less then that required. The obvious contribution that strategic planning makes to coherency management is the determination of organizational priorities and direction through the use of methodologies such as SWOT and PEST and the measurement and management of performance against these targets using methodologies such as the Balanced Score Card. However, there are some obvious similarities between the process of enterprise architecture and that of strategic planning. The environmental scanning that is typically understood as a preliminary step to undertaking strategic planning undoubtedly mirrors the enterprise architecture current state description. It could be argued that the use of tools such as the Zachman Framework (Zachman, 2005) represents a more rigorous and comprehensive approach to understanding the current environments that are external and internal to the enterprise. Moreover, the elements in each of the four perspectives identified by Kaplan and Norton (2004) in their Strategy Map (i.e. Financial, Customer, Internal, Learning and Growth) relate readily to the artifacts, models and descriptions developed by the enterprise architecture process.

Information management has a reciprocal relationship with both strategic planning and enterprise architecture. Management of information as a business function must be strategically aligned with the organization's goals and objectives. Furthermore, from the perspective of enterprise architecture, information management represents one of a number of core functions within the enterprise that must be designed to enable the enterprise target design state. However, frequently overlooked is the fact that information management is also a prime enabler of the organization's strategic planning and enterprise architecture capabilities. Both the strategic planning and enterprise architecture processes require robust management of information in order to be effective.

Given the separately identifiable but inter-related roles of enterprise architecture, strategic planning and information management, the following framework (see Figure 4) seeks to clearly delineate their respective roles in enterprise coherency management.

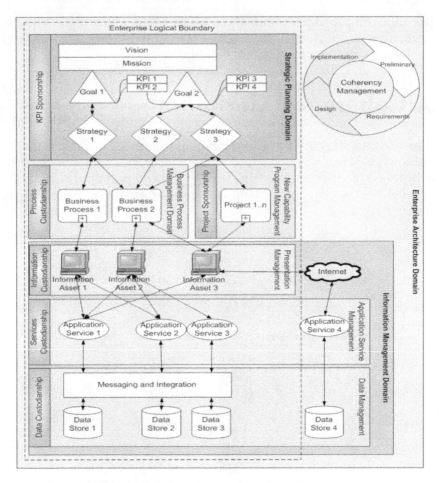

Figure 4. Improving Enterprise Coherency

Figure 4 illustrates the functions of strategic planning, enterprise architecture, and information management and their relationship to one another and other whole-of-enterprise coherency functions such as process and program management.

Figure 4 positions enterprise architecture as the frame of reference for strategic planning, business process management, program management and information management. Enterprise architecture enables the business to determine the enterprise design and transition plan components. Strategic planning defines the enterprise priorities and overall direction, as well as the management of the transition plan performance. The transition plan is implemented via the portfolio and program management function. Information management provides a central support role to enterprise architecture, strategic planning and program management.

A Coherency Methodology

Figure 5 illustrates a set of processes that together represent a methodology to enhance enterprise coherency. The model is largely comprised of enterprise architecture process steps, but also includes aspects of the strategic planning and information management functions.

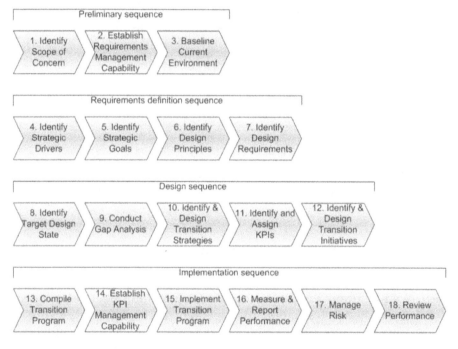

Figure 5. A Coherency Methodology

The processes are grouped into four sequences which follow a cycle of requirements definition, design and implementation. The process model is drawn from models such as TOGAF (The Open Group, 2006), ZIFA Quick Start Methodology (Holcman, 2008), Treasury Board of Canada's Business Transformation Enablement Program (2004) as well as the author's own experience in IM&ICT strategic planning. It is intended that the cycle be implemented repeatedly over time to iteratively improve enterprise coherency. In a volatile environment the cycle may need to be repeated frequently, possibly with cycles overlapping or run in parallel. The process model is also scalable and might therefore be equally used by an enterprise or a business unit within the same enterprise. A detailed description of the processes contained in each sequence is provided below. The process descriptions are accompanied by excerpts from a fictitious but hopefully instructive case study involving a large public health service provider.

HealthSec is a large public sector government-run health provider. HealthSec provides health services to a population characterized by increasing population numbers, of which the aged and elderly are an increasing percentage. Other external factors include an aging and reducing workforce, together with increased demand for acute and sub-acute health services. HealthSec has some 60,000, employees, 85% of whom are health professionals who work in 120 health facilities. These include five large tertiary teaching hospitals, 30 medium sized facilities and 85 community health facilities and small rural hospitals. The remaining 15% of employees make up a central corporate area and regionally based corporate services units. The corporate areas in HealthSec include population health, corporate strategy and policy, health service planning, financial and human resource management and an IM&ICT section. The Government has come under increasing public pressure to provide more adequate health services. A Government commissioned enquiry into HealthSec identified a number of structural and systemic changes together with a series of anticipated target gains in performance. Recently, the HealthSec Executive Directors met and during a heated meeting expressed their respective frustrations at achieving the performance targets. A significant amount of the criticism was directed at the CIO as the aging ICT infrastructure and core patient information system, and lack of quality information to inform planning decisions, were cited as fundamental inhibiters to HealthSec realizing the anticipated gains identified in the Commission's report.

Preliminary Sequence:

This sequence deals with a set of processes that provide a foundation to the rest of the cycle. Some of these processes (e.g. requirements management) may already be in existence, in which case they can be simply noted as having a role to play.

1. Identify scope of concern

This initial process involves establishing the scope of the issue to be addressed in this iteration of the cycle. Experience has shown that an enterprise architecture process is more likely to succeed where the initial scope is restricted to some issue or aspect of the enterprise that is likely to deliver quick gains, rather than attempting to tackle the whole enterprise. The development of a simple information model of the core concepts and their relationships may assist in identifying the scope of the problem domain. The scope might also be better understood by identifying any relevant industry reference models. These models may provide insights into related aspects of the enterprise.

2. Establish requirements management capability

This step assumes that there is not an already existing requirements management capability. This information management capability is essential to the enterprise architecture process and represents an ongoing knowledgebase of reference information that supports all subsequent process steps.
A requirements repository provides the means to define and track the requirements identified at various stages in the enterprise architecture process. It involves separately identifying requirements and recording them in a standardized way. It also provides a means to undertake analysis to identify common or conflicting requirements and inter-dependencies.

3. Baseline current environment

This process involves benchmarking the current internal and external environments and identifying the current design state. The process will typically involve identifying current strategic priorities, policy, roles, organizational structure, business services and processes, logistics, information assets and data stores, and supporting applications and technologies. The Zachman Framework (Zachman, 2005) is an excellent tool for identifying the dimensions of the enterprise and the various aspects from which they can be described and understood. One approach would be to identify the relevant Zachman Framework cells associated with the scope of concern established in step one, and then populating these cells with descriptions based on the current environment.

COHERENCY MANAGEMENT

It is important to recognize that the current state does reflect a particular design. However, the factors influencing this design may be more or less apparent or lost over time with changes in the corporate history of the enterprise. The business operating models described by Ross, Weill and Robertson (2006) are likely to provide a useful means to identify the current business model where this is not currently explicitly stated.

*The embattled HealthSec CIO knew that she had in effect been given an ultimatum by her colleagues to table a 'solution' at next month's meeting of the executive or start looking for alternative employment. The CIO, familiar with coherency concepts, spends the next three weeks in close consultation with her Chief Architect and other members of a newly established Enterprise Architecture Office. The EA Office was part way through conducting a baseline of the HealthSec strategic drivers, core clinical and administrative processes, information requirements, applications, and infrastructure. The EA Office has implemented a repository tool and has used this to store the baseline findings and map the strategic drivers to processes, information requirements, applications and infrastructure services and components. Together, the CIO and Chief Architect decide to present a 'program of transition' at the next executive meeting entitled "HealthSec 2.0". The presentation has a central message – HealthSec must be explicitly **designed** to achieve the Commission's Report's targets. In the weeks leading up to the presentation, the baseline is completed and the results incorporated into the presentation.*

At the next meeting of the executive the CIO tables "HealthSec 2.0" and leads the group through a review of the current environment, the Commission's targets, and a transition process of Requirements Definition, Design, and Implementation. The core message of explicit design meets with nodding approval from more than one of the other Executive Directors. However, there is concern that the process outlined would not mean that targets are met within the timeframes specified in the Report. The CIO uses the baseline material to 'focus on the facts' and to suggest that the scope of the HealthSec 2.0 design effort needs to be extended to include core business processes highlighted in the baseline such as patient intake, workforce recruitment, and procurement as well as the IT systems they use. "The best designed IT system in world cannot improve a business process that is fundamentally inefficient". The CIO challenges the other executives to review the baseline material with the view to identifying and agreeing on a set of priority areas to form the scope of the transition process at their next meeting. The CIO is commended by the Director-General for shifting the discussion from a 'blame game' to a more holistic, factual and constructive approach.

Requirements Definition Sequence:
This sequence deals with processes to establish the requirements that the goal state design will need to fulfill. The sequence includes processes from both the enterprise architecture and the strategic planning functions.

4.   Identify strategic drivers

This process uses the baseline data collected in the previous step to identify those aspects of the external environment which will act to constrain or move the organization in a particular direction. These might include legislative change, new competitors in the market place, new market opportunities due to technology advances, or changes in the customer stratification.

This process will usually involve some form of SWOT Analysis. The Weaknesses identified through this process might then be the subject of a further Root Cause Analysis to identify the underlying or systemic problems responsible. These analyses will then provide a thorough consideration of the current drivers, both positive and negative, which need to be taken into account when identifying the organization's strategic goals.

5.   Identify strategic goals

This is the key process for determining the future direction and priorities for the organization. This process will take into account the data collected during the baseline together with the strategic drivers identified in the previous step. The strategic goals are broad statements about how the organization wishes to be perceived by its customers and competitors (e.g. as a market leader in a particular market niche).

The Business Motivation Model (BMM (OMG, 2006) provides a useful set of defined strategic planning concepts and relationships. The BMM potentially provides a means to reliably model strategic planning concepts, and also to position strategic planning methodologies with respect to one another in terms of their outputs.

6.   Identify design principles

In order to develop the target design state for the organization, it is important to be explicit about the principles that will be used to guide the design. These principles will be high level generalized statements such as the principle of cost effectiveness, or the principle of modularity or the principle of component re-use. Good design principles are those that can be readily tested to determine whether the principle has been applied or not (i.e. design principles need to be objective statements). One way to identify principles is to preface statements with "The target design will need to conform to the principle of ..." An excellent example of the use of the of design principles in a strategic context is the concept of the operating model in Ross, Weill and Robertson (2006). Ross et al., present four fundamental business models determined by the combination of high or low process standardization and process integration (i.e. Coordination, Diversification, Unification, Replication). Each operating model in essence captures a particular set of process design principles (e.g. high integration but low standardization is represented by the Coordination model). In line with the view that design principles are an important part of requirements definition, Ross et al., suggest that identifying an operating model is a necessary first step in building a foundation for execution, and is a feature of successful companies. The principles identified in this step will be used in later steps to design strategies and initiatives within the transition program.

7.   Identify design requirements

Design requirements refer to the features or capabilities the organization will need to exhibit in order to meet the strategic drivers and fulfill the strategic goals identified in previous steps. These include both functional and non-functional design requirements. The design features or capabilities should be independent of the design principles identified in the previous step.

The design requirements describe those things that need to be true of the enterprise without defining an end solution or implementation (e.g. Statewide or national product distribution, Compliance with privacy legislative requirements, 24 x 7 customer support). Design requirements are often described in planning documentation within the enterprise in terms of goals or outcomes. The role of the enterprise architect in relation to these descriptions is to identify the various authoritative sources within the organization and to begin to collate and integrate the design requirements within the requirements repository. The Reference Models identified in Step1 might also be productively used as a comparison to ensure that all relevant design requirements or features have been considered.

The meeting of the HealthSec Executive went well, however, the month ahead is characterized by frantic activity on the part of the EA Office. The Chief Architect together with the CIO meets with the other Executives, their senior managers, and advisors to establish an agreed scope and set of requirements. The discussions revolve around agreement on the priority strategic drivers and the key strategies to address these drivers. The Chief Architect also uses the CIO's presentation message to ensure the discussions also cover the issue of explicit design principles, and design features for 'HealthSec 2.0'. By the third week into the month the EA Office presents the CIO with a draft set of agreed strategic drivers, goals, business design principles and design requirements. These are distributed to the other Executives prior to the next meeting of Executive Directors.

Unfortunately, the next meeting gets off to a bad start with the CFO leading the discussion and refuting the insinuation on the part of the ED for Clinical Services that the Procurements Unit is a major impediment to the organizational change he is attempting within all five major hospitals. The CIO enters the argument by tabling the draft Requirements Document and referring both the CFO and ED for Clinical Services to the design principles of 'Maximizing Public Value' and 'Process Standardization' agreed to by them and their advisors, and suggests that the discussion has reflected the tension between these two principles. The rest of the meeting focuses on the draft document and discussion shifts to agreement on the drivers, strategies, design principles and design requirements. At the conclusion of the meeting the CIO summarizes the agreed scope and outlines the next phase of the HealthSec 2.0 transition program in more detail. She requests that the executive agree to the EA Office working with the Corporate Services Strategy and Service Planning Unit and staff from Clinical Services to develop a draft target state description to be tabled at the executive meeting in two months time. The meeting agrees but again concern is expressed at the lack of any tangible progress and a process that "sounds fine in theory but may not deliver". The CIO counters with the suggestion that for the executive to better demonstrate to the organization as a whole their commitment to the Government's priorities and to improve accountability, each member be assigned responsibility for at least one target identified in the Commission's Report. The CIO notes that the target state de-

scription will provide the basis for developing the strategies that will realize the Report's targets. The meeting agrees in principle and concludes on a rather subdued note.

The next two months are again a period of intense activity on the part of the EA Office. The Chief Architect decides to offer his two Business Architects to work in the Corporate Strategic Planning Unit for 3 days a week for the next 3 weeks. The Business Architects work with the Corporate Strategists and Health Service Planners to apply the design principles and requirements to develop a series of models which succinctly describe future service types and delivery models. The Business Architects provide this information to the Information Architects who engage with the Health Records Management staff and key clinical thought leaders in the Clinical Services section to identify a future state information architecture. Meanwhile, the Business Architects conduct an initial gap analysis between the business process baseline and the target state service models to identify the main points of difference and potential candidates for business process change management. The Business Architects and Information Architects also meet with the Application and Technology Architects to begin to map out the future application and infrastructure requirements and the gaps between these and the current state using the baseline data. Finally, the Business Architects also meet with the HR section to work through the staffing requirements to support the proposed service models. During this period the EA Office Repository Librarian is busy ensuring the new models, requirements and mappings are included in the repository.

Design Sequence:
This sequence takes the outputs from the previous processes and uses these to design a target state, strategies and a set of transition initiatives.

8. Identify target design state

This process applies the design principles and requirements from previous steps to describe a target design state. In some instances, these descriptions may also already exist either wholly or in part within the organization (e.g. existing Strategic Plans, HR Plans, Financial Plans). However, to promote coherency, these existing descriptions must be assessed against the design principles and design requirements, and may therefore require further refinement as a result. The role of the enterprise architect will be to promote greater consistency by fostering discussion between stakeholders about target state business artifacts that have been developed in isolation or with little or no reference to each other or to any overarching design principles. The role of the enterprise will most often not be that of content matter expert regarding the target state descriptions for various areas of the enterprise. The enterprise architect will typically play the roles of facilitator, linker, collator and re-structurer of business artifacts.

Again the Zachman Framework is a useful tool to use to structure and position existing descriptions with respect to one another, identify gaps and to progressively develop the overall target state description. Target state descriptions need to be identified for each of the relevant Zachman Framework cells identified in previous steps. Each target state description needs to demonstrate how it complies with the design principles, and how it meets the design requirements. For example, if the design principle of loosely coupled systems has been identified as an important principle, then the relevant cell primitives need to demonstrate a 'plug and play' ability. Note that this principle might be equally applied to organizational units as to technology or software components.

9. Conduct gap analysis

A gap analysis needs to be completed in order to understand what differences exist between the current state and the target design state. Gaps can be capabilities that exist in the target that do not exist in the current state. Gaps can also include aspects of the current state that are important to continue with, but that have not been identified in the target state design. In this case it is likely that a strategic goal or design requirement has been missed which needs to be factored into the target state design. TOGAF (The Open Group, 2006) describes an excellent gap analysis methodology. Note that the purpose of the gap analysis is only to identify differences. Subsequent steps will identify what needs to be done to address the gaps and transition to the target state.

10. Identify and design transition strategies

Each gap identified in the previous step will reflect a need for the enterprise to adopt a strategy to transition to the target design state. One strategy however, may address several gaps. The design of the strategies will again draw on the design principles and design requirements identified in previous steps. A strategy statement is a statement that reflects an agreed course of action.

It does not describe actual implementation, but rather describes how the enterprise will behave (e.g. will pursue cost reduction in production processes, will undertake greater product diversification, will implement a decentralized distribution network, will standardize the customer experience). Again it should be noted that each strategy should be worded in a way that clearly associates it with the previously identified design principles.

11. Identify and assign KPIs

This process is responsible for identifying appropriate key performance indicators and assigning these to strategies identified in the previous step. KPIs should be readily measurable and relate obviously to the anticipated outcome of the applicable strategy (e.g. 10% increase sales by 2008 end of financial year, at least three new product lines within the next 2 years, 90% of deliveries within 2 days of initial order, 100% of outlets accredited within the next 12 months). Identifying suitable KPIs can be assisted by applying the SMART test and ensuring that KPIs are:

S = Specific: Are clearly and concisely worded.
M = Measurable: Are able to be quantified.
A = Attainable: Are achievable, reasonable, and credible.
R = Realistic: Fit within constraints and are cost effective.
T = Timely: Are time bound.

The selection of KPIs should consider the measurement of the performance of both design and implementation. Performance can be affected by both the overall design approach adopted by a strategy and by the choices regarding how the strategy or design is physically implemented. A given design or strategy might be implemented using one of many possible physical implementations. Therefore, KPIs need to be selected to measure the effectiveness of the design or approach described by a strategy (i.e. the suitability of the strategy), as well as the performance of the actual chosen implementation.

12. Identify and design transition initiatives

Having identified design principles and requirements, and a set of strategies consistent with these principles, specific initiatives or projects and solutions can now be identified. The identification of projects should be relatively straightforward at this point. The review should encompass an assessment of existing projects and their support for the principles, requirements and strategies. Importantly, the detailed solution design does not necessarily need to be undertaken at this time. The intent is that individual projects are constrained and specified based on the strategies, design requirements and principles. Any given initiative or project should be able to readily identify the design principles and strategies which it supports. The detailed solution design and implementation will be undertaken within the program management function, and may actually form the subject of individual KPIs.

The CIO meets with the Director-General and outlines the progress made to date on the HealthSec 2.0 transition program and planning. She makes the case that the program's success will depend on shared executive responsibility, and that it will require the Director-General's clear endorsement. The CIO undertakes to provide the Direct-General with a short presentation to be given by him at the next executive meeting in a few weeks time to reinforce his endorsement of the program and the requirement for each executive to be assigned responsibility for at least one target from the Commission's Report.

At last the two-month deadline arrives and the CIO is ready to present the draft target design state to the rest of the executive. The CIO tables the target design state document which describes the future desired business, information application and infrastructure architectures. The CIO also tables an initial gap analysis and an initial list of transition strategies based on the design principles and requirements. The assignment of executive members to the Report targets (as tentative KPIs) is taken up by the Director-General as a separate meeting agenda item. The meeting endorses the target state description but requests further time to consider the transition strategies. The CIO requests that they agree on a core set of the draft strategies so that work can begin on identifying the actual initiatives which will constitute the transition program. The meeting agrees to this, and to a draft set of all initiatives to be tabled at the next meeting.

Again the EA Office swings into top gear. The Chief Architect meets with each of the Executive Directors and their advisors to firm up the list of transition strategies. The initial design principles are a key input into these discussions. The meetings also identify tentative process owners, information, application and data custodians. The Business, Information, Applications and Technology Architects include the outcomes in their ongoing development and refinement of the gap analysis. Additional KPI's are identified and aligned with the Commission's Report targets. The final list of strategies, KPIs, custodians and initiatives is developed and provided to the executive members prior to their next meeting.

Implementation Sequence:
This sequence takes the projects and initiatives identified in previous steps and then develops them into a transition program which is then performance managed. This sequence promotes coherency by ensuring that the projects and initiatives are managed as a program that takes account of inter-dependencies, corrects for performance inconsistencies across projects, and aims to ensure project and initiative efforts are aligned with the organization's strategic goals and design principles.

13. Compile transition program

This process takes the list of all the required projects identified in the previous step and organizes them according to inter-dependencies, priorities and timeframes. The outcome of this process is a defined program of projects. Once compiled and approved, the program forms the basis of the 'hand off' between the enterprise architecture process and the program management process.

14. Establish KPI management capability

Up until this point there has been no requirement to actually use and measure the strategy KPIs. However, in order to evaluate the effectiveness and coherency of the transition program, it is necessary to implement a capability to measure performance. This will necessitate the establishment of a KPI database and identification of data sources to be used to populate the measures. This database would ideally be implemented as a section within the Requirements Repository established in Step 2. KPIs will typically need version control and an identified sponsor.

This process step echoes Kaplan and Norton's (2008) requirement that organizations need to invest specifically in creating a strategic management capability in order for the strategic program to be successful.

15. Implement transition program

This process represents the program management of the transition program and as such falls outside the scope of this chapter.

16. Measure and report performance

Using the KPI management capability this process entails the measurement and reporting of the KPIs. Typically the report is provided to the executive management team within the enterprise. The report needs to be an objective assessment of performance against the stated KPIs. Areas of poor performance are candidates for further investigation.

17. Manage risk

A risk assessment should be conducted for areas of poor performance. The risk assessment process will identify threats, risks and mitigation strategies. These strategies should then be fed back into the Requirements Definition sequence and will possibly generate additional projects or initiatives to be included in the transition program.

18. Review performance

The review of performance needs to be conducted for a defined time period. The review is a more holistic process than the measurement and reporting process covered earlier. The review will determine the degree to which the transition program has moved the organization toward the goals identified in Step 5 by examining performance against the KPIs and implementation of the design principles. The review may well identify new areas of concern and initiate the next iteration of the cycle. The review should culminate in a set of specific recommendations to move the transition program forward.

At their next meeting the executive approves the assignment of KPIs and endorses the initial list of initiatives, process owners and custodians. The CIO outlines the detail of the Implementation Phase and requests the other members of the executive give consideration to the relative priority of initiatives which contribute to the performance of the KPIs for which they are responsible.

Following the meeting the Chief Architect meets with the Execute Directors and their advisors to prioritize the initiatives which will be included in the finalized transition program. The Chief Architect provides an initial draft list of initiatives to his Solution Architects for review and assessment in terms of dependencies and sequencing. The KPIs and associated meas-

ures are implemented within the EA Office Repository and initial reports compiled and provided to the relevant Executive Director. At the following executive meeting the final initiative listing is presented for approval. The list includes several IM&ICT initiatives as well as a significant number of business process initiatives. The CIO offers temporary Solution Architect and Business Analyst support to the other areas of HealthSec to assist the Program Managers responsible for implementing the initiatives in each area. The offer is enthusiastically taken up by the CFO and Executive Director for Clinical Services. The HealthSec 2.0 Transition Program is officially signed and approved by the Director-General.

Over the following months each Program Manager provides performance measures to the EA Office. These measures are used to compile regular progress reports for the executive members. Initiatives which fall behind schedule are readily identified and remedial action is taken. After 12 months the executive decides to undertake a thorough review of the transition program. Although there has been significant progress and a number of the Commission Report targets have been met, there are other areas where progress has been slow. The executive decides to take these areas and use them as the scope for a second iteration of the Requirements Definition, Design and Implementation process.

Table 1 provides a high level summary of the processes within the coherency methodology. Each process is described in terms of its inputs and outputs, as well as the governance that would be typically employed and the stakeholders that would usually be involved.

Table 1. Process summary

Step	Inputs	Outputs	Governance	Stakeholders
Preliminary Sequence				
Identify Scope of Concern	Problem statements Reference Models	Scope statement	Scope statement approved by Sponsor	Sponsor
Establish requirements management capability	Scope statement	Repository	Repository Librarian Artifact owner approval	EA Team Artifact owners
Baseline current environment	Repository Scope statement	Current business models Baseline description	Baseline description approved by Sponsor	Artifact owners
Requirements Definition Sequence				
Identify strategic drivers	Baseline description SWOT Analysis	Strategic drivers	Business stakeholder endorsement	Business stakeholders
Identify strategic goals	Strategic drivers Baseline description	Strategic goals	Sponsor approval of Strategic goals	Sponsor Business stakeholders
Identify design principles	Strategic goals Baseline description	Design principles	Design principles approved by Sponsor	Sponsor Business stakeholders
Identify design requirements	Strategic goals Baseline description Reference Models	Design requirements	Design requirements endorsed by business stakeholders	Business stakeholders
Design Sequence				
Identify target design state	Baseline description Strategic drivers/ goals Design principles Design requirements Existing target state artifacts Repository	Target state description	Target state description approved by Sponsor	Sponsor Business stakeholders
Conduct gap analysis	Baseline description Target state description	Identified gaps	Business stakeholder endorsement	Business stakeholders
Identify and design transition strategies	Identified gaps Design Principles Design Requirements	Transition strategies	Sponsor approval of Transition strategies	Sponsor Business stakeholders
Identify and assign KPIs	Transition strategies	KPIs assigned to Transition Strategies KPI Sponsors identified	Sponsor approval of KPIs and Sponsorships	Sponsor KPI Sponsors Business stakeholders
Identify and design transition initiatives	Transition strategies KPIs Design principles Design Requirements	Listing of Transition initiatives	Business stakeholder endorsement KPI Sponsor approval	KPI Sponsors Business stakeholders
Implementation Sequence				
Compile transition program	Listing of Transition initiatives	Transition Program	KPI Sponsor endorsement Sponsor approval of Transition Program	Sponsor KPI Sponsors Business stakeholders
Establish KPI management capability	Transition Program KPIs Repository	KPI Management Capability	KPI Sponsor endorsement	KPI Sponsors EA Team
Implement transition program	Transition Program Program Management Capability	Implemented Transition Program	Program Manager Approval	Program Manager Project Managers Business stakeholders
Measure and report performance	KPI Management Capability Transition Program KPIs	Performance Report	Sponsor approval of the Report KPI Sponsor endorsement	Sponsor KPI Sponsors Program Manager Project Managers Business stakeholders
Manage risk	Performance Report	Risk Assessment Threats, Risks Mitigation Strategies	KPI Sponsor approval of mitigation strategies	KPI Sponsors
Review performance	Target state description Performance Report Risk Assessment	Review recommendations	Sponsor approval of recommendations	Sponsor Business stakeholders

COHERENCY MANAGEMENT

Conclusion

This chapter has explored the relationships between enterprise architecture, strategic planning and information management, and their contributions to coherency management. This chapter has outlined an approach which provides a means to describe the delineation between these three functions. This chapter has also presented a methodology aimed at improving organizational coherency by combining enterprise architecture processes with strategic planning and information management processes. The result is a comprehensive, flexible and integrated approach to improving organizational coherency. The approach outlined in this chapter could be readily extended by adding other enterprise functions such as human resource management, capital asset management and financial management.

Concluding remarks

Central to this chapter is the notion that enterprise architecture has the capacity to effectively provide a frame of reference for the management of coherency within the contemporary enterprise. However, as enterprise architecture becomes more accepted as a legitimate business activity and not one solely undertaken by the IT department, it is evident that there are aspects of the discipline which may require greater degrees of sophistication.

As stated earlier, enterprise architecture has an engineering heritage. This heritage is evident in the use of the construction industry, or town planning as an analogy for describing the enterprise architecture endeavor. This is apparent in terminology such as the naming of the Zachman Framework rows, TOGAF's 'building blocks', and indeed the term 'architecture' itself. Given the highly dynamic nature of human organizations, it could be argued that enterprise architecture needs to adopt a fundamentally different analogy or paradigm. More suitable candidates might be those found in the sciences of meteorology or social psychology which have developed around the study of highly dynamic systems, and which might consider that a successful human enterprise is something that is developed or grown rather than constructed.

The engineering heritage of enterprise architecture is also evident in its apparent preoccupation with enterprise state. State based 'snapshots' of highly dynamic systems typically reveal little about their internal workings. For example, the organizational charts of most enterprises reveal little about the true powerbroker relationships within the organization. Sciences like meteorology or the 'soft sciences' such as social psychology or sociology routinely study dynamic systems using observational methodologies and system simulations. Enterprise architects might therefore stand to gain from a deeper appreciation of the research literature and methodologies these disciplines use and have refined. For example, social psychologists have known for some time that by simply randomly assigning a group of people into two sub-groups and providing an arbitrary dimension of group comparison (e.g. preference in artistic style) is sufficient to elicit competitive behavior between the sub-groups (Tajfel & Turner, 1986). This tendency is one of many human characteristics that could usefully be taken into consideration when determining the optimal organizational structure, operation and design.

Documenting the enterprise at excruciating levels of detail is often cited as the reason for enterprise architecture failure. Perhaps there are more profound reasons for these failures such as the lack of credibility that a 'construction-based approach' has with those in an organization who better understand human behavior. This is not to diminish the importance of the design contribution of enterprise architecture but rather to suggest that there are other disciplines from which enterprise architecture needs to leverage and integrate with if it is to mature.

References

Bernard, S, A. (2005). An Introduction To Enterprise Architecture: Second Edition. AuthorHouse: Bloomington, Indiana.

Bernus, P., Nemes, L., & Schmidt, G, (Eds.). (2003). Handbook on Enterprise Architecture. Springer: Berlin.

Newman, D., and Logan, D. (2006). Spotlight on Enterprise Information Management. Gartner Research.

Henderson J. C., and Venkatraman, N. (1993). Strategic alignment: leveraging information technology for transforming organizations. IBM Systems Journal. Vol 32, 1.

Holcman, S., (2008). Pinnacle Business Group-Results Driven Enterprise Architecture Implementation, Unpublished workshop materials.

Humphrey, A. S. (1970). The Theory and Practice of Planning, unpublished report.

Office of Government Commerce. (2007). Information Technology Infrastructure Library Version 3, United Kingdom.

Object Management Group (OMG). (2006). Business Motivation Model (BMM) Specification – Adopted Specification, dtc/2006-08-03.

Porter, M.E. (1979) How competitive forces shape strategy. Harvard Business Review. March/April.

Kaplan, R. S., Norton, D. P. (2008). The Execution Premium, Linking Strategy to Operations for Competitive Advantage. Harvard Business Press: Boston, MA.

Kaplan, R. S., Norton, D. P. (2004). Strategy Maps: Converting Intangible Assets into Tangible Outcomes. Harvard Business School Press: Boston, MA.

Kaplan, R. S., Norton, D. P. (1996) The Balanced Scorecard: Translating Strategy Into Action. Harvard Business School Press: Boston, MA.

Ross, J. W., Weill, P., Robertson, D. C. (2006). Enterprise Architecture as Strategy–Creating a Foundation for Business Execution. Harvard Business School Press: Boston, MA.

Tajfel, H. & Turner, J. C. (1986). The social identity theory of inter-group behavior. In S. Worchel & L. W. Austin (Eds.), Psychology of Intergroup Relations. Chicago: Nelson-Hall.

The Open Group. (2006). The Open Group Architecture Framework. Version 8.1.1, Enterprise Edition.

Treasury Board of Canada. (2004). Business Transformation Enablement Program. http://tinyurl.com/de73yh

Weill, P., & Ross, J. (2004). IT Governance: How Top Performers Manage IT Decision Rights for Superior Results. Harvard Business School Press: Boston, MA.

Zachman, J. A. (2005). The Zachman Framework for Enterprise Architecture: A Primer for Enterprise Engineering and Manufacturing. The Zachman eBook. Zachman International, http://tinyurl.com/3hx82j.

About the Author

Chris Aitken currently works as Enterprise Architect at QIC in Brisbane, Australia. Over the last 15 years he has held a variety of government agency positions. In the last 6 years he has held the positions of Business and Information Architect, Information Security Architect, Enterprise Architecture Coordinator, and Manager Enterprise Architecture and Information Management. Chris is a contributing author for the book *Advances in Government Enterprise Architecture* (ed. Saha, 2008). Chris' clinical business and applied research background means that he brings the combination of a strong human service delivery perspective and a keen logical rigor to his approach to enterprise architecture and IM & ICT implementation. Chris' current interests include topics as varied as: the development of an abstract enterprise metamodel, IM & ICT policy and standards development, enterprise interoperability, and the integration of IM & ICT strategic planning with enterprise architecture. Chris holds a PhD in Psychophysiology, a Post Graduate Diploma in Psychology both from the University of Queensland, Australia and a Bachelor of Arts Degree in Psychology and Sociology from the University of Auckland, New Zealand. Chris can be reached at chris_aitken@exemail.com.au.

Acknowledgements

I would like to acknowledge my friends and colleagues at Queensland Health whose conversations and discussions and patience helped shape my thinking and contributed to the refinement of many of the models and frameworks presented in this chapter.

Chris Aitken
12 Winchester St,
Hamilton
Brisbane QLD 4007
AUSTRALIA
E-mail: chris_aitken@exemail.com.au

Chapter 6

THE STRATEGIC DIMENSION OF ENTERPRISE ARCHITECTURE

Tanaia Parker

Editors' Preface

Ever since Ross, Weill and Robertson's seminal book on Enterprise Architecture (2006) where they made the case for EA to be part of organizational strategy, plenty of current research focuses on how this can be operationalized. This chapter adds to the growing literature in this regard. It starts with a brief overview of strategic management and its constituents (analysis, formulation, execution and governance).

The chapter decomposes strategic management into its core elements and presents their associations and linkages to EA. This allows readers to view the connections in a more holistic manner. Furthermore, it provides insights into the ramifications of not taking advantage of EA in various activities of strategic management, and it elaborates how organizations can operationalize the strategic management and enterprise architecture combination. This is done by a proposed Strategic Enterprise Architecture Framework (SEAF). The proposed framework provides a structured way for organizations to take advantage of this integration. There is no dearth of literature on the technical / engineering aspects of EA. This chapter takes a purely business-oriented view of the EA.

We foresee EA (especially in the 'extended' and the 'embedded' modes) being used in organizations as an overarching management approach to enhance enterprise coherency and being used as a way to integrate and make sense of myriads of business improvement initiatives (Six Sigma, BPR, Business Transformation, Restructuring, Consolidation etc.) is already happening.

Introduction

When discussing the use of enterprise architecture (EA) to achieve the coherency management by-products of alignment, agility and assurance, we must give credit to the role strategy plays. When we refer to the strategic dimension of EA, many immediately connect with the inclusion of mission statements, org charts and strategic goals that are often included in the business layer of an EA. Although the movement to allocate EA "real estate" to the strategic elements of an organization reflects a maturing of the discipline, the incorporation of EA in organizations' strategic management (SM) activities has not gained traction.

Through the coherency management discussion, the three EA modes of Foundation Architecture, Extended Architecture and Embedded Architecture represent maturation in the intent, application and management of EA and provide a perfect segue into the strategic dimension. Earlier discussions in this book addressed these three modes, highlighting both the characteristics and the benefits of progressing toward an Embedded Architecture. Addressed in greater detail throughout this chapter, we will see that a direct link exists between the progression in modes of EA and the effective integration of EA and SM. Through an Embedded Architecture, the strategic dimension of EA is exemplified in that it encompasses an integration of EA and SM.

Acknowledging the tremendous value that EA has brought to business process, applications, data and technology planning and management, we must still be aware that not one of these dimensions would exist if not for the strategic dimension. Business process, applications, data and technology all exist to support the mission, goals and objectives of an organization. It is for this reason that we believe that an omission or lack of rigor in the strategic dimension of EA represents misaligned EA and thus inhibits sound coherency management.

As practitioners, we need to begin to acknowledge through practice and contributions to the discipline the authoritative position the strategic dimension has in the development and maintenance of EAs. In 2006, Jeanne Ross, Peter Weill and David Robertson published a groundbreaking book that boldly aligns enterprise architecture with business strategy (Ross, 2006). This book has forced organizations, practitioners and enterprise architecture naysayers to take another look at enterprise architecture as a discipline that can truly be leveraged for non-IT purposes. With their work and the work of others, we are definitely making strides in presenting enterprise architecture as a view of the business rather than that of the IT infrastructure. In that same vein, here we will demonstrate EA's strategic value to organizations by identifying the linkages between EA and SM, thus presenting EA as a discipline that can be leveraged for the strategic analysis, formulation, execution and governance phases of SM. In this chapter, we will also present the Strategic Enterprise Architecture Framework (SEAF) as a tool and resource for operationalizing the integration of SM and EA and reinforcing coherency management. The strategic dimension of EA enables stakeholders to better understand, align, communicate, execute, and govern the strategic direction of an organization. We refer to these as the Know-It, Tell-It, Align-It, Do-It and Govern-It benefits of a strategically-aligned EA, topics to be discussed in more detail in the sections to come.

Strategic Management as the Strategic Dimension

To discuss the "strategic dimension" of any topic is to address that topic within the context of the SM process. To that end, and for the purposes of this chapter, "strategic dimension" refers directly to the SM process.

SM is an enterprise-wide task that involves a proactive and continuous cycle of *analysis, strategy formulation, strategy execution, and governance* activities. SM enables organizations' ability to navigate change. It provides a deliberate and formalized process for ensuring

Figure 1. The Strategic Management Process

that the organization has appropriately planned for the environment in which it operates and that it effectively implements those strategies. SM involves ensuring that the organization's focus, approach and internal infrastructure are relevant, realistic and implemented such that the synergy created between them yields a well-positioned and results-generating organization.

Many view SM and strategic planning synonymously. That is a material flaw. The impact of this misconception is institutionalized in many organizations as their strategic planning efforts typically only involve strategic analysis and strategic formulation activities giving very little (if any) attention to strategy execution and governance which are critical to getting results. How many times has your organization embarked upon its "strategic planning season" to find that after all of the activity (and a well-put-together strategic plan that does no actionable good) that no one hears about it again until the next period? This is where strategic planning and SM differ.

In the next few paragraphs, we will briefly address each of the key activities within the SM process in order to set the stage for discussing their relationship to EA.

Strategic Analysis

Strategic analysis is the pre-strategy due diligence required to obtain the necessary information for strategy formulation and execution. This step within the SM process is typically a tremendous information gathering undertaking that spans across the enterprise and frequently delves deep into key aspects of the business. There are a number of tools, templates and information gathering techniques available to assist in this activity; however, the key factor here is ensuring that the data gathering and analysis effort is commensurate with the scope of the enterprises' strategic objectives. The information gathered and the analysis conducted varies from organization to organization.

Strategy Formulation

Strategy formulation is about crafting the best course of action based on where the organization desires to go, where it currently stands and the factors that impact the organization's reality. For strategy formulation to be successful, the most accurate, timely and relevant information must be available. Effective strategy formulation results in a framework for making operational decisions which ultimately guides the organization to where it desires to be. The output of strategy formulation is typically referred to as the "strategic plan." Strategy formulation is where traditional strategic planning often ends.

Strategy Execution

A surprisingly low percentage (less than 50%) of executives noted that they were satisfied with the results of their organizations' strategic planning activities and raised concerns about how their organizations execute, communicate, align and measure performance against it (Dye, 2006). Taking these results into consideration, there is no surprise that, historically, 90% of well-formulated strategies fail due to poor execution (Charan, 1999). Strategy execution is the bane of many organizations' strategic planning efforts. Consequently, strategy execution has become a discipline in its own right. Due to the complex nature of strategy execution, we devote a bit more time in addressing it in this section.

Strategy execution involves all of the activities required to "make happen" and manage the effectiveness of the strategies identified in the strategy formulation stage. Strategy execution requires a level of action planning that takes into account appropriately communicating the strategic plan to all who need to act against it and making the right resource, asset, time and energy investments. In order for strategy execution to be successful, it is important that the plan is not only made available and clear to all who have a hand in making the strategies happen, but that the plan also incorporates measurable points of progression such that monitoring is not merely a schedule and cost checkpoint but an "effectiveness gauge".

Making the plan available and clear means ensuring that the plan is accessible and communicated in a way (or ways) that is comprehendible across multiple perspectives to include varying functions (e.g., HR vs. Marketing vs. Finance), levels of seniority (e.g., executives vs. middle management vs. junior employees) and scopes of understanding (e.g., technical vs. non-technical). Ensuring a proper "effectiveness gauge" means that the strategies must be properly decomposed into measurable components. How else will management know when the organization has "arrived"? Execution and governance go hand-in-hand to ensure a deliberate and structured implementation of the organization's strategic plan.

Strategic Governance

Strategic governance is the management structure that ensures that the SM process (especially strategic execution) occurs in a deliberate and formalized manner. It consists of the policies, procedures and processes necessary to effectively manage the SM process and view progress along the way. Strategic governance requires proper and timely reporting, decision making and action accountability. With most strategic planning efforts lacking strategic governance, organizations rarely know where they are going wrong or even what is working really well until the reality (good or bad) is upon them. This often results in missed opportunities and debilitating blindsides.

Coherence in Strategic Management

We learned earlier that coherency management *is about using enterprise architecture to advance the alignment within an organization to create agility and assurance in promoting transformation and delivering value.* Through this definition, it is clear that coherency management through EA is in itself the SM of organizational alignment, agility and assurance. What does this mean? Earlier in this chapter, we discussed the fact that:

Strategic management enables organizations' ability to navigate change. IT provides a deliberate and formalized process for ensuring that the organization has appropriately strategized for the environment in which it operates and effectively implements those strategies. Strategic management involves ensuring that the organization's focus, approach and internal infrastructure are relevant, realistic and implemented such that the synergy created between them yields a well-positioned and results-generating organization.

Embracing this definition of SM, we will now relate SM to the three primary goals of coherency management (i.e., alignment, agility and assurance).

Alignment

Alignment refers to the need for similarity in EA methods at all levels/areas of the architecture (Doucet et. Al., 2008). As we will continue to unveil throughout this chapter, alignment cannot occur without SM. When SM is combined with EA, organizations achieve alignment on many different fronts. First, when a proper relationship between SM and EA exists in the development of an EA, a strategy-aligned EA will always result. A strategy-aligned EA is one that clearly shows the linkages to the organization's strategies, makes clear the dependencies and relationships across all pertinent layers of an organization and has been developed with strategic action and implementation in mind. Second, a strategically-focused EA framework combined with a disciplined SM process will result in the alignment of strategy down through the operational and enabling capabilities of an organization.

Agility

Agility refers to an enterprise's ability to manage change (Doucet et. Al., 2008). In the beginning of this chapter, we mentioned that SM enables organizations' ability to navigate change. To that end, SM is about promoting an organization's ability to move in a timely and coordinated fashion (i.e., be agile). The degree to which SM enables an organization to do so depends greatly on how mature its SM process is and how well the SM process and EA process are integrated.

Assurance

Assurance addresses control and speaks to confidence and fidelity in the sources and use of enterprise products and services (Doucet et. Al., 2008). Assurance, within the construct of SM, becomes a reality when an organization has: (1) performed all of the necessary strategic due diligence it can possibly perform, (2) formulated the best strategy based on what is known at the time (3) communicated the strategy in such a way that clarity in function, actions and dependencies exist among the executors and (4) established a governance structure through which the SM process will be effectively managed in tandem with EA. When SM and EA are performed properly and well-integrated with one another, assurance is an automatic by-product.

The Fundamental Elements of an Enterprise Architecture

This section is not intended to provide a remedial lesson in the key components of EA nor is it intended to comprehensively define these components. Instead, the goal of this next section is to continue setting the stage for the discussion that follows which addresses the relationship between SM and EA. Here we define the very basic components of EA within the context of the strategic value they provide to an organization.

The As-Is Architecture

The As-Is architecture is the set of artifacts which represents the organization's "today." Depending on the context, scope and EA framework used, the As-Is architecture can reveal *organizational and operational challenges* (e.g., a burdensome bureaucracy identified through documented business processes), *strengths* (e.g., technological capabilities identified through technology inventories), *deficiencies* (e.g., unmet business requirements identified through dissatisfied customers) and *opportunities* (e.g., untapped capacity identified through performance results). Through a well-defined As-Is architecture, each of these insights (individually and collectively) serves a tremendous strategic value in that they provide a tangible starting point for where strategy formulation can begin. Too often, organizations begin the strategy formulation phase with information that is subjective, incorrectly interpreted and/or not widely vetted, resulting in strategies that are not credible. Leveraging a well maintained As-Is Architecture in strategy formulation would contribute significantly to resolving the strategy credibility problem.

The To-Be Architecture

The To-Be architecture is the set of artifacts which represents what the organization wants to "look like" at a predetermined point in the future. This component of the EA is, by definition, strategic in itself in that it represents a plan for the future. However, the To-Be architecture is not to be confused with a Strategic Plan. Within the discipline of SM, the To-Be architecture represents a more detailed, operational representation of the organization's future state than what we would see in any traditional strategic planning document.

The Transition Plan

The Transition Plan is the piece that links the As-Is architecture and the To-Be architecture together. Highlighting capability gaps and providing an actionable roadmap for how an organization transforms from its As-Is to its To-Be, the Transition Plan is a dynamic resource which details the progression of changes that must occur in order to fill functional, data and technical gaps. The Transition Plan not only provides the details of the initiatives required to "transition" the organization from one state to another, a good Transition Plan also outlines the timelines, prerequisites, dependencies and owners.

The Transition Plan differs from the Strategic Plan in that it provides a much lower level of detail about the activities that must occur and spans across all layers of the enterprise (strategy, business, people, application, data and technology). A Strategic Plan, on the other hand, typically keeps the level of instruction and level of guidance at the enterprise level. The Strategic Plan serves as a higher level guidance tool that provides the organization's direction in terms of the "strategic rules" and strategic "to do" lists versus the operational "how to" that is in the To-Be architecture.

Strategic Management and Enterprise Architecture

Earlier in the book, we established that the primary goals of coherency management are alignment, agility and assurance in organizations through the use of EA. Particularly, when we look at the strategic execution and strategic governance components of the SM process, we see a very obvious synergy in function (and in some respects, form) between SM and EA. On the one hand, SM is the discipline that "owns" the activity surrounding the determination, execution, continued monitoring and management of the business focus and strategy while also setting the framework for how to move the organization in the appropriate strategic direction. EA, on the other hand, serves as the discipline that "owns" the activity surrounding the development and maintenance of the information needed to conduct SM (particularly, strategy formulation and execution). EA also provides a roadmap for transforming the organization's operational capabilities. An effective EA captures enough of the strategic/business level and operational level detail (via artifacts) to "inform" the entire SM process. The level of detail and the type of artifacts depends on what the organization needs in order to effectively strategize and execute.

In the paragraphs that follow, we will probe into the relationship between EA and SM within the context of the phases of the SM process. In the discussion, we will highlight the benefits one brings to the other and their points of integration.

Enterprise Architecture and Strategic Analysis

As we mentioned earlier, strategic analysis involves gaining a deep understanding of the organization's reality across many facets. Similar to the decisions made in EA, the "facets" addressed in strategic analysis depend on the organization, intention and scope of the effort. During the strategic analysis phase of the SM process, both strategy level and operational level information is critical. Appropriately scoped, maintained and accessible by the SM process, strategically-focused EA artifacts supply a great portion of the information needed during strategic analysis.

Enterprise Architecture and Strategy Formulation

Strategy formulation, which relies on the information obtained from the strategic analysis phase, involves determining the best approach for moving the organization from one position to another. Strategy formulation is not only about coming up with a plan for how to accomplish the end goal, it is a deeper activity that results in a decision-making framework. Strategy formulation brings coherency to day-to-day operational decisions by providing decision-making guidance through predetermined strategic principles. EA not only enables strategy formulation by providing informative details about the organization during the strategic analysis phase, but it also serves as a feasibility "sounding board" through its presentation of the organization's current, intermediate and future operational and technical capabilities. This injection of EA into the SM process prevents strategy from being formulated in a vacuum.

Enterprise Architecture and Strategic Execution

Figuratively speaking, strategic execution is where all of the SM activities converge to either deliver results (good or bad) or come to a screeching halt. For this reason, we will again pay a bit more attention to execution in this section.

Strategic execution involves all of the activities required to put the strategic plan into action. When properly integrated, EA enables three functions of the strategy execution phase: (1) strategy communication, (2) strategic action planning, and (3) strategic progress reporting. As an enabler to strategy communication, EA presents business strategies and overall strategic direction in views that are comprehendible by the players. As an enabler to strategic action planning, the EA (via the Transition Plan) provides a time-based outline of the activities that must occur immediately, intermediately and in the future. Finally, as an enabler to strategic progress reporting, EA provides a dynamic representation of where the organization stands at any given point in the execution of the organization's strategic initiatives. This is achieved as the "As-Is" set of artifacts for the organization are continuously modified/updated to accurately reflect the current state. Through all of these SM roles, EA serves as an inherent change management tool to the enterprise.

Enterprise Architecture and Strategic Governance

Strategic governance has to do with the process management and oversight activities in place to ensure that operational processes and strategic outcomes are proactively and effectively managed. This includes ensuring that each phase within the SM process is adequately performed and that corrective action takes place when unfavorable results are presented, as well as ensuring that business operations are representative of the direction set forth and the outcomes expected. Strategic governance requires continuous, structured and diligent monitoring versus serving as only a glorified status-reporting function. Strategic governance is directly related to EA in that it exists to ensure that the actions taken by an organization align with the operational direction, technical standards and transitional architecture set forth in the EA. Consequently, the strategic governance function of the SM process respects the organization's EA as an authoritative resource against which governance decisions are made. The challenge for the EA process (particularly within Foundational and Extended EAs) becomes ensuring that its own governance promises accurate and timely updates to the EA.

The Benefits of Integrating EA and Strategic Management

Although a number of benefits and points of tangible value about integrating EA and SM practices can be pulled from what has already been stated, we would be remiss if the specific benefits of leveraging EA for SM were not explicitly outlined. The key benefits to integrating the two disciplines can be summarized by how they help stakeholders relate to the strategic direction of the organization. Simply stated, the benefits include helping stakeholders *know-it, tell-it, align-it, do-it* and *govern-it* ("it" refers to the strategic direction of the organization). Let's look at each of these in a bit more detail.

Know-It
(know and understand the strategic direction)
In a survey conducted in 2001, an average of ninety-five percent of an organization's employees were unaware or did not understand the organization's strategy (Kaplan, 2001). More recent assessments have revealed that not much has changed since that survey. "Know-It" refers to EA's ability to make plain the business and strategic direction of an organization as defined through the SM process. Through the presentation of the business in many views across a number of different perspectives, EA helps organizational players know and understand the strategy they must implement.

Tell-It
(accurately and effectively communicate the strategic direction)
Related but different from, "Know-It," "Tell-It" refers to EA's ability to clearly communicate the strategic directions, directives and information of the organization while also existing as an enterprise-wide accessible resource. One of the fundamental issues with EA is its ability to adequately communicate with all stakeholders (Schekkerman, 2004). Consequently, it is imperative that the strategic requirements for an organization be correctly interpreted and appropriately presented in EA views such that the message is cohesive and understandable by those who need to execute.

Align-It
(properly identify the strategy-to-operations-to-enablers "line of sight")
Fifty-nine percent of those surveyed who worked in companies that had formal strategic planning processes responded that their HR and strategic plans are either only slightly integrated or not integrated at all (Dye, 2006). "Align-it" refers to the combined SM and EA benefit of making clear the relationships between seemingly disconnected or separated components and functions within an organization. EA builds the bridges that connect each of the layers within an organization. An effective EA will build the bridges between the strategy, business, people, data, technology layers of an enterprise making clear the dependencies, the business gaps and the redundancies. Many EA approaches fall short in making this alignment clear and actionable.

Do-It
(execute what needs to be executed)
"Do-It" refers to EA's enabling role in strategic execution. As discussed previously, by helping organizations "know-it" and "tell-it," through actionable views, EA provides the information needed by stakeholders to transform the organization from its As-Is state to its To-Be state. In addition to the views, an EA Transition Plan provides an executable framework by setting forth a work plan for execution that is presented in the language of those who have to execute it.

Govern-It
(ensure that the appropriate measures are taken to keep progress on track)
"Govern-It" refers to EA's role as an authoritative sounding board. By leveraging an organization's strategically-focused EA to evaluate and validate strategic alternatives, organizations achieve the coherency that is typically absent in IT-focused EAs.

Additional Benefits of Integrating Enterprise Architecture & Strategic Management
The purpose of this section is to discuss the additional benefits realized when EA and SM are effectively integrated. However, before addressing these benefits, it is helpful to revisit the role EA plays in each of the SM phases and highlight the risks an organization takes on when the linkage between the two disciplines is not present.

Strategic Management Phase	Role of EA	What Happens When the Linkage is Absent
Analysis	Provides timely, accurate and relevant data and information	The data upon which analysis is based may be flawed The data upon which analysis is based may not be relevant
Strategy Formulation	Provides timely, accurate and relevant data and information Serves as a feasibility "sounding board" for organizational strategies	Strategy risks getting formulated in a vacuum Bogus Strategy Syndrome (strategies that are not feasible or relevant for the organization)
Strategy Execution	Communicates the strategy to the appropriate audience in the appropriate language Provides the action plan Serves as a "status report" against the target architecture	Execution of strategies are left up to staff's interpretation of the strategic plan Execution management is often only measured at the senior levels of the organization vs. at the grassroots where most leverage exists
Governance	Serves as the "yardstick" for how an organization is to operate and how the organization's resources are to be managed	No solid guidelines exist for making operational decisions

Table 1. Strategic Management and Role of Enterprise Architecture

Other key benefits that can be realized with the integration of EA and SM include:

- the development of common taxonomy and semantics across the enterprise

- improved collaboration

- an all encompassing, multi-dimensional view of enterprise activities

- enforced alignment to the strategic direction of the organization

- exposure of relationships, dependencies, impacts and conflicts

- improved communication of the strategic plan

- improved priority management

Leveraging a Strategically-focused Enterprise Architecture Framework

There exists a plethora of effective EA frameworks. Of these frameworks, most focus the value, analysis and artifact attention on the information technology aspects of an organization. Then there are some up-and-coming frameworks which place more focus on the strategic and business aspects of an organization. With the new (and welcomed) EA attention to the "business of the business" (vs. just information technology), organizations are now left to figure out how to leverage EA frameworks to truly *execute* business versus merely documenting it. The professional discipline of EA has done a phenomenal job in helping organizations strategically plan and execute technology. Our task now is to position EA in such a way as to enable the discipline to also help organizations strategically plan, execute and transform *business*.

The Strategic Enterprise Architecture Framework^{sm} (SEAF)

In order to address the current need to leverage EA in business planning and execution, a framework specifically geared toward better distinguishing the drivers of an organization (namely the mission, strategy and how the business is intended to operate) from its enablers (i.e., the means through which business is accomplished) is needed. Though many frameworks exist that include strategy-related artifacts, most fall short in making the direct linkages between the strategic components and the operational and enabling components. These linkages are critical to having an actionable EA that delivers value in strategic transformation. The Strategic Enterprise Architecture Framework[sm] (SEAF) was created for this very purpose. Although deep specifics about the SEAF will not be discussed here, we will review enough of its elements to present a well-rounded example of a strategically-focused EA framework.

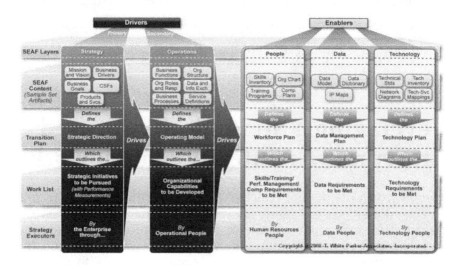

Figure 2. The Strategic Enterprise Architecture Framework[SM]

The SEAF presents a structure for organizing EAs while also providing a different perspective for how to leverage other EA frameworks. The SEAF is a framework that is solely concerned with creating a "line of sight" from the strategic elements of the enterprise down through the operations and enabling elements of the enterprise. Consequently, the SEAF is best suited for organizations in which alignment with an enterprise strategy is a must in order to be successful.

The SEAF leverages the power of EA as a SM discipline to ensure that strategy is properly articulated and aligned across all layers of an enterprise. The SEAF decouples the purpose, strategic direction and "ways of doing business" of an organization (i.e., drivers) from the manner in which these things are achieved (i.e., enablers). Properly executed, the SEAF approach to EA will transform the performance of organizations' SM efforts. Set apart from traditional EA frameworks, the SEAF has three key differences:

1. **Separates the strategy component from business operations and enablers**
   Justification: to truly depict strategy as a driver of the entire business, the strategic dimension of an organization cannot be combined with other components. Additionally, the strategic dimension of an enterprise does not represent the same level of abstraction in its purpose to the organization; thus, there is not an apples-to-apples relationship to other content usually combined with it in traditional frameworks.

2. **Includes "People" as a distinct enabler of the enterprise** Justification: people represent the single most critical factor in the success of an organization. Any business-oriented tool that ignores the impact of and to people in organizational transformations cannot be considered a business resource. Like data and technology, people are critical enablers to the business and must be included in the EA.

3. **Combines business process and applications into one layer called "Operations"**
   Justification: a principle of the SEAF is to identify the common denominator elements that make up the structure of an organization. To this end, an application is actually an automated business process (or combination of processes); thus, we believe it is redundant to have an additional layer that speaks to applications.

The SEAF Structure

The SEAF structure is tri-faceted comprised of the following elements: (1) enterprise context (i.e., driver vs. enabler), (2) EA content (i.e., artifacts, transition plan, work list and strategy executor lists) and (3) enterprise anatomy (e.g., strategy, operations, people, data and technology). The enterprise context exists at the highest level and makes the distinction between the "driving" anatomic parts and "enabling" anatomic parts. A "driver" represents the force behind why the business exists and how it operates (e.g., business purpose, strategy and operational details). An enabler, on the other hand, represents the resources and capabilities needed to operate in a manner that achieves the strategies which will result in the achieved vision (e.g., people, data, and technology).

The EA content represents the artifacts, documents and action planning resources that make up the EA. Though the SEAF does not dictate specific artifacts, it does require that artifacts that are relevant to those who need to execute be created. This aides tremendously in strategy execution and well-positions the EA value proposition within the minds of organizational players. SEAF EA content consists of carefully selected work products (i.e., Transition Plan, Work List and Strategy Executor List) that are execution-oriented and directly linked to each layer of the EA.

The third facet of the SEAF is represented by what we call the "enterprise anatomy." The anatomy is a strategically simplified representation of the make-up of an organization. Consisting of five vertical "layers", the anatomy of the enterprise is comprised of strategy, operations, people, data and technology with the intent to set apart strategy and operations as drivers of the other three enabling layers of people, data and technology.

Considering the Strategic Dimension When Selecting Enterprise Architecture Approaches

As mentioned previously, there are a number of effective EA frameworks that currently exist. Though most focus attention on the information technology of an organization, a few do indeed take the strategic elements and hard-core business aspects of an organization into consideration. The table below presents some key factors in considering EA approaches for SM.

Strategic Dimension Considerations for Enterprise Architecture Approaches
Strategic Elements Are Set Apart
Inclusion of Strategic Artifacts
Strategic Relevance of Artifacts
Enabling Layers of the Enterprise are Linked to Strategy
Strategic "Actionability"
Evidence of Strategic "Line of Sight" Among Enterprise Architecture Artifacts
Linkages Between Enterprise Architecture Development/Maintenance Activities and Strategic Management Processes

Table 2. Strategic Considerations for EA Approaches

Operationalizing the Integration of Strategic Management & EA

The strategically-focused and execution-oriented construct of the SEAF helps organizations to "operationalize" the integration of SM and EA. Designed to ensure that the strategic dimensions of an organization (vs. only the operational/tactical dimensions) drive the development and maintenance of EA, the SEAF provides an actionable roadmap for embarking upon an EA effort while also embedding, as prerequisites, the SM activities discussed previously. Although the SEAF is just one option for organizations seeking to operationalize the integration of SM and EA, the use of any strategically-focused and execution-oriented EA framework and/or methodology that addresses the operational requirements of the organization would also suffice. The key is ensuring that an organization's "drivers" and "enablers" serve as the underlying intent of the approach while also ensuring that "strategic actionability" is present.

The table below summarizes the extent to which each of the coherency management modes of EA meets the needs of the strategic dimension elements discussed earlier in this chapter. In reviewing the table below, it will become obvious that an Embedded Architecture is the goal of any organization seeking to properly address the strategic dimension of EA by effectively integrating the two disciplines.

Fully ● Partially ◗ Not at All ○	Strategic Dimension Elements	Foundation Architecture	Extended Architecture	Embedded Architecture
Strategic Management Process	Analysis	○	○	●
	Strategy Formulation	○	○	●
	Strategy Execution	○	○	●
	Governance	○	◗	●
SEAF "Layers" *The Enterprise Anatomy*	Strategy	○	◗	●
	Operations	◗	○	●
	People	○	○	●
	Data	●	●	●
	Technology	●	●	●

Table 3. Mapping Strategic Dimension Elements to Coherency Management

The Outlook for the Strategic Dimension of Enterprise Architecture

There is a lot of promise in EA continuing to mature into a discipline truly leveraged for business transformation and strategic execution. We are seeing on a more frequent basis EA information being leveraged in enterprise-level decision-making. In addition to EA information becoming a more respected and useful tool in enterprise planning, enterprise architects are now also being pulled into organizational planning initiatives. In a survey conducted in 2007, forty-nine percent of the enterprise architects who responded stated that they were involved in long-term organizational decision-making (Orbitz, 2007). This number increased to sixty-five percent for organizations of 50,000 or more employees (Orbitz, 2007).

For the practice of EA to keep up with the increased business use of EA, we must now put more focus on maturing EA practices, tools, frameworks and methodologies to support the strategic dimension. That being said, we must find a satisfactory middle ground that transcends the needs of both technically-focused architects and business-focused architects.

Conclusion

When speaking of EA and SM, neither discipline exists as a substitute or replacement of the other. Instead, the two disciplines complement one another and should be integrated to bring higher levels of coherency to an organization. With that said, there are three key summarizing points that we would like to close this chapter with: (1) the strategic dimension of EA represents an integration of EA and SM, (2) proper integration of EA and SM produces the coherency management goals of alignment, agility and assurance as automatic by-products and (3) an EA framework that embraces strategy as the authoritative driver of an organization is key to realizing the business transforming capabilities of the discipline.

References

Charan, R., Colvin, G. (1999). Why CEOs Fail?. Fortune. Vol 39. pp 69 – 78.

Doucet, G., Gøtze, J., Saha, P., and Bernard, S. (2008). Coherency Management: Using Enterprise Architecture for Alignment, Agility, and Assurance. Journal of Enterprise Architecture. Vol 4, No 2.

Dye, R. (2006). Improving Strategic Planning: A McKinsey Survey. The McKinsey Quarterly. August. pp. 2.

Kaplan, R., and Norton, D. (2001). The Strategy-Focused Organization: How Balanced Scorecard Companies Thrive in the New Business Environment. Harvard Business School Press: Boston, MA.

Orbitz, T., Doddavula, S. K., and Aziz, S. (2007). Findings from the Enterprise Architecture Survey 2007. June. pp. 6.

Parker, T. (2007). Enterprise Architecture as a Discipline for Strategy Execution. Cutter Consortium. December. Vol. 10, No. 12.

Ross, J., Weill, P., and Robertson, D. (2006). EA as Strategy: Creating a Foundation for Business Execution. Harvard Business School Publishing: Boston, MA.

Schekkerman, J. (2004). How to Survive in the Jungle of Enterprise Architecture Frameworks. Trafford Publishing.

About the Author

Tanaia Parker is president of T. White Parker, a management consulting firm specializing in "enterprise problem solving" and "strategic management" (www.twhiteparker.com). Ms. Parker has worked as a management consultant, enterprise architect, and advisor to various levels of management within the public and private sectors. Her experience has helped to create a unique approach to strategic management and enterprise architecture. Ms. Parker is an experienced speaker, lecturer, trainer and facilitator and holds a B.S.B.A. from American University and an MBA from George Washington University. Ms. Parker is currently the National Capital Area Chapter President of the Association for Strategic Planning.

Acknowledgements

A special thanks to: Jesus Christ, my Lord and my strength, my husband, Lloyd, my family, Dr. Scott Bernard, and all of my colleagues in this great work and in the wonderful field of enterprise architecture.

Tanaia Parker
2325 Dulles Corner Blvd., #500;
Herndon, VA 20171
United States of America
tanaia.parker@twhiteparker.com

Chapter 7

ENGINEERING THE SUSTAINABLE BUSINESS: AN ENTERPRISE ARCHITECTURE APPROACH

Ovidiu Noran

Editors' Preface

Environmental sustainability is fast becoming as important as economic viability for businesses to stay relevant and profitable. However, at present none of the architecture frameworks explicitly include environmental perspectives. As a work around organizations typically handle EA and Environmental Management (EM) as two distinct and separate programs or initiatives. More often than not, this leads to a lack of synergy and consistency between the two. Needless to say there are benefits of integrating the two by extending traditional EA programs to include aspects of EM. However this proposed integration brings forth several challenges.

The chapter clearly goes in-depth in demonstrating the benefit of using EA to address issues concerning sustainability and EM. This is unique and contributes to the EA literature. Furthermore, by including EM related issues within the realms of EA, it allows organizations to extend the role and influence of EA into non-IT areas. This, we believe, is a promising entry point to the extended architecture mode. Though not explicitly depicted in the chapter, the idea of developing and adopting environmental reference models is utilitarian. These reference models when fully mature would have the ability to provide organizations with the tools and mecha-

nisms to adopt and take a more inclusive view to EM in general. The chapter proposes a meta-methodology for operationalizing the integrated approach. This, we believe, is useful as it allows organizations and architects to see how enhancing traditional EA programs to take-on EM related issues impacts the architectural activities and their associated artifacts.

Environmental Sustainability – The Other Issue of the New Century

One of the main concerns of businesses of all times has been their capacity to survive and adapt to changes in the commercial environment and thus to remain productive for their entire envisaged life span – hence, to be an economically sustainable business. History has shown however, that the continued existence of businesses also strongly depends on their impact on the natural environment and the way they treat their workers. This basic truth was emphasized by Elkington's (1998) Triple Bottom Line (TBL) approach to business sustainability: one must achieve not only economic bottom-line performance but environmental and social performance as well. Blackburn (2007) compares economic sustainability to air and environmental and social sustainability to food: the first is more urgent but not more important than the second. Blackburn also rightfully asserts that 'the 2Rs' – Respect for humans (and all life) and judicious management of Resources – form an essential component of overall sustainability of the business (in this chapter also called 'enterprise', 'company' or 'organization').

Hence, a successful enterprise must take a whole-system, integrated approach towards sustainability, understood in this chapter as an abbreviation for the Brundtland Report notion of *sustainable development* that "...meets the needs of the present without compromising the ability of future generations to meet their own needs." (UN World Commission on Environment and Development, 1987).

Tackling Environmental Sustainability Challenges

The current mainstream consensus is that climate change is real and happening at a rate faster than initially thought. In these conditions it is to be expected that environmental legislation will become considerably more restrictive, customer and stakeholder expectations will be much higher and environmental damage clean-up and prevention expenses will increase substantially. On the opportunity side however, sustainability will become an even more effective device to manage intangible but essential assets such as corporate image, brand and reputation (Australian Department of Environment and Heritage, 2003).

In the opinion of the author, it appears that, presently, the main challenges brought by sustainability are *integration and coherence*. Thus, environmental responsibility must permeate all aspects and levels of the business and the environmental constraints must be consistently understood and managed *across* the organization, in an integrated manner, in order to preserve the coherence of the business units.

Meeting these challenges requires setting up an environmental management (EM) project with:

- top-management support for the project champion(s) (CEO can be one, however not the *only* one);
- sufficient authority and appropriate human / infrastructure resources allocated;
- a suitable environmental strategy, integrated in the general company strategic direction;
- a cross-departmental approach, horizontally and vertically;

These prerequisites are essential if the project is to trigger organizational culture change (to determine permanent changes in the way people do things) and to include changes in the enterprise's information system (IS) for effective access to environmental information facilitating the decision-making process (Molloy, 2007; Nilsson, 2001).

The above-mentioned issues match to a good extent the scope of a typical 'extended' (i.e. applying to the entire organization, not only to its IS / IT subsystem (Doucet et al., 2008)) enterprise architecture (EA) project. This match may provide a solution to an integrated, coherent approach to the introduction of environmental issues in the management and operation of all business units. This is desirable because a company whose architecture includes environmental management, competencies and responsibilities in an integrated fashion will have the necessary *agility* and *preparedness* not only to cope with, but even to *thrive* on the challenges brought about by climate change and global warming, thus turning a potential weakness into a strength. Hence, changes in the economic, natural and/or social environment will produce less knee-jerk, interventionist management behavior and organizational turbulence, since the capacity to cope with change will be built-in rather than imposed. The company will be able to adapt promptly and naturally, according to well-defined and effective policies including environmental adaptability.

Environmental Sustainability and Enterprise Architecture

The quest to evolve a business towards environmental sustainability occurs in a complex environment: there are risks, legal and financial constraints, government agencies, non-governmental organizations (NGOs), public opinion, stakeholders and corporate social responsibility (CSR) considerations. On the other hand, there is also a growing body of specialized literature, current and emerging standards, reporting frameworks and consultant companies, all offering to help and guide towards business sustainability assessment, design, implementation and reporting / monitoring in various degrees of detail. This has the potential to assist but at the same time compound what already constitutes a complex enterprise engineering (EE) task.

The project to create or evolve the environmentally sustainable business involves several typical steps, such as: identifying the business processes and understanding their impact on the environment (the AS-IS), defining a vision and concept(s) for the future state (the TO-BE), eliciting and specifying requirements to reach the selected TO-BE state, (re)designing the processes, policies and often the entire organization according to these requirements, implementing them, continually monitoring the effects and applying some of the previous steps for correction and enhancement. These phases reflect the continuous improvement Plan-Do-Check-Act cycle (Shewhart, 1986) which is underlying the majority of the mainstream environmental sustainability support artifacts available nowadays. Of course, in order to ensure focus and feasibility, the effort to identify the AS-IS and propose TO-BEs must concentrate on the environmental aspect of the processes and not try to 'boil the ocean'.

As in any project start-up, the stakeholders and the project manager are faced with several immediate problems. What is the state of the business now (AS-IS), and how *sustainable* (TBL-wise) is it? What are the requirements and the baseline? What is it that the business wants to achieve (TO-BE state): minimum compliance with the law in the short term, or forward-looking policies and processes, with the afferent risks and unknown productivity effects in the short term? How are they going to get to the desired TO-BE state, namely *what do they actually do next?* And if help is available, which artifacts can be used, when and where? Should they require outside help (e.g. sustainability consultants) - and then what to ask for?

This chapter argues for the necessity and benefit of integrating the proposed EM project into the ongoing EA initiative present in all successful companies (note that in this chapter, EA is understood as *extended EA* unless otherwise stated). For example, strategic integration of EM is only achievable if necessary information is quickly available and is of high quality (Molloy, 2007). Thus, information must be at the fingertips of managers in the form and level of aggregation they need as agility is not compatible with delays due to digging out and filtering suitable information separately for each request. Moreover, companies need the environmental aspect to be present on all levels of management, which effectively calls for an environmental decision support system. For such reasons, the ongoing EA project needs to be fully aware of the environmental sustainability project so that all information / process / organizational / technical aspects are taken care of in a coherent and integrated manner.

The target audience of this chapter is the CxO, management, enterprise architect and anyone interested in a better approach to managing sustainability issues based on EA-specific artifacts.

Current Problems and Some Proposed Solutions

While initially environmental activities were mostly triggered by legal action and involved addressing the effect (compensation, treatment, etc) rather than the cause, climate change, changing regulations and growing public awareness and pressure have resulted in the environmental aspect being considered in all life cycle phases of the company and its products. In addition, the intended environmental scope has gradually extended from the operational level (reflex reactions to regulations and law suits) to tactical and strategic level. However, to date most of these efforts are still disjointed, i.e. specific to business units and not properly supported by the ICT infrastructure. This means that a) the company loses coherence as different units approach environmental sustainability in different levels of detail and at a different pace, b) there is a possible loss of combined or aggregate capabilities due to the various departments not 'understanding' each other's approach to sustainability and c) top management cannot effectively use the information generated by the environmental reporting functions due to language, format, level of aggregation etc.

The Environmental Management System: A Silver Bullet?

Companies typically address the mandated and / or perceived requirement to introduce environmental responsibility in their business units by attempting to implement some type of environmental reporting and environmental management system (EMS). An EMS is intended to be part of an organization's management system that is used to develop and implement its environmental policy and manage its environmental aspects (ISO, 2004). Thus, it is typically seen as an add-on to the existing management that also enables the organization to benchmark its environmental performance and evaluate its performance and improvement (note that in this chapter, environmental measurement and reporting are seen as functions of the EMS acting as a decision support system).

While an EMS is a significant step in the right direction, when implemented in isolation it will not trigger the cultural change necessary to make environmental responsibility 'stick' in the company. Some authors (Coglianese and Nash, 2001) argue that the implementation of an EMS alone (especially if imposed on the organization for various reasons), is irrelevant if the company does not have a real commitment to environmental improvements as a prerequisite. For example, ISO 14001:2004 only requires that EMS-s be designed in such a way that companies can work toward the goal of regulatory compliance and seek to make improvements, not that the company actually achieves environmental excellence or even full compliance with existing laws! Hence, it appears that to be effective, EMS-s must be backed by regulation and enforcement by e.g. environmental protection agencies (EPAs).

Various reference models (frameworks, methods etc) for EMS design have emerged. However, each company is different and therefore EMS implementations using such reference models require their customization - which needs knowledge of those artifacts and may result in 'locking' the company in a particular proprietary solution.

Methods, Frameworks, Standards ... and other Artifacts

Generally, the available definitions of sustainability do not provide enough detail to translate into action effectively. Blackburn (2007) addresses this problem by proposing a 'Sustainability Operating System' (rather than an EMS) which is in fact a management method to achieve sustainability based on the Brundtland report, the '2R's and the TBL approach applied to sustainability. Willard (2002) also recommends a TBL-based approach encompassing economy / profit, environment / planet and equity / people with seven benefits: easier hiring and retention, increased productivity, reduced manufacturing / commercial sites expenses, increased revenue / market share and reduced risk. Clayton and Redcliffe (1998) propose a systems approach to integration of sustainability aspects into the business and define the concept of environmental quality as capital (and thus the feasibility of 'tradeable pollution').

EM frameworks aim to provide a structured set of artifacts (methods, aspects, reference models, etc) specialized for the EM area. Some examples are The Natural Step (TNS) Framework, using a systems-based approach to organizational planning for sustainability (Upham, 2000), The Natural Edge Project (TNEP, 2007) which proposes a holistic approach ('Whole System') taking into account system life cycle and Life Cycle Management, a framework of concepts, techniques and procedures aiming to achieve continuous environmental improvement from a life cycle perspective (Hunkeler et al., 2001).

Assessment and reporting frameworks aim to assist the measurement and reporting functions of the EMS. For example, the Life Cycle Assessment (LCA) method measures the environmental impacts of products or services relative to each other during their life cycles (EPA, 2008). The Global Reporting Initiative's Sustainability Reporting Framework (GRI, 2002) contains reporting principles, guidance and standard disclosures that are claimed to be applicable to all types of businesses.

International Standards also cover the EM issue. ISO 14000 is a set of reference models for setting up EMS-s, life-cycle assessment, environmental auditing of processes, environmental labeling and environmental performance evaluation. ISO 14001:2004 deals specifically with EMS-s, aiming to provide a framework for a holistic and strategic approach to the organization's environmental policy, plans and actions (ISO, 2004). Standards provide a good starting and reference point for design and assessment; however, current EM standards do not define EM performance levels that the company should meet.

As can be seen, many frameworks, methods, etc recognize the need to analyze the life cycle of the products. However, as many enterprises go through a *continuous* change process ensuring their agility and overall sustainability, it is often required to take into account other life cycles – e.g. of the host company, of the project set up to create the EMS and especially of the EMS itself - and analyze the interactions between these entities in that context. This approach provides a holistic approach allowing the representation and clarification of the business, EM project, EMS and product AS-IS and TO-BE states and identify potential problems and aspects that may not be otherwise obvious. Suitable frameworks describing systems during their entire life (not just at particular points in time), or *life cycle architectures* are commonly used in EA. Therefore, in this chapter we argue that EA artifacts (such as modeling frameworks and methodologies) can systematize and provide guidance and coherence in implementing an EMS. Thus, if the considerations of EM are built into the standards, models, languages and structure of EA, its artifacts can contribute to the understanding and management of the enterprise to support an EM goal. This would provide an integrated solution for environmental, social and economic sustainability.

Enterprise Architecture Frameworks, GERAM and GERA

Enterprises are highly complex systems. Therefore, sets of models (sometimes aggregated in architectural descriptions corresponding to viewpoints (ISO/IEC, 2007b)) are produced using various languages in order to control this complexity and allow the enterprise architect and other stakeholders to focus on various aspects of the business. As models themselves can get complex, modeling frameworks (MFs) are often used to structure them according to various criteria. In addition, several other types of artifacts are commonly used in EA practice, such as methods, reference models (synonymous with 'partial models' in this chapter), ontologies, meta-models, glossaries, etc. All these are typically organized in architecture frameworks (AFs), some of which have underlying metamodels formally describing their structure. Currently there are several mainstream AFs, generic (e.g. PERA (Williams, 1994), TOGAF (The Open Group, 2006)) or aimed at various domains such as manufacturing (CIMOSA (CIMOSA Association, 1996), ARIS (Scheer, 1999), GRAI (Doumeingts, 1984)), defense (DoDAF (DoD Architecture Framework Working Group, 2003)) and information systems (Zachman, 1987) to name a few.

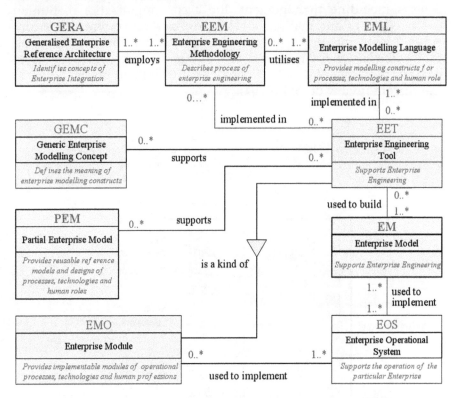

Figure 1. A Possible High-Level Metamodel Of GERAM
(Based on ISO, 2000)

In this chapter we have selected a reference AF obtained by generalizing other AFs and thus considered to be expressive enough to contain all the elements necessary for the EE task at hand, namely achieving environmental sustainability using EA artifacts. This AF is GERAM (Generalised Reference Architecture Framework and Methodology), described in Annex C of ISO 15704:2000. Despite its name (owing to historical reasons), GERAM contains several other elements in addition to its reference architecture (GERA) and methodologies (EEMs, see Figure 1). Among others, GERAM has been used in practice to guide EE projects (Bernus et al., 2002; Mo, 2007; Noran, 2004c) and in theory to assess other enterprise AFs (Noran, 2003, 2004a, 2005a; Saha, 2007) and to build a structured repository of AF elements for a proposed decision support system (Noran, 2007). GERAM is fully described in (ISO, 2000).

The main component of the Reference Architecture of GERAM, called GERA (see Figure 2), is an MF containing an extensive set of aspects including management, life cycle, organizational, human (with extent of automation) and decisional – all of which are considered instrumental for the following analysis. These aspects and their subdivisions correspond to various stakeholder concerns (a concept present in ISO 42010 (ISO/IEC, 2007a) and are included in the current review of ISO 15704).

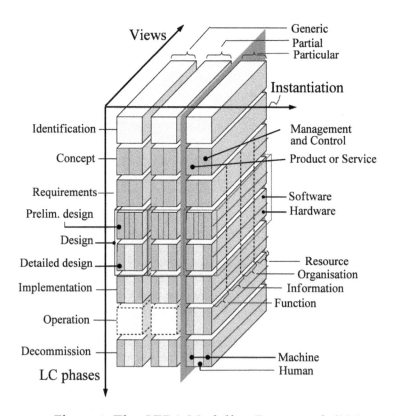

Figure 2. The GERA Modeling Framework (ISO, 2000)

COHERENCY MANAGEMENT

An Enterprise Architecture approach towards Environmental Management Projects

A Meta-methodology for Enterprise Engineering Projects

To illustrate the EA approach towards setting up and operating the EMS and the EM project we propose to use the set of steps described in (Noran, 2005b, 2007) that are structured in a meta-methodology, i.e. a method to build methods applicable for specific types of EE tasks. The proposed meta-methodology comprises three major steps and a set of sub-steps. In the first step, the user is prompted to create a list containing entities of interest to the project in question, making sure to include project participants, target entities (organizations, other projects) and importantly, the EE project itself. The second step comprises the creation of business models showing the relations between the previously listed entities in the context of their lifecycles, i.e. illustrating how entities influence each other within each life cycle phase. The third step assists the user in inferring the set of project activities by reading and interpreting the previously represented relations for each life cycle phase of the target entities. The resulting activities must be detailed to a level deemed as comprehensible (and thus usable) by the intended audience.

The first meta-methodology sub-step calls for the selection of suitable aspects (or views) to be modeled in each stage; the life cycle aspect must be present since it is essential to the meta-methodology. The selection of a MF is also recommended, as MFs typically feature structured collections of views that can be used as checklists of candidate aspects and their intended coverage. This sub-step also calls for the identification and resolution of any aspect dependencies. The second sub-step asks the user to determine if the present (AS-IS) state of the views previously adopted needs to be shown and whether the AS-IS and future (TO-BE) states should be represented in separate or combined models. Typically, the AS-IS state needs to be modeled when it is not properly understood by the stakeholders and / or the TO-BE state is to be evolved from the AS-IS (i.e. no radical re-engineering is likely to occur). The third sub-step requires the selection of suitable modeling formalisms and modeling tools for the chosen aspects, according to the target audience of the models and to competencies and tools available in the organization.

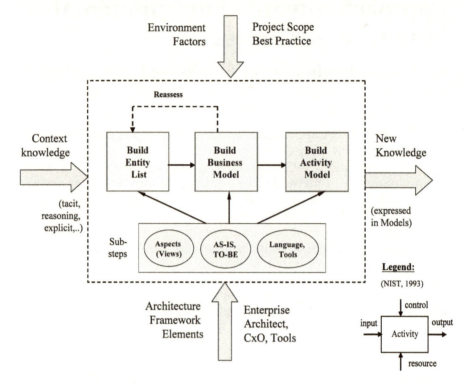

Figure 3. Simplified Meta-Methodology Concept (Noran, 2007)

Note that all the above-described steps and sub-steps have an underlying logic that can be used to automate the meta-methodology (Noran, 2007) and to guide the user in the decision-making process. This task is also assisted by additional models and artifacts built and adopted during the second stage. A full description of the meta-methodology is beyond the scope of this chapter and can be found in (Noran, 2004b, 2008).

In this particular case, the main meta-methodology deliverable would be a model of a method to set up the EM project and the EMS taking into consideration the internal and external business life cycle context. Since the management of the organization and all other entities (business units, other organizations, agencies, laws, etc.) that need to be involved in the EM project and the EMS are to be included in the entity list (the first step in Figure 3, left), their influence will be taken into account throughout the lifecycle of the EM project and the EMS. An important initial premise for EM integration into the organization is thus fulfilled.

As can be seen from Figure 3, the meta-methodology assists in creating new knowledge – in this case, how to go about setting up and operating the EM project and the EMS – based on *context knowledge* – i.e. know-how of running the business including its corporate culture ('how things are done around here'), relations with suppliers, clients, authorities etc, typically available at middle and top management level and within CxO and enterprise architect roles. The involvement of these roles in the methodology creation process establishes the conditions for management buy-in and support for the upcoming EM project and early involvement of the EA department in the EM project. This will create the best conditions for integrated development of the EMS and supporting functions of the IS.

First Step: Creating the Entity List

Often, selecting views or an MF (as required by the first sub-step) is unnecessary in this early stage, as too many details can in fact be counter-productive. The AS-IS and TO-BE states (sub-step two) can be represented in a combined manner, as the low complexity of the models does not justify the overhead of consistency checking. The modeling formalism chosen in sub-step three can be simply text at this stage. As a result, an entity list can be built in the first meta-methodology step using text to represent a combined AS-IS and TO-BE state. Proposed members in the entity list are the company as a whole, business units, the EM project, the EMS, environmental reports, NGOs, the government, EPA, EM Principles (e.g. 2R, TBL), EM laws, EM standards, EM frameworks, assessment and reporting frameworks, social responsibility standards, Quality Standards and EM consultants.

Second Step: Building the Business Model

This step requires the creation of a business model showing interactions of the entities previously elicited in the context of their life cycle phases. In sub-step one the life cycle, management, decisional and organizational aspects are selected to be modeled for the entities participating in the project. This choice is obvious due to the nature of the system being designed (management) and also due to the importance attached to the decisional and organizational aspects as essential factors in the integration of the EMS and the intent to trigger cultural change. The GERA MF (see Figure 2) is adopted as the most likely to provide a suitable formalism for the mandatory life cycle dimension and for the other selected aspects.

In this case, the TO-BE state is incremental and based on the AS-IS rather than representing radical change. Therefore in sub-step two, it can be decided that the AS-IS state needs to be represented for all aspects. While there is no tangible advantage in showing separate AS-IS and TO-BE states in the business model, it is very useful to do so in the decisional / organizational structure. This is because as previously shown, in this particular EE task it is imperative to show where and how the functions of the EMS interact with the existing system so as to ascertain the degree of integration and effects of the EMS on the decisional and organizational structure of the host company. Separate AS-IS / TO-BE decisional / organizational models may also help define several TO-BE ('what-if') scenarios.

A modeling formalism based on the GERA MF is chosen for the business model in sub-step three (see Figure 4). GRAI–Grid (Doumeingts et al., 1998) is selected to represent decisional and organizational aspects, together with a plain graphical editor as a modeling tool. GRAI-Grid is optimal in this case due to its ability to represent both the decisional and organizational aspects on the same diagram (minimal number of languages and formalism reuse in building the models, as best-practice, is one of the rules attached to the selection criteria within the automated version of the meta-methodology).

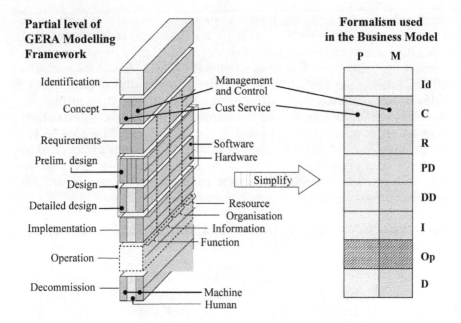

Figure 4. Formalism Used For The Business Model

As previously shown, the business model is constructed based on context knowledge (often tacit and requiring eliciting (Kalpic and Bernus, 2006)) owned by stakeholders, i.e. CxO, enterprise architect, top management, etc. Any partial models that can help in this effort are considered for use, e.g. high-level guidelines contained in the EMS standards, EM assessment and reporting frameworks, etc. Note that before use, all such artifacts should be first assessed using the GERAM reference AF to determine their actual scope and usefulness. A Structured Repository containing AF elements organized based on the results of such assessments exists and is being further developed (see Noran (2008) for details).

A possible outcome of this second step is shown in Figure 4. As can be seen, the relations between the relevant entities can be explicitly represented for each life cycle phase. Note that some entities' life cycle representation has been reduced to the phase(s) relevant for the EM project. For example, we are only interested in the Operation life cycle phase of Auditors, EM Standards and EM assessment / reporting frameworks since they are not being designed / built as part of the EM project. The figure also shows the relations between the company, the EM project and the EMS, which allows the building of consensus, achieving a common understanding and explicitly representing what needs to be done, phase by phase, at a high level. A few examples: the EMS is built by the EM project; however, EM consultants may also be involved in the design. The company is lobbied by NGOs and has to abide by EM Laws. Auditors perform either certification audits (affecting the concept and design of the EMS) or surveillance audits (to check if the EMS is still compliant). The EPA will look into the EMS operation and receive information from external auditors. Importantly, the EMS should be able to re-design itself (arrow from Mgmt operation to the other life cycles) to a certain extent and thus be agile in the face of moderate EM regulation and market changes. Reaction to major changes should be however delegated to the upper company management.

The influences of other entities on the EMS and EMP shown in Figure 5 can also be interpreted as stakeholder concerns that translate in particular areas of interest being modeled and addressed. Thus, for example the client may want to know how the mission and vision of the Company (the Concept area of Comp entity in Figure 5) addresses its environmental concerns, and the government will want to ensure that the Company abides by its environmental concerns expressed in EM laws (EML in Figure 5).

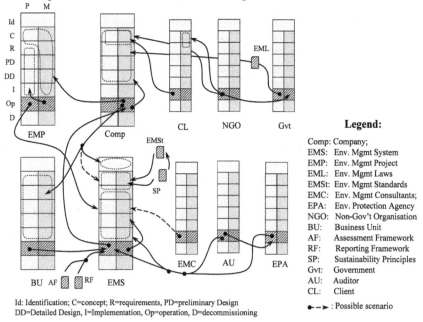

Legend:

Comp: Company;
EMS: Env. Mgmt System
EMP: Env. Mgmt Project
EML: Env. Mgmt Laws
EMSt: Env. Mgmt Standards
EMC: Env. Mgmt Consultants;
EPA: Env. Protection Agency
NGO: Non-Gov't Organisation
BU: Business Unit
AF: Assessment Framework
RF: Reporting Framework
SP: Sustainability Principles
Gvt: Government
AU: Auditor
CL: Client

Id: Identification; C=concept; R=requirements, PD=preliminary Design
DD=Detailed Design, I=Implementation, Op=operation, D=decommissioning

●--► : Possible scenario

Figure 5. Business Model Showing Relations of Relevant Entities in the Context of Their Life Cycles.

COHERENCY MANAGEMENT

Modeling Additional Aspects: Decisional and Organizational Models

The formalism selected for the decisional / organizational aspect allows for the presentation of essential concepts present in the design and implementation of an EMS (e.g. as specified in ISO 14001:2004) in an integrated manner (see Figure 5). The GRAI-Grid is based on Decision Centres (DCs) that operate within the boundaries of Decisional Frameworks (DFs) set by the upper echelon. DCs can provide feedback on the DFs allocated via information links (IL) to the upper echelon. Planning in GRAI-Grid means balancing the management of resources and products and is represented in the central column of the grid to reflect its paramount importance. In this particular case, the GRAI-Grid allows the clear representation of the EMS planning requirements for products, services and activities. Legal requirements, policies, etc can also be represented as DFs consisting of constraints, objectives (fixed) and decision variables (that the target DC can manipulate). Horizons and Periods represent the extent of time that the decisions at a particular level (Strategic, Tactical etc) aim to cover and are to be revised at, respectively.

The resources and products are represented in two columns adjacent to planning. Resources can be further split into e.g. budget, people and infrastructure, while products can also be subdivided depending on the specific profile of the company (see Figure 7).

The representation of the DFs will ensure that EM problems are spotted early. Such problems may include narrow and paternalistic management – whereby EM may be isolated from other relevant management aspects, or the EM DCs are not given enough authority, respectively. As previously shown, these are aspects considered essential to the effectiveness of an environmental sustainability initiative and if neglected may indeed produce a 'toothless' EMS, useful to obtain certification to a standard or ease EPA scrutiny, but not to make the organization more environmentally sustainable (and thus profitable).

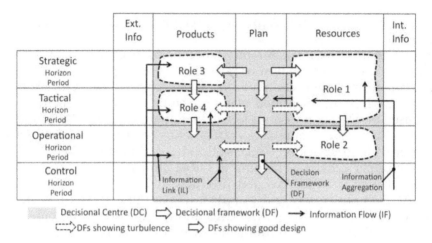

Figure 6. GRAI Grid Formalism And Notations

A large number of horizontal DFs from the planning DCs to product and resources DCs at all levels would indicate an interventionist management style (see Figure 6). This is detrimental to the EMS and the company as a whole as it involves the Planning DC (sometimes the CxO) spending valuable time 'putting out fires' (resolving urgent, short-term surges and imbalances between resources and production) due to the incapacity of the DCs to deal with the problem (typically owing to a defective strategy). This management style creates turbulence and incoherence in the entire organization as there is no stable and effective overarching strategy reflecting the EM and other goals. In contrast, vertical DFs indicate that the DCs can cope with the objectives allocated and the balance is maintained without intervention – i.e. the organization (including its integrated EMS) is agile and can thus adapt 'naturally' to a certain amount of changes (including environmentally triggered) in regulations, resource and product requirements.

Communication / information flow is also present in the GRAI-Grid in the columns adjacent to Product and Resources. Information aggregates in a bottom-up fashion and reaches the DCs via ILs. Thus, environmental reports for example can be tracked and checked to originate in the right DCs so that they contain the required information and also reach the intended target DCs so that appropriate corrective action is taken if required. Direct communication between DCs is achieved via ILs as well (see Figure 6).

COHERENCY MANAGEMENT

Roles can be represented in the GRAI-Grid by areas covering one or more DCs (see Figure 6). The organizational structure can then be obtained by allocating human resources (HRs) to these roles. For example, a role may be fulfilled by a CxO or an entire department.

Competence, training and awareness can be represented in the DCs content as HR management, for example, at the strategic level, decide on necessary competencies and at the tactical level decide on a training / hiring plan. The EMS documentation aspect is reflected in the need to maintain internal information on each level, e.g. operationally to report; tactically to aggregate reports and trends; and strategically, to decide on an action plan based on policies, regulations and objectives.

It must be noted that the actual sustainability issues are *instances* of objectives – therefore the GRAI-Grid in fact shows DFs that consist of *types of* objectives, constraints and decision variables, which define the management roles. These types are instantiated when implemented (in every period, or if triggered by a significant event), thus the instances of objectives can be different from time to time. The DC (management role) has to decide (based on higher level objectives and the inputs it received from the outside world and EM reporting entity) what the objectives for its horizon are. For example, the constraint type may be 'abide by the current emission regulations', while the constraint instance is the set of actual values that the current regulations prescribe. The objective type may state 'abide by current ISO and country standards', while the instances are actual current standards.

One may ask: well, what about the organizational culture aspect that triggers behavioral change and makes changes 'stick'? The culture is often a consequence of the type of organizational design (who does what), staff training and management style / strategy. For example, the feedback provided in the environmental reporting can be used to set a strategy that encourages and rewards excellence in EM and that implements it at tactical and operational levels.

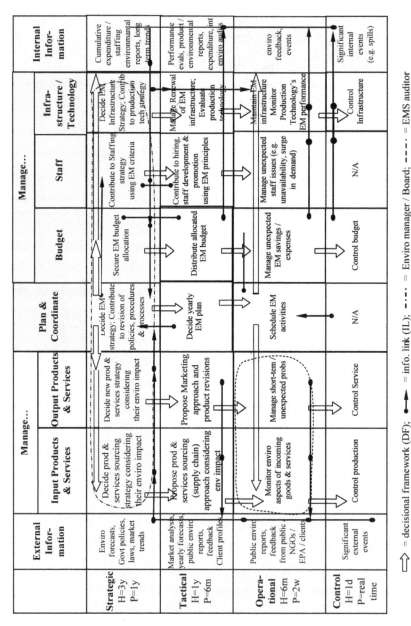

Figure 7. Sample GRAI Grid

COHERENCY MANAGEMENT

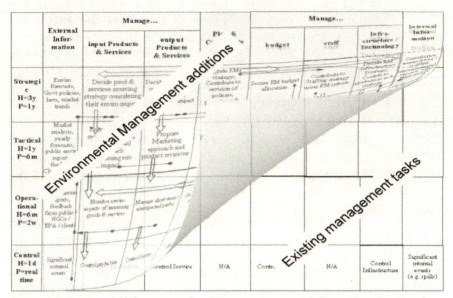

Figure 8. EM Addition To The Host Company Management Tasks

Figure 7 shows a sample GRAI-Grid and Figure 8 shows (symbolically) the way the EM DFs would overlay the host company management tasks. In practice, DCs need to be further detailed using a functional model (for example expressed in IDEF0 (NIST, 1993) or UML (Rumbaugh et al, 1999) activity diagrams), down to the level of understanding of the HR(s) fulfilling the role covering those DCs.

Third Step: The Functional Model

The main deliverable of the third (and last) meta-methodology step is an activity model describing the creation and operation of the EM project and of the EMS. This is achieved by analyzing the life cycle representation of the entities in Figure 5 and expressing the interactions shown in that figure in terms of the aspects selected from the chosen MF.

In terms of the first meta-methodology sub-step, the type of deliverable (a method) mandates the functional aspect. However, to be understood and enacted, the activities represented in a functional model must be detailed using other aspects and views contained in the MF selected in step two – in this case management / service, human / machine and software / hardware. The present state will be represented (sub-step two) and it will be shown in a common diagram with the TO-BE, since the activity model depicts in fact the transition from the AS-IS to the chosen TO-BE state. As for sub-step three, the IDEF0 language is chosen to represent the functional model and the AI0Win tool (KBSI, 2007) is selected to support model creation. The choice is justified in the following section, along with a brief generalization.

Important Side Note: The Benefit of using EA languages and tools in EM tasks

The overarching and cross-departmental features of EA are reflected in the languages and tools used in this domain. Families of languages (some integrated by meta-models) and tools aware of the implemented languages' syntax and often featuring a common repository underlying all models depicting various enterprise aspects, provide the premise for integrated development. We have attempted to illustrate the advantage of using such EA artifacts in the sustainability effort by selecting a sample EA tool and language for the third meta-methodology step applied to the EM project.

IDEF0 provides for complexity control by implementing multiple model levels. Thus, model components and levels can be independently developed; however, their interfaces called ICOMS (inputs, controls, mechanisms and outputs, see Figure 9) must be kept consistent. This essential feature can enforce coherence and discipline in the EMS life cycle design process. For example, management, business unit teams and EA personnel can work on various aspects / levels of a model in a (quasi-) independent fashion, knowing that the overall coherence of the model is preserved at all times. 'Aware' tools implementing this language (such as the one selected) will enforce such conditions and automatically carry through and provide the ICOMS necessary for a particular level.

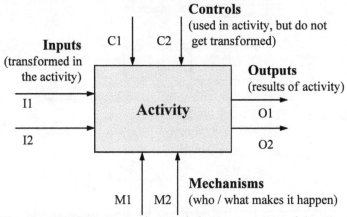

Figure 9. IDEF0 Generic Model, Context Level (A-0)

Back to the Method Model: The Context Level

This level provides a bird's eye view of the EM project and its outcome (i.e. the EMS). Such a simple model may look trivial; however, it is very useful for high-level management, the enterprise architect and other stakeholders to quickly grasp the big picture and make sure that all the necessary elements are present, e.g. necessary inputs, adequate resources, mandatory constraints and required deliverables. Getting a common understanding of 'what is to be done' and agreeing upon this overall picture can make a significant difference in achieving a favorable attitude and commitment towards the EM project.

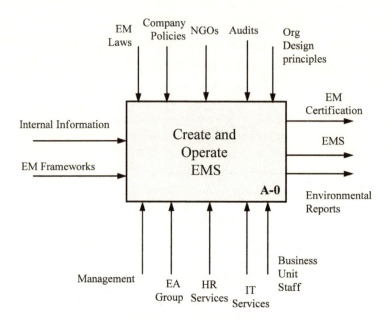

**Figure 10. Context (A-0) Level Of The EMS
Creation And Operation Model**

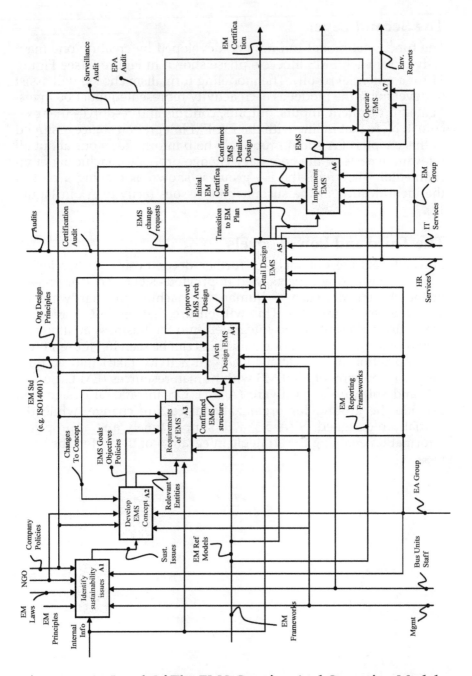

Figure 11. A0 Level Of The EMS Creation And Operation Model

The Second Level

The functional model can now be developed by creating one main activity for each EMS lifecycle phase shown in Figure 3 (see Figure 11 for a potential result). The modeling formalism chosen will assist in developing the model as each activity represented must be investigated for content, inputs, outputs, controls and resources that execute it. Note that in line with the EA-EM integration stance assumed in this chapter, EA should routinely help inform decisions about all relevant aspects of the necessary change processes, including environmental. Therefore, the EA group is shown as playing a part in the identification of the sustainability issues (activity A1 in Figure 11).

The Third and Lower Levels

Lower levels are obtained by further decomposing each relevant activity considering aspects used in previous steps and / or present in the chosen MF, such as human vs. machine and hardware vs. software (see Figure 12). This will ensure that the EM(S) requirements are represented and integrated into the business at all necessary levels and aspects. For example, as can be seen in Figure 11, the decomposition of the Detailed Design activity takes into account proper resourcing of the EMS with human resources (EM Group, A 5.2) and software / hardware (A 5.1). Organizational design will provide the ground for organizational culture change, while the partially redesigned IS (A 5.3) will supply timely and appropriate information enabling the strategic integration of the EM in the business.

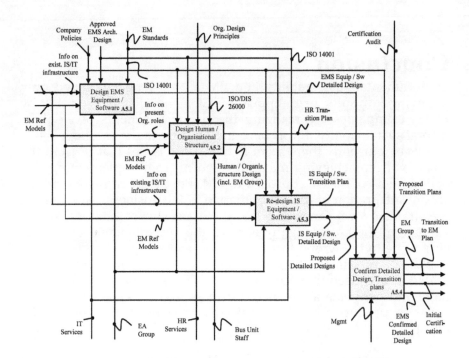

**Figure 12. One of the A1 Levels (Detailed Design)
of the EMS Creation and Operation Model**

How far will the decomposition go? The activities must be detailed down to the level where they are understood, and thus can be executed by the human(s) and/or machine(s) that need to perform them.

A full decomposition of the example is beyond the purpose of this chapter, which aims to introduce the approach and test the concept rather than to perform a complete design of the EMS. In addition, each business is different; therefore, additional specific information is required to enable deeper level decompositions. For the interested reader, several worked examples are contained in Noran (2008).

Conclusion

Environmental sustainability and EM are no longer pursued only following law suits, or to appease NGOs and alleviate scrutiny by EPAs. Companies are realizing the financial benefits of environmental sustainability; EM is becoming a commodity (Molloy, 2007). However, currently there seem to be several issues that prevent the business from achieving maximum return from implementing and operating a concerted approach to EM. Firstly, there seems to be a lack of integration of the EM initiative in the business, especially at the strategic level - meaning that the management cannot take advantage of the knowledge present in the environmental reporting, either due to the wrong format and/or level of aggregation, or due to stale data content - hence the need for automation and an integrated IS architecture. Secondly, the EMS needs to be driven internally and permeate all areas of business in a consistent manner in order to produce organizational culture change ensuring lasting effects.

In this chapter we have argued that these needs are best addressed by integrating EM in the ongoing EA initiative present in one form or another in every successful and agile enterprise. EA can provide the necessary artifacts and the prerequisites for a coherent, cross-departmental and culture-changing approach ensuring business sustainability and profitability in the long term.

References

Australian Department of Environment and Heritage. (2003). Corporate Sustainability - an Investor Perspective: The Mays Report. Available at http://tinyurl.com/cc6web.

Bernus, P., Noran, O. and Riedlinger, J. (2002). Using the Globemen Reference Model for Virtual Enterprise Design in After Sales Service. In I. Karvoinen and R. van den Berg and P. Bernus and Y. Fukuda and M. Hannus and I. Hartel and J. Vesterager (Eds.), Global Engineering and Manufacturing in Enterprise Networks (Globemen). VTT Symposium 224. Helsinki / Finland. pp. 71-90.

Blackburn, W. R. (2007). The Sustainability Handbook. EarthScan Publishers: Cornwall, UK.

CIMOSA Association. (1996). CIMOSA - Open System Architecture for CIM,. Technical Baseline, ver 3.2. Private Publication.

Clayton, A. and Redcliffe, N. (1998). Sustainability - A Systems Approach. Earthscan Publications: Edinburgh, UK.

Coglianese, C. and Nash, J. (Eds.). (2001). Regulating from the Inside: Can Environmental Management Systems Achieve Policy Goals? : RFF Press.

DoD Architecture Framework Working Group. (2003). DoD Architecture Framework (Vol I-II; Deskbook). US DoD.

Doucet, G., Gøtze, J., Saha, P. and Bernard, S. (2008). Coherency Management: Using Enterprise Architecture to Achieve Alignment, Agility and Assurance. Journal of Enterprise Architecture. Volume 4, Number 2. pp. 9-20.

Doumeingts, G. (1984). La Methode GRAI [PhD Thesis]. Bordeaux, France: University of Bordeaux I.

Doumeingts, G., Vallespir, B. and Chen, D. (1998). GRAI Grid Decisional Modelling. In P. Bernus and K. Mertins and G. Schmidt (Eds.), Handbook on Architectures of Information Systems. Heidelberg: Springer Verlag. pp. 313-339.

Elkington, J. (1998). Cannibals with Forks: The Triple Bottom Line of 21st Century Business.

EPA. (2008). Management Tools. Environmental Protection Agency, South Australia. Available at http://tinyurl.com/dbrrnz.

GRI. (2002). Sustainability Reporting Guidelines. In Global Reporting Initiative (Ed.), Sustainability Reporting Framework: Global Reporting Initiative.

Hunkeler, D. (Ed.). (2004). Life-cycle Management: Society of Environmental Toxicology & Chemist.

ISO. (2000). Annex C: GERAM, ISO/DIS 15704: Industrial automation systems - Requirements for enterprise-reference architectures and methodologies: International Standards Organisation.

ISO. (2004). ISO 14001:Environmental management systems - Requirements with guidance for use: International Standards Organisation.

ISO/IEC. (2007a). ISO/IEC 42010:2007: Recommended Practice for Architecture Description of Software-Intensive Systems.

ISO/IEC. (2007b). ISO/IEC 42010:2007: Recommended Practice for Architecture Description of Software-Intensive Systems (IEEE1471).

Kalpic, B. and Bernus, P. (2006). Business process modeling through the knowledge management perspective. Journal of Knowledge Management, 10(3).

KBSI. (2007). AI0Win Software Product, [White Paper]. Knowledge Based Systems, Inc. Available at http://tinyurl.com/cedxhv.

Mo, J. (2007). The use of GERAM for Design of a Virtual Enterprise for a Ship Maintenance Consortium. In P. Saha (Ed.), Handbook of Enterprise Systems Architecture in Practice. IGI Global Information Science Reference: Hershey, PA. pp. 351-366.

Molloy, I. (2007). Environmental Management Systems and. Information Management – Strategic- Systematical Integration of Green Value Added. In J. M. Gómez and M. Sonnenschein and M. Müller and H. Welsch and C. Rautenstrauchm (Eds.), Information Technologies in Environmental Engineering ITEE 2007 - (proceedings of the 3rd International ICSC Symposium).

Nilsson, I. (2001). Integrating Environmental Management to Improve Strategic Decision-Making. Chalmers University of Technology, Götteborg, Sweden.

NIST. (1993). Integration Definition for Function Modelling (IDEF0) (Federal Information Processing Standards Publication 183): Computer Systems Laboratory, National Institute of Standards and Technology.

Noran, O. (2003). A Mapping of Individual Architecture Frameworks (GRAI, PERA, C4ISR, CIMOSA, Zachman, ARIS) onto GERAM. In P. Bernus and L. Nemes and G. Schmidt (Eds.), Handbook of Enterprise Architecture. Springer Verlag: Heidelberg. pp. 65-210.

Noran, O. (2004a). A C4ISR Reference Architecture Assessment using GERA. In O. Vasilecas and A. Caplinskas and W. Wojtkowsji and W. G. Wojtkowsji and J. Zupancic and S. Wrycza (Eds.), Advances in Theory, Practice and Education (Proceedings of the 13th International Conference on Information Systems Development (ISD2004). Vilnius: Vilnius Geminidas Technical University. pp. 47-58.

Noran, O. (2004b). A Meta-methodology for Collaborative Networked Organisations. Unpublished Doctoral Thesis, School of CIT, Griffith University.

Noran, O. (2004c). A Meta-methodology for Collaborative Networked Organisations: A Case Study and Reflections. In P. Bernus and M. Fox and J. B. M. Goossenaerts (Eds.), Knowledge Sharing in the Integrated Enterprise: Interoperability Strategies for the Enterprise Architect (Proceedings of ICEIMT '04). Toronto / Canada: Kluwer Academic Publishers.

Noran, O. (2005a). An Analytical Mapping of the C4ISR Architecture Framework onto ISO15704 Annex A (GERAM). Computers in Industry. Volume 56, Number 5. pp. 407-427.

Noran, O. (2005b). A Meta-methodology Prototype for Collaborative Networked Organisations. In L. Camarinha-Matos (Ed.), Collaborative Networks and Breeding Environments (Proceedings of the 6th IFIP Working Conference on Virtual Enterprises - PROVE 05). Valencia / Spain: Springer Verlag. pp. 339-346.

Noran, O. (2007). Discovering and modelling Enterprise Engineering Project Processes. In P. Saha (Ed.), Enterprise Systems Architecture in Practice (pp. 39-61). IGI Information Science Reference: Hershey, PA.

Noran, O. (2008). A Meta-methodology for Collaborative Networked Organisations: VDM Verlag.

Rumbaugh, J., Jacobson, I. and Booch, G. (1999). The Unified Modelling Language Reference Manual. Reading, MA: Addison-Wesley.

Saha, P. (2007). A Synergistic Assessment of the Federal Enterprise Architecture Framework against GERAM (ISO15704:2000 Annex A). In P. Saha (Ed.), Enterprise Systems Architecture in Practice. IGI Global Information Science Reference: Hershey, PA. pp. 1-17

Scheer, A.-W. (1999). ARIS-Business Process Frameworks (3rd ed.). Berlin: Springer-Verlag.

Shewhart, W. A. (1986). Statistical Method from the Viewpoint of Quality Control: Dover Publications.

The Open Group. (2006). The Open Group Architecture Framework, (TOGAF 8.1.1 'The Book') v8.1.1.

TNEP. (2007). The Engineering Sustainable Solutions Program Whole Systems Design Suite. The Natural Edge Project (TNEP). Available: http://www.naturaledgeproject.net/.

UN World Commission on Environment and Development. (1987). Our Common Future (Brundtland Report). Oxford University Press: Oxford.

Upham, P. (2000). An assessment of The Natural Step theory of sustainability. Journal of Cleaner Production. Volume 8, Number 6. pp. 445-454.

Willard, B. (2002). The Sustainability Advantage: Seven Business Case benefits of a Triple Bottom Line. New Society Publishers: Gabriola Island.

Williams, T. J. (1994). The Purdue Enterprise Reference Architecture. Computers in Industry. Volume 24. Number (2-3). pp. 141-158.

Zachman, J. A. (1987). A Framework for Information Systems Architecture. IBM Systems Journal. Volume 26. Number 3. pp. 276-292.

About the Author

Ovidiu Noran holds a PhD in Enterprise Architecture, a Masters in Information and Communication Technology and an Engineering degree in Building Services and Automation. He has worked as an engineer and business architecture/management consultant for companies in Europe and Australia and is currently lecturing in Enterprise Architecture and Systems Engineering at Griffith University. He is a member of several professional bodies (Engineers Australia, Australian Institute of Management, etc) and standardization committees ISO/IEC/SC7/WG42 and ISO/TC184/SC5/WG1. His seminars, publications and regular involvement in conferences and journals highlight research interests in Artificial Intelligence, Software Engineering and Enterprise Architecture and a preference for Action Research.

Ovidiu Noran
N44 1.23 Nathan Campus
Griffith University
Brisbane QLD 4111
O.Noran@griffith.edu.au

Chapter 8

ENTERPRISE ARCHITECTURE FORMALIZATION AND AUDITING

Scott Bernard & John Grasso

Editors' Preface

This chapter has been included in the book because it focuses on the importance of formalizing and auditing enterprise architecture programs as a way to improve their value to public and private sector organizations. The authors discuss the formalization of an EA program as centering on the establishment and maintenance of six basic elements: governance, methodology, framework, tools/repository, and associated best practices. The EA Audit Model (EA2M) is an emerging element of the practice of EA and builds on established best practices including the CMMI and the U.S. Government Accountability Office's EA Management Maturity Model. The EA2M is presented as the basis for an audit procedure that reviews EA programs for maturity in three general categories: completeness, consistency, and utilization. The basic steps of the EA2M are described as a comprehensive and repeatable method for conducting EA program audits. Basic and advanced forms of the EA2M audit are also introduced as a way for organizations to have the option of doing preliminary reviews prior to comprehensive audits. The training and certification of EA2M auditors is in the beginning stages, with courses and additional reference materials planned for release in 2009.

Introduction

Enterprise Architecture (EA) is a management and technology discipline that has emerged during the last two decades. In this timeframe, EA has evolved from a concept for improving the use of information technology (IT) to a holistic approach for all dimensions of an enterprise: strategic, business, and technology. This is done by linking strategic drivers, business requirements, and technology solutions within and between all of an enterprise's lines of business. Today, the primary goal of EA is to improve performance by achieving and maintaining coherence, which is a clear understanding of an enterprise's current capabilities and future options.

During the past twenty years, formal EA programs have been established in many public, private, military, academic, and non-profit organizations around the world. This is especially true for large, complex enterprises that continually deal with issues of aligning strategic goals and integrating business requirements across a broad spectrum of stakeholder interests. The popularity of EA programs has grown with the increasing importance of IT within organizations, especially in the form of e-business and e-government applications. Nevertheless, EA programs have produced varying degrees of value for different stakeholder groups, some of whom tend to view a formalized architecture as expensive to develop, light on returns, and a threat to project or system-specific interests.

The fact that some EA programs have not produced desired levels of value is an indication that requirements and/or expectations for EA development and use are often not sufficiently articulated. Also, even with twenty years of investment, the EA discipline is still evolving toward a useful meta-architecture, so perceptions of low value delivery among some stakeholder groups is to be expected and is not an indication of EA's ultimate capability. Additionally, it should be recognized that the very act of 'structuring' an organization (or other type of enterprise) inherently creates an architecture, which may remain undocumented and therefore may not be available as a reference for planning and decision-making. The lack of a formalized architecture that can help to manage change and create agility is arguably more of a problem than are the issues associated with the creation and use of a documented EA.

Having said this, two concepts are discussed in this chapter that can improve EA program development and use in public and private sector organizations:

Architectures Must Be Formalized. Harnessing the power of an enterprise-wide architecture requires that it be formally documented and maintained on an ongoing basis through an EA program that meets criteria for formalization and completeness.

Architectures Must Be Audited. EA program performance and value can be enhanced through a formal audit process that is applied on a periodic basis through annual reviews and no-notice spot checks. The "EA Audit Model" is presented in basic form for the first time in this chapter, builds upon and extends prior methods, is current in that it accommodates EA approaches developed since 2005, and is comprehensive in auditing three primary areas: completeness, consistency, and utilization.

Background

The widely-acknowledged initial description of what was to become the practice of EA was published in a 1987 article entitled "Information Systems Architecture" by John Zachman in the *IBM Systems Journal*. His approach began with a set of data, function, and network artifacts (artifacts are models and other types of documentation) that were expanded in 1992 to include people, time, and motivation-related artifacts (Zachman, 1997; Zachman & Sowa, 1992). In 1992, a book on "Enterprise Architecture Planning" by Steven Spewak (Foreword by John Zachman) presented the first EA development methodology and a framework that called for the development of current and future views of an enterprise's business, data, application, and technology sub-architectures using Zachman's initial artifact set. What was different about the writings of Zachman, Spewak, and Sowa is that they moved the initial thinking about IT architecture from a systems-centric view to an enterprise-wide view.

While this new architecture thinking expanded the focus beyond the individual system, most practitioners continued to treat the development of an architecture as an IT activity. This IT-centric view continued until the mid-1990s when business requirements were increasingly recognized as the driver for IT solutions, and EA began to be described in more business/mission-centric terms for use in the public and private sectors (Cook, 1996; Federal CIO Council, 1999). The expansion continued when a decade later a strategic level of the architecture was specified apart from the business layer. Indeed, strategic goals and initiatives were recognized as being the context and rationale for identifying business workflow requirements and technology solutions at the application, system, and infrastructure levels (Bernard, 2004, Ross et al., 2006). Additional topics such as security and workforce planning also began to emerge in several EA approaches (Bernard, 2004; Federal EA Security and Privacy Profile, 2005).

During the past decade, a parallel development was the emergence of methods to assess the maturity and effectiveness of EA programs, led primarily by the U.S. Federal Government. This movement began in 1996 with the passage of the Clinger-Cohen Act , which mandated the development and maintenance of an IT architecture by each Federal Agency (Public Law 104-106). From this, two government approaches were articulated: (1) the "C4ISR Framework" published in 1997 and re-released in 2001 as the Department of Defense Architecture Framework (DODAF) which is mandated for use in defense agencies, and (2) the Federal CIO Council's publication of the Federal EA Framework in 1999 for use in civilian agencies.

The General Accounting Office, later renamed the Government Accountability Agency (GAO), is an organization in the Legislative Branch of the U.S. Government that supports Congress by performing various assessment functions, including audits of Federal Government agencies in the Executive Branch to determine if the mandates of laws passed by Congress are being correctly and effectively implemented by the agencies. To do this GAO develops assessment and audit methods, some of which become best practices in the public and private sectors. In 2002, GAO developed the EA Management Maturity Framework (EAMMF) for use by GAO and Federal Government agencies to assess compliance with the EA-related provisions of the Clinger-Cohen Act and the maturity of managing agency EA programs. The EAMMF identifies five stages of architecture management maturity and four sets of success attributes for an EA program, as well as nineteen core elements that must be achieved for an agency's EA program to be ranked at the top stage of maturity. The EAMMF was updated in 2003 to extend to thirty-one core elements and has been used in subsequent government-wide surveys and EA program audits conducted by GAO. The maturity levels, success attributes, and core elements of the EAMMF are shown in Figure 1, and the general evaluation purposes of the EAMMF (governance, content, measurement, and use) are shown in Figure 2 (GAO, 2007).

In 2004, the U.S. Office of Management and Budget (OMB) developed the EA Assessment Framework (EAAF) that has been used on an annual basis as a self-assessment tool for Federal Agencies. OMB is part of the Executive Office of the President and provides budget and program policy, guidance, and procedures to all of the agencies in the Executive Branch of the U.S. Federal Government (there are over two-hundred Departments, Agencies, Boards, and Commissions). The EAAF was updated in 2006 and 2007 to reflect new initiatives and guidance developed within the Federal EA community. The EAAF is organized into three capability areas: Completion, Use and Results.

	Stage 1: Creating EA awareness	Stage 2: Building the EA management foundation	Stage 3: Developing EA products	Stage 4: Completing EA products	Stage 5: Leveraging the EA to manage change
Attribute 1: Demonstrates commitment		Adequate resources exist. Committee or group representing the enterprise is responsible for directing, overseeing, and approving EA.	Written and approved organization policy exists for EA development.	Written and approved organization policy exists for EA maintenance.	Written and approved organization policy exists for IT investment compliance with EA.
Attribute 2: Provides capability to meet commitment		Program office responsible for EA development and maintenance exists. Chief architect exists. EA being developed using a framework, methodology, and automated tool.	EA products are under configuration management.	EA products and management processes undergo independent verification and validation.	Process exists to formally manage EA change. EA is integral component of IT investment management process.
Attribute 3: Demonstrates satisfaction of commitment		EA plans call for describing both the "as-is" and the "to-be" environments of the enterprise, as well as a sequencing plan for transitioning from the "as-is" to the "to-be." EA plans call for describing both the "as-is" and the "to-be" environments in terms of business, performance, information/data, application/service, and technology. EA plans call for business, performance, information/data, service, and technology descriptions to address security.	EA products describe or will describe both the "as-is" and the "to-be" environments of the enterprise, as well as a sequencing plan for transitioning from the "as-is" to the "to-be." Both the "as-is" and the "to-be" environments are described or will be described in terms of business, performance, information/data, application/service, and technology. Business, performance, information/data, application/service, and technology descriptions address security.	EA products describe both the "as-is" and the "to-be" environments of the enterprise, as well as a sequencing plan for transitioning from the "as-is" to the "to-be." Both the "as-is" and the "to-be" environments are described in terms of business, performance, information/data, application/service, and technology. Business, performance, information/data, application/service, and technology descriptions address security. Organization CIO has approved current version of EA. Committee or group representing the enterprise or the investment review board has approved current version of EA.	EA products are periodically updated. IT investments comply with EA. Organization head has approved current version of EA.
Attribute 4: Verifies satisfaction of commitment		EA plans call for developing metrics for measuring EA progress, quality, compliance, and return on investment.	Progress against EA plans is measured and reported.	Quality of EA products is measured and reported.	Return on EA investment is measured and reported. Compliance with EA is measured and reported.

maturation

Source: GAO.

Figure 1. GAO's Enterprise Architecture Management Maturity Framework (EAMMF), Version 1.1

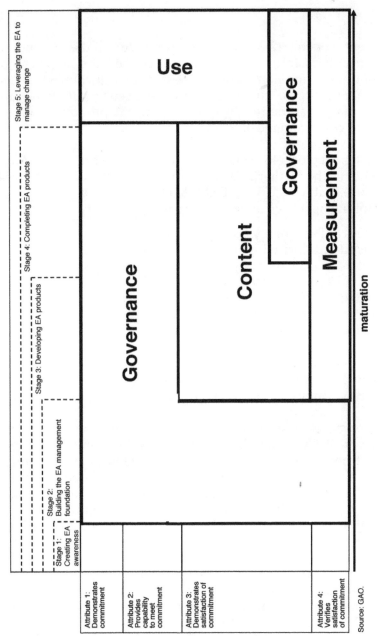

Figure 2. EAMMF – General Evaluation Categories

The current version (2.2) of the EAAF reduced the number of evaluation criteria from 17 to 13, and increased the emphasis on completion of mission-focused segment (functional/service-specific) architectures, integration of cross-agency initiatives, and the measurement of the results of having an EA program (e.g. cost savings and cost avoidance).

Also in 2004, Jaap Schekkerman, founder of the Institute for EA Developments in the Netherlands developed the Extended Enterprise Architecture Maturity Model (E2AMM) that has six maturity levels and the following eleven areas for measuring maturity:

- Business & Technology Strategy Alignment
- Extended Enterprise Involvement
- Executive Management Involvement
- Business Units Involvement
- Extended Enterprise Architecture Program Office
- Extended Enterprise Architecture Developments
- Extended Enterprise Architecture Results
- Strategic Governance
- Enterprise Program Management
- Holistic Extended Enterprise Architecture
- Enterprise Budget & Procurement Strategy

Many approaches to evaluating process maturity were influenced by the work of Philip Crosby (1979) and Watts Humphrey (1989). Crosby introduced the concept of a "quality management maturity grid" with five stages of maturity for initiatives intended to manage quality in organizations, and Humphrey applied this to the task of managing quality in the domain of software development. In 1991, Humphrey's efforts at Carnegie Mellon University's Software Engineering Institute (SEI) bore fruit in the form of the publication called the Capability Maturity Model® (CMM®; see Paulk, et al., 1991). The CMM contained five levels of maturity for software development organizations, along with an auditing method useful to guide their self-improvement or as a framework for a formal, external capability determination. In 2002 the newer CMM Integration[SM] (CMMI®) model was introduced, along with training components and a family of appraisal methods (the Standard CMMI Appraisal Method for Process Improvement, SCAMPI[SM] Class A, Class B, and Class C). Class A appraisals are complete in documenting and verifying objective evidence and in validating findings. They provide reliable and repeatable rating results. Class B and C appraisals are less intensive, using fewer resources and smaller teams, for example, to perform a preliminary analysis of an organization's processes.[6]

Since 2002, the CMMI product suite has expanded to include model components, training components, and appraisal components organized by areas of interest called "constellations." As is shown in Figure 3, three of SEI's constellations are "CMMI-DEV" for organizations that develop products or services, "CMMI-ACQ" for organizations that are acquiring products and services, and "CMMI-SVC" for organizations that are service providers or their clients. The current set of constellations contains 16 common core process areas, plus additional process areas that are unique to each constellation. Taken together, the process areas encompass the ways an organization performs its work, so the set of process areas comprises a framework to implement best practices and thereby gain expected improvements in cost, schedule, productivity, quality, and customer satisfaction. SEI reports that, since 2002, more than 80,000 people have received training on CMMI models, and more than 3,000 SCAMPI appraisals have been conducted by organizations in over 60 countries around the world (for more information see www.sei.cmu.edu). Stimulated by this approach, many other capability models and/or maturity models have emerged in many different application domains.

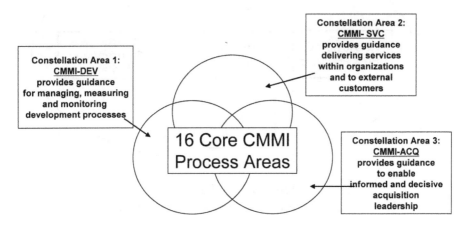

Figure 3. CMMI Constellation Areas and Core Processes

[6] ® The terms Capability Maturity Model, CMM, and CMMI are registered in the U.S. Patent and Trademark Office by Carnegie Mellon University.
SM The terms CMM Integration and SCAMPI are service marks of Carnegie Mellon University.

Enterprise Architecture Formalization

For an EA to be effective and authoritative at all levels and in all dimensions of an enterprise, the EA must integrate the strategy, business, and technology aspects of the architecture through a formal, ongoing program and an approach that has six basic elements: (1) an EA governance process that integrates with other management processes; (2) a repeatable methodology that supports program implementation and maintenance: (3) a framework to establish the scope of the architecture and the relationship of sub-architectures and other components; (4) a comprehensive and integrated set of documentation artifacts; (5) documentation tools to assist with modeling, and configuration control that uses an on-line repository for storing the documentation; and (6) associated best practices to guide EA documentation and use. Figure 4 shows the six basic elements of an enterprise architecture approach.

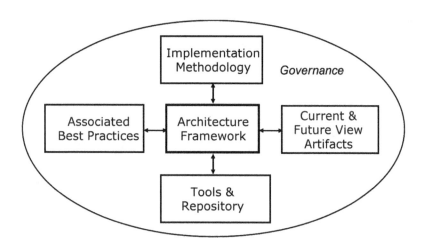

**Figure 4. The Essential Elements of an
Approach to Enterprise Architecture**

Each of these six basic elements plays an important part in the development, maintenance, and use of the architecture. The elements must not only be present, but they must be designed to work together to make the EA approach useful in the strategic, business, and technology dimensions across all lines of business. Their pres-

COHERENCY MANAGEMENT

ence is also key to enabling the EA to serve as the meta-architecture for an enterprise and is essential to achieving higher levels of architecture maturity. Therefore these elements are a foundational part of the EA audit procedure described later in this chapter. A number of current EA approaches do not have all six of these elements and therefore are lacking in fundamental ways. For example, without a prescribed artifact set that covers all areas of the framework, it is not possible to document and relate the strategic, business, and technology areas of the architecture in a consistent way across all lines of business. Without a specified way to select associated best practices for use within the EA approach at various sub-architecture levels, there can be confusion about which one is the meta-approach and which one is the supporting approach (e.g., Balanced Scorecard™, service-oriented architecture methods, object-oriented database design methods, CORBA software integration standards, and IT Infrastructure Library™ standards).

EA has evolved to be a meta-approach, which stands in contrast to other planning, design, analysis, modeling, and management methods – which are best suited to serve in a supporting role in the strategic, business, data, application, infrastructure, and/or security areas of the EA. Figure 5 provides an example EA approach called the "EA^3 Cube" (Bernard, 2004) which contains all six elements in a way that is designed to integrate the elements (e.g., the framework organizes the artifacts; the repository is designed to align with the underlying framework; and best practices are identified for use at each sub-architecture level defined in the framework).

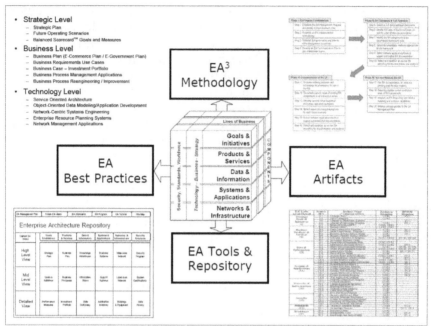

**Figure 5. Example of the Basic Elements of a
Complete EA Approach – EA³ Cube**

Auditing an Enterprise Architecture Program

Since the primary purpose of an EA program is to document an enterprise in current and future states to improve performance and coherency, the process for auditing an EA program must include general areas for completeness, consistency, and utilization. The Enterprise Architecture Audit Model (EA2M) follows generally accepted audit procedures and can be used with public and private sector EA programs based on any specific approach (e.g., Zachman, TOGAF, DODAF, FEAF, EA3, and GERAM) to measure maturity in the three areas: Completeness, Consistency, and Utilization. For example, in the 'Completeness' audit category the six basic elements of any EA approach are evaluated. In this way, the audit method can be consistently employed and resulting maturity scores can be used to track progress. Figure 6 shows the basic format, audit categories, maturity levels, and indicators of the EA2M approach.

Enterprise Architecture Audit Model (EA2M)					
	Level 1	Level 2	Level 3	Level 4	Level 5
Maturity Level	No Formalized Architecture	Foundational Architecture (General Indicators)	Extended Architecture (General Indicators)	Embedded Architecture (General Indicators)	Balanced Architecture (General Indicators)
Audit Category #1: Completeness					
Governance		EA Governance process selected	Governance initial implementation	Governance full implementation	Ongoing integration with management processes
Methodology		EA Methodology steps selected	Methodology initial implementation	Methodology full implementation	Methodology repeatable and steps optimized
Framework	Default initial level	EA Framework design selected	Framework initial implementation	Framework full implementation	Framework design optimized
Artifacts		EA Artifact set selected	Artifact initial implementation	Artifact full implementation	Artifacts used to support planning/decision-making
Tools / Repository		EA Tools & Repository selected	Tool & Repository initial implementation	Tool & Repository full implementation	Tool use & Repository design optimized
Best Practices		Best Practices selected	Best Practices initial implementation	Best Practices full implementation	Ongoing integration of Best Practices
Audit Category #2: Consistency					
Program		EA program approved	EA program initial implementation	EA program full implementation	EA program optimized
Policy	Default initial level	EA policies selected	EA policy initial implementation	EA policy full implementation	EA policy optimized
Resources		EA resources identified	EA resource requirements met	EA resources fully utilized	EA resources optimized
Training		EA training requirements identified	EA training initial implementation	EA training full implementation	EA training optimized
Audit Category #3: Utilization					
Strategic Value		Strategic goals & metrics identified	Strategic goals & business svcs mapped	Strategic goal attainment supported by the EA	Strategic goal attainment optimized via the EA
Business Value		Business services & requirements indentified	Business requirements and IT solutions mapped	Future business service scenarios established	Business services optimized via the EA
Technology Value	Default initial level	Current technology solutions identified	Future technology solutions refined	Future technology scenarios established	Technology use optimized via the EA
Risk & Security Management		Risk & security areas identified	Risk & security solution initial implementation	Risk & security solution full implementation	Risk mitigation optimized via the EA
Coherency		Coherency goals & metrics identified	Coherency goals initially met	Coherency goals fully met	Coherency optimized via the EA

Figure 6. The Enterprise Architecture Audit Model (EA2M)

The EA2M's five maturity levels are based on the progressive stages of development that architectures go through, and which is described in the beginning chapter of this book (Doucet et al., 2008). Table 1 shows the five levels and it should be noted that reaching subsequent levels is a cumulative process in that the key elements of the architecture at each maturity level are retained as the organization's EA program progresses upward toward Level 5 - where all of the elements are working synergistically to optimize EA completeness, consistency, and utilization.

EA Program Maturity Level 1	EA Program Maturity Level 2	EA Program Maturity Level 3	EA Program Maturity Level 4	EA Program Maturity Level 5
No Formalized Architecture	**Foundational Architecture**	**Extended Architecture**	**Embedded Architecture**	**Balanced Architecture**
Maturity Level 1 is the 'default' level for all enterprises that do not have an established EA program and/or documented architecture.	At Maturity Level 2, the 'foundational' elements of the EA are being put in place. EA is documented for the entire enterprise in its current and future states. The focus is on well-architected, well-designed IT systems with enterprise-level alignment, efficiency, and interoperability. Accordingly, EA at this level is very IT-centric, and for many people the EA would be viewed as a data and technology architecture, except that it is being implemented at the enterprise level. This perspective does help to leverage concepts such as federated patterns, but under-delivers from an enterprise-wide strategy and business perspective. Also, the value of EA is measured according to the success of IT investments.	At Maturity Level 3, the architecture is 'extended' to focus on engineering an entire enterprise from an integrated strategy, business, & technology perspective. To support this, approaches and tools are developed to provide standardized, repeatable methods for describing the enterprise in all dimensions - beyond just the IT perspective. Whereas foundation EA used architecture methods and tools to capture business requirements in order to design IT systems, the Extended EA approach uses architecture methods and tools to capture strategic goals and related business requirements in order to design the enterprise.	At Maturity Level 4, EA tools, methods, and models become 'embedded' in the normal (usually existing) processes of the day. Rather than relying on processes and people extraneous to the business programs (and their processes), the architecture is produced by the processes themselves. In this way the architecture is organic and is renewed on an ongoing basis as a natural outcome of normal business processes.	At Maturity Level 5, the elements of architecture at the three previous levels are 'balanced' and are all working synergistically to optimize EA completeness, consistency, and utilization. In so doing, the EA helps the organization to be more agile and competitive as various future operating scenarios are envisioned on an ongoing basis and appropriate courses of action are chosen and implemented in ways that effectively mitigate risk and help to manage change, innovation, and continuous improvement

Table 1. Maturity Levels of the EA Audit Model

EA2M Audit Procedure

Auditing is an essential aspect of most program/process quality assurance approaches (including CMMI), as well as a number of public laws that seek to improve accountability, accuracy, and service delivery. These include the U.S. Government's Federal Financial Management Improvement Act of 1996 (FFMIA), the Sarbanes-Oxley Act of 2002, and the Federal Information Security Management Act of 2002 (FISMA). Auditing of EA programs has been occurring in U.S. government agencies since 2002 and EA audits were included as a mandate of the Korean Government's IT Architecture Act of 2006.

The EA2M audit is designed to help organizations to identify the strengths and weaknesses of their EA program, reveal crucial risks, set priorities for improvement plans, derive ratings, and support realistic benchmarking. The EA2M is the evaluation 'framework' to

COHERENCY MANAGEMENT

be used for the collection and analysis of information, and to generate accurate and valid level ratings to be reported to the organization.

The EA2M Audit Procedure (EA2M-AP) is the method including all steps necessary for objective evaluation, including preparation, collection of evidence, formulation of preliminary findings and ratings, finalizing findings, reporting, and follow-on activities. As with SCAMPI Class A, B, or C appraisal methods, which vary in their intensity and resource consumption, each organization should tailor their audit plans on dimensions including the goals to be served, the amount of objective evidence to be gathered, the resources to be allocated, the size of the team to be involved, and the nature and use of final reports to be prepared. The following is the set of steps covering the basic elements of the EA2M-AP:

1. Plan and Prepare for the EA Program Audit
1.1 Set Goals, and Analyze the Objectives and Requirements

1.2 Develop an Audit Plan and Schedule

1.3 Select and Prepare an Audit Team

1.4 Obtain and Inventory any Initial Objective Evidence

1.5 Prepare for Conduct of the Audit

2. Conduct the EA Program Audit
2.1 Prepare Participants

2.2 Examine and Collect Objective Evidence

2.3 Document Objective Evidence

2.4 Verify Objective Evidence

2.5 Prepare and Validate Preliminary Findings

2.6 Generate Audit Results

3. Report Audit Results
3.1 Deliver Audit Results

3.2 Package and Archive Appraisal Assets

The EA2M-AP is intended to be implemented at both a basic and an advanced audit level to allow organizations to choose the depth to which they want the audit analysis to occur. A basic audit provides an organization with an initial estimate of the maturity of the program, or may be used to assist in establishing an EA program, with no 'official' maturity rating being given. The advanced audit provides a comprehensive look at all aspects of the EA program using the audit categories and indicators in the EA2M model, and results in an 'official' maturity level rating. Repeated annual audits and periodic spot checks that use the EA2M are the best way to ensure consistency in evaluating the EA program and progress in attaining higher levels of maturity. A summary of these audit levels is provided in Table 2 as follows:

	Basic EA Program Audit	Advanced EA Program Audit
Audit Team	1-2 People	2-5 People (Depends on EA Program Size)
Timeframe	2-4 Days	5-10 Days (Depends on EA Program Size)
Depth of Analysis	Cursory	Complete
Recommended Groups	Beginning EA programs and all initial audits. Provides feedback but no official rating.	After the basic audit is done and for subsequent audits. Allows for consistency in maturity tracking. Only way to get official rating.

Table 2. Basic and Advanced EA2M Audit Characteristics

The final aspect of the EA2M-AP to be covered is the training and credentialing of the auditors. To maintain consistency and respect for the audit procedure, findings, recommendations, and ratings it is important that the auditors be experienced senior enterprise architects who are trained in the EA2M-AP process. At present, the authors are the only approved EA2M auditors, yet auditor training courses are planned for the mid- to late-2009 timeframe. Links with existing quality assurance groups are also in coordination to promote consistency in the training levels and integration with other quality approaches.

Conclusion

This chapter focused on the importance of formalizing and auditing enterprise architecture programs in order to improve their value to public and private sector organizations. Formalization of an EA program centers on the establishment and maintenance of six basic elements: governance, methodology, framework, tools/repository, and associated best practices. The EA Audit Model (EA2M) was presented as the basis for an audit procedure that reviews EA programs for maturity in three general categories: completeness, consistency, and utilization. The basic steps of the EA2M Audit Procedure were introduced which create a comprehensive and repeatable method for conducting EA program audits. Basic and advanced forms of the EA2M audit were also introduced as a way for organizations to have the option of doing preliminary reviews prior to comprehensive audits. The training and certification of EA2M auditors is in the beginning stages, with courses and reference materials planned for release in 2009. Subsequent research in this area and application of the EA2M audit process will provide the basis for additional writings, an EA2M Auditor's Handbook, and applied case studies.

References

Bernard, Scott (2004). An Introduction to Enterprise Architecture. Authorhouse Publishing: Bloomington, IL.

Cook, Melissa (1996). Building Enterprise Information Architectures: Reengineering Information Architectures. Prentice Hall: Upper Saddle River, NJ.

Crosby, Philip B. (1979). Quality is Free: The Art of Making Quality Certain. New American Library, a division of Penguin Books: New York.

Federal CIO Council (1999). The Federal Enterprise Architecture Framework. September 1999.

Humphrey, Watts (1989). Managing the Software Process. Addison Wesley Professional Series: Cambridge, Massachusetts.

Paulk, Mark C.; B. Curtis, M.B. Chrissis, et al. (1991). Capability Maturity Model for Software. CMU/SEI-91-TR-24, August 1991. Carnegie Mellon University, Software Engineering Institute. Pittsburgh, Pennsylvania.

Schekkerman, Jaap (2004). Extended Enterprise Architecture Maturity Model. Institute for Enterprise Architecture Developments. http://tinyurl.com/c76rcn

Software Engineering Institute (2001). Appraisal Requirements for CMMI (SM), Version 1.1 (ARC, V1.1). CMU/SEI-2001-TR-034. Carnegie Mellon University, Software Engineering Institute. Pittsburgh, Pennsylvania.

Software Engineering Institute (2006). Standard CMMI® Appraisal Method for Process Improvement (SCAMPI) A, Version 1.2: Method Definition Document. CMU/SEI-2006-HB-002. Carnegie Mellon University, Software Engineering Institute. Pittsburgh, Pennsylvania.

Software Engineering Institute (2006). Capability Maturity Model Integration, Version 1.2. Carnegie Mellon University, Software Engineering Institute. http://tinyurl.com/5jjxrm.

Spewak, Steven (1992). Enterprise Architecture Planning: Developing a Blueprint for Data, Applications and Technology. John Wiley & Sons Publishers: New York.

U.S. Congress (1996). The Clinger-Cohen Act of 1996 (formerly known as the Information Technology Management Reform Act). Public Law 104-106.

United States General Accounting Office (2002). Information Technology: A Framework for Assessing and Improving Enterprise Architecture Management, Version 1.1. Report #GAO-02-6. February 2002.

United States Government Accounting Office (2003). Information Technology: Leadership Remains Key to Agencies Making Progress in Enterprise Architecture Efforts, Report # GAO-04-40. November 2003.

United States Government Accountability Office (2006). Enterprise Architecture Remains Key to Establishing and Leveraging Architectures for Organizational Transformation. Report #GAO-06-831. August 2006.

United States Government Accountability Office (2007). Gauging an IT Organization's Maturity, An Overview of GAO's Approach. Briefing given to the U.S. Department of Defense, August 2007.

United States Office of Management and Budget (2007). Federal EA Program, Enterprise Architecture Assessment Framework (version 2.2). October 2007.

Zachman, John (1987). A Framework for Information Systems Architecture. IBM Systems Journal. Volume 26, Number 3. pp. 276-290.

Zachman, John, and John Sowa (1992). Extending and Formalizing the Framework for Information Systems Architecture. IBM Systems Journal. Volume 31, Number 3. pp. 590-616.

About the Authors

Dr. Scott Bernard is the founding editor of the *Journal of Enterprise Architecture* and teaches at Syracuse University and Carnegie Mellon University. In 2004 he wrote the book *An Introduction to Enterprise Architecture* that presented the 'EA^3 Cube' architecture framework, the 'Living Enterprise' repository design and an associated implementation approach. Dr. Bernard has over 20 years of experience in IT management, including work in the academic, government, military, and private sectors. He's held positions as a Chief Information Officer, management consultant, line-of-business manager, network operations manager, telecommunications manager, and project manager for several major IT systems installations. Dr. Bernard has developed enterprise architectures for public, private, and military organizations, started an EA practice for an IT management consulting firm, developed his own consulting practice, and taught EA at a number of universities, businesses, and agencies. He holds a Ph.D. in Public Administration from Virginia Tech (2001); a M.S. in IT Management from Syracuse University (1998); a M.A. in Business Management from Central Michigan University (1984); a B.S. in Psychology from the University of Southern California (1977), and a CIO Certificate from the U.S. National Defense University (2000). Dr Bernard can be reached at sabernar@syr.edu.

Dr. John Grasso is the Director for Strategic Development and Distance Learning, in the Institute for Software Research International (ISRI), in the School of Computer Science at Carnegie Mellon University. In addition to his administrative role, he is appointed as Special Faculty in the School of Computer Science. He joined Carnegie Mellon after serving as Professor and Director in applied research at West Virginia University (WVU) for 17 years. His research career includes topics in technology, human resource development, and their contributions to productivity. His clients included telecommunications, manufacturing, mining, and software industries, U.S. and global companies, U.S. State and Federal Government, and other universities. In the area of software engineering, Dr. Grasso has taught the Management of Software Development, a core course in Carnegie Mellon's Master of Software Engineering program. In the area of quality management, he developed and delivered training for small and mid-sized companies, ranging from requirements management through acceptance testing and final evaluation. In software engineering, he was the WVU team leader on a large project ("AdaNET") for the NASA Johnson Space Center, on certification of software objects for software re-use in the space shuttle program. This project has evolved into the current Electronic Library Services and Applications (ELSA) project, the operational part of the Repository Based Software Engineering (RBSE) program sponsored by NASA at the University of Houston - Clear Lake. Dr. Grasso holds a B.Sc. in Computer and Information Science and Ph.D. in Human Resource Policy, both from The Ohio State University (1970, 1975). Dr. Grasso can be reached at john.grasso@cmu.edu.

Section II

COHERENCY
MANAGEMENT IN
ACTION:
INSIGHTS FROM
ENTERPRISE
ARCHITECTURE
IMPLEMENTATIONS

Chapter 9

ISSUES IN USING ENTERPRISE ARCHITECTURE FOR MERGERS AND ACQUISITIONS

John P.T. Mo & Laszlo Nemes

Editors' Preface

Mergers and Acquisitions (M & A) are complicated affairs requiring incredible amounts of analysis before and after the purchase. The chapter explores the use of EA to help with these processes. It is primarily a research-based chapter with an interesting exploration of a DNA based modeling approach. It is also worth noting that M & As share many similar challenges to large organizations simply trying to optimize their operations or act more horizontally, such as is the case with many national governments.

As Editors we believe that EA can definitely help with M & As and there is literature that explains this in detail. However, there are some real challenges we need to address to make this more effective and easier. The idea that EA could use DNA type approach is worth exploring. The componentization of the enterprise has been a long mission of EA, the most obvious example being Service Oriented Architecture (SOA). The field of EA is still emerging in some ways and the ultimate way we will describe our enterprises from an EA perspective is still evolving. This represents an avenue of exploration worth the effort in our estimation. Coherency Manage-

ment is better made as the EA tools (such as the models discussed in this chapter) improve. If more enterprises start to use common models, then the ability to analyze merger opportunities as well as the ability to execute on those mergers greatly improves. The agility element of the coherent enterprise helps with M & As just as with any other change or in the consideration of change. It is important to keep in mind that as the new models of EA propagate they should also be considered for how they will support the embedded concept.

Introduction

Global trade has driven enterprises to participate in inter-enterprise collaboration in order to satisfy customer requirements as well as to remain competitive or achieve further market advantage. One of the dynamic practices for expanding business is through mergers and acquisitions (M&A). There are many reasons for that. Swaminathan et al (2008) suggested that strategic emphasis alignment is a key construct that facilitates value creation. Alignment here means the extent to which the resource configurations of acquirer and target firms are similar to or distinct from one another. Tsai and Hsieh (2006) argued that M&A played a significant role in technological strategic deployment. Their study showed that the application can effectively assist corporations in controlling selections of technological assets and tailor technological asset investment mode for them.

Grimpe (2007) cited that a major reason for carrying out M&A is to gain access to technological knowledge and to increase new product development (NPD) capabilities. To achieve the desired effect of improving a firm's capacity for innovation, this knowledge must be combined with the acquiring firm's existing resources. The study on 35 M&A cases showed that a common organizational structure serves as a basis for realizing innovative resource combinations and streamlining the NPD process. This underpins the importance of measures to build-up a common corporate culture.

Mergers and acquisitions aim to achieve synergy between enterprises. However, M&A cases have significant challenges in the integration of the initially separated entities into one bigger enterprise. Enterprise Architecture (EA) provides a fundamental and comprehensive mechanism for corporate executives to define their M&A framework and design their systems in the new environment. A key to good EA design is coherency (Doucet et al, 2008). EA should be adopted as a tool for coherency management across the merging enterprises and as an ongoing, overarching blueprint for the design and engineering of the new enterprise.

In this chapter, we start with a literature review, where references are made to international efforts in studying M&A. We then explore the issues of existing enterprise architectures in modeling and guiding the formation of new enterprises from M&A, and hence propose a new way to handle this issue.

Challenges and Opportunities

One may argue that the major objective of M&A is to expand the business by absorbing other similar entities. This is often a painful process with grieving from those who lose out in the chain of actions. In Taiwan, M&A activities affected corporate performance in the telecommunications industry. The study by Li et al (2007) revealed that M&A strategy did not seem to enhance corporate performance, whilst an internal growth strategy could do better. Working independently, King et al (2008) confirmed that acquisitions did not lead to higher performance on average, instead, complementary resource profiles in target and acquiring firms were associated with abnormal returns.

Barmeyer and Mayrhofer (2008) examined the contribution of inter-cultural management approaches to the success of an international merger and illustrated the impact of cultural differences due to conflicts in managerial situations. The impact of cultural difference is more serious in Japan. Froese and Goeritz (2007) reported that in recent years, Japan has seen a sharp increase in foreign cross-border M&A transactions. Among the larger ones, a few multinational companies are already struggling with their acquisitions. Findings indicated that human and organizational integration were strongly interwoven in Japan, with human integration being a necessary prerequisite for organizational integration.

The sale or merger of any company could affect its employees seriously (Halpin and Bishara, 2006). Though it is merely a hassle adapting to a different enterprise, the sudden uncertainty about health-care coverage and pensions can be truly stressful. For plant managers, the impact is even greater - adapting to a new budgeting process and reporting requirements, not to mention answering hundreds of subordinates' questions about the future, even before the deal closes. The major concern is the organisational unrest affecting morale and job performance of staff. Lin and Wei (2006) used a structural equation modeling approach to empirically test their hypotheses based on 264 samples from financial companies. The data analyses indicated that ethical conduct in M&A was significantly correlated with employee job performance.

The most persuasive but not necessarily voluntary reason for companies to pursue M&A is due to change of government policy. Kaen et al (2008) reported that many power utilities, as a response to the deregulation of the electricity industry, adopted a strategy of acquiring other electricity or gas utilities. However, they found little evidence that M&A created long-term value for a fully diversified investor because the acquirers operated a portfolio of utilities that did not engage in merger activity.

Acquisition in the public sector takes a different format. Clifton and Duffield (2006) applied alliance principles to manage a public private partnership project and achieved improved service outcomes. Capron and Shen (2007) reported that the lack of information on private targets limits the breadth of the acquirer's search and increases its risk of not evaluating properly the assets of private targets. At the same time, less information on private targets creates more value-creating opportunities for exploiting private information, whereas the market of corporate control for public targets already serves as an information-processing and asset valuation mechanism for all potential bidders.

One of the crucial requirements in M&A is the adequacy of financial and accounting reporting in the new enterprise. Downes (2008) used two case studies to illustrate that centralised information governance had a significant positive factor in both IT integration and government regulation compliance. When considering M&A, large publicly listed companies would have greater degree of compliance and hence consistency within their enterprises. However, when a public company seeks to acquire a large private entity, due diligence must be done to assess the status of control of the target company. On the contrary, Kwon et al (2007) reported that enterprises going through significant organisational change such as M&A could result in downsizing IT functions. The outcome is not simply elimination of some workers in the IT department; it also eliminates communication and information-processing conduits necessary for effective communication and coordination. This finding further confirms the need for EA to ensure a coherent integration process that could realize expected synergies.

M&A activities inevitably require changes in the enterprise. The uncertainty in this business environment presents many research opportunities in enterprise engineering. Yin and Shanley (2008) proposed a three dimensional model that could assist decision makers to merge or form alliances. Oberg et al (2007) presented the concept of "network pictures" as the modeling framework to illustrate and analyse changes in managerial sense-making and networking activities following a merger or acquisition. They concluded that following a merger or acquisition, managers may need to adapt their previous network pictures in a radical way.

The dynamics of merger was analyzed by Marino and Zabojnik (2006). In their model, if new firms can enter the market quickly, it is more likely that merger is motivated by efficiency as opposed to increased market power. Thus, there is less reason to challenge the merger. On the other hand, if the entry of new firms becomes less costly, firms may have a stronger incentive to monopolize the industry through horizontal merger. We observe that many M&A cases had serious problems and they generally lacked overarching human, organization and engineering principles. It is our conclusion from these studies that issues on M&A should be dealt with in a systematic organized fashion, supported by a methodology with strong engineering disciplines. The use of enterprise architecture will assist in fostering an orderly transition.

Problems With Existing Enterprise Architectures

In a merger or acquisition event, it is normal that a single enterprise is formed from several independent enterprises. There are many risks in this event. For example, there are risks in collaboration, confidentiality, intellectual property, transfer of goods, conflicts, opportunity loss, product liability and others. On the other hand, the study of enterprise architecture requirements in the last decade has been on how enterprises can be designed and operated in an environment when the enterprise missions and objectives are not changing rapidly due to the relatively slowly shifting external business conditions, or when the facilities are specialized for a limited number of products. These enterprise engineering researches shared a common starting point. They assumed that one can follow the common engineering practice of well established sequences of steps: design – implementation – operation and decommission phases. To reduce the work associated with each step (e.g. design) the researches built multi-dimensional enterprise modeling and design methodologies. They have general models, which contain the most logical steps applicable to all kind of enterprises. These are generic models that can offer logical guidance but have limited practical value to general users. The partial model is extended from the generic model and contains more industry specific information (e.g. discrete production characteristics in automotive industry). Hence, if an automotive company would like to create an enterprise model, they do not create the model from scratch. Instead, they take a partial model and put the company relevant information into that. This architecture is shown in Figure 1.

The rationale to use enterprise engineering methodologies to guide these steps is to minimize enterprise design modifications and associated rework of the system governing information and material flows. Any unplanned change to the enterprise is an impact of uncertainty to enterprise performances. The Enterprise Architecture approach provides a structured system to manage M&A activities, for example, promote planning, reduce risk, and implement new standard operating procedures and controls, rationalizing manufacturing facilities.

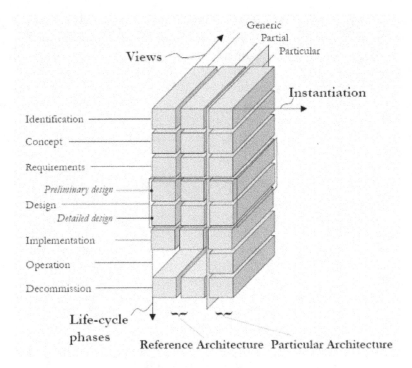

**Figure 1. Generic Enterprise Reference Architecture (GERA) –
Stepwise, multi-dimensional characteristics
(IFIP-IFAC Task Force, 1999)**

Since 1980s, much research has been done in search of suitable EAs for different industries and organizations. An EA is a blueprint for good enterprise planning, modeling, management and implementation. However, due to different backgrounds and basis of investigations, different EAs cover different things. Some EAs define architecture as well as tools. Some EAs focuses on functional constructs. PERA (Williams, 1994) describes how to design an enterprise through its lifecycle. CIMOSA (Didic, 1995) describes what should be in an enterprise. GRAI (Chen et al, 1997) describes how the components of an enterprise are linked. Normally, the application of EAs starts with substantial integration effort in design and implementation. The formulation of EAs is described tacitly with the assumption that the present state of the enterprise does not change during the life cycle of the "enterprise engineering project". This used to be the case when establishing or modifying large, one-of-a-kind installations, such as an oil refinery or a fertilizer plant or a navy ship.

On the other hand, enterprises going through an M&A process are effectively dissolving the original enterprises into a new enterprise. The volatility in the merger and acquisition process violates many fundamental principles that enterprise architecture theories are based on (Bernus and Nemes, 1996). For example, enterprise architecture assumes a consistent mission for the enterprise. The outcome of a merger will be a new enterprise with a mission either adapted from one of the merging entities or changed from any of the existing ones due to new opportunities.

In an acquisition process, depending on the size of the transaction, the architecture design and early modeling should be started in parallel with the feasibility studies to be completed usually by investment banks. These financial institutions work frenetically against the clock to complete the task before any other competitor might become interested in buying the same target. The analysis usually covers the financial situations and the possible product mix (enterprise profile) and they do not cover the issues related to the operation of the new entity. Therefore, it is expected the architecture building and operation modeling should be started in concert with the investment analysis. It is obvious that the speed of transactions in the new communication era is enormous and does not allow enough time for any detail enterprise modeling studies using the established practices. Many developments in the newly formed enterprise are unpredictable. There is room to improve the existing enterprise engineering toolbox to manage such changes, but unfortunately, there are restrictions. The most significant restriction is time. The question is: how fast changes could be made?

A solution is to modify the existing architectures, making them suitable for adapting to the new global business environment. We need to understand their shortcomings, for example, what is missing from them and how to incorporate the missing issues in the modified structure.

However, traditional enterprise architectures are based on top down approach. They emphasize uniformity throughout the organization. As such, the structure is inflexible and will not be able to respond to fast changing dynamic issues. Changing the structure would take too long to fix any problem. The top-down approach has inherent resistance to change. This is evident from the studies on virtual enterprises such as the RELINK project (Mo et al, 2005). The RELINK initiative aims to demonstrate the methodologies and systems that will enable small firms in the tooling and automotive

COHERENCY MANAGEMENT

component industry to work with medium and large firms in turn-key projects as part of a broader global supply chain. The resistance from change came from the reluctance of the tool manufacturers, in particular, the smaller enterprises, to establish effective communication platforms in order to collaborate. The project concluded with the identification of an open communication framework for the virtual enterprise defining a continuity of functionality in the communication process that enables B2B operations to be performed satisfactorily. Individual companies could decide how they would like to participate within a virtual enterprise with varying levels of communication capabilities. The result is far from satisfactory.

Virtual enterprise methodologies can be regarded as a toolset that has the characteristics for assisting multiple enterprise interaction such as M&A. The ground work for modeling inter-enterprise collaboration was done in a number of international studies and modeled by virtual enterprise reference architecture (Zwegers et al, 2003). The theory of enterprise design and life cycle management was established in order to understand the essence in these cases. Several key properties can be identified immediately (Van den Berg and Tolle, 2000). First, the operating conditions of the business environment are characterized by frequent changes in products, services, processes, organizations, markets, supply and distribution networks. Second, in the enterprises there are autonomous teams performing tasks in such networks. They form a temporary alliance to deliver a project or product and they dissolve when the job is completed. The teams work together as one entity for a goal, but the relationships among them and the individual companies where they come from, often rely on trust and industry practices. Success in achieving the goal therefore demands well-coordinated agility in all internal and external aspects of the virtual enterprise.

The theory of virtual enterprise is not however sufficient to provide a guideline for understanding enterprise performance in M&A. The virtual enterprise evolution cycle has three major life histories which take a while to complete (Figure 2). In addition, it does not model the path of change. The changes are also quite restricted, for example, current enterprise engineering does not allow change of the mission statement.

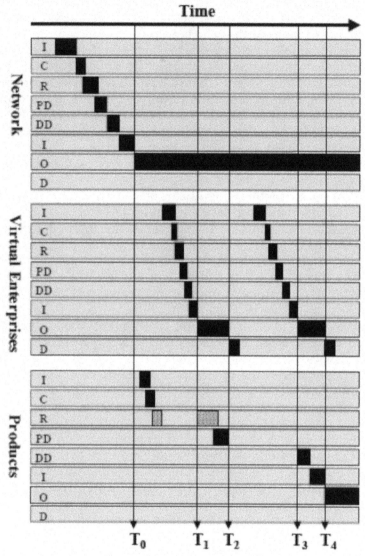

Figure 2. Virtual enterprise life history diagram
(Vesterager et al, 2002)

The situation is further compounded by the advancement in network technologies that flattens the organizational structure in many enterprises. In a virtual enterprise, a flat many-to-many communication architecture is a fact that is given rather than one that is designed. New technologies have tremendous advantage over past

COHERENCY MANAGEMENT

practices, particularly in the flow of information and the management of knowledge. However, there are also undesirable consequences. For example, there is no apparent method to handle reassignment of roles and responsibilities in a virtual enterprise. A lot of information and personal knowledge is buried in personal email folders and not accessible or even lost to the rest of the enterprise. Issues can be made to surface quickly. Control mechanisms do not work and in many cases, do not actually exist within the loosely linked virtual enterprise architecture. It is almost a universal phenomenon that any change in personnel, such as new appointments or relocation could change the course of the project. The challenge to future enterprise architectures is not to prevent changes, but rather to foster fast changes in the required direction.

Requirement for Enterprise Architecture in M&A

An enterprise architecture defines methods and tools which are needed to identify and carry out change. Enterprises need life-cycle architecture that describes the progression of an enterprise from the point of realisation that change is necessary through the setting up of a project for implementation of the change process. Therefore, it is crucial that the enterprise resulting from M&A should be supported by a systematic design methodology. This helps the management develop well defined policy and process across the organizational boundaries prior to the merger process, and to implement the changes in all enterprises concerned during the process.

However, this view is one sided, primarily from the point of view of the larger organization taking over smaller companies. If we use a more generic approach and consider stories from both sides, the major objective of M&A is to develop a new enterprise which is:

- more agile

- reduces (eliminates) errors (less mistakes and less rework)

- more efficient (cheaper to run, less waste)

Therefore, the fundamental requirements for enterprise architecture in M&A should have five key characteristics:

1. *Understanding the cost of merging production, information systems, and human organization*
   Any change to the enterprise means the maximum use of resources and minimal disruption to normal businesses. These activities should be fully costed and understood, and preferably optimized to maximize the benefit of change.
2. *Modeling risks in all areas*
   Risk is the chance of something happening that will have negative impact on the objectives. The purpose of risk modeling is to define, analyze, treat, and monitor risks inherent in the enterprise processes of management policies, practices, and procedures. It involves achieving an appropriate balance between realizing opportunities for gains while minimizing losses.
3. *Modeling the time necessary for the merger, identifying the optimum, best and worst case scenarios*
   Time management is a vital part of good project management, especially in the changing environment of M&A. It is necessary to ensure the strictest control of activities that are on the critical path of change implementation.
4. *Maximizing the re-use of best practices and resources in all areas*
   The ultimate objective of enterprise engineering is to identify best practices through the modeling framework of enterprise architecture. The requirements of enterprise architecture in M&A are not only to understand, but also to allocate scarce resources to the most effective area.
5. *Understanding the difficulties, identifying the bottlenecks in all areas*
   We discussed the difficulties in M&A previously, mostly related to people and information compatibility. A merger process creates new opportunities for people who would like to move upwards. There are also issues related to the change of thinking styles in generations, for example, GenY. The requirement for enterprise architecture is to be able to foresee these issues in the architecture as bottlenecks during implementation.

It is necessary to understand that everything in the business environment is driven by business goals and mission. Engineering an enterprise using architecture is about meeting the enterprise goals. The difficulty in engineering an enterprise through a merger or acquisition type of change is that the enterprise goals are affected by the change itself.

Possible Solution

Given the dynamism in M&A, we propose an alternative solution, viz, to create a new type of modeling tool that is highly flexible and has the ability to enforce the five key characteristics. Observations in science have demonstrated that biological organisms are the most adaptable structures in the world. Penrose (1952) used the analogy between biological and enterprise systems to explore possible development of enterprises based on better known biological theories. Three analogies were identified: a 3 stage life cycle, a natural selection process and homeostasis (to maintain certain equilibrium). Miller and Friesen (1984) further strengthen the enterprise development theory to a 5-stage life cycle: birth, growth, maturity, revival and decline. These concepts are primarily focused on drawing upon the knowledge of biological organisms' development to explain natural changes of enterprises.

We use an analogy from DNA (Deoxyribonucleic acid) (Biotechnology Australia, 2008). DNA is the foundation building block for all living cells. DNA looks like an incredibly long twisted ladder. This shape is called a double helix. The sides of the ladder are a linked chain of alternating sugar and phosphate molecules. The strands connect to the sugar molecules and are known as bases. There are four bases - adenine (A), thymine (T), guanine (G) and cytosine (C). It is through the permutation of these bases that DNA contains information used in everyday metabolism and growth and influences most of our characteristics.

Among the first few researchers using DNA as an analogy for exploring enterprise characteristics, Baskin (1995) represented the enterprise DNA with two interwoven "strands": identity and procedure. The enterprise identity represents its vision, values and accepted behavior. The procedure is externalized as the corporate knowledge that everybody should know. Sireesh (2006) further developed the concept on compliance and risk management culture within organizational DNA.

Spear and Bowen (1999) published DNA coding for the Toyota Production System (TPS) using a four-level prism model comprising vision, principles, toolbox, and learning organization. A series of material flow propositions relating to this model are advanced. This includes the smoothing of production, the strategic use of inventories, and the exploitation of industrial engineering techniques. These help explain and rationalize the apparent impact of TPS on a wide range of industries. Towill (2007) identified a well-trodden improvement path from 'traditional' to 'seamless' operations based on uncertainty reduction leading to smooth material flow. Furthermore, TPS readily passes the predicated 'transferability test' between enterprises and between market sectors.

The simplicity of DNA and yet the complexity of the organisms that resulted from the combination of the four bases stimulated the thinking around enterprise systems. Enterprises are complex entities formed through human activities and relationships and yet they are built from foundation blocks in the three domains: equipment, information and people. If enterprise models can be described in the three basic domains, is it possible that "Enterprise Engineering" in merging and acquisition can be view as "Genetic Engineering" of the new enterprise? Similarly, as biological DNA is a blueprint of living organisms, the "Enterprise DNA can be viewed as the "blueprint for enterprise".

When considering the new way of thinking, we need to define the fundamental building blocks of an enterprise. Williams et al (1994) studied and mapped most EAs into a generic architecture. This work showed that the enterprise DNA can be defined from 3 foundation elements: *data*, *people* and *assets* (*machines*). In such DNA thinking, these building blocks should be itemized to enable free combination in any order for creating new EAs.

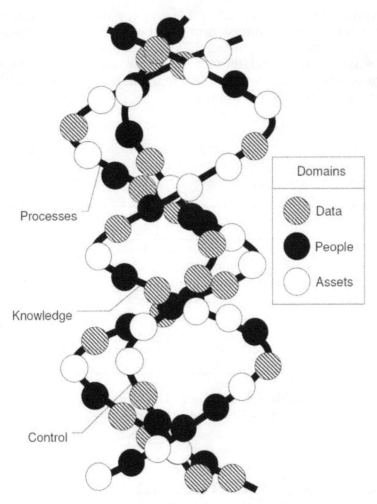

Figure 3. Strands of enterprise DNA

If we regard these building blocks as equivalent to DNA bases, combination of these building blocks into the anatomy of the enterprise can be realized as three strands of basic enterprise constructs:, control, knowledge and processes (Figure 3). Information about how the enterprise is built will be encoded in these strands and can be studied, if the appropriate analytical methodologies are applied. Subsystems of the enterprise are therefore characterized by the genes in the form of departments, products, services and other tangible entities.

The advantage of this approach is that the formation of enterprises becomes a way of permuting the bases. The characteristics of the enterprise are also governed by the way the bases are grouped together in the genes. Understanding of the performance of the enterprise is a matter of diagnosing the permutation of the bases in each of the genes. This modeling approach can also meet the five key characteristics requirements. A comparison of the concept with the requirements is shown in Table 1.

	Key Characteristics	How DNA EA models
1	Understanding the cost of the merging of production, information systems, and human organization	By examining and comparing the genes in the new enterprise and where they originate from (the parent enterprises).
2	Modeling risks in all areas	By behavioral studies of enterprises of similar genes
3	Modeling the time necessary for the merger, identifying the optimum, best and worst case scenarios	By mapping and evaluating the development processes of enterprises of similar genes
4	Maximizing the re-use of best practices and resources in all areas	Genes can be re-used, re-organized, and refreshed (re-trained)
5	Understanding the difficulties, identifying the bottlenecks in all areas	Introduce new genes

Table 1. Mapping of DNA modeling capability to key characteristics

M&A as Reproduction

Using the DNA model, the agility and flexibility for M&A could be visualized. The DNA model can provide an explanation of the state of the enterprises before and after the merger. Before the merger, the enterprises to be merged are represented by different EA genes. Each of them will have special characteristics due to different permutation of the bases. At the time of merger, the genes are broken into different parts and re-assembled with the genes from other organizations. A new enterprise is then formed with the new genes.

M&A is like a "fertilization" or a "genetic engineering" process. Either it clones the dominant enterprise or it takes the common strands from both but selects one from the differing genes. The key event is the creation of a new enterprise with the sacrifice of the old.

Hence, if the EA strand formation theory is acceptable, cloning of the newly acquired enterprises can be done from the most effective one, most likely to be the enterprise that dominates the merger process. It is also possible to create plug and play (i.e. by replacing genes) information systems that fit the new enterprise. Optimization of production (whatever the delivery output is going to be: manufacturing, banking, health care, government services. etc) can be done by mix and match value adding activities irrespectively from localities ("making" ad "moving" are interchangeable "objects"). People skills and their opportunities for creativity can be maximized rather than considered from their present positions for the merged enterprise. It is also worth noting that the inheritance of genes may not be entirely controllable by the enterprise designer, for example, one may not have the freedom to select products or services due to historical reasons.

This modeling method does not replace the existing lifecycle architectures and modeling tools. It serves a different purpose. Here we assume that the two or more enterprises are already in their operating phase of their respective lifecycles and the unified one (after merger or acquisition) will be a combination of them. The mission, values, etc. will be adopted from the dominant one. So the DNA blueprint can be viewed as the description and documentation of certain phases of the lifecycles. This is therefore an extension of the "normal" mission-oriented enterprise engineering method rather than its replacement. The mission elements can be changed by replacing very specific genes in each enterprise. There are uncertainties in this approach, for example, there are bases that are to be identified. More research is required to map current types of enterprise architectures in the new triple helix models.

A Case Study

We use a case study to illustrate the concept of using DNA EA model in M&A circumstances.

Since the early 1990s, the Australian electricity industry has undergone a series of transformations. Separate commercial structures were developed for the monopoly transmission and distribution ('wires') functions and the competitive generation and retailing functions of the industry. The major reform in the Australian electricity industry involved the establishment in southern and eastern Australia of the National Electricity Market (NEM). The NEM operates in the eastern states of Australia with one of the world's longest interconnected power systems of more than 4000 km. Over $A11 billion of electricity is traded annually in the NEM to meet the demand of almost eight million end-use consumers. Exchange between electricity producers and electricity consumers is facilitated through a spot market where the output from all generators is aggregated and scheduled every half an hour to meet demand through a centrally-coordinated dispatch process by the National Electricity Market Management Company (NEMMCO). The owners of the company are the five States and the Territory within which the NEM operates.

The National Electricity Market commenced operation in December 1998 under a detailed set of rules administered by the National Electricity Code. In December 2003, the Australian Government made further changes to the NEM by establishing two new statutory commissions:

- an Australian Energy Market Commission (AEMC) for rule-making and market development in relation to the NEM; and

- an Australian Energy Regulator (AER) for enforcement of the National Electricity Law and National Electricity Rules.

Both commissions commenced in July, 2005. The reforms led to the disaggregation of the vertically integrated government-owned electricity authorities into separate generation, transmission, distribution and retail sales sectors in each State. The goal of the reform process was to increase competition in the industry and provide greater choice for end-use electricity consumers. Due to these reforms and in conjunction with the privatization of energy assets, there were many M&A activities in the decades from 1995 to 1992.

According to a benchmark survey carried out by Caslon Benchmarking, there were 56 major acquisition transactions in the world since 1995 (Caslon, 2008). For this case study, we focus on the M&A activities related to the changes of the State Energy Commission. Our discussion here is not on whether the M&A activities were reasonable or managed well. Our focus is to examine how DNA EA can be applied to understand the changes that occurred. The series of events relevant to our discussion are:

- PacifiCorp buys Powercor from the Victorian government for $2.1bn in 1995

COHERENCY MANAGEMENT

- Victorian government sells CitiPower to Entergy for $1.57bn in 1995

- Entergy sells CitiPower business to American Electric Power (AEP) for $1.7bn in 1998

- ScottishPower buys PacifiCorp for US$10.3bn in 1998

- Cheung Kong Infrastructure (CKI) and Hongkong Electric buy ETSA from the South Australian government for $3.4bn in 1999

- ScottishPower sells Powercor to Cheung Kong and Hongkong Electric for $2.31bn in 2000

- ScottishPower sells PacifiCorp to Warren Buffett's MidAmerican for US$9.1bn in 2000

- CKI and Hongkong Electric sell Powercor electricity retail business to Origin Energy for $315m in 2001

- CKI buys CitiPower from AEP for $1.5bn in 2002

CitiPower and Powercor Australia are two of Victoria's five electricity distribution companies created in the State's restructure of the electricity industry in 1994. It can be seen from the series of M&A transactions that the two companies CitiPower and PowerCor changed hand at least 3 times in 7 years. According to the 2003 annual report of the two combined companies, there was instability in the two companies until 2002. The EA for the companies is designed such that while each operates its own electricity distribution network with its own brand and customers, the companies plan, manage and develop their operations as a group under a common joint ownership. In addition to operating electricity distribution networks, they also provide services to external markets in network design, construction and maintenance, telecommunications, information technology and customer services. The joint CitiPower and Powercor group operates through six main business streams (Figure 4). The six business units are supported by a centralized group of business units providing strategic and operational support functions. The network businesses are physically separated.

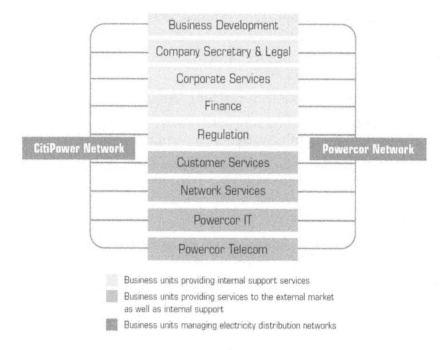

Figure 4. Business units (CitiPower and Powercor Australia, 2003)

These business units have their own specific business objectives but they are dependent on each other as well as the remaining business units. The business units cannot exist by themselves and yet they are in many respects autonomous in operation. We model these units as strands in the DNA EA (Table 2).

Process	Knowledge	Control
• CitiPower Network • Powercor Network	• Customer Services • Network Services • Powercor IT • Powercor Telecom	• Business Development • Company Secretary & Legal • Corporate Services • Finance • Regulation

Table 2. DNA EA mapping for business units

To support these business units, the two companies describe their company structure by a number of elements as shown in Figure 5.

**Figure 5. Joint company structure
(CitiPower and Powercor Australia, 2008)**

The company structure can be analyzed by DNA EA if we segment the domain elements in Figure 5 as shown in Table 3.

Business Units	Data	People	Assets
Electricity and Networks	• Business Performance and Improvement • Safety and Environmental Compliance	• Control and Operations • Customer Projects	• Asset Strategy and Performance • Engineering Asset Inspection and Maintenance • Regional Asset Management
Powercor Network Services	• Design engineering, construction & Field Services • Logistics / Supply Chain Management	• Business Development • Resource Management	• Project Management
AMI Services (metering)	• Metering and Communication Technologies		• Advanced Interval Meter Rollout • Metering Services
Information Technology	• Information Technology	• Business Information Systems	
Finance	• Finance • Taxation • Financial Business and Strategic Planning	• Treasury • Corporate Risk Management	• Purchasing and Contracts • Property Services • Fleet and Logistics
Human Resources & Corporate Affairs	• Quality Management	• Human Resources • Corporate Affairs • Health and Safety • Industrial Relations • Training and Development	• Environment and Sustainability
Company Secretary & Legal Services	• Legal • Audit	• Company Secretary	• Real Estate
Regulation	• Regulation • Price Reset		• Network Pricing • Business Development and Innovation
Customer Services	• Revenue Management • Data Management	• Customer Response • Retailer and Customer Relations	• Connection Services • Customer Service

**Table 3. Domain elements of CitiPower
and PowerCor merged enterprise**

CitiPower joined Powercor under common ownership, when the parent companies acquired the CitiPower distribution business in August 2002. The governance of the newly acquired company would need to be adjusted to fit that of the existing EA. The M&A further reinforced the need for a common EA. Since then the companies have made significant progress integrating CitiPower and Powercor processes, while maintaining their respective legal enti-

COHERENCY MANAGEMENT

ties, brands and distribution licenses. We examined the series of company annual reports from CitiPower and PowerCor. The changes after 2003 were gradual and the same management team was in charge. This shows that the company was stabilized after major reforms in 2003 when the merger with CitiPower occurred and the domain elements are distributed to different strands of the enterprise structure.

Research Opportunities

The case study is used to illustrate the concept of DNA EA. The classification of process, knowledge and control are specific to this group of companies. However, it is useful even for people external to the companies to understand the rationale behind this EA and how it is formed. There are many possible ways forward for the companies but whatever the changes are, the DNA in Table 4 will not change.

This case study and DNA EA formulation lead us to the next question: what should we do next? Given the relatively easy and natural modeling of the case by DNA EA, our conclusion is that the new approach has great potential to provide guidance to enterprises when they are involved in M&A transactions. From the DNA's perspective, the characteristics of the company formed by the M&A event would inherit some, if not all, characteristics of the parent companies. We can understand the EA of CitiPower and Powercor as they are captured at this point. However, there is insufficient information on the parent companies so it is not possible for us to prove that the DNAs of the two companies are inherited.

We examined the structure of the sister company in this case, viz, ETSA. There is evidence that a similar EA has been adopted, for example, the existence of a consultancy and engineering services business unit that not only supports internal (ETSA's) requirements, but also provide business services to other electricity and distribution companies. It seems that due to inheritance of DNA, this knowledge strand is an essential part of the EA of infrastructure companies. Hence, if one can analyze the DNA of the parent companies, it is possible to determine the EA for the new company after M&A. Further research will explore why this EA is formed and how various DNA structures come into existence.

Conclusion

This chapter examines how EA can be used in M&A processes which are fundamentally different from a static enterprise design based on lifecycle design methodology. The proposed EA forms the foundation for defining a new coherent enterprise that can benefit from the synergy of M&A and build on the structured foundation to grow. In this chapter, we point out the peculiar issues by providing a literature review, where references are made to international efforts in studying M&A. We explore some of the shortfalls of current enterprise architectures in the modeling of changes and guidance for designing a new enterprise architecture in the M&A process. We examine the need for enterprise coherency management during M&A but there are issues in existing EAs due to their static modeling nature. The enterprise model that exhibits most but not all of the required characteristics in a M&A turmoil is virtual enterprise reference architecture. However, it has substantial issues due to speed of change and fundamental principles. By elaborating the new requirements for enterprise architectures, we propose a new thinking in enterprise architecture, based on the biological analogy of DNA. The new modeling approach has shown advantages, for example, the ability to foreshadow a suitable EA prior to making enterprise changes. However, there are still a number of questions to be addressed and these will be explored in future EA research.

References

Barmeyer, C., Mayrhofer, U. (2008). The contribution of intercultural management to the success of international mergers and acquisitions: An analysis of the EADS group, International Business Review, 17(1):28-38

Baskin, K. (1995). DNA for corporations: Organizations learn to adapt or die. The Futurist, 29(1), Jan-Feb, 68

Bernus, P., Nemes, L. (1996). A framework to define a generic enterprise reference architecture and methodology. Computer Integrated Manufacturing Systems, 9(3):179-191

Biotechnology Australia. (2008). What does DNA look like? http://tinyurl.com/chxegs (accessed June, 2008)

Capron, L., Shen, J.C. (2007). Acquisitions of private vs. public firms: Private information, target selection, and acquirer returns. Strategic Management Journal, 28(9):891-911

Chen D., Vallespir B., Doumeingts G. (1997), GRAI integrated methodology and its mapping onto generic enterprise reference architecture and methodology. Computers in Industry, 33:387-394

CitiPower and Powercor Australia. (2003). Annual Report 2003.

CitiPower and Powercor Australia. (2008). Joint management team. http://tinyurl.com/ddmo5a, accessed 25 October, 2008.

Clifton, C., Duffield, C.F. (2006). Improved PFI/PPP service outcomes through the integration of Alliance principles. International Journal of Project Management, 24:573-586

Didic, M.M., Couffin, F., Holler, E., Lamperiere, S., Neuscheler, F., Rogier, J., de Vries, M. (1995). Open engineering and operational environment for CIMOSA. Computers in Industry. 27:167-178

Doucet, G., Gøtze, J., Saha, P., Bernard, S. (2008). Coherency Management: Using Enterprise Architecture for Alignment, Agility, and Assurance. Journal of Enterprise Architecture, Vol.4, No.2, May 2008, pp.9-20

Downes, G. (2008). Enterprise Architecture and IT Governance Considerations for Mergers & Acquisitions in Integrating Sarbanes-Oxley, Journal of Enterprise Architecture, Vol.4, No.1, February 2008, pp.41-61

Froese, F.J., Goeritz, L.E. (2007). Integration management of Western acquisitions in Japan. Asian Business and Management, 6(1):95-114

Grimpe, C. (2007). Successful product development after firm acquisitions: The role of research and development. Journal of Product Innovation Management, 24 (6): 614-628

Halpin, P., Bishara, A. (2006). Mergers present challenges - and opportunities - for plant managers. Power, 150(6):96, Jul-Aug

IFIP–IFAC Task Force (1999). GERAM: Generalised Enterprise Reference Architecture and Methodology. Version 1.6.3, Annex to ISO WD15704, Requirements for enterprise-reference architectures and methodologies, Mar 1, 39 pages

Kaen, F.R., Goldberg, L.G., Becker-Blease, J.R. (2008). Mergers and acquisitions as a response to the deregulation of the electric power industry: value creation or value destruction?" Journal of Regulatory Economics, 33(1):21-53 FEB 2008

King, D.R., Slotegraaf, R.J., Kesner, I. (2008). Performance implications of firm resource interactions in the acquisition of R&D-intensive firms. Organization Science, 19(2):327-340

Kwon, D, Oh, W, Jeon, S. (2007). Broken ties: The impact of organizational restructuring on the stability of information-processing networks, Journal of Management Information Systems, 24(1):201-231

Li, H.H., Chen, T.Y., Pai, L.Y. (2007). The influence of merger and acquisition activities on corporate performance in the Taiwanese telecommunications industry, Service Industries Journal, 27(7-8):1041-1051

Lin, C.Y.Y., Wei, Y.C. (2006). The role of business ethics in merger and acquisition success: An empirical study, Journal of Business Ethics, 69(1):95-109

Marino, A.M., Zabojnik, J. (2006). Merger, ease of entry and entry deterrence in a dynamic model, Journal of Industrial Economics, 54(3):397-423

Miller, D., Friesen, P.H. (1984). A longitudinal study of the corporate life cycle. Management Science, 30(10):1161-1183

Mo, J.P.T., Beckett, R.C., Nemes, L. (2005). Technology Infrastructure for Virtual Organisation of Toolmakers. Collaborative Networks and Their Breeding Environments: IFIP TC5 WG 5.5 Sixth IFIP Working Conference on VIRTUAL ENTERPRISES, PRO-VE'05, Editors: Luis M. Camarinha-Matos, Hamideh Afsarmanesh, Angel Ortiz, Valencia, Spain, 26-28 September, ISBN: 0-387-28259-9, pp.493-500

Oberg, C., Henneberg, S.C., Mouzas, S. (2007). Changing network pictures: Evidence from mergers and acquisitions. Industrial Marketing Management, 36(7):926-940

Penrose, E.T. (1952). Biological analogies in the theory of the firm,

The American Economic Review, 42(5):804-819

Sireesh, S. (2006). Embedding enterprise compliance and risk management culture into organizational DNA. InFinsia, 120(1), Feb-Mar, 48-51

Spear, S., Bowen, H. K. (1999). Decoding the DNA of the Toyota Production System, Harvard Business Review, 77(5), Sep-Oct, 96-106

Swaminathan, V, Murshed, F, Hulland, J. (2008). Value creation following merger and acquisition announcements: The role of strategic emphasis alignment, Journal of Marketing Research, 45(1):33-47

Towill, D. R. (2007). Exploiting the DNA of the Toyota Production System. International Journal of Production Research, Aug, 45(16):3619-3637

Tsai, Y.T., Hsieh, L.F. (2006). An innovation knowledge game piloted by merger and acquisition of technological assets: A case study. Journal of Engineering and Technology Management, 23(3):248-261

Van den Berg R.J., Tolle M., (2000). Assessing Ability to Execute in Virtual Enterprises. In IFIP TC5 WG5.3/5.7/5.12, Fourth International Working Conference on the Design of Information Infrastructure Systems for Manufacturing (DIISM 2000), Ed. Mo, J.P.T., Nemes, L., 15-17 November, Melbourne, Australia, pp.38-45

Vesterager, J., Tølle, M., Bernus, P. (2002). VERA: Virtual Enterprise Reference Architecture. Global Engineering and Manufacturing in Enterprise Networks - GLOBEMEN, VTT Symposium 224, 9-10 December, Helsinki, Finland, 39-52

Williams T.J. (1994). The Purdue Enterprise Reference Architecture. Computers in Industry, 24(2-3):141-158

Williams T.J., Bernus P., Brosvic J., Chen D., Doumeingts G., Nemes L., Nevins J.L., Vallespir B., Vlietstra J., Zoetekouw D. (1994). Architectures for integration manufacturing activities and enterprises. Computers in Industry, 24:111-139

Yin, X.L., Shanley, M. (2008). Industry determinants of the "merger versus alliance" decision. Academy of Management Review, 33(2):473-491

Zwegers A., Tolle M., Vesterager J. (2003). VERAM: Virtual Enterprise Reference Architecture and Methodology. Global Engineering and Manufacturing in Enterprise Networks - GLOBEMEN, VTT Symposium 224, 9-10 December, Helsinki, Finland. (Ed) I. Karvonen, R. van den Berg, P. Bernus, Y. Fukuda, M. Hannus, I. Hartel, J. Vesterager, pp.17-38

About the Authors

Professor John Mo is the Discipline Head for Manufacturing and Materials Engineering at the RMIT University, Melbourne, Australia. Prior to this, John was the Team Leader of the Manufacturing Systems and Infrastructure Networks research group in the Division of Manufacturing and Infrastructure Technology of Commonwealth Scientific and Industrial Research Organisation (CSIRO). John led several large scale international projects involving multidisciplinary teams in the development of advanced project collaboration systems for designing one-off facilities such as chemical plants and high value computer controlled assets. His team of 15 professionals had completed projects on developing methodologies for risk analysis, critical infrastructure protection modeling, electricity market simulation, wireless communication, fault detection and production scheduling. He also led the National EPC Network Demonstrator Project and its extension, which were the first EPC implementations conforming to the EPC Global standard. He obtained his PhD from Loughborough University, UK. John is a Fellow of the Institution of Engineers, Australia. John Mo can be reached at john.mo@rmit.edu.au.

Dr. Laszlo Nemes was Chief Research Scientist and Science Director in the Division of Manufacturing and Infrastructure Technology of the Commonwealth Scientific and Industrial Research Organisation (CSIRO) Australia. He led a research program with more than 50 staff working on enterprise integration, machine vision, autonomous robotics, signal diagnostics and process control. In addition, he also led complex international research teams to complete large, industry related R&D projects in the area of computer aided design and manufacturing, within the international Intelligent Manufacturing Systems program. His achievements are hallmarked with six industry related patents; over 100 papers published internationally, and six books/monographs. His major achievement, the development of the Generic Enterprise Reference Architecture, was developed in a team of international experts and was endorsed as the Annex to ISO enterprise engineering standard. Dr Nemes is a Fellow of the Australian Academy of Technological Sciences and Engineering, and Fellow of the Institution of Engineers, Australia. Laszlo Nemes can be reached at laszlo@nemes.com.au.

Chapter 10

APPLYING ENTERPRISE ARCHITECTURE FOR CRISIS MANAGEMENT: A CASE OF THE HELLENIC MINISTRY OF FOREIGN AFFAIRS

Leonidas G. Anthopoulos

Editors' Preface

In most Governments, the response to crises is largely reactive. Applying EA, governments develop their plans and largely follow them to transition to the target architecture. Following the plan makes things relatively easier as outcomes are usually predictable. Hence the focus tends to be more on efficiency and effectiveness (alignment and assurance). Management of crises, where organizations must learn to deal with unpredictable situations can make things challenging and complex. In addition to alignment and assurance, responsiveness to the crises becomes an imperative.

The application of EA has been largely under conditions of 'normalcy' or 'business-as-usual' type of scenarios. However, in many scenarios, organizations must fine-tune their processes, services and policies to enable crisis management methods and integrate them into their EA. This chapter is an application of EA for crises management with special focus on the Hellenic Ministry of Foreign Affairs (Greece). There is very little literature on how EA can be leveraged in situations of crises. The chapter is particularly unique because it presents the case study of a government organization that is specifically tasked to manage crises [unlike the US Government's Federal Emergency Management Agency (FEMA) for instance]. This uniqueness brings forth several interesting insights and also proposes a 'crises architecture'. The chapter elaborates on how 'crises architecture' demands different practices, mechanisms and approaches as compared to the normal EA. The key success factor for EA applied in situations of crises is agility, i.e. how quickly the organization can respond decisively. It is beyond doubt that, in such cases, organizational coherence is critical.

Introduction

Enterprise Architecture (EA) evolves as the key element in the implementation of an organization or enterprise's mission. According to (McGovern, Ambler, Stevens, Linn, Sharan and Jo, 2003) for an enterprise or organization, the EA defines the blueprints of the Information Technology (IT) infrastructures that will be installed and used for the production of new services or products. For a public organization, the EA defines the architect principles and standards for the IT – analyzed in different layers, in order for the strategic mission of the organization to be safely implemented – and secures the alignment, agility and assurance of the architecture at all levels (Doucet, Gøtze, Saha and Bernard, 2008).

EA is becoming a critical part of every e-Government strategic plan. Most well known e-Government plans (US, British, Canadian and German) have adopted different EAs, analyzing their IT architectures in different layers of interest and considering e-Government from different points of view. EAs used for e-Government plan implementation have many similarities and deal with comparable considerations.

In this chapter, it is considered that the political/business perspective of an EA has implications beyond the targets of a strategic plan. These implications arise during or after the implementation of various projects contained in the plan, basically extracted from crises. Most crises can be predicted during the project planning and can be handled as risks. However, in many cases unpredicted scenarios demand crisis management methods. Since EA is designed with the involvement of multiple stakeholders (supervisors, politicians or public seniors), the incorporation of crisis architecture in EA is proposed.

The incorporation of crisis architecture embeds crisis management in EA and can secure the coherency among projects, and the organization's coherency. Crisis management can support the avoidance of project re-engineering - as can be seen in the presented case of the Hellenic Ministry of Foreign Affairs -, which can affect EA standards and organization strategic targets.

Chapter's Background

According to (Chief Information Officers (CIO), 2001) "Enterprise Architecture (EA) is a strategic information asset base, which defines the mission, the information necessary to perform the mission and the necessary technologies, and the transitional processes for implementing new technologies in response to the changing mission needs. EA includes a baseline architecture, target architecture and a sequence plan". EA is accompanied by a specific framework (CIO, 1999) containing the proper procedures that a given public Agency needs to follow in order to implement the EA. EA within this context seeks to solve for intellectual manageability (McGovern et. al., 2003). Architecture of large projects is complex, large, and it is influenced by novelty and by state-of-the-art technology in some cases. EA aims to provide a way to hide unnecessary detail, simplify difficult-to-understand concepts, and break down project goals into better-understood components.

The US mission for e-Government was mapped on a US strategic plan and it is supported by the Federal Enterprise Architecture (FEA) (CIO, 2001). FEA was inspired by Zachman's model (Zachman, 1987) and adopted the National Institute of Standards and Technology (NIST) model (CIO, 1999), containing the business, information, information systems, and data and delivery systems architectures layers. British Government approved its EA in 2005 (UK CIO, 2005) calling it the "cross-Government Enterprise Architecture (xGEA)", describing the common "business-led vision" and procedures for British Administration. German EA is called the SAGA Framework (KBSt Publication Series, 2003) and contains centrally selected, common solutions and standards for IT projects in the German Administration. Furthermore, the framework presents different perspectives that the IT architecture designers in public Administration must follow for e-Government projects. The Federal Government of Canada designed its e-Government Strategic plan – "Government on-Line (GOL)" (Treasury Board Secretariat, Government of Canada, 2001) – in 1999. GOL strategy has evolved into the Service Oriented Architecture (SOA) Strategy (Treasury Board Secretariat, Government of Canada, 2006). Service orientation is defined as "the planning and delivery of all services by formally componentizing each of the services and their subordinate services such that the overall collection of services work as a whole and supports a high level master-plans." The Canadian SOA can be considered as its EA since it contains the vision, the rules and the methods for e-Government, to be complied with by all public agencies.

All of the above strategic plans are analyzed in projects. A project does not define an EA. Instead, projects are components of a strategic plan, aimed at specific targets of the global political mission, and have to follow the EA defined by the mission stakeholders. According to (Project Management Institute, 2004), a project is "a temporary endeavor undertaken to create a unique product or service". Temporary means that the project has an end date. Unique means that the project's end result is different than the results of other functions of an organization. Project Management (Philips, 2004) is the supervision and control of the work required to complete the project vision. The project team carries out the work needed to complete the project, while the project manager schedules, monitors, and controls the various project tasks. Projects, being the temporary and unique things that they are, require the project manager to be actively involved in the project implementation. They are not self-propelled.

Within a project, risks (Philips, 2004) "are unplanned events or conditions that can have a positive or negative effect on its success. Not all risks are bad, but almost all are seen as a threat. In order to handle risks, risk management is applied". Risk Management (Philips, 2004) "is a process undertaken by the project manager and the project team, by which risks are identified, analyzed and evaluated, and actions are applied to deal with these threats".

According to the above definition, risks are unwanted threats, which, if they occur, cause crises. There are many definitions of crisis. Wordnet (WordNet, 2008) defines crisis as "an unstable situation of extreme danger or difficulty". In (Wikipedia, 2008) crisis is considered as "an incident that may occur on a personal or societal level. It may be a traumatic or stressful change in a person's life, or an unstable and dangerous social situation, in political, social, economic, military affairs, or a large-scale environmental event, especially one involving an impending abrupt change. More loosely, it is a term meaning 'a testing time' or 'emergency event'".

Different crises are treated by different means. However, the manipulation of a crisis is based on crisis management methodologies. According to (NATO, 2008), crisis management, "stands for coordinated actions taken to diffuse crises, prevent their escalation into armed conflict and/or contain resulting hostilities. The crisis management machinery provides decision-makers with the necessary information and arrangements to use appropriate instruments (political, diplomatic, economic, and military) in a timely and coordinated manner". The above definition considers crisis as an event that can lead to armed conflicts. Extending the NATO approach, crisis management can be considered as "coordinated activities using political, diplomatic, economic and military tools and methods for handling crises and avoiding further unwanted situations". A crisis management plan contains critical decisions (Lund, 2002) that can be grouped as a) when is action taken, b) what action is taken, c) who takes action, d) how is action taken, and e) where is action most likely to be effective.

It is obvious that crises can occur in everyday life and usually concern social, political, economic, environmental and military phenomena. However, crises can occur during IT project implementation, causing unwanted results on a regional or wider level, since internet growth changes geopolitical balances. From this point of view, EA in e-Government strategies has implications beyond local or national visions.

Enterprise Architecture and Political Implications

Every enterprise or organization plans its strategy for evolution. E-government can be seen as a public organization's transformation by information technologies, aiming at simplifying public transactions, securing citizen satisfaction and minimizing operational costs (Wimmer, Traunmuller, 2000), (Devadoss, Pan, Huang, 2002). EA can support public organization transformation (Doucet et. al., 2008): *Foundation EA* provides the organizing logic and the IT capabilities (policies and technical choices) of a public agency or an enterprise, in order to align IT to the operational processes. *Extended EA* offers tolls and approaches for engineering an entire organization, to align on common standards and methods. With the extended approach, EA is recognized as a key change management tool that provides methods to align new, growing non-IT business functions coherently. By following the extended EA, public organizations can effectively transform their units and internal procedures, mostly in order to conform to top-down strategic planning

(Anthopoulos, Siozos, Tsoukalas, 2007). With *Embedded EA*, tools, methods and models become embedded in the daily workflow of the organization.

The transformation of an enterprise or a public organization has political results, some of which have been predicted in the EA: an enterprise that minimizes operational costs can see its shares rise on the stock market. Moreover, an enterprise can deliver new products and services as outcomes of its transformation. A public organization that delivers more and better public services, achieves citizen satisfaction. Political supervisors of such organizations expect their popularity to grow when EA succeeds in establishing coherency in the organization's operations, and in delivering services effectively, or they can see their popularity fall after EA failures in securing a coherent environment.

However, some political fallout cannot be predicted during strategic planning. For instance, blogs and other social networks evolved independently after the broadband revolution – which was part of almost all e-Government strategic plans – and deliver social participation and free dialogues quicker than e-democracy projects. Today, social networks and bloggers affect policy-making and a politicians' popularity.

The Case Study of the Hellenic Ministry of Foreign Affairs

The case study of a small project of the Hellenic Ministry of Foreign Affairs is presented in this chapter, in order to show how the political implications of an IT crisis can impact EA and influence the policy of an organization. For reasons of national security, technical details regarding the project and the incident are not given, and they are beyond the purposes of this chapter.

The Hellenic Ministry of Foreign Affairs conducts Greek foreign policy, represents Greece before other states and international organizations, participates on its behalf in international cooperation initiatives and mechanisms at the international, European and regional levels and advocates Greek interests, both public and private, abroad. The Hellenic Ministry of Foreign Affairs (MFA) planned its IT strategy in the late 1990s. The MFA's plan had to conform to the Greek Information Society Framework Program (Greek Ministry of

Finance, 2002) and e-Europe action plan (European Commission, 2002) and consisted of multiple projects aimed at internal transformation and modernization. The MFA plan contained several information systems and infrastructures, together with software and solutions for interoperability.

The MFA strategic plan was initially not based on a specific EA. However, in 2005, during a project concerning the development of a user-friendly central web portal (www.mfa.gr), the project team investigated EA literature, defined architectural standards for further projects and composed a draft EA. Moreover, the project team considered the System, Software and Service Oriented Architecture (SOA) architectures (McGovern et. al., 2003) and provided the following principles: a) all information systems should follow n-tier architectures establishing availability, scalability and security at all layers, b) all applications should follow thin-client architecture and c) SOA should interconnect novel with legacy applications in the organization. Furthermore, the draft EA version incorporated the FEA (CIO, 2001) perspectives for IT deployment.

The central web portal was online by the end of 2005, offering public information concerning Greek foreign policy, news and announcements regarding foreign policy activities, and contact points with the MFA and with Greek Authorities abroad. The central web portal is running under the supervision of the MFA spokesman and the Information Service of the Greek MFA.

By 2007, the MFA political leadership requested the homogenization of all the web sites of Greek Missions Abroad with the web portal and hosting on the central infrastructures of the Ministry. A new project was designed, extending the MFA strategic plan and it's EA, with the incorporation of rules and standards for Greek Missions Abroad. The initial purpose of the project was to increase the infrastructures of the information system of the central portal, following the MFA EA. A sub-project was initiated to deliver a huge, scalable and extensible n-tier information system for the web portal and for the other MFA web sites. Project management techniques were selected and applied for project planning, supervision, scope, cost and time management (Philips, 2004), succeeding in sub-project design, funding and contract. A risk management plan was structured, containing all possible risks regarding the project, grouping them into technical, organizational and external risks (Philips, 2004). The risk management plan was compatible with organization policies and rules: the new system, like the old one, should be a subnet of the general information system, operating in a Demilitarized Zone (DMZ), using domain restrictions, considering the further network environment secure, and being itself unsecured until the end of the project. The contractors, who would install the new information system, had to migrate applications and data from the old system to the new one and carry out all possible tests and verifications that could confirm the stability of the new system. The new system was to go online and replace the old one only after all confirmation tests were completed.

The project had a strict time line of one-month duration, because the capacity of the old system was nearing depletion. Crisis management defined the following as possible technical risks: a) project could not be finished in a month due to delayed delivery of the infrastructures, b) application migration might fail, since the Content Management System (CMS) software that was migrated from the old system was out-of-date, and c) data migration could fail due to compatibility problems between the old and the new RDBMS. The project team that was identified by the contractor, considered as a potential organizational risk the unavailability of MFA staff during project implementation. Finally, external risks were defined, regarding possible disasters in the MFA computer room, where the project was implemented. Responses to the above risks were also planned: a) the project team executed a simulation of the project implementation in contractors' areas and was successful. The team had written specific guidelines to be followed for the project execution. b) Hardware failure should be overcome with the availability of spares.

When all the above planning was finished, the project was initiated. During the application and data migration, a hardware failure occurred in the old system and the project team was ordered by MFA officials to deliver the new system online, before the end of the project. Risk management was initiated again and the project manager was concerned about all possible external risks, seeking methods to tackle them. However, an unexpected problem occurred: the brand new system was hacked, because system strengthening was not completed and because the project team considered the network environment – beyond the system – secure. Crisis management was instantly initiated. The crisis was handled entirely by the project team and had to deal with: a) the attack and severity recognition, b) system recovery and assurance until project completion, c) suggestion of extra security methods after project completion, meaning a project extension. Until the recognition of the attack and its severity,

COHERENCY MANAGEMENT

the team was considering the redesigning and re-execution of the project as possible scenarios. Moreover, the hijack was going to harm the organization's coherency and the existing MFA EA, since project deliverables were considered unsecure to existing infrastructures and to other project deliverables. Although all technical problems were resolved and the existing EA's standards were followed entirely, the coherency between the new information system and the other ministry IT environment was harmed: the new system was under suspicion for its consistency to EA standards, such as compatibility to security and availability values.

Furthermore, the hacking incident caused the web portal to be out of order for two days, a fact that caused a political crisis in some bilateral relations. This political crisis was unexpected and the project team could not deal with it. The new crisis was handled through diplomatic channels by Ministry officials.

The incident caused the EA of the Greek MFA to be reconsidered and brought about the participation of security officials in the strategic planning. MFA incorporated crisis architecture into its EA, and involved different staff categories to predict different kinds of risks and crises that can occur during mission implementation.

Incorporating Crisis in EA

The case study of the Greek MFA shows that crises are unexpected even in cases where project teams are coordinated and where organizations support project implementations. The Greek MFA extended its EA with the incorporation of crisis architecture, in order to secure the completion of future projects, to maintain MFA's EA and secure the organization's coherency. The new MFA EA is inspired by the US Federal Enterprise Architecture (FEA) (CIO, 1999), by (Sowa, 2000) and by the Collaborating Enterprise Architecture (Anthopoulos, 2008), and consists of the following architecture layers placed in the columns of (Table 1):

a) The *organization architecture*, dealing with organization's physiognomy and vision, and national EA.

b) The *crisis architecture* that refers to the prediction of possible crises, the involved parties, the cooperating schema of the involved participants in the strategic planning and crisis management phases.

c) The *technical architecture*, which contains the technical standards for the development and interoperability of the architecture's subsystems.

d) The *data architecture* describing physical storage and repositories, file and record structure, semantics for information exchange, copyright and securing options.

e) The *user satisfaction* architecture that describes the efficiency of the architecture, since its vision and implementation are being evaluated by members of their target groups.

Architecture / Perspectives	Organization	Crisis	Technical	Data	User satisfaction
Authority	Structure	Crisis definition	SOA	Existing file and records structure	End user definition
Business	Framework, procedures	Participating processes, decision making	Process simplification	Re-usability and migration where possible	Public service definition
Financial	Budget, operational costs	Crisis costs and cost savings from crisis avoidance	Time and cost savings from investments	Storage optimization. Statistical analysis methods over data	Operational costs from transactions
Political	Organization vision	Crisis implications	Compliance with national interoperability standards and legal framework	Compliance with data accessibility initiatives	Improve user satisfaction and Agency's responses
Implementation	Representatives definition	Crisis assignment for handling	Maximize potential from existing national initiatives: Innovating where possible	Common Semantic model for data description	Case studies about usability and accessibility
Technical	Existing systems	Crisis management tools	Compliance with international standards.	Physical data models	Web and voice accessibility
Project Manager	Change management	Role assignment. Inform political officials.	Management and tools	Collect data during implementation procedures	Evaluate accessibility during implementation procedures
Administrative	Testing period definition, levels of access	Crisis evaluation and handling procedures.	Monitoring tools	Methods for statistical analysis and data monitoring.	Evaluation and improvement

Table 1. The Enterprise Architecture of the Greek Foreign Ministry

The EA presented above achieves coherency at the following axes of precedence:

a) All projects that are implemented by the Greek MFA align to the organization's vision and strategic targets defined by the political perspective.
b) All projects follow common standards, complying with organization and national technical standards, defined by the technical perspective.
c) Coherency is established among all projects, since they all focus on SOA and they all conform to interoperability standards defined by the technical architecture.

Moreover, even in crises cases, agreed processes will be followed, EA will be maintained and coherency will be secured in the organization's operations and among projects' deliverables.

The *crisis* architecture can be applied in organizations that deal with crises in their common procedures or in cases where the strategic planning has political implications. The perspectives defined in the MFA EA are not strict and can vary according to custom conditions.

A) Authority's Perspective: Defining crises

Organization stakeholders are not familiar with IT in detail, but they define mission goals, and they must maintain a "leading role" in the initiative. Stakeholders cooperate with other organization officials or with other experts who are invited for the strategic planning and its implementation (e.g., academics and professionals). All of them comprise the planning team that deals with crises. They exchange their views and their experiences from their roles in other projects they have participated in and they define possible crises. They should not underestimate risks, even in small project cases. Moreover, the team can plan crisis management, defining how they can engineer the organization services, processes and policies when crisis occurs, in order to maintain coherency during and after crises and secure project deliverables. Furthermore, the team can identify all normal (non-EA) processes to include the necessary elements (organization units involved, necessary information to be delivered, processes etc.) to deal with crises.

B) Business perspective: Participating processes, decision making

The planning team defines a collaborating schema with specific roles in crisis management. The schema must align at least the following roles: a) crisis manager who control the whole team, b) public relations leader who communicates with mass media representatives and with other parties affected by the crisis, c) engineer who will diagnose crisis results and recovery methods and d) leaders from teams of experts (e.g., engineers, diplomats, journalists etc) with whom the organization transacts. All of the teams of experts must have representatives in the planning team. The collaboration of the planning team will be based on a specific protocol with communicating and decision-making rules.

C) Financial perspective: crisis costs and cost savings from crisis avoidance

Tools and methods are required in the handling of a given crisis. The planning team must secure funding for crisis management and must estimate the costs of a crisis and of its possible resolution.

D) Political perspective: Crisis fallout

Crisis in itself affects the popularity of politicians and can damage the involved parties. However, the potential fallout from a crisis must be identified and rated, in case the planning team has to decide between risk scenarios.

E) Implementation Perspective: Crisis assignment for handling

Each crisis has a physiognomy and covers specific areas. The treatment of a crisis must be assigned to the engineer of the planning team, who is aware of the technical details of the crisis. The engineer will select the professionals who can support the handling of the crisis case. However, the leading role must be assigned to the political official who stands to lose by a given crisis. Both of them can exploit the experience of similar worst crisis cases.

F) Technical perspective: Crisis management tools

Both legacy and novel systems can generate risks in architecture. Monitoring and minimizing risks are the most important tools for the avoidance of crises. When a crisis occurs, the whole process must be centrally coordinated and monitored. The coordinator must be aware of the available resources (e.g. human resources, spares, mass media and other teams that can be approached, etc.) and allocate them instantly to avoid further unwanted results.

G) Project Manager's perspective: Role assignment. Inform political officials.

The project manager of a project that causes a crisis must have a specific role in the crisis management team. The project manager must inform the competent political officials in detail about the incident, in order for the proper crisis management team to be structured. He then informs the team members of the risk that caused the crisis, of the skills that are demanded and of possible further unwanted situations that have to be avoided.

H) Administrative perspective: Crisis evaluation and handling procedures.
When crisis occurs, all pre-evaluated costs must be allocated for handling procedures. During a crisis, the manager (political leadership) carries full responsibility and controls the management procedures. At the end of the crisis, the damage must be assessed and recovered, blame must be assigned to the responsible team members, and both reasons and treatment methods must become experience for future occasions.

Considering the Crisis Architecture in a Crisis Incident

The crisis architecture presented above, was considered and simulated in the crisis incident in the Greek MFA, in order to secure future project completion in cases with crises. For the purposes of this chapter we present how the project planning and the management of the specific crisis scenario would comply with the crisis architecture.

A) *Authority's perspective*: the crisis management team would be structured and participate in the project planning, in order to become familiar with the project, and possible security risks not to be underestimated. The team would demand detailed alignment to the organization's IT security policies during the project planning. Moreover, an official pre-defined crisis reaction schema (stakeholders, reaction rules and processes) would be incorporated in the project planning, agreed by all project stakeholders (contractor and project team).

B) *Business perspective*: the hijack event would initiate the crisis management team. The team would have to follow all pre-defined rules and processes. The successful execution of the processes would be recognizable by all organization's units and would secure the coherency among project deliverables and the organization's IT infrastructure.

C) *Financial perspective*: funding would be estimated and be secured before the project initiation. The crisis management team would use this funding to apply extra security infrastructure on the system (e.g. the installation of a web application firewall), in order to protect the system until the crisis was overcome and the project completed. This process would guarantee that during crisis management the project deliverables would be secure against further attacks.

D) *Political perspective*: the crisis management team would identify the possible political affects of the decision-making. In case the ministry web portal would stay out-of-order, possible unknown assumptions would be made by all visitors (local and international users). On the other hand, if the ministry web portal would stay online, this could cause new hijacks, with possible unwanted results. The team would propose the publishing of a temporary web page – from a different, secure system - displaying that the portal is out of order temporarily due to technical reasons. Moreover, the team would inform all missions abroad about the malfunction, in order to strengthen the avoidance of possible diplomatic implications.

E) *Implementation perspective*: the incident's technical recognition and handling would be assigned to the pre-defined engineer, who would have the flexibility to invite specials from the private sector to identify the severity and the necessary updates in the projects (e.g. the system's strengthening). The whole process would be written down and be communicated and agreed by the crisis management team.

F) *Technical perspective*: a coordinator of the crisis management team would be identified; to supervise the involved stakeholders, to be aware and secure the necessary resources, to monitor the whole management process, and to keep memos from all involved partners and executed processes.

G) *Project manager's perspective*: the project manager would participate in the crisis management team and support the decision making. He would inform the organization's political officials of the caused damage - directly after the incident - providing detailed information, while he would propose tools and methods to handle the crisis.

H) *Administrative perspective*: the political leadership (*manager*) would be informed directly by the project manager about the incident and its damage, and would secure funding for the crisis management requirements. The *manager* would support the results from the political perspective, would stay aware of the crisis management process and assign blame (e.g. would lay charges against the contractor).

Conclusions

Each EA consists of perspectives and architectures that guide the implementation of the organization's mission. However, IT projects delivering products and services can exceed technical limits and achieve political and other results. Moreover, during the implementation of a given project, risks that were not foreseen or were underestimated can become crises. Crises can impact the unique project or the entire mission. Crisis management is a tool that can deal with unwanted results or come into play when a risk occurs. This chapter described the case of a risk that could not be predicted during a small IT project in the Greek MFA. The risk became a crisis in foreign relations and officials who did not belong to the project team had to undertake management of the crisis. The presented case resulted in the extension of the Greek MFA enterprise architecture, incorporating crisis architecture into its considerations. A Foreign Ministry takes all crises seriously and deals with crises of many natures on a regular basis. The presented architecture is considered optimal for similar cases of organizations that deal with crises and where the implications of projects can damage deliverables or the credibility of stakeholders themselves. Moreover, crisis architecture can incorporate crisis management methods - such as the one of the presented case -, securing the completion of projects with risks, maintaining the EA, and establishing assurance, agility and alignment with other future, ongoing or legacy projects. Furthermore, crisis management can secure organization's coherency and coherency among projects, since project re-designing or re-engineering that can affect EA's standards and organization's operations can be avoided. The application of the crisis architecture in the crisis scenario presented above, shows that all of the organization's stakeholders would agree on specific processes and standards concerning crisis management. The agreement would obligate them when considering the crisis overcome as a fact and guarantee coherency between project deliverables and the organization's other infrastructures.

References

Anthopoulos L., Siozos P., Tsoukalas I. A. (2007) Applying Participatory Design and Collaboration in Digital Public Services for discovering and re-designing e-Government services. *Government Information Quarterly*, Volume 24, Issue 2, April 2007, Pages 353-376, Elsevier.

Anthopoulos, L. (2008) Collaborative enterprise architecture for municipal environments. In Saha, P. (ed.) *Advances in Government Enterprise Architecture*, IGI Global, Hershey, USA.

Chief Information Officer Council (1999). Federal Enterprise Architecture Framework. http://tinyurl.com/ctw6fp

Chief Information Officer Council (2001). A Practical Guide to Federal Enterprise Architecture. Version 1.0.
http://tinyurl.com/cmceo3

Devadoss, P., Pan, S., Huang, J., (2002). Structurational analysis of e-Government initiatives: a case study of SCO. *Decision Support Systems*, vol. 34, p. 253-269, Elsevier.

Doucet G., Gøtze J., Saha P., Bernard S. (2008). Coherency Management: Using Enterprise Architecture for Alignment, Agility, and Assurance. *Journal of Enterprise Architecture*, May 2008.

European Commission (2002). eEurope 2005: An information society for all. European Commission, COM 263.
http://europa.eu.int/eeurope

German Federal Government (2003). BundOnline 2005. 2003 Implementation Plan. http://www.bunde.de

Greek Ministry of Finance (2002). Greece in the Information Society. Strategy and Actions. Secretariat for the Information Society. http://www.infosociety.gr

Lund M. (2002). What Kind of Peace is Being Built? Taking Stock of Post-Conflict Peacebuilding and Charting Future Directions. What Kind of Peace Workshop, September 2002. http://tinyurl.com/dnm7uo

McGovern J., Ambler W. S., Stevens M., Linn J., Sharan V., Jo K. E., (2003) Practical Guide to Enterprise Architecture", Prentice Hall PTR, New Jersey, USA.

North Atlantic Treaty Organization (1997) NATO Logistics Handbook, October 1997, http://tinyurl.com/cohvu5

Philips, J. (2005). PMP Project Management Professional Study Guide, McGrow-Hill, Emeryville, USA.

Project Management Institute, Inc., (2004). A Guide to the Project Management Body of Knowledge, Third Edition (PMBOK Guides), Pennsylvania, USA.

Sowa, F. J. (2000) Levels of Representation. Knowledge Representation. Logical, philosophical and computational foundations. Brooks Cole Publishing Co., Pacific Grove, USA.

Treasury Board Secretariat, Government of Canada (2006). Service Oriented Architecture Strategy. http://tinyurl.com/cpyrj3

UK Chief Information Officers Council (2005). Enterprise Architecture for UK Government. An overview of the process and deliverables for Release 1. http://tinyurl.com/yvcvtn

Wikipedia (2008). Crisis Definition. http://tinyurl.com/yv9ppt. June 10, 2008

Wimmer, M., Traunmuller, R. (2000). Trends in Electronic Government: Managing Distributed Knowledge. In the Proceedings of the 11th International Workshop on Database and Expert Systems Applications 2000 (IEEE, DEXA'00).

Wordnet (2008). Crisis Definition. http://tinyurl.com/darl88. June 10, 2008

Zachman, J. A. (1987). A Framework for Information Systems Architecture, *IBM Systems Journal*, vol. 26, No. 3, 1987. http://tinyurl.com/kj2xz

About the Author

Dr. Leonidas G. Anthopoulos is an Expert Counselor at the Hellenic Ministry of Foreign Affairs, in the areas of e-Government and e-Diplomacy. He holds a BSc in Computer Science and a PHD in e-Government. In his previous position as IT researcher and manager in the Research Committee of the Aristotle University of Thessaloniki (Greece), Municipality of Trikala (Greece) and Information Society S.A. (Greece), he was responsible for planning and managing the development of multiple IT systems for the Greek Government and public organizations. He is the author of several articles published in prestigious scientific journals. His research interests include e-Government, Enterprise Architecture, Social Networks.

Acknowledgments

I would like to thank Mr Michael McCormak, executive of the Information Service of the Hellenic Ministry of Foreign Affairs, for his contribution in English reviewing and editing of this chapter. I would also like to thank Mr George Koumoutsakos, Spokesman of the Hellenic Ministry of Foreign Affairs, for his contribution during the presented case's manipulation.

Chapter 11

BRIDGING THE GAP BETWEEN EA GOALS AND TECHNOLOGY REQUIREMENTS WITH CONCEPTUAL PROGRAMMING

Jorge Marx Gómez & Thomas Biskup

Editors' Preface

Small and Medium Enterprises (SME) form the backbone of most econo-mies. One of the criticisms EA often faces is that it seems to favor large enterprises. There may be some truth in that criticism, because architec-ture by its very nature brings greater benefits to organizations that are large. John Zachman asserts that the two fundamental reasons EA is an imperative is its ability to deal with 'complexity' and 'change'. Large or-ganizations usually are more complex. However dealing with 'change' is precisely the reason why SMEs should be looking at EA. SMEs by and large have to be more responsive, agile and flexible given the unique chal-lenges they face.

The 'Conceptual Programming' approach presented in this chapter specifi-cally analyses the unique needs of SMEs and discusses how EA can be made equally useful for such enterprises. This is important, as current management and technology literature has a gap in this aspect. 'Concep-tual Programming' allows SMEs to develop and deploy IT solutions with-out having to traverse the high-ceremony EA methodologies (that as men-tioned earlier) are skewed towards the needs of large organizations. This chapter is about making EA more accessible to SMEs through the use of Conceptual Programming.

*As a realization of Model Driven Development, early results of the appli-
cation of CP are presented in this chapter. This is an excellent example of
EA in the Foundation mode, where the key intent still remains 'doing EA
to build better systems'. This, however, ought not to be underestimated as
SMEs face unique challenges.*

Enterprise Architecture and SMEs

Enterprise Architecture (EA) provides many benefits to companies
understanding this discipline as a strategic tool for business development – as many of the following chapters of this book illustrate.
Thus Enterprise Architecture should be a discipline valued by enterprises of all sizes and kinds. But as we will see the majority of the
businesses operating in current markets – that is: small to medium
sized enterprises (SMEs) – are in a difficult position in order to
make use of EA approaches and methodologies. This is particularly
critical as these enterprises might be the most hard pressed to adapt
EA due to urgent needs resulting from the way market developments exert pressure on them (Taylor 1995).

What is more, the lack of success in establishing Enterprise Architecture in SMEs creates an even greater problem with the much
needed discipline of coherency management (Doucet, Gøtze, Saha,
Bernard, 2008): SMEs are missing out on a highly successful tool for
introducing an aligned enterprise architecture that includes both IT
and business assets. Combined with the rather chaotic and extremely speedy nature of day to day business governed by the need
for continuous tactical adaptations while considering strategic perspectives, SMEs face great danger to their continuing welfare and to
their ability to compete with larger enterprises.

This chapter will explain the particular challenges faced by SMEs,
show how they could benefit from adapting EA, and present Conceptual Programming as an approach that allows the effective
adoption of EA for SMEs despite their limited financial, organizational and technological resources. Conceptual Programming fur-
thers coherency management by concentrating on introducing
foundational Enterprise Architecture to SMEs with an affordable
and workable methodology. Conceptual programming utilizes a
model- driven approach (MDD) in order to provide a coherent
documentation of the organization's IT architecture, thus allowing
SMEs to achieve the first maturity level of Foundational Enterprise

Architecture. It combines the model-driven approach with Domain Driven Design (DDD) to help them reach the second level of maturity by capturing the business of the enterprise in a standardized and consistent model-based description.

The state of small to medium sized enterprises

Small to medium sized enterprises by European standards are defined as enterprises with up to 500 employees and up to 50 million EUR annual turnover (European Commission, 2003). Taking statistical numbers from e.g. Germany, the average SME actually only generates 500.000 to 4 million EUR in annual turnover – the size pyramid of SMEs is obviously balanced towards the smaller ranged enterprises (Günterberg, Kayser 2004, pp. 15-16). The resulting restrictions on all kinds of budgets – especially IT budgets if the actual core business is non-IT-related – are obvious. Nonetheless SMEs compete – quite often in the role of market leaders for highly specialized niche solutions – with companies from all over the world and of all sizes. Consequently they must face a number of critical challenges:

- They need to operate and effectively compete in globalizing markets despite their rather local upcoming and organization.

- They compete with other SMEs from diverse countries, each operating under a vast variety of differing market and legal contexts, some advantageous, some disadvantageous.

- They need to adapt ever faster to market conditions also changing at an ever growing speed.

- They need to comply with the organizational and technological changes necessary in order to survive in e.g. supply change scenarios of complex industries (like automotive) in which they are important (although small) building blocks.

The same holds true for larger enterprises – but larger enterprises also enjoy benefits not available to SMEs that allow them to counter these challenges in a more strategic way:

- They have far more technological, organizational and financial resources at their disposal.

- Global enterprises benefit from being able to move critical processes more easily to countries in which they can operate and produce with better efficiency.

- Large enterprises possess much larger brain pools with accumulated experience in specialized technological areas when compared to SMEs.

In summary, SMEs face almost the same challenges as large enterprises in our expanding global market situation but suffer from the fact that their resources are far more limited. SMEs nonetheless so far have managed to compete as they can rely on standard software for most daily challenges. They usually need to concentrate on procuring solutions which strengthen both their unique selling propositions and the underlying internal advantages. Surprisingly this seems to be a pretty complex problem – statistics for e.g. German SMEs show that more than 50% of the software solutions used by almost 40% of all SMEs have been developed by individual programming. 15% of all SMEs rely on individually developed software for more than 75% percent of the solutions they use (TechConsult 2006). Comparing this with the limited budgets indicated by the figures beforehand, this shows a pretty dramatic situation:

- SMEs have very limited budgets, yet rely to a major part on individually developed software solutions to drive their businesses.

- The ever increasing speed with which markets and the resulting challenges to SMEs change will present a serious problem to remain competitive when considering the high degree of individually developed software together with the rather limited budgets of SMEs.

The following table summarizes the essential differences between SMEs and large enterprises:

Area	Small to medium-sized enterprises	Large enterprise
Market type	Usually a niche market or a highly specialized part of a broad market	Broad markets
Budgets for IT and business modeling	Very limited	Large
IT expertise	Usually low	Usually high
Markets	Both local and global	Usually global
Prevalent type of IT solutions for core business concerns	Individually developed solutions	Customized standard products

Table 1. Differences between SMEs and large enterprises.

Since SMEs usually are very informed about their specialized sphere of work, one can assume that this situation is caused by the fact that very few standard solutions exist for niche markets – which is obvious since standard solutions rely on economies of scale. Niche markets (especially those held by smaller companies) just don't provide the required scale effects. Consequently SMEs face no other choice but to develop individual solutions for particular niches. The methodologies applied by SME to develop software mirror the tight budget restrictions: experience in developing elaborate solutions is rare, consulting usually is not affordable (or highly limited) and solutions are thus mostly influenced by pragmatic concerns rather than a strategic perspective. This pragmatic approach naturally hinders any attempts to build a coherent architecture for IT specifically – not to mention the overall business.

The logical consequence would be to look up to scientific disciplines like software engineering, enterprise architecture and related branches in order to provide methodologies and approaches that facilitate solution development for small to medium sized enterprises. While in some areas this is happening, most scientific approaches in the still young discipline of computer science are concerned with providing effective approaches to developing solutions for complex large scale scenarios. The increasing speed of market changes thus threatens to undermine the ability of SMEs to survive in a global economy. This is a particularly dire perspective as SMEs are the foundation of our economy (Klett, Pivernetz 2004).

The Road to EA Accessibility for SMEs

Based on the aforementioned observations we decided to look into the needs of SMEs in more detail in order to distill key requirements based on the general work context of SMEs. The next section will provide the brief results of our requirements analysis. Based on this requirements analysis we will introduce our "Conceptual Programming" methodology which focuses on making the key benefits of Foundational Enterprise Architecture available to SMEs and also enables them to quick-start on the road towards an Embedded Enterprise Architecture once the basic principles of Conceptual Programming have been firmly established. We will explain the design of the methodology, the underlying principles and approaches and explain – based on experimental evaluation in the area of food surveillance – the preliminary results and effects of the approach.

IT Methodology Requirements of SMEs

As elaborated before, SMEs are characterized by heavy reliance on individually developed software solutions despite mostly very constrained budgets and limited IT expertise. The relevant experts will be under heavy strain due to the need to balance strategic projects with day to day tasks (it is e.g. quite typical for SMEs to use the available programming resources at the same time as system administrators, help desk managers, etc.). Additionally most SMEs are still owner-managed and the owners of the businesses are heavily invested in day to day decisions and work. This usually results in a very close relation between strategic planning and tactical execution of plans.

When trying to introduce Enterprise Architecture principles into such SME organizations there are obvious consequences:

- From a positive point of view the road to realizing an Embedded Enterprise Architecture is rather short – strategic IT projects usually enjoy immediate management attention and will be very tightly coupled to the core business. Additionally most actual IT projects are strategic in nature – thus it is very easy to connect IT interests with the business interests of the management board if there is an actual business case (which we assume – otherwise it would not be sensible to introduce EA).

- From a negative point of view the almost immediate management attention to such projects exerts pressure to provide tangible positive results in a short amount of time. The limited budgets of owner-managed SMEs enforce this requirement even more since there is neither time nor budget for experiments and the welfare of the individual business depends heavily on the efficient and successful use of the available resources.

- Methods must be grounded in pragmatic thinking – approaches that are too theoretical in nature usually will not be accepted due to the required investments to build up sufficient knowledge to use them (if at all). External consulting is not likely an alternative for solving this problem since the limited budgets rarely allow for extensive external consulting. On the contrary, they require building up internal competence in new tools and approaches very quickly in order to achieve self-sustainability.

COHERENCY MANAGEMENT

In summary, SMEs provide a particularly challenging environment for Enterprise Architecture approaches since they exist in as highly dynamic environments as large enterprises but in many respects are even more chaotic in their operations because the overall competence in IT related methodologies is usually weaker compared to large enterprises. Additionally, roles are less clear: business expertise often is tightly coupled with top management, guaranteeing management attention for better or worse at all project stages while introducing new strategic IT concepts. Methodologies for introducing coherent enterprise architectures thus need to be particularly careful to take into account the resulting requirements of the target audience.

Despite these challenges we regard coherency management as one of the most important IT topics for SMEs due to a simple fact: as explained above, the global market environment becomes more and more challenging for SMEs due to their inherent structural limitations – thus a methodology streamlining IT concerns, architectures and technologies is extremely valuable because it simplifies future changes and allows better adaptation to changing market requirements. Effectively, SMEs embracing and mastering the discipline of coherency management will thus become a lot more competitive and in their particular niches and will even enjoy advantages compared to large enterprises which usually are much slower to adapt to new circumstances. Thus a weak start position could be turned into a very strong mid-term position for SMEs occupying coveted niches.

We will introduce Conceptual Programming as one methodology facilitating the introduction of coherence management into SMEs as a strategic discipline.

Conceptual Programming (CP) as an EA Enabler

Our methodology of Conceptual Programming is firmly grounded in the basic tenets and beliefs of foundational EA: We strive to provide a development methodology that greatly simplifies the development of domain-specific applications while at the same time generating formal and precise specifications due to the strict use of a model driven approach (for an actual example concerning semantic web technologies see Biskup, Marx Gómez, 2006).

The basic idea of our Conceptual Programming methodology is to model systems through intuitive models on a strong conceptual level. These models must not be based on one global theory (like e.g. MDA with the Meta Object Facility, see Object Management Group 2006) but rather utilize the most pragmatic theoretical foundation suitable for the problem at hand. Additionally, the models should abstract the technological details as much as possible and focus on the conceptual business facets of one particular domain wherever feasible. Detailed models are aggregated into more general models while great care is taken to provide a simple transformation from the individual model to the runtime representation of the model. This allows software developers and architects to work together with customers and business experts concentrating on the business side of the system.

Of greatest importance is the way in which CP based models are made available to the conceptual experts at hand: we require that models use a language that comes as close as possible to the tools and ways used by the target audience to express their concepts. Thus the way of modeling will differ between areas of expertise. While this might at first feel like a disadvantage because software engineers will have to learn various differing modeling languages, we regard this as an advantage: the rules for transforming and executing these models need only be understood by a very small number of persons – namely persons who build the actual transformations or interpreters. In contrast the user base for the concepts modeled typically will be very large in comparison. Thus it seems more reasonable to build models which are intuitive for the end user base and not the (intermediate) developers. Additionally it benefits the developers by forcing them to concentrate on the conceptual aspects of development while hiding the technical details.

One might argue that this is just a step back to the "model wars" in the years from 1990 to 2000 before the advent of UML. We argue that UML and similar OMG approaches did not really solve those problems as far as the actual specification of conceptual tasks goes. UML provides very effective models in order to specify technical details – but those technical details mostly are of no interest at all to the conceptual experts at hand who require a solution for their (non-technical) problems. The gap between available tools for specifying technical aspects and the lack of suitable tools for formally specifying the purely conceptual parts of a problem leads to a high number of failing software projects (failing software projects are those that fail to meet their goals in time, money or quality, see Hartmann 2006).

Studies concerning the success and failure of software projects seem to prove this point (Standish Group 1994): more than 75% of all unsuccessful software projects failed due to problems with requirements analysis and errors in the resulting specifications. We thus argue that more problem-oriented models are a necessity in order to facilitate the communication between technical and non-technical experts.

Since our CP methodology additionally requires Rapid Prototyping (Reilly 1996) as a means to be easily able to verify specifications, we implicitly provide a means between the Enterprise Architecture notions of Foundational Architecture, Extended Architecture and Embedded Architecture:

- The conceptual makeup of the model allows all business levels to become immediately involved in the solution design process. There is no artificial barrier that requires starting the introduction of Enterprise Architecture on a technical project level (Foundation Architecture) and from there taking the arduous path of extended and embedded architectures. Right from the start the foundations for an embedded architecture are provided.

- The prototyping approach easily overcomes important psychological boundaries when introducing new technological architectures: for non-IT experts the true benefits of a new architecture are hard to discern and the fear of change slows or even completely inhibits the required alterations to business processes. Rapid prototyping provides immediate results ("things to touch") and exemplifies the benefits of the Conceptual Programming approach to Enterprise Architecture by actions instead of by words and presentation slides.

We have experienced the latter benefit quite often with customers who initially were not convinced of introducing EA concepts into their business – as soon as results were easy to understand due to the conceptual model design and provided almost immediately tangible results, the overall mood and energy required for the business transformation process changed to a much more favorable level. The resulting projects benefited from this benevolent stance throughout the project lifecycle.

In the following sections we will explain the CP approach in more detail and illustrate its benefits for introducing Enterprise Architecture approaches into businesses.

The Basic Methodology: CP = CMDSD + CDPM

Conceptual Programming (CP) consists of two parts:

- Conceptual Model Driven Software Development (CMDSD) describes how to build model-based generative frameworks and tools that facilitate the domain driven (conceptual) specification of software solutions at a high abstraction level.

- Concept Driven Project Management (CDPM) explains how to utilize the CMDSD based tools and frameworks in projects in order to enable the creation of flexible software architectures and solutions for SMEs based on a highly agile, model driven project methodology.

Conceptual Programming thus enables the introduction of formalized and coherent enterprise architectures by combining the strengths and advantages of the following four basic software engineering principles:

- Conceptual Programming is based firmly on Domain Driven Design (Evans 2004) in that it relies on terms and concepts from the customer domain wherever available. This helps to directly connect to the target audience and allows communicating in a most immediate manner about the actual business purposes of the underlying target architectures. The return on invest (ROI) usually becomes much more tangible due to this approach since the target audience is directly shown that the methodology is not just a means to introduce more complex IT solutions but rather helps to formalize the business needs of the particular company. Additionally the domain driven approach helps to create coherence by using terms and relations from the actual problem domain instead of mapping technical terms and concepts in an error-prone way to domain terms (like e.g. quite often happens with classical approaches, Standish Group 1994). The domain centricity of Conceptual Programming thus solves the isolation problem many of today's EA efforts are experiencing since it basically enforces close communication with business experts and prevents the IT experts and consultants from hiding behind complex IT topics.

- Conceptual Programming uses agile software development processes to model the business requirements. CP has been especially inspired by Extreme Programming (XP, Beck, Andres 2005). We take the "on site customer" practice one step further by defining conceptual pair programming) as one of the essential methods of our approach: The business experts and the IT experts model the future architecture and solutions in tightly coupled processes, working together as teams for the whole time. This provides a deeper understanding for both the IT and business requirements and enables the team to manage changing requirements in a most immediate way. Additionally the agile approach (especially due to its iterative and evolutionary take on solution modeling in combination with rapid prototyping as the central means to validate models) helps to make utmost use of the aforementioned rather limited budgets of SMEs. Return on invest is immediate and models can be evaluated in a very effective way since the resulting IT consequences can be reviewed in a most immediate manner. This immediacy is only possible due to the highly domain centric approach and the somewhat more limited complexities faced by SMEs.

- To facilitate the need for coherence and alignment we rely on model driven generative approaches (Czarnecki, Eisenecker 2000): With CMDSD domain specific models are developed in a specialized way that focuses the domain driven approach and abstracts from technical concepts as far as possible (e.g. the models hide both an underlying standardized IT architecture and the technical implementation details from domain experts). Models can be transformed directly into executable solutions (as we will explain by example in the final sections of this chapter). Thus the need to use manual programming for solution development is strongly reduced. Since general transformations and generators are used to create specific solutions we automatically achieve alignment: all levels of the business will be modeled in a similar fashion thus winning over all levels of business units with a method that supports intercompany communication and exchange of experiences. Additionally the model driven approach takes care of one of the greatest weaknesses of the EA approach: With more classical methodologies EA often feels "just like creating a lot of documentation with no tangible results" – with Conceptual Programming the model based documentation is directly used to generate architectures and specific solutions and thus immediately becomes a valuable and cherished artifact.

- To stress the idea of coherence, Conceptual Programming is development-wise based on the ideas of Software Product Lines (SPLs) which support creating variant instances from a coherent and orderly foundation (Clements, Northrop 2002). Since a domain specific SPL is used as the basis for model transformation a unified architecture can be achieved despite taking into account the individual requirements.

In summary, Conceptual Programming introduces Foundational EA in a most immediate and direct manner due to its model driven rapid prototyping approach: IT systems are generated from models in a simple and efficient approach (only possible due to its high domain centricity) usually leading to a quick adoption on all business levels. After initial evaluation of projects, this usually leads to an Extended EA in a rather short time period since the success of the initial prototype projects compel business experts to extend the Conceptual Programming usage to strategic, business and technological solution modeling.

The Road to Embedded EA

Evaluation projects conducted together with the QuinScape GmbH have proven the viability of this approach in several dozen SME related projects. The final step of establishing an Embedded EA is more involved and, due to space constraints, beyond the scope of this chapter: its chances for success highly depend on the company culture of the individual SME and the management support gathered in the initial steps – in some cases support was so strong that an Embedded EA seemed like a natural consequence and evolved in a most immediate way, in other cases the approach was not adopted by a sufficient amount of business users due to communication problems between the early adopters and the rest of the company. Preliminary results show that it is most important to win over respected and domain centric early adopters when trying to be successful in establishing an Embedded EA – if early adopters are too IT centric or belong to niche departments the overall probability of introducing an Embedded EA is strongly reduced.

As mentioned before, Conceptual Programming uses Software Product Lines (SPLs) as a structural foundation for establishing a basic architecture and an evolutionary path for more involved architectures. Additionally, it includes tools to design a coherent enterprise architecture and system landscape due to its inherently model driven approach as well as facilitating business design because of its strong grounding in a domain driven design based approach for its tools. Thus it establishes a spawning ground for embedded EA.

In the next two sections we will briefly show how Conceptual Programming with its subsystems of CMDSD and CDPM is integrated with the SPL approach by extending two of the three essential activities of SPLs: Core Asset Development and Product Development. Figure 1 exemplifies this.

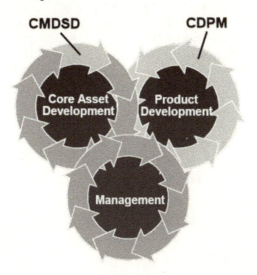

Figure 1. CMDSD and CDPM as Extensions to SPL Activities

Conceptual Model Driven Software Development (CMDSD)

Conceptual Model Driven Software Development extends the *Core Asset Development* activity defined for SPLs by adding an additional phase that we have termed "Model Modeling". The key idea behind this phase is the necessity to find model representations that fulfil the following requirements:

- The models refer to the domain terms used by the domain experts.

- The models use a high abstraction level so that domain experts will not be adversely affected by technical details.

- The models can be represented by simple yet powerful – preferably graphical – notations so that documentation can be easily understood.

- The models are designed in a top down manner – from the most abstract overviews to more specific models. Usually one model represents but one important domain concept.

Concept Driven Project Management (CDPM)

Concept Driven Project Management is a micro model for the implementation phase of SPLs' product development activity. It is based on an iterative model-based rapid prototyping approach that stresses the communication between domain and IT experts about the problems to be solved. Figure 2 shows the simple proposed control loop designed to maximize conceptual communication.

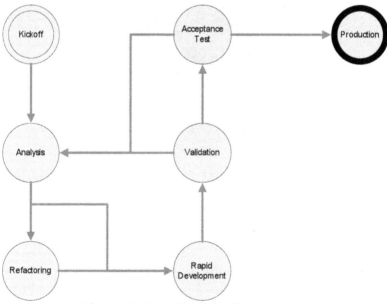

Figure 2. The CDPM micro process

After the implementation kick-off, an analysis phase determines the initial stories to be implemented. Analysis is followed by either an optional refactoring phase (starting with the second iteration) or a rapid development phase. During rapid development the method of conceptual pair programming (as explained in previous sections) is used to model the required solutions and establish the necessary architecture. Rapid development is again succeeded by a validation phase. In this phase the generated prototypes will be used to validate the modeled concepts. When all stories have been tackled, acceptance tests are conducted. When the acceptance test phase is finished successfully, the solution is turned over into production.

As can be seen, the CDPM micro process is an evolution of existing phase models that focuses and refines particularly successful aspects garnered from various agile approaches (especially by combining the "on site customer" idea of Extreme Programming with the notion of "Pair Programming" and a rapid prototyping approach into "conceptual pair programming"). Conceptual pair programming in actual projects is one of the strongest points of CDPM because it greatly simplifies communication and builds even more trust between developers and customers resulting in far less stressful projects.

It should be noted that this micro process is part of an iterative macro process so that further evolutionary refinements required by strategic goals will result in iterative refinements on the micro level. Additionally, we would like to stress the effect of the above process model on communication: we have taken great care to involve both domain experts and IT experts in all phases of the micro process to create a feeling of understanding for both the problems and solutions concerning each individual group. As explained before, this tight connection helps to facilitate the assimilation of complex technical issues like Enterprise Architecture into the business mainstream.

Additionally, the approach stresses one of the fundamental outcomes of coherency management – agility – by optimizing service delivery with the combination of several highly successful development methodologies:

- It uses rapid prototyping for quick feedback.
- It directly involves the customers in conceptual pair programming in order to improve project team communication.
- It employs model driven development in order to align the prototypical systems into coherent system architectures.

During the development of our CDPM micro process we considered subsuming it into some larger accepted project management approach like e.g. the Rational Unified Process (RUP). After some early experimental attempts we refrained from this idea since we quickly had to recognize that e.g. the RUP is highly unsuited for the main target group of our approach, namely SMEs. The main reason for this is the rather complex and time-consuming setup of a tailored RUP process which does not fit very well into the contextual limitations of SMEs explained in prior sections. Future research work will cope with the question of how Conceptual Programming can be fitted into approaches like RUP in order to be easily integrated into such IT processes for larger enterprises.

Evaluation of Conceptual Programming

To prove the benefits of Conceptual Programming, we transferred our theoretical design to several problem areas. This work was conducted in cooperation with several German companies: the Quin-Scape GmbH, an expert for portal based solutions (QuinScape 2008) and the BALVI GmbH, a market leader for IT solutions in food surveillance for the public sector (BALVI 2008) together with the faculty of business informatics at the University of Oldenburg (Wirtschaftsinformatik Universität Oldenburg, 2008). Here we will present some results gathered while designing the next food surveillance product generation for the BALVI GmbH.

BALVI has been providing such solutions for about 15 years and its flagship product BALVI iP is used throughout Germany. The current product is based on Windows Client technology, developed in the Delphi programming language and only takes into account the German context. Nonetheless a lot of experience concerning food surveillance has been accumulated and is going to be introduced into the next product generation – BALVI iP International.

Requirements Analysis

In 2007 BALVI decided to introduce the next generation of their flagship product "BALVI iP". Central requirements for designing and developing the new product generation "BALVI iP International" are:

- The need to provide portal based solutions for a growing and more dynamic user base.

- The ability to provide solutions not only on a German level but rather for international scenarios.

- The necessity to enhance the flexibility of internal structures in order to be able to model more diverse international scenarios.

- The ability to work closely with the existing team of domain analysts and experts who have been designing the business requirements of BALVI iP for the past ten years.

The Strategic Implementation Methodology

Various options for an appropriate development and design process were evaluated. The setup of BALVI as a product company made it clear from the beginning that a coherent enterprise architecture would need to be provided for a unified product line despite the highly varying organizational differences of food surveillance on a global level. Finally Conceptual Programming was chosen as the methodology to use for the following reasons:

- The model driven approach provides for high flexibility in the face of ever changing technological requirements. At the same time it allows for a tight involvement of the available domain experts due to its domain driven nature.

- The agile rapid prototyping approach most efficiently employs the existing (limited) budgets for developing the next generation solutions because evaluation feedback can be garnered immediately by examining the prototypes and then evolving the models in the desired directions.

- The grounding in software product lines is a natural fit for a product company that needs to rely for its business model on a unified infrastructure for individualized solutions.

Since the BALVI domain experts were accustomed to designing software solutions within the concepts of data structures, screen designs and workflows (while describing the more complex domain tasks in a written manner), the CMDSD methodology of Conceptual Programming was used to develop models that allow the continuation of this practice on a high abstraction level.

The Model Design Approach

We will give an overview of these domain centric models below – before doing this we must stress that the technological consequences of generating executable solutions from these models are completely hidden to the domain experts: the fact that JavaEE based multi-tier web applications employing AJAX, DHTML and object relational mapping frameworks (for example) are used by the automatic transformations to actually provide executable solutions is mostly unknown (and not of interest) to the domain experts. Nonetheless, the generative approach used by Conceptual Programming creates a completely coherent and aligned architecture for food surveillance organizations since the transformations are defined centrally and all models are handled in a unified manner.

To allow for a most immediate involvement of the existing domain experts (who throughout were neither accustomed to model driven approaches nor to web applications as a technology platform) the models were created in such a way as to hide almost all technological implications and allow for a straightforward top down design approach. Initial models will structure the application and its modules on a very high level, follow-up models slowly drill down into more detailed depths of the application.

Model Examples

Food surveillance software basically contains two major parts of functionality: on one hand flexible means to input data for a vast variety of processes are required; on the other hand powerful reporting functionality needs to be provided. Consequently, interface designs and workflows make up a major part of the model design while reporting requirements usually are specified by legal documents.

On the topmost level the various processes supported by the food surveillance solution are structured with a model quite similar to mind maps that allows defining process groups and subgroups in a very simple manner. Obviously, navigation hierarchies can be easily generated (which e.g. must contain additional sub models defining access permissions to individual processes). Figure 3 shows part of the application as an example.

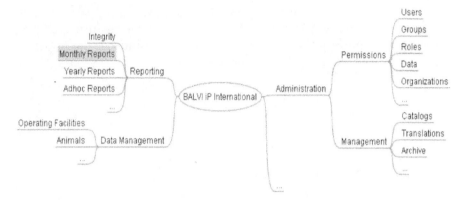

Figure 3. Navigation Model

Each node in the navigation model can point to a process model – if necessary several nodes can point to the same process model (but with e.g. differing access permissions). For brevity we leave out the permission models – picture them as simple access control lists.

Process models in turn use a limited number of states to model user workflows: (sub) process start states, view states, decision states and (sub) process end states. Arrows represent transitions between states and are annotated with so called transition models that contain further sub models like e.g. action models representing the actual activities executed during a transition (for the sake of brevity simply imagine transition models as a kind of action list with standardized actions from the food surveillance domain). Figure 4 shows a small example.

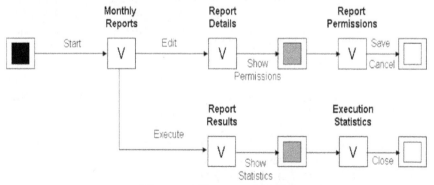

Figure 4. Process Model

Each view state in turn is described by a view model which basically is equal to a WYSIWYG representation of the resulting UI and contains all the required information for data binding etc. Figure 5 shows an example.

Figure 5. View Model

Further models include filter models (for logical conditions), interface models (for inter-process communication), agent models (to describe background processes), permission models (to model access control lists, etc.) and more.

Preliminary Results

So far the introduction of a CP based approach has been very successful. Early adopters of BALVI were able to start almost immediately with the design of the next generation product line. Architectural decisions could be evolved during the process, extension points have been introduced into the architecture to take care of future requirements. The coherent architecture resulting from the model driven approach already yields many benefits, since recurring patterns are identified again and again and allow for a high component reuse throughout the resulting architecture. The agile approach produced tangible results early on which in turn helped in winning over the whole of BALVI to the approach and provided a convincing business case for its viability. During the first seven months since the start of the project in October 2007, not only the basic models explained above were designed, but the transformations to executable solutions have also been implemented to a large degree. Additionally, the domain experts became directly involved in the project from day one and in a short time were able to use the models derived during the initial modeling phase to specify solution modules for the core product. This strategy will be continued, the first milestones being pilot installations of the new software generation in Germany during 2009. The short period of time from the initial decision to use Conceptual Programming to the release of the first pilot solutions based on the new approach stresses the strengths of Conceptual Programming: despite the highly involved methodology, the focus on a specific business domain and the generative approach allowed for the creation of actual results in a very short period of time.

Summary

This chapter has introduced Conceptual Programming as a strategic foundational tool in order to align IT systems into a coherent system architecture and landscape, especially suited for the context of small to medium sized enterprises. SMEs are characterized by having to compete in as dynamic environments as large scale enterprises, yet suffering from even more chaotic operating environments due to rather limited resources and tight coupling between management and business expertise (resulting in more tactical and less strategic business perspective). We have shown how a combination of agile rapid prototyping, a model driven and generative approach grounded on software product lines and a highly focused domain centric view of the business domain results in a coherent and more easily aligned enterprise architecture approach for SMEs.

Additionally we have explained how Conceptual Programming supports the five main advantages of establishing Enterprise Architecture in an enterprise (Doucet, Gøtze, Saha, Bernard 2008):

1. CP helps to understand business operations much better by explicitly modeling the business domain on a high conceptual level and setting up the whole development approach as an inherent model driven methodology.

2. CP treats information as a core asset by directly involving the business experts in the process of information accumulation and formalization due to its discipline of conceptual pair programming.

3. CP narrows the gap between the needs of the business and the deliveries of IT departments by setting up an immediate and di-

rect feedback channel, again through conceptual pair programming.

4. CP creates synergies between existing and emerging technologies by allowing the developers to evolve the technological foundation of the modeled systems because due to the chosen approach implementation technologies can be exchanged without requiring any changes to the business models.

5. CP helps in the discovery of new business opportunities and optimizations by allowing the quick evaluation of new business approaches due to its foundation in rapid prototyping processes.

Thus Conceptual Programming also guarantees the third expected outcome of successfully established Enterprise Architecture approaches – assurance – to non-IT management stakeholders by providing a formal and unified (model driven) development approach.

Future work focuses on transforming Conceptual Programming into a highly specialized method template to be able to evolve domain specific instances in an even more efficient manner. A Ph.D. thesis and various master thesis works at the University of Oldenburg continue to evolve this approach while working closely with various industry partners in order to validate the theoretical foundation of the methodology.

References

BALVI GmbH (2008). http://www.balvi.de.

Beck, K., Andres, C. (2005). Extreme Programming Explained. Embrace Change. Second Edition, Addison-Wesley, Boston.

Biskup, T.; Marx Gómez, J. (2006). Conceptual Model Driven Software Development (CMDSD) as a Catalyst Methodology for Building Sound Semantic Web Frameworks; in: Radaideh, M. (ed.): Architecture of Reliable Web Applications Software. Idea Group Publishing Hershey (PA), London.

Clements, P., Northrop, L. (2002). Software Product Lines. Practices and Patterns, Addison-Wesley.

Czarnecki, K., Eisenecker, U. (2000). Generative Programming: Methods, Tools, and Applications, Addison-Wesley Professional.

Doucet, G., Gøtze, J., Saha, P., Bernard, S. (2008). Coherency Management: Using Enterprise Architecture for Alignment, Agility, and Assurance. Journal of Enterprise Architecture, May 2008.

Evans, E. (2004). Domain Driven Design — Tackling Complexity in the Heart of Software, Pearson Education, Inc., New Jersey.

European Commission (2003). Recommendation 2003/361/ KMUDefinition, http://tinyurl.com/czjj9a

Günterberg, B., Kayser, G. (2004). SMEs in Germany, Facts and Figures 2004, Statistisches Bundesamt Bonn.

Hartmann, D. (2006). Interview: Jim Johnson of the Standish Group. InfoQ. http://tinyurl.com/zgqkr

Klett, C., Pivernetz, M. (2004). Controlling in kleinen und mittleren Unternehmen. Ein Handbuch mit Auswertung auf der Basis der Finanzbuchhaltung, 3. Auflage, NWB Verlag.

Object Management Group (OMG), OMG's MetaObject Facility (MOF) Home Page, http://www.omg.org/mof

Reilly, J.P. (1996). Rapid Prototyping: Moving to Business-Centric Development. Coriolis Group (Sd). 1996.

Standish Group (1994). Chaos Chronicles Version 3, http://tinyurl.com/y6uhpy

Taylor, D. A. (1995). Business Engineering with Object Technology, John Wiley & Sons.

TechConsult GmbH (2007). IT im Mittelstand. Sicherung von Marktanteilen unter gestiegenem Wettbewerbsdruck. Deutschland 2005–2007, http://tinyurl.com/d35oy9

QuinScape GmbH (2008) http://www.quinscape.de.

Wirtschaftsinformatik, Universität Oldenburg, Fakultät II der Informatik. http://tinyurl.com/cfshtz

About the Authors

Prof. Jorge Marx Gómez studied Computer Engineering and Industrial Engineering at the University of Applied Sciences Berlin (Technische Fachhochschule Berlin). He was a lecturer and researcher at the Otto-von-Guericke-Universität Magdeburg (Germany) where he also obtained a PhD degree in Business Information Systems with the work Computer-based Approaches to Forecast Returns of Scrapped Products to Recycling. In 2004 he received his habilitation for the work Automated Environmental Reporting through Material Flow Networks at Magdeburg University. From 2002 till 2003 he was a Visiting Professor for Business Informatics at the Clausthal University (Germany). In 2005 he became a full Professor and Chair of Business Informatics at Oldenburg University (Germany). His research interests include Very Large Business Applications, Federated ERP-Systems, Business Intelligence, Data Warehousing, Interoperability and Environmental Management Information Systems.

Thomas Biskup studied Computer Science from 1990 to 1997 at the University of Dortmund. He finished "cum laude" and was granted both the Hans Uhde award and the German Software Engineering Award of the Denert foundation. In 2001 he co-founded the QuinScape GmbH (http://www.quinscape.de). He specializes in intranet and extranet systems, model driven software development, domain driven design and agile methods. His Ph.D. thesis focuses on agile methods and models in order to simplify requirements engineering with cooperative rapid prototyping approaches for non-technicians in the form of "Conceptual Programming" as a foundational Enterprise Architecture methodology. In both roles as a researcher and a practical enterprise architect he has been active as a speaker and author for various publishers and conferences.

Univ.-Prof. Dr.-Ing. habil. Jorge Marx Gómez
Carl von Ossietzky Universität Oldenburg
Department für Informatik, Abt. Wirtschaftsinformatik
Ammerländer Heerstr. 114-118, 26129 Oldenburg, Germany
jorge.marx.gomez@uni-oldenburg.de

Dipl.-Inform. Thomas Biskup
QuinScape GmbH
Wittekindstr. 30, 44139 Dortmund, Germany
thomas.biskup@quinscape.de

Chapter 12

THE EVOLVING ROLE OF ENTERPRISE ARCHITECTURE WITHIN SYNGENTA

Peter Hungerford

Editors' Preface

Enterprises are starting to realize the criticality of EA. General EA practices are improving and maturing. Enterprises are expending lots of resources and time in establishing full time EA offices, governance processes, selecting the most relevant frameworks and methodologies, creating architecture artifacts and building business awareness. Despite all the good work that is being done, there is a growing realization that to sustain an EA practice, organizations need to link it to other management practices and approaches (strategic planning and solutioning). These linkages obviously extend the role of traditional architects to now understand and be intimately involved in aspects that were previously not thought of as architecture activities in the classical sense.

The chapter positions EA within the context of IS strategic planning. Using Syngenta as a case study, it starts with a good description of the role of the EA office. The evolving role of the EA office is evident in the fact that it is shifting away from the emphasis purely on technology to include business and information aspects. This shift can be seen in the context of the EA Design Model presented in chapter 2 of this book. It is critical to appreciate the impact of this shift as it has deep impact in the EA program and to the organization in general.

The chapter shows how Syngenta plans its IT systems as part of the IS Strategy Review. Interestingly, the chapter goes on to demonstrate the linkage from the IS Planning to its execution by linking it down to execution mechanisms. This allows the approach to be holistic and complete. These together address issues like:

- *How is the IS strategy formulated?*

- *How is the IS strategy operationalized? Where are the touch-points between the planning and the execution phases?*

- *What feedback mechanisms have been incorporated to ensure that planning and operations are in sync?*

- *What metrics are used to assess individual projects? How are these metrics then rolled-up to link to strategic goals?*

- *What are stress-points in this whole chain? Where does it break down?*

Introduction

You are a member of an Enterprise Architecture group, or perhaps you are leading one, and an executive board member meets you by the elevator. In the brief conversation, the topic of the company's overall business strategies and long terms plans arises and you are asked, rather pointedly, about your contribution. You reply....

This chapter aims to investigate the question of what entitles an Enterprise Architecture group truthfully to be able to consider itself strategic and to work at the enterprise level. In order to answer this question we will be looking at two key areas of the overall strategic lifecycle: the creation of the strategic plans and the ability of large projects or programs of work to drive strategic change. These extremes are particularly interesting since they address the *what* and the *how* of strategy; the *theory* and the *reality*. We are of the firm belief that Enterprise Architects must be involved in projects in order to keep their credibility, avoid the ivory tower label and to be able to influence and govern from *within* the project.

This chapter is a case study to show how Syngenta has used Enterprise Architecture to promote coherence within its organization. A thread running through this chapter is that we will look at our evolution from a Foundation mode of EA to include the Extended mode (see the Introductory Chapter) elements; we will attempt to provide best practice recommendations and maturity guides for the various aspects of EA in relation to the IS strategic plan and strategic projects.

Since we are dealing with EA within a company, we are always conscious of having to be pragmatic and aware of the compromises and tradeoffs that have to be made around resources, time, quality and risk. These compromises should be rational and made as evidenced-based decisions as advocated by Pfeffer and Sutton (2006). Finally, we will talk about the human element: the role of the architect. His or her skills both personal and formal are changing; acknowledging this and addressing these correctly is critical for business success. For a discussion of some of these aspects, see Saha (2007).

Setting the scene

In order to provide an overall context for the subsequent discussions we will provide a brief background to Syngenta as a company. In addition, we will present an overview of the IS department, and specifically the evolving role of the Global Strategy and Architecture group, the custodians of EA.

The Company

Syngenta (www.syngenta.com) is a world-leading agribusiness committed to sustainable agriculture through innovative research and technology. The company is a leader in crop protection, and ranks third in the high-value commercial seeds market. Sales in 2007 were approximately $9.2 billion. Syngenta employs some 21,000 people in over 90 countries at more than 420 sites.

The Syngenta business includes crop protection, seeds, seed care products as well as turf, garden, home care and public health products. Each of these lines has different business drivers: cost leadership, focus and differentiation as discussed by Porter 1998. As an aside, we believe that the EA characteristics, as exemplified by qualities (see Malan and Bredemeyer 2002) for each of these drivers would be different.

The Information Services Function

Syngenta is supported by a Global IS Function. For details, organizational approach, governance etc. see Saha 2007. A simplified view of the continuing evolution of the IS Function since the establishment of Syngenta is encapsulated in a strategic agenda. This agenda sees that an IS organization needs to progress through a series of steps in order to maximize its business contribution.

The first steps are to make certain that we have the right in-house capabilities and that IT suppliers are managed to ensure guaranteed delivery of quality IS services, which are benchmarked, scalable and sustainable. All these aspects must be well established before we can address the next stage. This is to forge a successfully partnership with the business to produce process excellence and concentrate on true information management. At Syngenta the IS function is on the journey through these stages. Interestingly this could just as well be described as the need for first providing architectural Assurance and Alignment before successfully being able to address Agility. These labels in turn acknowledge the need to master Foundation architecture before being able to successfully tackle the Extended mode.

Enterprise Architecture

Our Global Strategy and Architecture (GSA) group is part of Global IS and is responsible for the development, maintenance, governance and communication of our EA. Within this chapter, to make it easier for the reader, we will use "EA Group" as a synonym for GSA.

The group has internally organized itself in six domains designed to provide a specific process, information or technical focus, and to provide a business constituency based on the way Syngenta is organized. The horizontal layers indicate common services supporting all business areas.

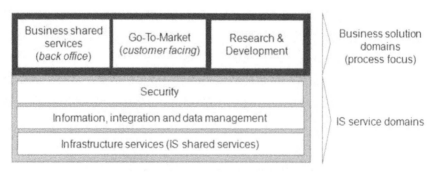

Figure 1. Syngenta EA Domains

The three business process focused domains highlight the increasing focus of architecture on the business. We do however recognize the importance of continuing to manage technology and services.

The group over the years has been shifting its emphasis away from a technology focus and more towards Business and Information Architecture. Technical Architecture is increasingly being assigning to strategic suppliers. This whole evolution aligns with the IS strategic agenda discussed earlier and, we believe, with the expansion of the EA modes from Foundation to include Extended.

Strategic Plans

Introduction

We could drown in the sheer quantity of business strategy research that is currently available and it most certainly will be added to in the future. Amazon, with over 12,000 books with "Business Strategy" in the title, illustrates this well. There are many references but the reader may want to try Mintzberg, Lampel, and Ahlstrand 2005, because of the excellent overview they give. There has been much less research published on IS strategy and specifically the IS strategic plan. The seminal book on EA and strategy is by Ross, Weill and Robertson (2006). We consider that the IS strategic plan is an essential EA artifact that is also undergoing transformation, morphing from an IS-focused planning device into an instrument that will provide a significant means to create coherency within the enterprise. It will need broader input and business dialogue and wider communication tailored to different audiences.

Within Syngenta we currently have a range of strategic planning activities with varying time horizons, all the way up to long-term reviews of emerging technologies and science and market opportunities that point to options for activities up to fifteen years ahead. Standard business strategy planning operates on a five year horizon with business function plans, including IS, harmonized at a company level. This process provides the basis for shorter operational planning activities and the cross linkage is extremely important in order to make the plan a living, breathing process.

We will examine our present IS strategic plan from various perspectives: the creation process, its major components, how it is communicated and its role in the overall IS planning cycle. A critical point is its alignment with the business, especially when the major activity is likely to be outside of the corporate HQ. We will consider the role of the Enterprise Architect in this process and judge what makes a successful plan. Finally, we will consider the improvements that we foresee to our current process in order to evolve from our current Foundation mode to include Extended mode elements.

The IS Strategic Plan
Process for its creation
The IS strategic plan is an integral part of the yearly IS planning cycle as can be seen in the following figure.

Figure 2. IS Planning Cycle

This can be summarized as follows. The rolling five-year plan is reviewed and updated at the beginning of the year; a major influencing factor is the agreed IS budget. The material that is created is subsequently used in the:

- CIO architecture reviews – Here the CIO and his leadership team review the yearly proposed changes to the architecture,

- Business strategy reviews – Reviews of individual business function strategy,

- CIO portfolio reviews – The CIO and IS - Business relationship managers agree on the proposed portfolio of IS activities for the coming year,

- IS budget – The IS budget for the coming year, agreed by the Syngenta executive committee.

A key point is that the corporate business budget planning process provides a fixed anchor point and a regular rhythm for the IS planning process, culminating in November when all parts of the business review and agree budgets for the coming year with the executive committee.

Content - The IS strategic plan contains several elements organized around a central unifying theme. For example, a synthesis of various IS functional plans: architecture, financial and supplier management, key external drivers.

Alignment with the business - The content is aligned with functional business CEOs and signed off by the Syngenta Executive Committee.

Communication - Currently the communication of the plan is somewhat limited, primarily because of the confidentiality of some of the pieces. However it is important that the messages depend on the audience (stakeholders).

Governance / ownership - The ownership of the plan is with the CIO and his leadership team, including the Head of Global Strategy and Architecture.

Role of the architecture function - Architecture is currently represented on the IS team by the Head of Global Architecture and Strategy.

Discussion

The current role of architecture and the general IS strategic plan process is more representative of the Foundation mode. We are currently reevaluating our strategic plan process and we believe Syngenta is evolving from the Foundation level (current) to include Extended mode elements of planning. We have also tried to "dream-the ideal" and foresee what an Embedded mode process might look like. We can see this in the following table.

	Current Process	Proposed Process	Future Process?
Mode of Enterprise Architecture	Foundational	Extended	Embedded
Strategic Drivers (why do we do it)	Alignment of IS strategy with business strategy Financial control System and service consolidation	Alignment of IS strategy with business strategy Simplification of business Information and knowledge exploitation	IS strategy is an integral part of the overall business strategy
Locus of Control (who leads the program)	IS Leadership team	Enterprise Architecture group as custodians Relationship Managers	Distributed control throughout business
Critical Management Innovation (How is it accomplished)	IS internal process	Interactive confirmation of plans with business (Gathering, Creation, Validation, Approval, Communication) Broad tailored communications	Embedded in a standard enterprise-wise planning process
Key Governance Mechanism (what is used to accomplish it)	IS leadership team Executive Committee	IS leadership team Business Process Owners Business Function Committee Executive Committee	Diffuse architecture team throughout IS and business
Program Metrics (How is it measured)	None direct	Agreed and monitored	Agreed and monitored, allowing self modification of the process
Benefits and outcomes (what do we get)	Visibility of IS plans to high level business management	Broad business and IS visibility of plan Broad input into plan Collaborative – adjustment of both business and IS plans to reflect joint issues and opportunities More aligned and coherent process	Coherent Enterprise-wide view of the plan, tailored to role within the organization Agile planning process

Table 1. Comparison of the IS Strategic Plan characteristics based on architecture maturity

Challenges to the participation of the EA group in the Strategic plan

To progress up the maturity curve EA must overcome two obstacles:

- *Confidentiality of information*
  To be effective the Strategic Plan must embrace information that is highly confidential in nature. There is an inevitable resistance within the organization for sharing the creation task, restricting access to information on a "need to know" basis, which traditionally excludes the EA group. This can be mitigated by using our CIO and senior business leaders to test concepts, validate principles and guide scenario developments whilst keeping confidential information disclosure to an acceptable level.

- *Getting a seat at the business table*
  The Relationship Manager is the designated IS contact with the business and the person who is naturally involved in business strategy discussions. It is not clear how architects can best fit into this relationship but the consequence is that their direct involvement with the business is currently limited. We are addressing this by using our relationship managers to open doors and get greater visibility for architects with senior business managers. Of course this opportunity carries with it a hefty price – namely that the enterprise architect must be able to discuss the implications of IS strategy and strategic choices in business language as well as be able to apply the EA set of tools and ideas to the broader business issues

Role of the EA group in the future process

We anticipate that our Enterprise Architects will:

- Create and maintain the architecture input

- Develop a picture of the projects/initiatives needed to deliver the strategic plan, their interactions, dependencies, cost/organization/skills, implications and priorities

- Maintain a clear direction in terms of IS technology, services and organizational structure, skills and capabilities, and cost impact

- Use IS governance processes to assess business impact and highlight key issues to IS and business management

- Understand external market dynamics and ensure that our strategy is aligned for maximum business advantage

- Use the IS strategic plan material as input into CIO reviews (Budget, Architecture and Portfolio need to be built into overall process)

In addition, they will support the strategic plan process by:

- Developing and promoting a solid (annual) process to develop/review/maintain the strategic plan

- Collating key IS and business targets that serve as input for the plan from a variety of stakeholders – extracting the IS and Architecture specific relevant material from our commercial plans. Moreover they can support and align the numerous process owners who are creating artifacts used in the overall EA.

- Providing communication materials on architecture issues for use by a variety of identified stakeholders

- Ensuring that the process runs smoothly

Summary

In this brave new world of the strategic plan, the skills that architects require are changing. They need to be recognized for their vision and experience in order to be trusted by IS senior management and, more importantly, by the business in giving input to their long-term plans. Personal skills and real business knowledge are essential to explain IS issues in a business context to senior management. It is also important for the architect to understand that it takes time for vision to become reality; he/she must anticipate and develop capabilities ahead of need. The art of the architect is recognizing the timing and the direction that the business wants to go, differentiating this from what is simply local, short-term hype.

There are many ways that the real world can influence plans, some foreseeable, others not. An important factor that long-term planners sometimes ignore is the way that technology can shape business. As an example, a company that deploys SAP as an integrated toolset across many parts of the business will find that selective business process outsourcing can raise serious problems.

We can say that our current IS strategic plan is more Foundational in nature than Extended. However, we are in the process of introducing improvements that we believe will build upon this Foundation approach, bringing in more Extended and Embedded mode elements.. We believe that the most critical change that we are making is broadening the number of actors in the process, not only IS but also business, allowing for a much more aligned and coherent approach. In time, we can envisage the IS strategic plan process becoming truly embedded in the organization, merging with the overarching corporate strategy and becoming much more reactive and capable of consistent change.

Strategic Projects

Introduction

If the strategic plan can be considered the *theory* or the *what* that an enterprise would like to achieve then its counterpart, the project or program, can be considered the *reality* or *how*. Here we are talking about those significant transformation programs that lie outside the normal business change activity; they tend to cut across and impact business silos, have high level executive sponsorship (CEO) and change *the fundamental way the business operates*. We would like to share our experiences by using two pairs of enterprise-wide projects separated in time and focus to illustrate the Foundational and Extended modes of EA. These discussions are based on projects that were / are being undertaken within Syngenta but have been simplified in order to highlight the essential elements.

Case Studies

The four projects that we will be looking at are summarized in the following table:

	Project: Biz2002	Project: Tech2005	Project: Biz2007	Project: Tech2008
Date (when was it undertaken)	2002	2005	2007	2008
Role of IS	Support	Lead	Partner with Business	Partner with strategic supplier
Role of EA group	Consultant to the technical needs of business Architecting the IS solutions	Governance of architecture Managing the IS architecture	Governance of IS architecture Managing the architecture	Governance of architecture
Role of Strategic Partners	Consultants	Partners	Partners	Lead
Mode of Enterprise Architecture	Foundational /Extended	Foundational	Extended / Embedded	Extended / Embedded
Strategic Drivers (why do we do it)	**Business Transformation** Increase revenues through customer focused programs Reduce cost and capital by transforming operations to best in class Streamline R&D operations and provide increased focus for innovation and delivery	**Technology Consolidation** Reduce by 40% the number of servers through consolidation and rationalization Create standardized infrastructure services Takes IS support activity out of business units into a central team, either saving costs or allowing local resources to focus on business growth	**Business Transformation** Process standardization and simplification embedded into organization Business services Business transformation and systems renewal Growth through differentiated processes	**Technology: Service Approach Business: Agility** Creation of next generation data center services The introduction of 'utility based' services and/or 'service based' SLA's. The implementation of best practice management methodologies and new technologies Leverage the market and gain economies of scale and institutionalize business change
Locus of Control (who leads the program)	Cross function business team	IS Organization	Cross function business team and significant IS	IS Organization and Strategic suppliers
Critical management innovation (How is it accomplished)	Independent business Project teams Organizational change Supporting Architecture	Independent IS Service teams (internal and supplier) IS exploitation team Supporting Architecture Mature relationship with supplier	Independent Business project Teams Organizational change Supporting Architecture	Independent IS Service Teams (internal and supplier) Supporting IS Architecture Mature relationship with supplier Mature industry environment
Key Governance Mechanisms (what is used to accomplish it)	Cross Business Functions	Joint supplier and Syngenta	Cross business functions. Dedicated Process owner committees	Joint supplier and Syngenta
Program Metrics (How is it measured)	Cost efficiency Sales growth Innovation and Learning Internal business	Cost efficiency Servers reduced	Cost efficiency Simplification achieved	Cost efficiency Utility (pay per use) services introduced
Benefits and Outcomes (what do we get)	Supply chain efficiencies Corporate function efficiencies Sales Growth optimizing within a functional silos,	Shared IS technology platforms Cost reduction Centralized services Reduced server count	Standardized business processes enterprise wide Common platforms Sustainable excellence Business agility Pervasive mindset of simplicity optimizing end-to-end processes which run across functional silos	Service Offerings, Further cost reductions Asset less IS infrastructure IS agility

Table 2. Summary of the Enterprise Architecture Dimensions of Projects

We have chosen these projects since we believe that they are representative of the different architecture modes and form congruent pairs in terms of *Strategic Drivers* and *Locus of Control*.

1. Project Biz2002 (business transformation, business led) & Project Biz2007 (business transformation, IS led)

2. Project Tech2005 (technology change, IS led) & Project Tech2008 (technology change, IS and supplier led)

Comparison of Projects Biz2002 and Biz2007
In these primarily business transformation projects, it is interesting to understand and analyze how the role of IS and Architecture has matured.

Biz2002
This was a business instigated project, with IS playing a supporting role. The key reason for this more limited role was that, although the CIO was visionary and saw the possibility of greater responsibility, IS was in the process standardizing, consolidating its services and generally getting its own house in order, "fixing the basics". There was limited EA group involvement and this was primarily at the technology level, mainly performing architecture tasks.

Biz2007
This project was catalyzed by IS and spearheaded by a very credible CIO. It could only happen in the context of a mature relationship between IS and business in which there is meaningful two-way dialogue. Furthermore, IS had demonstrably optimized operations in line with business requirements and was already able to respond quickly to changing business needs. As a result, business management understood and accepted the impact of complexity in business operations on the IS cost base. Within the project IS was actively involved with business, with IS holding several leadership positions. The EA group is extensively involved not just on a technical level but also helping to shape the work and its ongoing business impact; their role was regarded as critical.

What had changed?
The most significant change that has enabled IS and the EA Group to play a much more important role is most decidedly organizational maturity. IS and the EA Group can lead by example, showing that it has transformed itself, simplifying its

processes, rationalizing its organization and fixing the basics: delivering quality services using strategic suppliers, e.g. our project Tech2005. Moreover, these consolidated and centrally managed services brought a mindset of standardization and simplification into key parts of the business.

An important factor is our improved ability to respond to changing business priorities; we are able to scale our operations in line with changing business needs, i.e. respond to growth and/or cut back where needed. One key aspect was a change in the balance of fixed vs. variable costs in IS. We now have a largely variable cost base, using our strategic suppliers, where we can respond flexibly to business peaks and troughs.

Tactically the astute IS leadership team picked the right time and means to launch the project. The EA group was able to decrease the architecture effort in the infrastructure space through support of the service organization, aided by strategic partners. Having already earned its spurs through previous work, the EA group has thus now been recognized as capable of playing a more important business-facing role.

Challenges to the EA Group during the course of the projects

Biz2002

- Having to use best-of-breed technical solutions because of the immaturity of standard solutions
- Fighting silo thinking, in both business and IS, which caused complexities in architecture
- Difficulties in understanding and being able to talk with business
- Initial lack of the knowledge/skills required to understand the way companies work and the way decisions are made at high managerial levels
- Idealism of the architecture approach verses pragmatic business reality

Biz2007

- Getting suppliers to assume responsibility, structuring contracts (risk/rewards) to encourage this

- Playing a broad architecture management role, managing multiple vendors and partners to in order to obtain the desired result
- Not necessarily having the detailed technical knowledge to be able to judge architecture solutions

What had changed?
The form of the challenges has evolved from technical, where the rational architect was master, to more unclear situations where the architect has to deal with ambiguity and many political factors. It is critical that the architect develops additional skills, mainly softer, to be able to guide and influence business decisions.

Comparison of Projects Tech2005 and Tech2008

In the primarily IS-led transformation projects we will review the points relevant to the changing role of business, IS and the EA Group.

Tech2005
This project was born out of the need to reduce the IS cost base and the IS realization that this could best be achieved by combining a server consolidation exercise with standardization of IS services. This encompassed a transition to predominantly variable costs in order to give flexibility and agility in response to growth. There was minor business involvement through the production of standardized collaboration services as part of the initiative. The EA Group had minimal participation in the contractual stage, but contributed to the high-level architecture. It was more deeply involved in managing the architecture and design governance, where the contributors were Syngenta's strategic suppliers.

Tech2008
The EA Group together with Purchasing and Services was actively involved in putting the business case together for the next generation infrastructure, service based, and utility computing project. Business acknowledges and approves this work but is playing no active part, regarding it as a license-to-operate activity within IS that will lead to savings and support business agility. The EA group is involved in the architecture governance, setting broad direction and challenging at critical stages of the implementation.

What has changed?

Through the delivery of infrastructure services delivered by strategic partners the EA group, focus has shifted from creating IS architecture to managing it. This has required, perforce, a focus on higher levels of abstraction and greater emphasis on commercial aspects such as negotiation skills, costs and the overall business case. The EA group is an accepted part of a broad multi-disciplinary team involving purchasing, strategic supplier management and IS services.

Challenges to the EA group during the course of the projects

Tech2005

- Since now we are working with suppliers, accepting the lack of control over technical details

Tech2008

- Challenge of using separate projects to drive part of the architecture proposals.

- The industry commercial models, for example licensing, may not be mature and this impacts the potential ideal architecture

- Understanding that commercial considerations overrule the ideal architecture

What had changed?

- The architecture view in this primarily technical area has moved from a technical architecture perspective to something much more holistic, where necessary compromises from the architectural ideal need to be made. It could well be that this phase of activity begins to mark the transition into the Extended architecture form even for IS-focused activities.

Linkage between the IS Strategic Plan and Strategic Projects

There clearly has to be a strong two way linkage between the IS Strategic Plan and Strategic Projects as the means to implement the plan in order to ensure a coherent approach. We will explore these linkages by trying to answer the following questions.

How is the IS strategy operationalized? Where are the touch-points to the actual projects?
The Annual CIO Portfolio review (see Figure 2), is used to prioritize and agree to the set of IS related projects across all business units based on cost (within overall IS budget targets), business value and urgency. Once portfolio shape is agreed, business units are then responsible for project initiation and planning. In addition, architecture reviews of projects at key stages to ensure architecture compliance and direction is embedded into standard project lifecycle methodology. Finally, Project Steering Committees with key stakeholders are used to continually monitor direction.

What feedback and feed forward mechanisms are used to ensure that the strategy and operations are synchronized?
Overall business strategy and IS strategy is aligned at the highest level by review at the senior executive committee. More detailed business strategy, IS strategy, architecture and project fit is undertaken by annual business strategy reviews. To synchronize project and operations the annual CIO architecture and portfolio reviews (see figure 2) are used.

What metrics are used to assess the individual projects? How are these metrics then rolled-up to link to strategic goals?
At the project level, financial, architecture and business fit metrics are recorded at key stages on the project lifecycle. These metrics are rolled up to form KPI's (e.g. IS cost to sales ratio) that are monitored on an ongoing basis. We are starting to record value-based metrics and monitor these on an ongoing basis with projects. This approach allows value (which goes beyond cost-benefit) to be captured, monitored and even to be used to shape implementations.

What are the challenges to this approach?
One useful aspect of the approach described above is the feedback loop that has been established via the IS planning cycle and the visibility to senior stakeholders of the strategy and project alignment. We do still need to broaden the use of metric, especially

around value and to improve the visibility of the strategy clear enough for middle management, who are largely responsible for implementation of projects. Where IS activities are fully integrated into business strategic agendas this is starting to improve.

Additional Observations

Overview of the Enterprise Architecture group evolution in Syngenta

The following table summarizes the past, current and (possible) emerging role of the EA group within Syngenta, looking at the group from a variety of aspects.

Aspect	EA Group in 2003	EA Group in 2008	EA Group in 2012?
Primary Architecture skills	Technical	Technical / Business	Technical / Business / Behavioral
Source of new skills	Internal development from a IS technical background	Internal development from a business facing IS background Strategic recruitment	Internal development from a business background Strategic recruitment Supplier base
Architecture roles	Single role in an dedicated EA organization	Multiple roles in an dedicated EA organization	Multiple roles in multiple organization groups
Governance (focus)	Technical Infrastructure	Technical Infrastructure, Applications	Technical Infrastructure, Applications, Information, Process
Communication	Top-Down cascade	Targeted	Targeted but also viral, marketing
Architecture Process	Developed in-house	Based on TOGAF	Agreed industry standard
Documentation	Word, Visio, PowerPoint	Word, Visio,, PowerPoint, multiple EA and BPM Tools	Harmonized BPM & EA Tool set
Collaboration approaches	Loose community within the company using email	Loose community within the company using SharePoint	Structured network within and external to the company using public infrastructure
Architecture Scope (focus)	1 year time horizon Global Infrastructure Physical, Technical abstraction levels	5 year time horizons, Global Infrastructure, Applications Physical, Technical, Logical abstraction levels	10 year time horizons Global Applications, Global Information, Global Processes Logical, Conceptual abstraction levels

Table 3. Evolution of the EA Group within Syngenta

In addition to the evolution of the architecture mode, we have observed the following.

Projects can have unforeseen impact on the Enterprise Architecture
Strategic projects, because of their size and importance, often make significant changes to the overall EA. At the start of the project, the ideal end state is envisaged, hopefully aligned with the strategic plan. Then the project all too often encounters difficulties that cause it to change scope, time or budget.

Changes of scope have the greatest impact on the EA. In our experience, a common situation is one where a large project is used as the vehicle for also introducing enterprise services that will be used later by other parts of the organization. When the inevitable project cost and time pressures arrive, it is tempting to cut back on the delivery of these enterprise services, either by removing them completely or by delivering them in a project centric way, rendering them unusable at an enterprise level. In this situation the architect has to demonstrate mature judgment and be able to hold strategic conversations with business and project management. Equally, the organization as a whole must have a governance model that can value enterprise wide benefits alongside project priorities. Careful judgment is needed at the point when the proposed change of scope is discussed. Is it to be accepted or should the architect make a stand, hoping to convince the organization that for the common good the original scope should be kept? There is a desperate need for more concrete guidelines for such a situation.

The skills of the Enterprise Architect are changing
We can see and feel for ourselves that the skills of the Enterprise Architect are changing. There is a clear need as we move from the Foundational to include Extended mode that our skill set becomes likewise enhanced. We must act as more than consultants; the IS organization and more often the business will look to the architects to take a leadership role. For this, we must have personal credibility. In addition, ability to communicate effectively with and influence business and third party suppliers is growing in importance. This requires architects to learn to communicate in a more sophisticated way, tailored to their audience. Other skills that are emerging with the Extended mode include: organizational awareness, leading change, effective influence, and the ability to resolve conflicts.

As more projects are used to architect the enterprise rather than just IT, it is important to recognize and formalize the changing roles of the EA group and the concomitant skills that are required if an organization is to raise its game.

Concluding Thoughts

We have looked at the changing role of EA and the architects that create it; we have considered the specific cases of the IS strategic plan and the strategic project within Syngenta. We see that there is an evolution within these areas, with the focus of the architects expanding from IT to the business at large. Moreover, in order to provide *sustainable* EA rather than one-off exercises, we foresee the next steps: we need a higher degree of institutionalization of EA within standard business processes. This is in agreement with the overall themes of this book. However, we have noted that this evolution does not come free; the IS organization and the architects specifically need to prove themselves by first delivering quality IT services and leading the business by example. With this *earned* trust and respect of business, we will get a seat at the business table.

An important common theme is that EA maturity, IS maturity and business/organization maturity are all interlinked and must develop coherently. One cannot get ahead of the other(s).

Two additional aspects also need to be consisted by any EA group: firstly, we operate in a real world that requires the correct frame of mind and sometimes the acceptance of the less than ideal; secondly, in order to support this changing world, the capabilities of the architect need to evolve as well.

Finally as practicing architects within an enterprise, we must be prepared to instigate our vital changes at the right time, in the awareness that they will inevitably take time to implement. Therein lies the conundrum in these days of limited resources, especially time: how will the architects know and convince the organization that it is the moment to move? The answer alas cannot be systematically determined - it lies in the skill and expertise of the architect and, irrespective of where you are on the EA journey, always will.

COHERENCY MANAGEMENT

References

Malan R. and Bredemeyer D. (2002). Architectural Requirements in the Visual Architecting Process. http://tinyurl.com/dhtac6

Mintzberg, H., Lampel, J. and Ahlstrand, B. Strategy (2005). Safari: A Guided Tour through the Wilds of Strategic Management, The Free Press, April 2005.

Pfeffer, J. and Sutton, R. (2006). Evidence-Based Management, Harvard Business Review, January 2006.

Porter, M.E. (1998). Competitive Advantage: Creating and Sustaining Superior Performance, Free Press, June 1998.

Ross, J., Weill, P., and Robertson, D. (2006). Enterprise Architecture as Strategy. Boston, MA: Harvard Business School Press.

Saha P. (2007) Handbook of Enterprise Systems Architecture in Practice, Information Science Reference, Chapter XX – The Syngenta Architecture Story – Hungerford P.

About the Author

Peter Hungerford is an Enterprise Architect within the Strategy and Architecture Group of Syngenta. Among his current activities are providing solution architect leadership on a significant business change project and fostering continual improvement of EA processes within Syngenta. His previous, diverse IT work, which has included architecting many enterprise-wide solutions, creation of infrastructure services and in the distant past application development, has been recognized by award of the title Syngenta Fellow. He holds a D. Phil in Nuclear Physics from the University of Sussex.

Acknowledgements

I would like to acknowledge thought provoking conversations with Martin Walker, Mark Peacock, and Nick Barron. Special recognition goes to Alec Fitton for his insightful comments and to his support over the years. To all my Global Strategy and Architecture colleagues I say a big thanks for all the stimulating and challenging dialogues over the years and for many of the ideas I have shamelessly included here. Val, as always, my heartfelt thanks...

Peter Hungerford
Syngenta AG
Schwarzwaldallee 215
CH-4058 Basel, Switzerland
peter.hungerford@syngenta.com

Chapter 13

REALIZING THE BUSINESS VALUE OF ENTERPRISE ARCHITECTURE THROUGH ARCHITECTURE BUILDING BLOCKS

Fred C. Collins & Peter De Meo

Editors' Preface

Enterprise Architecture is a challenging endeavor. Organizations often express inability to embark on and sustain the resources and adequate management attention needed to take full benefit from EA programs. Given such serious impediments to EA, a formal and disciplined approach to EA provides organizations with the much needed guidance that they strive for. A formal, structured and disciplined approach to EA is usually captured as a methodology.

This chapter presents IBM's EA Methodology. It does briefly discuss the various phases (neighborhoods), but the focus of the chapter is not so much the methodology per se but the value it brings to EA practice. The authors describe the purpose and key deliverables within the context of how they bring value to the organization. The chapter makes a good effort in showing an integrated approach of how IT gets linked up to business and how the transition from business to IT can be made as seamless as possible. In building the case for an integrated approach, the chapter puts forward the idea of 'upstream' and 'downstream' EA. It provides a very good description of how the EA is linked downstream to solution architecture.

We believe this is critical in the foundation mode as it allows organizations to operationalize the EA and save it from becoming 'shelf ware'. Again, aspects of such linked approaches can be enhanced to improve its utility in the 'extended' and 'embedded' modes. Furthermore, to reinforce the key points the chapter uses example snippets from the US Department of Interior and the US Federal Government.

Introduction

When you consider the business value provided by EuroControl, NavCanada, or the US Federal Aviation Administration (FAA), do you think about the value as expressed in air traffic density (e.g. moving more people and cargo in a shorter period of time) or do you think about the business value as in terms of the commerce air travel enables on the wider economy? Or perhaps you don't really think about air travel at all until such a time that you need to actually board a plane. Even when you are flying, you are not paying much attention to all of the interconnected activities, events, processes, people, organizations, locations, and technology that make the flight possible, indeed, you are probably just hoping for an adjacent empty seat and thinking about how stingy the airline is about food. So when the enterprise architecture (EA) of air travel works well, all of its constituent parts work together so smoothly that you could say from your point of view that it is delivering its value in a stealth mode.

In their article, *Coherency Management: Using Enterprise Architecture for Alignment, Agility, and Assurance*, Gary Doucet, John Gøtze, Pallab Saha, and Scott Bernard argue three forms of Enterprise Architecture (EA) including: foundation, extended, and embedded. The authors argue that "Embedded EA" manifests itself in organizational culture and "everyday" artifacts such as strategic plans, human resource organizational charts, job role training materials, catalogs, and standards etc. Further, the authors argue that these embedded EA artifacts deliver real business value because they are intrinsically used by decision makers and solution designers.

Explicit EA requires a governance regime, EA framework, method, program office, evangelistic enterprise architects, a repository, and adequate funding and executive commitment to make everything work. In the air travel analogy, it is commensurate to trying to build a plane every time you want to fly somewhere, which may be one reason why explicit EA has never really delivered on its expectations.

We at IBM concur with the authors that embedded EA intrinsically causes an organization to gain market share, and establish credibility with its customers or citizens, if a government agency, and build better IT along the way. Indeed, there are a plethora of examples of the best ideas coming from the far edges out in the "field" that once adopted by "corporate" really begin to change the culture and organization itself. But how do you know what idea to choose? How do you know what impact a marketing decision will make on the corporate IT infrastructure? How do you "connect the dots" in such an organic EA environment without calling attention to yourself so as to remain stealthy? Much like Latin is the basis of the Romance Languages, we believe that it takes an EA "lingua franca" to provide an architectural foundation to make Embedded EA a functioning reality.

From our perspective, the concept of Embedded EA is a state of EA maturity. Today we are seeing our government and corporate clients' think of "useable EA" as something that becomes a common language and frame of reference between the IT organization and its customers. We argue that, regardless of what EA development method you choose, you should deconstruct your organization into its constituent parts, catalog them, and organize them in new ways to drive business value. We call these parts architectural building blocks (ABBs), and the best way to think of them is to use the Lego analogy as illustrated Figure 1 below. The following sections will put these blocks into the context of our EA method to demonstrate how the concept can be put into practice. Since the IBM EA method heavily influenced the industry standard, The Open Group Architecture Framework (TOGAF) and the burgeoning US Government standard Federal Segment Architecture Method (FSAM) by virtue of IBM helping develop its predecessor, the Department of Interior's (DOI) Method for Business Transformation (MBT), we feel that the IBM EA method can serve as a lingua franca for explaining how the ABB concept can make Embedded EA possible.

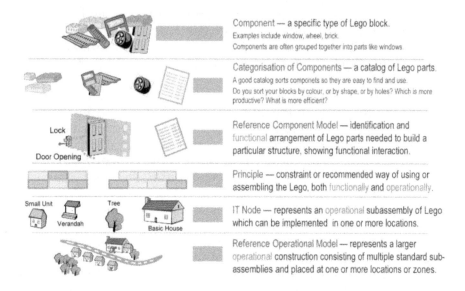

	Component — a specific type of Lego block. Examples include window, wheel, brick. Components are often grouped together into parts like windows.
	Categorisation of Components — a catalog of Lego parts. A good catalog sorts components so they are easy to find and use. Do you sort your blocks by colour, or by shape, or by holes? Which is more productive? What is more efficient?
Lock Door Opening	Reference Component Model — identification and functional arrangement of Lego parts needed to build a particular structure, showing functional interaction.
	Principle — constraint or recommended way of using or assembling the Lego, both functionally and operationally.
Small Unit Tree Verandah Basic House	IT Node — represents an operational subassembly of Lego which can be implemented in one or more locations.
	Reference Operational Model — represents a larger operational construction consisting of multiple standard sub-assemblies and placed at one or more locations or zones.

Figure 1. Architecture Building Blocks

The IBM EA Method

We consider EA to be much more than the collection of IT and other standards that must be adhered to by projects developing and implementing IT based business solutions. EA must address aligning IT initiatives with business strategy and optimally select and sequence those initiatives (Doing the Right Things). It must also ensure IT systems are built in accordance with enterprise standards and contribute towards the realization of the client's strategy (Doing Things Right). We define Enterprise Architecture as the framework, including architectural models and processes, needed to plan, coordinate and control the IT related activities of a (large) number of semi-autonomous groups and/or individuals towards a common goal or interest. Within our context, EA consists of:

The Architecture - "This is the way our projects should be architected"

> EA provides a specification of the IT and other standards and products that must be adopted by IT projects, including the overall business, application and infrastructure architectures that must be followed together with the principles and guidelines needed to ensure these standards are exploited properly.

The Governance of Projects & Programs - "Are we doing these projects the way we said we wanted them done?

> EA provides an organization and associated processes designed to ensure these specifications are adhered to or – when appropriate – exceptions allowed.

The Governance of the Architecture – "Are our target architectures still right?" / "Are we still moving in the right direction?"

> EA's architecture cannot be defined at a single moment in time - there needs to be a vision on how its constituent parts will evolve over the short and long term and how it, as a whole, will change to meet the changing demands of the business – i.e. how it is kept vital and appropriate for the enterprise?

The Transition - "These are the projects we should do"

> A collection of processes and tasks designed to support the selection and execution of the right projects to realize the EA vision, in concert with the business-as-usual IT project prioritization planning processes.

The IBM EA Method focuses on the development of a number of EA deliverables, organized according to a number of distinct domains or "neighborhoods". This is shown in Figure 2 below. Each deliverable has an associated work product description (WPD) and technique paper (TP) to ensure consistency in its delivery from engagement to engagement and across consultants.

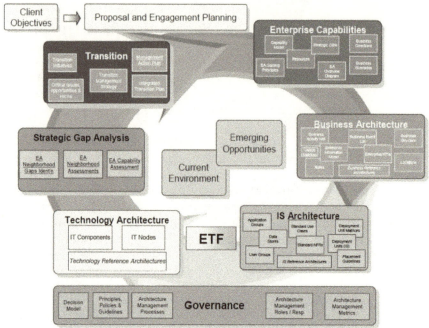

Figure 2. IBM EA Method Framework

In the context of the IBM EA Method, the Enterprise Capabilities neighborhood captures the strategic intent of the enterprise. The Enterprise Capabilities neighborhood provides the bridge from the organization's business strategy to the architectural building blocks that enable and help realize the strategy. The Business Architecture is the structure or structures of a business, which comprise processes, resources, goals, and information, the externally visible properties of those parts, and the relationships amongst them. Both the Enterprise Capabilities and Business Architecture are technology independent. The Information Services architecture describes the automated elements of business functionality and business data and the relationships between these elements. The Technology Architecture describes the automated elements of infrastructure functionality and data and the relationships between these elements.

The method defines several sets of building blocks that are designed to meet these enterprise capabilities, and which are then used by multiple (often independent) business and IT projects. In broad terms, these ABBs are either associated with the overall Business Architecture, IS or the IT Architecture. IBM's definition of an

ABB is somewhat broader than the TOGAF[7] definition which has a stronger technology focus.

To use EA appropriately, it is necessary to design and implement a Governance mechanism, based on number of well-defined management processes owned and executed by an Architecture Management Team. To work well, governance must ensure solution projects use the EA appropriately, as well as keeping the EA itself current and vibrant.

Most IT oriented projects are triggered by a direct business need, and are prioritized and scheduled accordingly. Additionally, an EA will, via a Strategic Gap Analysis, identify the crucial areas of existing business structure and IT investments that must be enhanced to conform with the EA and therefore meet the business' objectives – contained within a set of Transition Initiatives.

Modeling Enterprise Capabilities

We address strategic goals and business requirements in our Enterprise Capabilities and Business Architecture neighborhoods. As stated previously, the Enterprise Capabilities neighborhood provides the bridge from the organization's business strategy to the architectural building blocks that enable and help realize the strategy. To focus the EA on delivering the right plan for the enterprise, it must be based on a detailed understanding of the Enterprise Capabilities the enterprise has decided it needs to achieve its business objectives. The definition of these capabilities may either be established during the creation of the EA, or may already be available as part of a defined business strategy. A number of approaches may be used to capture the strategic intent of the enterprise including IBM's Component Business Modeling[8] and Strategic Capability Networks (SCN). SCN depicts the strategic capabilities and associated enablers of a business, their interrelationships and their combined roles and significance in supporting value exchanges with external players on the value net of a business. SCN is a proprietary IBM modeling technique[9]. Figure 3 shows a SCN as created in the System Architect modeling tool.

---

[7] http://www.opengroup.org/togaf/

[8] http://www.research.ibm.com/journal/sj/444/cherbakov.html

[9] US Patent 6249768

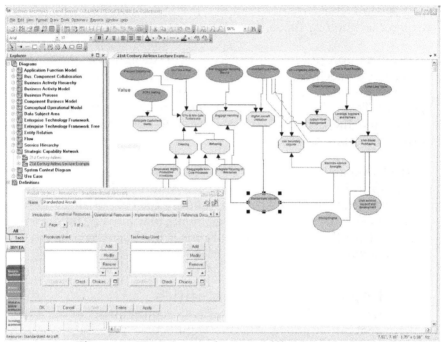

Figure 3. IBM Strategic Capability Network

As seen in Figure 3, the SCN depicts an integrated framework of a firm's capabilities. This integrated framework shows how, and to what extent, these capabilities interact with and affect one another, in serving the value exchanges (where a product or service is exchanged for something of value) between the firm and its customers and other external value net players (Partners, Suppliers, Channels, etc.). The framework also shows the degree to which capabilities positively reinforce one another, or negatively impede one another, and the direction of cause and effect between related capabilities. In its most detailed form, this integrated framework shows how enablers (resources) combine to serve one or more capabilities.

Component Business Modeling (CBM) is a way of assessing and designing a business. It is an evolution of traditional views of a business, such as the business unit, function, geographic area, or process view. By combining both horizontal and vertical integration, the Component Business Model methodology identifies the basic building blocks of a business. Business components are the equivalent of interchangeable manufacturing parts but are instead composed of processes, functions, activities, and services, collectively referred to as capabilities. Each building block includes the

COHERENCY MANAGEMENT

resources (including human resources), activities, and technology needed to produce a service valued by another component, or by an external customer. After a comprehensive analysis of the composition of each business, the individual building blocks, or components, are mapped onto a single page. Figure 4 shows a CBM map created in the System Architect modeling tool.

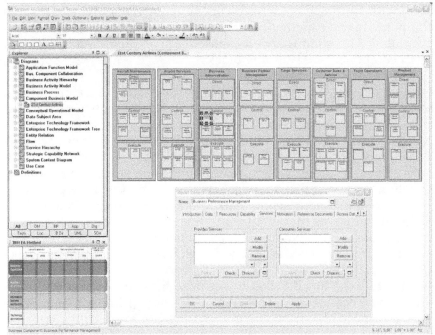

Figure 4. IBM Strategic CBM Map

A component map is a two-dimensional view of a business. The rows of the component map represent different event horizons and "accountability levels." The accountability levels are the directing, controlling, and executing levels. The different levels typically require unique skills and often operate over different time scales. The columns of the component map represent competencies and define what critical capabilities an organization needs in order to be successful. Which competencies are required depends on the industry and the business strategy of the company.

The CBM technique, when applied to IT, represents a new way for CIO's to approach fundamental questions by viewing the IT function as a business unto itself. Examination of the components can help identify specific ways in which such "business" operations could be improved. At a large US government agency, IT managers used their "Business of IT" CBM map as a way to: 1) define IT across business units in standard way, 2) define standard roles and responsibilities, 3) represent existing resource allocations, 4) discuss existing organizational responsibilities, and 5) where to improve for strategic differentiation and return on labor. CBM helped the CIO determine how efficiently the IT service management (ITSM) infrastructure was operating and how well the IT service "business" was helping to support and drive business value. By applying the same component-based methodology as is used elsewhere in the enterprise, the IT function was decomposed into a unique, yet integrated, set of components or building blocks.

For that agency, neither the CBM map itself, nor the technique that went with it, were as important as the value IT managers derived from being able to have cross-organizational conversations using a common taxonomy. As such CBM and the EA engagement acted as a facilitator of communication. The IT managers themselves combined resource allocation and their opinions on effectiveness, differentiation, and criticality to reveal areas for action that were not previously visible. The outcome was a roadmap of prioritized and sequenced initiatives that would take the IT organization from a centralized model to the matrix model they knew would best establish and maintain customer intimacy. For example, the IT managers recognized that they needed to become process based instead of functionally based. They decided to organize themselves around the Information Technology Infrastructure Library (ITIL) for their standard IT processes, participate in the American Productivity & Quality Center (APQC) benchmarking program, and develop the necessary EA guidance and enabling technology to make that ITIL-based approach work for them and their customers.

For the DOI Human Resource (HR) Modernization Blueprint, a number of techniques were used by IBM to capture and model the Enterprise Capabilities domain. An internal survey of DOI HR executives and managers was performed to assess the challenges facing the DOI HR business area. Each Bureau was solicited for participation in the survey. The survey was designed as a starting point for the DOI HR Blueprint data collection and subsequent analyses. The survey proved to be an effective means of engaging business leaders and capturing their challenges. From a modeling perspective, we employed a Strength, Weakness, Opportunities, and Threats (SWOT) diagram to summarize a subset of what was gathered during the survey sessions with the stakeholders.

Modeling the Business Architecture

The IBM EA Method defines the Business Architecture as "the structure or structures of a business, which comprise processes, resources, goals, and information, the externally visible properties of those parts, and the relationships amongst them." The Business Architecture describes the current and futures states of the business. Building blocks for modeling the Business Architecture are captured and modeled during creation of Enterprise Capabilities. Enterprise resources (skills, activities, and information) captured using the SCN technique form the basis for roles, business activities, and enterprise information building blocks used in modeling the business architecture.

IBM uses a number of modeling techniques to capture the Business Architecture, including process narratives, business scenarios, organizational charts, and enterprise information models. One work product, the Business Activity Model (BAM) is used to help define how a business currently operates or would like to operate in the future. It provides a decomposition of all levels of business activities in the enterprise or within the scope of the business unit. It may be modeled as a node tree or as an embedded hierarchy diagram (as shown in Figure 5).

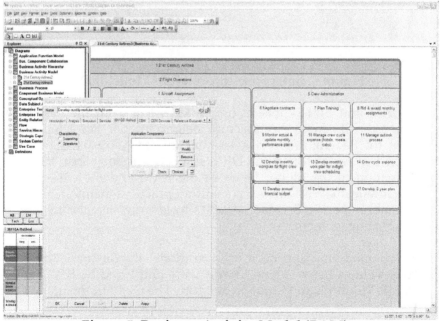

Figure 5. Business Activity Model (BAM)

The Enterprise Information Model work product, shown in Figure 6, represents the strategic information requirements of the enterprise. It depicts, in both graphical and textual form, the structure and content of the key categories, or "subject areas" of persistent data that need to be managed by the enterprise.

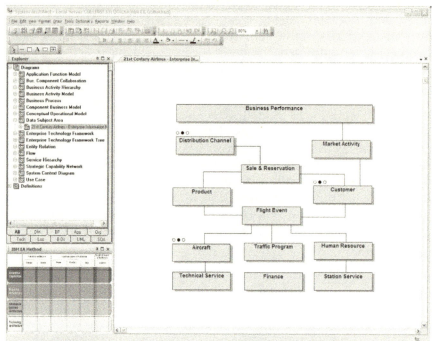

Figure 6. Enterprise Information Model (EIM)

The BAM and EIM represent only a subset of available models to capture the Business Architecture neighborhood. For US Federal clients, the Federal Enterprise Architecture (FEA) business and data reference models[10] (BRM and DRM respectively) may form the basis for creation of the higher levels of the BAM and EIM. As part of IBM's intellectual capital, our consulting practices maintain a library of industry-specific BAMs and EIMs to leverage as starting points for client engagements.

Another modeling approach used to model the Business Architecture is Value Chains. Value Chains were employed by IBM for the DOI HR Modernization Blueprint effort. The DOI HR Business Area

---

[10] http://www.whitehouse.gov/omb/egov/a-2-EAModelsNEW2.html

"As-Is" value chain visually depicts the high level functions that are performed in the current state for the DOI HR business area. The value chain diagram is a mandated work product of the MBT approach. The work product depicts the high level functions that are leveraged in the current state. The value chain was created from information gathered from DOI HR stakeholders via the stakeholder survey and is based on the Office of Personnel Management HR Business Reference Model. The value chain, depicted in Figure 7, shows HR provides four main products or services: HR Strategy & Planning, Staff Acquisition, Sustaining Employees, and Employee Separation. Largely, these products or services are created via the provision of a collection of Bureau HR services. These services, in turn, are supported by a common DOI / Bureau infrastructure and a collection of Bureau-specific and enterprise (DOI / Government wide) HR information technology applications. The business of HR is guided by Title 5 Code of Federal Regulations and a number regulations / laws by the OPM, DOL, Unions, and even certain presidential mandates.

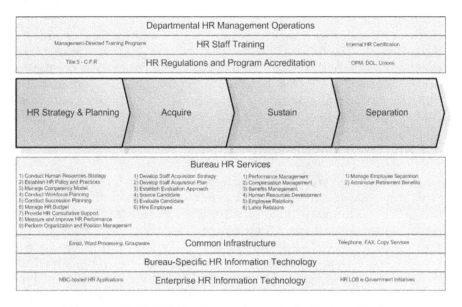

Figure 7. DOI HR Business Area As Is Value Chain

We find that techniques such as Value Chains in conjunction with Business Activity Models and Enterprise Information Models are effective in modeling the Business Architecture domain.

Modeling the Information Services and Technology Architectures

The Information Services (IS) architecture describes the automated elements of business functionality and business data and the relationships between these elements. The Technology Architecture describes the automated elements of infrastructure functionality and data and the relationships between these elements. In the IBM EA methodology, the Information Services and Technology Architecture combined represent the "digitized" elements of the EA and are referred to as the IT Architecture.

One of the challenges we face in EA is taking the artifacts captured in the development of the Enterprise Capabilities and Business Architecture domains and using them to create the foundations of the IT Architecture. Sometimes EA programs are criticized for lacking specifics with respect to solution implementation. Some EA programs simply capture artifacts at the granularity of IT investments. As EA programs mature, more is demanded from EA. Within the US Federal EA community the mantra calls for 'actionable architectures' with tangible linkages between EA planning and solutions. According to the Office of Management and Budget (OMB), Segment architecture development is a collaborative process forming a bridge between enterprise-level planning and the development and implementation of solution architectures. Within the context of IBM's EA Methodology (EAM), enterprise-level planning is termed 'upstream EA' whereas solution architecture development and implementation is termed 'downstream EA'.

The Technology Architecture describes the basic technology infrastructure needed for efficient & effective automation of the business. The Technology Architecture work products complement IS Architecture artifacts to provide a complete set of building blocks and guidance for IT Solution projects. These building blocks are categorized and grouped together into a catalog of parts called an Enterprise Technology Framework (ETF). This ETF, shown in Figure 8, is used as a repository for all information about the IT capabilities and enablers required to implement the desired business objectives and capabilities. It defines the technology services and functions (IT capabilities) required to support the business applications and data. The framework in total is the ETF whereas the components which comprise the ETF are the ABBs.

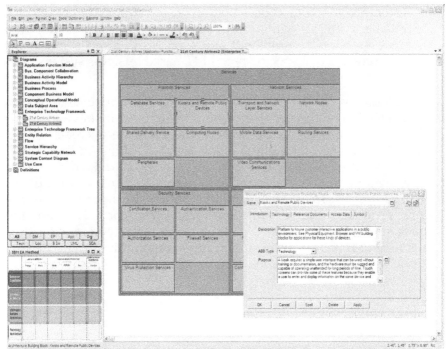

Figure 8. Enterprise Technology Framework Work Product

ABBs feature a taxonomy like OMB's Federal Enterprise Architecture (FEA) Technical Reference Model (TRM), but also embody work products (WPs), WP dependencies and workflow all in the context of a metamodel and method. This taxonomy is shown graphically as the ETF. Principles provide guidance on ABB assembly. Pre-assembled ABB collections (called reference architectures or patterns) guide solution development. Standard patterns, describe pre-defined solution IT architectures that must be adopted for various types of business application. Depending on circumstance, these patterns may take several forms, including:

- **Logical Functional Environments**, which describe various "standard builds" for all permitted hardware platforms (such as a "high performance workstation" or "small departmental server") and the permitted ways in which these can be deployed. These LFEs may be constructed from specified ABBs (i.e. they are technology neutral) or particular implementations of ABBs (in which case permitted ranges of non functional requirements such as workload or availability characteristics must be given for each technology set).

- **Reference Architectures**, that describe complete IT systems (maybe with or without application level components) that must be tailored, combined and extended to directly match the requirements of a specific type of IT based business system.

Figure 9 shows the relationship between enterprise architecture (shown circled on the right) and solution architecture (shown on the left) is simply a matter of scale. Enterprise Architects create coarse-grained guidance, and guide the development of fine-grained guidance by solution architects. The key to success is to have an underlying metamodel to categorize various architecture work products, work product descriptions, technique papers for the creation of the work products, and a work product dependency diagram and which shows the influence of one work product upon another thus establishing line-of-sight from enterprise capabilities down through technological implementation.

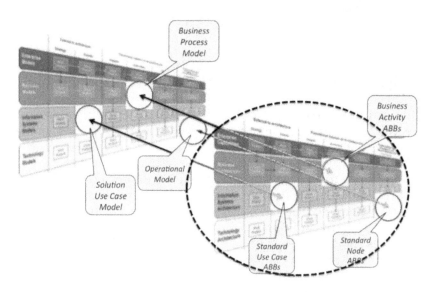

Figure 9. Mapping of EA to Solution Architecture Work Products

This decomposition from enterprise to solution scale does not just occur between the Information Systems Architecture and the Technical Architecture. Indeed, Figure 10 illustrates how the Activity and Information Resources from the Business Capabilities decompose further into Business Architecture Business Activity and Enterprise Information Models which in turn define Application

Groups, Deployment Unit Matrices, and Data Stores in the Information Systems Architecture.

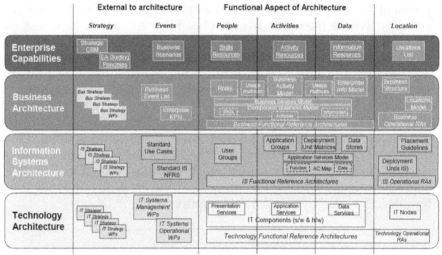

Figure 10. Decomposition of Architecture Work Products

The following EA process is predicated upon the ability of the IT organization to control their entire legacy portfolio from an operations and maintenance perspective. The first step is to conduct a standard application assessment on the portfolio to determine which applications hold the greatest return on investment and/or customer priority. The assessment reviews each application from a business value perspective, measuring such things as alignment with strategic objectives, alignment with business processes, effectiveness accomplishing business objectives, and sensitivity to external factors. The assessment also reviews from a cost of ownership, information quality and accuracy, technical alignment with the TRM, as well as the "ilities" such as:

- Maintainability
- Flexibility
- Interoperability
- Availability
- Usability

The chosen applications are then deconstructed into standard categories with a focus on addressable issues shared by many applications. The EA program worked closely with solution architects using the ABBs and other EA related guidance for how to write up the project change requests that would ultimately become funded change orders. These changes orders became the mechanism for incrementally rationalizing the legacy portfolio to the target environment. If this process completes as planned, it will also result in a situation where business owners only have to specify business requirements and not worry about the enabling application, data, and technology architecture and infrastructure. While still a long way from reality, the agency is steadfastly adding coherency as a means for controlling "shadow IT" and empowering the IT organization.

User Groups, shown modeled in Figure 11, are categories of users who have similar application and data access requirements. User Groups are a natural refinement of the Roles defined in the Business Architecture. The User Groups' work product, shown in Figure 8, combines business roles into categories of users with similar characteristics, IT experience and usage requirements.

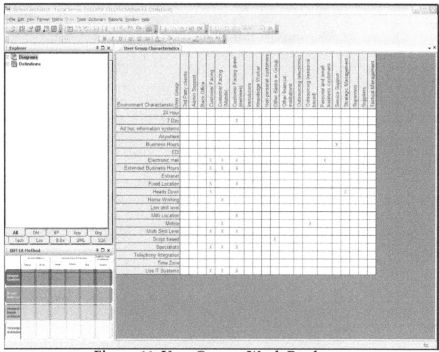

Figure 11. User Groups Work Product

User Groups, Application Groups, and Data Stores, along with Standard User Cases, Non Functional Requirements, Deployment Units, and Placement Guidelines go on to define the IS Architecture domain. The creation of User Groups from Roles, Application

COHERENCY MANAGEMENT

Groups from the BAM, and Data Stores from the EIS model involves clustering based on common attributes. We took what was a heuristic approach and codified it as an affinity analysis algorithm in System Architect. This algorithm assists the consultant in creating the IS work products and helps to standardize the process. There is still a subjective aspect of the affinity analysis as the consultant must select weights associated with the clustering attributes, but the process is now documented and more defensible.

Governance

Embedding EA into the organization requires leaders with two very different sets of skills: it formally connects Business and IT Architecture, and focuses the combination on achieving an effective response to business needs through coherency management. We see coherency in creating implementable EA guidance for solution architects (i.e. standards, reference models, and architecture building blocks) and in establishing robust IT governance (i.e., setting enterprise-wide standards and ensuring their continued vitality, regular business-led reviews, and implementing an EA roadmap).

Without Solution Architecture Guidance and EA Governance	With Solution Architecture Guidance and EA Governance
Legacy applications maintain dependencies on a broad range of obsolete technologies and the skills to maintain them.	A smaller number of enabling technologies enabling skill standardization.
Systems always behind the state of the art.	Highest priority systems working on the latest, highest function, most robust, lowest cost technologies.
Slow and unpredictable turnaround times.	Rapid responses to many functionality requests. Timely responses to more unusual functionality requests.
Redundant solutions across the enterprise.	Fostering of and exploitation of commonalities between solutions.
Struggling to get by in the face of change.	Focused on fulfilling changing to business needs.
A restraint on business change.	An enabler of business change.

Table 1. Guidance and Governance

The deliberate governance of solution development projects is the EA means for ensuring the use and usability of standards. After all, standards are only truly valuable when they are used and usable. Governance processes include architectural and design reviews, as well as variance management. Reviews not only identify nonconformance, but enable EAs to add value to the solutions under development. Explicit variance management is important, since it is impossible with an EA to anticipate all possible situations and thus all relevant architectural standards and needs. The explicit granting of variances not only allows quality control of solution developed projects, but acts as a feedback mechanism to those seeking to ensure the vitality of the EA.

The ongoing review and revitalization of standards is just one of many forms of solution portfolio review. More critical, perhaps, are reviews focused at meeting business needs, and in enabling forms of business interaction that are newly feasible because of technological advances. While reviews may lead to single solution development projects, their enterprise-wide scope often results in the launch of medium term initiatives to manage the coordinated development and roll-out of many solutions. Initiatives may be proactive (for example, to reduce costs), or reactive (for example to respond to a disaster of some kind, from a power failure to something on the scale of 9/11). They may be long term and strategic (for example, to support the provision of "business functionality on demand in a utility environment") or short term and tactical (to determine an interim architecture while a promised technology standard matures).

EA requires a level of discipline and organization that has been lacking in most IT organizations. The creation of EA governance is a significant organizational hurdle, and so requires both justification (cost/benefit) and explicit executive sponsorship. The early stages of embedding EA governance typically include a mixture of standard adoption and portfolio documentation and evaluation. Early initiatives may include: determining standards based on internal best practices and published standards; performing an inventory to bootstrap portfolio management; and determining initial sets of applications to migrate so that they conform to newly set EA standards.

The Role of the EA Repository

Our contention is that without effective integrated tooling support, implementation of complex methodologies such as the DOI's MBT, FSAM, and IBM's own EA Method is difficult if not impossible. It is possible to use a collection of business process, data, and architectural modeling tools, but the end result is a collection of work products. Line-of-sight analysis is difficult across such a collection of disparate work products created by different tools from a myriad of vendors. It is true that some EA repositories and modeling tool integration products offer the promise of being able to integrate such a disparate collection of EA artifacts, but our experience is that such an approach can be time consuming and costly. Our approach was more simplistic in that we elected to have all the work products created and maintained in a single tooling environment.

For the most part, enterprises have collections of information on hand from which to derive value and drive modernization. The value of this legacy data is often called into question, but you can always find some value in the data when it is integrated with other sources of information. The key to the derivation of business value is the collection, integration, normalization and presentation of this data as information to stakeholder groups. A repository based on a relational database architecture is key to the integration and normalization of this data. Most organizations can immediately derive positive ROI on the repository investment from the elimination of redundant data stores. This approach yields quick results to a broad base of stakeholders, increasing the odds of program success.

The business case for the investment in an EA repository is based on the elimination of the myriad of current data stores of EA and EA-related artifacts. The repository must integrate, normalize, and facilitate the lifecycle of EA and EA-related information. The ability to finally extract and publish integrated reports that cut across previous stovepipes of information should be emphasized. The key to success is to get various stakeholders to agree to give up their current spreadsheets, MS Access databases and ad hoc data stores, provided this new repository meets their needs.

As the scope of EA analysis grows from technology to business, to strategy, and to financial data stores, this notion of replacement and elimination of the other data stores is unrealistic. Most EA and EA-related data stores fall under the domain of the CIO and thus, in theory, can be consolidated if it makes business sense. These other data stores contain information and/or meta-data of interest to EA, but are owned and maintained by other business units. For such a scenario, a federated architecture is most appropriate. Federation is the concept that a collection of resources can be viewed and manipulated as if they were a single resource while retaining their autonomy and integrity. Federation creates a temporary "view" by integrating up-to-date data from multiple sources on the fly. Federation allows clients to combine data from different databases. Data need not be copied, but replication can be used to create a centralized view of enterprise information and to support time series analysis. Within a federated database architecture, the central EA repository can query data from other autonomous heterogeneous data sources which can be structured or unstructured. The key to fostering cooperation with these other business domains is to demonstrate the value of information-sharing and to demonstrate the ease of a federated architecture over labor intensive data calls.

EA repositories have evolved from collections of non-integrated architectural artifacts to elaborate decision-support systems. There are significant differences, however, among EA repositories. Before selecting a given repository one should consider:

- Relational versus Object-Orientated versus Hierarchical designs
- The ability to perform true SQL-based queries
- The ability to manage the lifecycle of data within the repository
- The ease of data management, data import and data export
- Role-based security features
- Ease of canned queries, ad hoc queries, standard reports, HTML generation
- Data-driven visualization of object relationships within the repository
- Integration with existing modeling tools and other data sources
- Pre-built dash boards and applications
- Portal interface
- Open database support versus dependency on a single vendor's solution
- Technical support, stability of the company and installation references
- Experience suggests the use of a relational repository over object-oriented or hierarchical designs. The ability to perform true SQL-based queries is predicated on a relational architecture. Reporting, data management, data integration and performance are all superior with relational-based repositories.

Summary

As enterprise architects, our role is to recognize the implicit organizational, political, business, information, and technical architectures that already exist in our organizations and add an element of coherency to them such that they can be related and built upon at an enterprise scale. This paper provided an overview of IBM's Enterprise Architecture (EA) consulting methodology and discussed its use in realizing tangible business value from EA engagements by thinking in terms of architectural building blocks. We also discussed the application of the method to Federal clients and how such a method can be used to augment a client's pre-selected methodology such as the DOI's MBT and FSAM. We also showcased support for the method in IBM's System Architecture modeling tool. We discussed the embedding of EA into organizational and business model architectures by thinking of the enterprise as a set of business components and teaching stakeholders how to use this perspective to introduce change on their own terms. We also discussed embedding EA into solutions as a means to make EA "implementable" thru architecture building blocks and decomposition of higher abstraction artifacts into design level guidance. This traceability helps EA provide the architectural models and governance mechanisms that help an enterprise guide its change programs to design their solutions in a consistent and integrated manner. Finally, we discussed the role of the EA repository and some guidance on how to choose one.

Acknowledgements

A shortened version of this article entitled "Realizing the Business Value of Enterprise Architecture" was published in Architecture and Governance Magazine[11]. This submission greatly expands upon the original piece with new material, an introduction to the EA method used, case studies, and lessons learned. The original word count was expanded from approximately 1,600 to 5,000 so this represents a significant expansion from the original source material. The title, however, remains the same.

About the Authors

Dr. Collins is an Executive Enterprise Architect supporting IBM's Public Sector Consulting Practice. He has extensive technical knowledge and leadership experience with enterprise architectures (EA) and EA modeling tools, EA repositories, and EA methods. He is one of IBM's Global Enterprise Architecture method instructors. He has been with IBM since 1995 and has over 20 years of information technology experience. He has a Ph.D. in Applied Math and Statistics, a Master's degree in Industrial and Systems Engineering, and a Bachelor's degree in Industrial Engineering and Operations Research. Fred has lead or supported Enterprise Architecture engagements throughout the public sector including engagements at the Department of the Interior, Department of Energy, Farm Services Agency, Forest Service, Bureau of Land Management, and the Department of Defense. Dr. Collins co-authored the Interior Department's Methodology for Business Transformation (MBT), which is currently being used within 8 DOI Bureaus and has been taught to hundreds of federal employees and support contractors. He led the IBM effort to place MBT into IBM's method authoring tool, Rational Method Composer. He is currently providing strategic direction on EA tooling for IBM and supporting IBM's Department of Agriculture account team.

Mr. De Meo leads IBM's Public Sector enterprise architecture (EA) practice. He provides guidance and thought leadership to senior executives and policymakers across several federal civilian and defense agencies currently including the Federal Aviation Administra-

---

[11] http://www.architectureandgovernance.com/articles/05-collins.asp

tion (FAA), Department of Homeland Security (DHS), and the Federal Deposit Insurance Corporation (FDIC). He has provided EA guidance to several foreign governments including Denmark, Japan, Singapore, Korea, and China. His primary responsibilities include new service offerings, EA best practice and research development, and support for FEA-PMO Solutions Architect Working Group (SAWG), Industry Advisory Council (IAC), and the Federal CIO Council. Peter authored an EA development method that fused the Federal Enterprise Architecture (FEA) with the Federal Enterprise Architecture Framework (FEAF) that was adopted by the FAA, Department of Transportation (DoT), and the United States Agency for International Development (USAID). Members of Peter's practice have instructed at the FEAC EA certification course. Peter also instructs IBM's standard EA training program and he regularly briefs domestic and international agencies at IBM's Institute for Electronic Government (IEG). Peter's 18 year professional and managerial consulting background has been spent predominantly in large scale custom systems development and integration for the Departments of Homeland Security and Defense. In addition, he developed a specialty in managed corporate travel and provided strategic business and technical consulting to travel agencies and airlines. Peter holds a BBA in Management Information Systems from the University of Notre Dame and a MS in Telecommunications from the John's Hopkins.

Dr. Fred C. Collins, Ph.D.
Executive Architect
IBM Business Consulting Services
fred.collins@us.ibm.com

Mr. Peter De Meo
IT Architect, Management Consultant
IBM Business Consulting Services
peter.demeo@us.ibm.com

Chapter 14

REFERENCE MODELS FOR GOVERNMENT

Neil Kemp

Editors' Preface

It is fair to say that Enterprise Architecture is in a bit of an identity crisis vis-à-vis its relationship to technology. Many prominent experts on the subject will often say that EA is about more than technology but their message has less impact than hoped because the examples tend to be quite focused on the technology view of solving the business problem and realizing true business value. It's not that business value is bad, it's that it primarily limits approaches to the value proposition of how IT will serve the business.

The change in thought we seek to support and advance (we don't take credit for inventing this idea) is that people think of EA as a way business people can architect their business regardless of what IT considerations might follow. EA is not invited after the business decisions, strategies and plans are made. It is brought in to help business leaders design their business; to shape the strategy and to ensure coherence of vision, capability and action by the business.

In this chapter Neil Kemp delivers his summary of a model for describing pubic services for governments in Canada. The interesting thing to note is that this public sector reference model supports the standardized and structured representation of the business for business design purposes, not simply to have captured the requirements effectively for the sake of systems development.

The other major learning we hope you take from this chapter is that Business Architecture is not only Process Reengineering. It involves (among other things) understanding the service value chain through modeling which takes a rather scientific view of how our actions benefit those we attempt to serve.

On our website. www.coherencymanagement.org, Neil Kemp presents a case study where GSRM was used in the Winnipeg Fleet Management Agency (WFMA) to support the organizational transformation of the Agency, to identify the essential capabilities required to serve its customers, the governance structures best suited to its operations, the distribution of work, the requirements for information, and the automation of information management across the organization.

Background

In the past, commercial, government, and social systems were far less complicated than they are today. As the complexity of the modern enterprise and its elements increases and exchanges between business components become more interactive, it becomes increasingly difficult for decision makers to maintain a clear, complete, accurate and shared image of an enterprise and the various system interfaces. This is the good news; the bad news is that these trends are likely to continue.

The ability of the modern business to adapt, change and respond to threats and opportunities has been hampered by the inability of decision makers and analysts to quickly and accurately communicate. Terms such as "objective", "outcome", "service", "process", and even "enterprise" all suffer from having multiple meanings and therefore, without clarification of intent, they lack the specificity needed to be useful in either analysis or decision-making. As it is necessary for the affected stakeholders to work out just what ideas are contained in these and many other words, this adds a significant overhead to the decision making process. Important thinkers such as Michael Porter (1996) put forward powerful ideas such as "service value chains" without providing a repeatable means of finding a "service". John Zachman (2001, pp. 38-40), who has laid much of the foundation for modern enterprise architecture, points out that it is not necessary to model an entire enterprise; that it can be done in manageable "slivers" and "slices", but he provides no means of either finding or managing such pieces of an enterprise. Information Technology theorists are concerned with building systems to respond to

COHERENCY MANAGEMENT

business needs, but are not provided with meaningful descriptions of the structure or nature of the business they are mandated to enable.

Given these challenges and the pressures to adapt, the ability to share the understanding of organizational mandates and systems becomes essential. It is imperative that the ability exists to represent and share the many views and business elements of the modern enterprise using a standardized framework based on rigor, akin to the models employed in airplane, building, bridge and road designs.

"Most enterprises have a wide definition of business architecture and business models. Typically, the definition includes strategies, missions, goals, critical success factors and other targets. The payback of identifying these factors and communicating them consistently across the enterprise has been studied and documented for more than a century" (Gartner, 2002). This is particularly true in the public sector, both because of the complexity of government and because of an increasing need to provide evidence in support of decisions.[12]

In the public sector, the implications of this complexity include:

- Departments and jurisdictions are not able to collaborate, therefore complex problems are not addressed in the time and manner required.
- Because the government is dependent on the proprietary methods and language of various vendors, no single system of record in the governance of design has been possible. Analysis is frequently redone, at great cost in money and time, just to serve the needs of the vendors.
- Analysis has been technology or process centric with no ability to scale up to either provide context to, or justification for investment.

In an effort to provide a framework for describing the strategic components of public sector institutions, and associating organizational activities based on a client service-centered paradigm, the

---

[12] Comparing any modern public sector organization to an equally large private sector organization will typically expose that the former have many more "lines of business" than the latter, are subject to more change (most public sector organizations go through a "hostile take over" every four to eight years), and are subject to far more oversight.

government of Canada has developed a standardized ontology and controlled vocabulary that draws on a defined set of patterns to both understand and describe business. The result of this work was the Governments of Canada Strategic Reference Model (GSRM), a non-proprietary, scalable, integrated and standardized business reference model[13] that provides a method for describing the business of government.

The GSRM began as the Municipal Reference Model, developed by the Municipal Information Systems Association (of Canada) and Chartwell IRM. Chartwell then worked with the province of Ontario to create the PSRM; Provincial Strategic Reference Model.

The experience in developing these early reference models was then leveraged to create the more generalized, powerful and mature GSRM.

Structured models[14] are core to the GSRM, providing standardized language, representation and methods for business people to share ideas about their operations, operational improvements, options for collaboration, and the strategic approach to both manage and invest in all business resources, including building computer systems that enhance their individual and collaborative processes.

The three Canadian orders of government: municipal, provincial/-territorial and federal, are now working to create a formal governing body which aims to be publishing agreed models some time in 2009.

Use of the GSRM

The concepts underlying the GSRM and the methods used in developing and propagating its creation and application are based on lessons learned from many sources. This includes a realization that the major reason that IT investments were underperforming was

---

[13] Ovidiu Noran's article on "Reference Models in Enterprise Architecture" asserts that "Reference models represent reusable templates for human roles (organizational), processes (common functionality) or technology (resources such as IT)." This in turn, supports an "enterprise engineering tool", which is used to build an "enterprise model".

[14] Models using a graphical representation, such as employed with UML, as compared to formal models which are based on mathematical representation.

that all IT methodologies assume that "the business" both fully understands "the business" and can express this understanding to IT in a form that is clear and complete enough to exploit the desired enabling technologies. Drawing on lessons from IT within the Government of Canada (GoC) and in other organizations an understanding emerged that:

- Commonly, reference[15] and strategic business models can provide context for business design decisions by representing strategic and tactical perspectives in the same basic terms, more efficiently than by any other means, at multiple levels of strategy – whole-of-government, departmental or program-level.

- Strategic business models can serve as systems of record for governing the design of the enterprise, more coherently and more efficiently than by other means.

- Strategic business models provide a means to link to more detailed models and designs (e.g. of business procedures, applications and databases).

These in turn resulted in the understanding that:

- Strategic business models must be championed and sponsored by business interests or they will not mature into an on-going asset. This means that the initial purposes may be for decision-making concerning information systems and technology, but models must offer on-going business benefits to policy and program managers or they will not be maintained. For example, business models should make it possible for business managers to explore and compare business alternatives in areas like HR and real property management.

- Strategic business models must be managed like a corporate resource. Business models must be accessible, useable and useful to many stakeholders, but managed by a central function to ensure quality and value.

The government also realized that whatever the solution, it could not exist as the property of a single vendor, that a lingua franca was needed if the government were to minimize rework by the business and systems services communities.

---

[15] "A reference model is a conceptual framework and may be used as a blueprint for information systems development" (Fettke & Loos, 2007, p.1).

The vision for applying the GSRM is that it is used to facilitate change management and to identify, scope, and coordinate multiple change initiatives and implementation projects. It will be used to develop application architecture strategies resulting in software that is coherent with business requirements.

A personal note on scalability
After working as a business analyst in a rapidly growing multinational corporation in the 1980s, I found that the analytical tools we had were not up to addressing the "big" problems that senior management asked me to take on. It was not until 2000, that I saw the first parts of the GSRM and immediately recognized that it was inherently scalable. This feature has been demonstrated on multiple assignments, making it possible to deal with a number of problems at the very top of the Government of Canada, as well as for a number of departments at the federal and provincial levels.

Advantages and Benefits of the GSRM

As a tool for supporting business decisions the GSRM provides:

- A business and client-centered means of developing shared understanding and establishing accountability.

- A highly scalable tool set for analyzing strategic business problems.

- A non-proprietary toolkit for expressing facts about business issues in a way that is rapidly consumable by decision makers.

- A public sector-centric language for addressing the "business of government".

In principle, the GSRM is used where and when it is necessary to make explicit any shared enterprise-wide business view – as a design tool and as the system of record for design governance at all levels including project, program/department, enterprise, and inter-enterprise. However, the GSRM goes well beyond a conceptual framework. As described previously, it contains specific design decisions and design constraints (e.g. the town plan and building code).

The GSRM offers benefits to the public, and to providers such as programs, departments, central agencies, partners, and other government jurisdictions. Benefits to the public arise from the GSRM's systematic and consistent representation of key elements of business in the design of all programs and services, so that the cross-program implications and impacts can be better understood, and a higher level of commonality, harmonization and client-centered integration can occur. Benefits to providers generally flow from the ability of a strategic business model to provide to all stakeholders an efficient, holistic/contextual and dependable basis for business analysis, design and transformation. Direct beneficiaries of the GSRM (and the whole-of-government models it produces) include government executives, who are therefore better able to identify redundancies and gaps to determine strategic opportunities for savings and investment, as well as areas where collaboration can improve and simplify service delivery. Business managers are able to use the models to describe their operations in the context of whole-of-government functions, and identify the other agencies or departments that play a role in their line of business to pursue opportunities for collaboration and cost-reduction.

In planning, the GSRM models provide tools to identify and analyze gaps, redundancies and opportunities for collaboration (e.g. with Canadian centric service delivery design), rationalize processes, bundle and or consolidate services, share information, better synchronize responses to events, and determine the implications of a policy change. This work typically occurs in studies at central agencies, department or program levels, and the models can be analyzed under different "what if" scenarios. Patterns and templates representing effective re-usable business designs, practices, etc. can be identified and recorded for later use.

In change management, the GSRM models can be used to help define the business scope and impact of GoC design change initiatives, and coordinate the interactions between these initiatives. To "use" the models means to describe the scope of each project in terms of standard elements (i.e. the specific programs, services, processes, information, etc. addressed by or implicated in the project) so that projects can be compared in similar terms.

In new designs, projects can take elements from the GSRM models, such as information about defined programs, services, types of communities, outputs, events, or processes, to create a specific design to carry out a business process or processes. Projects can use their business designs as starting points for more detailed models leading to applications, databases, technology, detailed business procedures, and so forth (working in different rows of the Zachman Framework for Enterprise Architecture). Projects are able to use patterns and templates to expedite their business design processes and improve the results.

In alignment, design change and new design initiatives meeting criteria for review can present their business designs to governance at the department, inter-departmental and/or central agency levels. Alignment with overall strategic designs[16] and coordination with other concurrent projects, as well as comparisons to the rest of the operating enterprise (when it is also described with GSRM), can be ensured.

External to government, stakeholders also benefit from a more coherent and consistent procurement process. Suppliers and service providers to government in specific fields are provided with clearer project requirements and specifications that use the same basic terminology, regardless of which administrative unit in the GoC leads the project. This makes it easier to generate accurate and reliable cost estimates, as well as improve the overall fairness and competitiveness of the procurement process for suppliers and government alike.

Parliamentarians and others who are responsible for overseeing and monitoring also benefit, because the many processes of government are more thoroughly and accurately "depicted" than through the simple narratives that are frequently used to date; the interdependencies between them becomes more evident, and areas of duplication and redundancy are easier to identify.

Elements of the GSRM

The elements included in the GSRM are broadly categorized into three groups:

- The semantics which define the core concepts of the GSRM including relationships among these concepts.

---

[16] A strategic design and plan is a long term plan of action designed to achieve a particular goal; its arguments are clearly linked to desired business outcomes and the way forward is described in just enough detail to trigger change and shape the result. It is not concerned with the actual deployment of resources through which objectives and, ultimately, the strategic intent is achieved.

- The controlled vocabulary and patterns which allow for extensive reuse.

- The models or composite constructs that link multiple concepts and relationships prescribed by the GSRM which may be used for analysis and / or design of business activities.

GSRM Semantics

The following is a semantic model showing some of the key concepts in the GSRM. There are of course, many more concepts in the GSRM, and still further numbers of concepts are required to fully describe an enterprise.

A note on the state of the GSRM specification

While the GSRM is in active use, both within the federal Government of Canada and across all other jurisdictions, a full specification for GSRM has not officially been released by the Government of Canada. While some aspects of the GSRM were published by the Chief Information Officer Branch in 2003, this was done as part of an effort to enable better transformation within and across government. The specification exists as a number of draft and working documents which are being incorporated / considered by the newly created pan-Canadian governance body. The material in this chapter draws on the most authoritative sources available from this body of work.

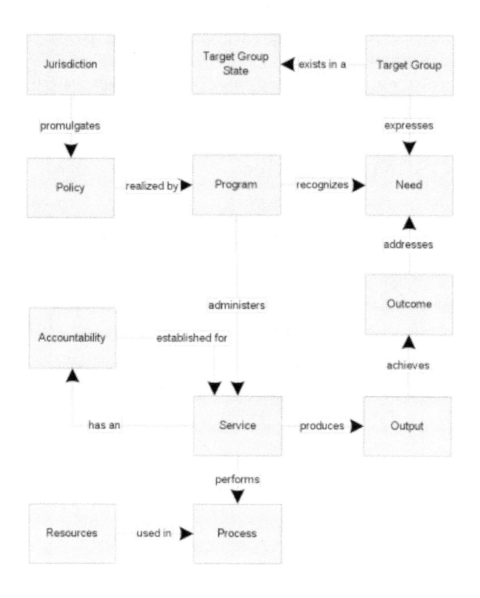

Figure 1. Partial Semantic Model of the GSRM

The boxes on the above figure represent concepts of significance to the GSRM, and the arcs show valid logical relations between the concepts. The arrow is included ONLY to assist the reader in understanding how the verb or verb phrase annotating the arc can logically be read to understand the relationship between the two concepts. For example, "Policy is realized by (a) Program", or "Program administers Service" are logical statements in this model, whereas "Output produces Service" is not.

Some of the key concepts set out in the GSRM are provided in the following section.

Accountability

Accountability is an obligation to demonstrate and take responsibility for performance in light of agreed expectations. The key distinction between responsibility and accountability is that responsibility is the obligation to act whereas accountability is the obligation to answer for an action. In other words "accountability" is a type of relationship in which the "accountable" party has accepted an obligation to report on and meet agreed performance targets and to accept the consequences if agreed targets are not met.

The accountability relationship between services identifies who receives the value, and places the accountability on the service.

The outsourced call centre

From the perspective of the GSRM the fact that a call center has been outsourced by a service provider is irrelevant to the provision of service to the end customer. The service provider is always accountable to the customer for the service. In a well designed accountability relationship, the call centre, even though organizationally separate from the service provider, should have all the tools to transparently meet the customer needs, and the two organizations would be able to separately carry out their respective processes without impacting the customer in any way. While the customer might obtain some output of value from the call centre, the key value relationship is that the call center is accountable to the service provider, and the service provider is accountable to the customer for the service experience. When these relationships are not recognized, the foundations are laid for poor service.

The value of understanding accountability as opposed to operating entirely in a process or information flow paradigm is that it exposes the contractual relations or commitments necessary to deliver value.

Need

A need is an acknowledged physiological condition of an individual person or a group of people requiring relief. It is manifested by a target group and recognized by a program (i.e. the portion of need[17] that the program will address). A targeted or recognized need is a target group condition or circumstance that the program is obliged or mandated to respond to when it occurs.

The value of using needs is that the acknowledgement of needs establishes a client centricity to the design and from this scope, a clear justification for the inclusion or exclusion of all components.

Outcome

An outcome is a desirable trend in the level of a recognized Target Group Need. It is an intended result of action, expressed in the normalized terms of a recognized Target Group Need and a desirable trend expected to manifest in measurements over time.

Program

A program is a mandate conferred from the governors of the enterprise to achieve goals and outcomes or the delivery of value that addresses the identified needs of a target group[18], to either keep a target group in a particular state or to move them to one that policy has identified as being more desirable. Programs are delivered through a collection of services that contribute to the program goals and comply with the program strategy. Programs are allocated funding and resources by the governors of the enterprise.

Public Programs have target groups external to the government — individuals, businesses and not-for-profit groups. Internal Programs have communities internal to government as their target groups.

---

[17] Needs are different from requirements; needs are recognized or acknowledged from first principles whereas requirements are determined or defined from alternatives.

[18] In the private sector, this could be expressed as "A line of business has a mandate conferred from the governors of the enterprise to generate profit by addressing the needs of a market segment."

The value of the program concept is that it provides the scope, context and motivation for the expenditure of resources and shows the benefits of such expenditure.[19]

Service

One of the core concepts of the GSRM is the idea of "service". A service is a means to address needs by managing the delivery of some valued output. As such, a service is a well bounded 'machine' capable of producing an output that is deemed to be complete and valuable in and of itself. It is both discrete and measurable, and from the client's perspective, it is independent from other services.

A service has a number of very important properties:

- It hides the details of work from the client.
- It affects the real world through the production of some real valued result.

The value of the service concept:

- Provides both motivation and context for process, thus providing justification for the existence of a process as well as establishing clear points at which a process starts and stops.
- Based on the service type, establishes a pattern of process required to deliver the value of the service.

The relation of the service concept to the Zachman primitives is subtle; a service is a container for a pattern of services that give the processes their motivation. Thus, while a service is not a "Zachman primitive", it provides justification to the list of processes that appears in Column 2 (the "what" column).

Within the GSRM there are nineteen service output types. These are capable of providing all the value delivered by government, and each provides, through its patterns, important information about the applicable performance metrics and process patterns required to deliver the desired value.

---

[19] The service paradigm offers one method to understand both what has been done and not done with confidence.

	Service Output Type	Service Type	Accountability	Service Delivery
Enhance Capability to Act	Funds	Acquiring & providing financial resources	Appropriate Use	Convey
	(Units of) Resource	Providing resources such as goods, equipment, accommodations (apart from funds)	Appropriate Use	Convey
	New Knowledge	Conducting research	Innovation	Discover
	Care & Rehabilitation Encounters	Providing care & rehabilitation to people & things	Restoration	Restore
	Educational & Training Encounters	Providing education & training experiences	Learning	Teach
	Recreational & Cultural Encounters	Providing recreational & cultural experiences	Values Expressed	Present
	Movements	Moving people & things	Delivery	Transport
Facilitate and Influence Actions	Advisory Encounters	Providing information & advice	Information	Advise
	Matches, Referrals & Linkages	Brokering, referring, connecting, matching	Obligations on Both Parties	Refer
	Advocacy & Promotional Encounters	Influencing, advocating, persuading, promoting awareness	Persuasion	Advocate
	Periods of Agreement	Creating collaborations, negotiating agreements, settling disputes	Commitment of All Parties	Negotiate
Regulation Actions	Periods of Permission	Regulating, licensing, permitting, certifying, identifying, authorizing	Ensuring Entitlement	Grant
	Findings	Inspecting & investigating	Diligence	Investigate
	Rulings & Judgements	Applying rules & dispensing justice	Fairness	Judge
	Penalties & Periods of Sanction	Enforcing compliance, meting out punishment, penalizing	Ensuring Compliance	Enforce
	Periods of Protection	Monitoring, warning, guarding, storing, eliminating threats, reducing risks	Vigilance	Guard
	Interventions	Intervening, responding to threats & emergencies, giving aid, restoring order	Readiness	Intervene
Core Actions	Rules	Creating & changing rules	Reflecting Mandate	Promulgate
	Implemented changes	Changing existing organization, practices, systems	Mitigating Risks	Implement

Table 1. Service patterns

The "service" concept is an incredibly powerful organizing concept. Because each service of a specific output type requires a similar pattern of processes, knowing the service provides the list of processes provides the justification for each process, and sets them at a similar level, giving each a defined start and end. Through the patterns established for each service output type (Government of Canada, 2004), important information about performance standards is identified. This information can be used in service contracts or service level agreements.

Target Group
A target group is a segment of a larger population having specific inherent characteristics (i.e. age, gender, unemployed) that is intended to receive the benefit of a program. When addressing a need, it is the target group that sets the scope of the response by the program.

Key Models

The GRSM provides business analysts with the means to develop the various models needed to support the analysis of business activities performed by large organizations. These models are of interest to decision makers as they provide a robust and evidence-based source of information to support decision-making. As all GSRM primitive components are internally consistent and unambiguous, each composite model provides a single perspective, and each view is consistent with all the other composite models or views, they provide a means for looking at any business in a consistent and rich basis designed to support business design and investment decisions in the overall enterprise context. The result is that decisions and investments are no longer locally optimized, but placed in terms of their net value to the overall business entity, be it government, department, program or project.

Some of the key models employed in the GSRM are:

- Program Service Accountability Model
- Service Integration and Alignment Model
- Semantic Model
- Target Group State Transition Model
- Logistics Model

While these models only represent a subset of the total toolkit available within the GSRM, they do constitute the key weapons in the architectural arsenal. Two of the strategic models in this toolkit are the Program Service Accountably Model and the Service Integration and Alignment Model.

Program Service Accountably Model (PSAM)

A PSAM documents the context of an operating business (i.e. government service) or a prospective business (i.e. program) specification by expressing the value that it is intended to deliver.

Imagine a program aimed at managing the transport of a controlled waste; the mandate for such a program might look as follows:[20]

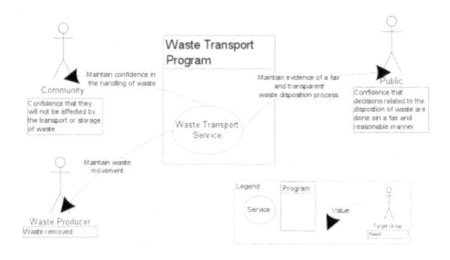

Figure 2. Example PSAM

Target Group	Essential Characteristics
Waste Producer	A party having waste that must be disposed of.
Community	Individuals or groups directly affected by the handling, transport and disposition of waste (i.e. on the route or at the destination).
General Public	Current and future parties that may be impacted or have an interest in the decisions related to the handling, transport and disposition of waste

---

[20] Examples are oversimplifications and for illustrative purposes only.

This program has a single target group facing service; the "Waste Transport Service", a service of service output type "Movement". This service responds to the recognized needs of:

- Waste Producers by maintaining waste movement
- Community by maintaining confidence in the handling of waste
- The Public by maintaining evidence of a fair and transparent waste disposition process

Each of these outcomes responds to a specific need that is recognized by the program and collectively they establish a client-centered description of its value. Indicators can be attached to each of these outcomes to measure the extent to which the desired results are being achieved.

The purpose of this model is two-fold:

1. To assemble the components and to specify the relationships between them in order to highlight the benefits that an existing or prospective program will deliver to an identified group.
2. To provide an organization independent context (i.e. define the scope) for describing a unit of government activities.

A PSAM:

- Provides a foundation for policy analysis and service requirements.
- Documents traceability between those getting value and the service output being delivered.
- Sets a foundation to support "client-centric" business design.[21]
- Identifies the policy that established the mandate for the program and the strategic outcome that is to be realized.
- Provides the information needed to compare and align multiple programs and services in terms of target groups and needs
- Makes explicit the link between service outputs and the value that is delivered to fulfill target group needs.

---

[21] The Conceptual blueprint of an enterprise, it shows interrelationships between the enterprise's major processes and main resources required in achieving its objectives and in providing value to its customers. Typically this will include the decision-making process (governance) of the enterprise.

- Identifies direct program outcomes for the program, its target-group facing services, target groups and needs.

- Identifies direct outcomes that are used in the development of the program's Program Logic Model to make explicit the links from direct outcomes to strategic outcomes.

- Establishes the full scope of the program objectives based on the response required or needs to be fulfilled, thus identifying the capabilities as well as the value of the responses.

- Identifies the service outputs that represent the final valued outputs that are designed to respond to identified needs.

- Sets the context at the top of the system of interest and from the outside of the enterprise looking in (from the perspective of those that derive value from the system), both expressed in terms of value. From this point on, everything is focused on meeting this context, providing the value.

- Identifies the final outcomes for which it is necessary to develop requisite capability to provide the responses at the necessary levels of service.

- Documents traceability between those getting value and the response.

- Provides a means for developing shared insight into how multiple programs compare to one another, integrate, and the benefits that each program is designed to deliver.

Service Integration and Alignment Model (SIAM)

A SIAM is a view of a business that represents the requisite organizational capabilities (i.e. services or process patterns) and the accountability relationships necessary to achieve a specified outcome[22] – the value of the enterprise (as set out in the PSAM).

As a chain of value, the SIAM depicts:

- All capabilities (services) within the scope of one or more mandates (programs), required to achieve the final valued output.[23]

---

[22] An "accountability" may be operationalised as a service level agreement, a contract or through some other performance based agreement. However, GSRM makes no provision for specifying or modeling these accountability mechanisms.

[23] Those relationships making up the value chain that assembles the raw materials to deliver the final valued output.

- All service outputs provided by the services that are in scope. In a service value chain the service output of one service is the raw material for another service or a service all along the chain, until the final valued output is delivered to the client or client recipient.

- All accountability relationships among service providers in scope. Rarely does a single service have all the capabilities needed to deliver its value proposition.

A SIAM may take one of three forms:

1. It may be an "abstract SIAM", which places no constraints on (horizontal) capabilities needed to fulfill a mandate.

2. It may be an "Unconstrained Design SIAM", which shows both horizontal and vertical accountability relationships (relationships to governance) between services independent of organizational context and which identifies opportunities for the creation of common[24] or shared[25] services that provides economies of scale in service delivery.

3. It may be a "Constrained Design SIAM", showing the implications of placing services in specific organizational configurations.

For the Waste Transport Program, the service and accountability relation shipments might be in the following form:

---

[24] Common services - Services that all parts of the enterprise must use.

[25] Shared Services - Services that parts of the enterprise may chose to use only when they deem it appropriate.

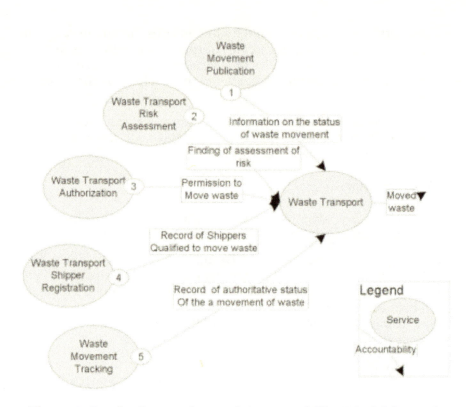

Figure 3. Service Integration and Accountability Model (SIAM) for Waste Transport

Ref	Service	Description	Accountabil-ity
	Waste Transport	Safely transports waste from the Waste Producer to a safe disposal site	Transport
1	Waste Movement Publication	Provides timely notification of what waste is being trans-ported were, when and by whom	Advice
2	Waste Transport Risk Assessment	Determines the risk associated with the transport of waste	Finding
3	Waste Transport Authorization	Provides the approval to transport waste and sets the terms and conditions for the movement of waste	Permission
4	Waste Transport Shipper Registration	Provides a record of the actual handling of waste	Periods of Protection
5	Waste Movement Tracking	Keeps track of the actual han-dling of waste	Advice

The SIAM shows that all the services in the Waste Transport value chain are accountable to the Waste Transport service; that the Safe Transport of Waste and the fulfillment of the outcomes identified in the PSAM are dependent on each of the enabling services meeting its obligations to the target group facing service, Waste Transport. Each vector shows the nature of the accountability relationship. These relationships are often initially confused with process relationships, but in this and all other cases, the processes which this portfolio of services is accountable for would make a very complex web which is hidden at this level of abstraction.

Assuming the SIAM provides full coverage of the required value chain, a wide number of decisions can be made. Examples of such decisions include:

- The service performance standard of each service required for the entire chain to properly function can be evaluated.

- Organizational design decisions can be made (i.e. can pieces of the value chain be outsourced, assigned to different organizations and if so, what risks might these entail and what options are available to mitigate the associated risk).

- Identifying the enabling technology might be appropriate to assist in the provision of service.

The SIAM also provides an important context to the behavior, structure and purpose of its components. The services each provide an organizing context and justification for their processes, semantics, and the states and events of affected resources.

Conclusion

The total toolkit of the GSRM is much more extensive than what has been presented here. The model coverage includes such areas as logistics, semantics, performance measurement, and the measurement of strategic outcomes. They individually and collectively take into account the repeatable patterns and relationships required to create a very powerful set of tools that can be used to address many of the significant problems of modern business. By using the GSRM, we have been able to address of complex business questions to rapidly identify gaps, inconsistencies, and opportunities with a high level of confidence that the analysis was correct and complete.

> "I lost sleep on a lot of occasions because of issues at work, but never because I did not have an architecture." Senior Executive
>
> The real question is: "How many good night's sleep might you have had if you had confidence that the architecture was going to provide the evidence to obtain a solution?" or
>
> "What would you do to know there was no problem because the architecture had long ago provided guidance on the optimal course of action?"

Lessons Learned

While the GSRM was built on lessons learned over time, its use has in turn spawned additional lessons. As a result of applying the GSRM, some of the insights we have gained include:

- The challenge for managers introducing or using Enterprise Business Architecture (EBA) is to find the balance to do enough analysis to improve decisions, while not allowing a search for the "perfect architecture" to get in the way of "better".

- The difficulty with EBA is that it flies directly in the face of the "quick fix" mentality that ignores the implications of poor designs, weak business integration across the enterprise, the inherently weak understanding of cause and effect within the business, and that seeks to show rapid apparent progress. Because many decision makers are used to and believe that they are proficient at making decisions drawn on complex design questions without evidence, they see no value in building or exploiting the shared understanding that comes from modeling.

From a management perspective, the models produced through GSRM style architectural analysis have been shown to be important tools for supporting business decisions by executives by ensuring:

- A client-centered focus is created as all analysis starts with the need for those for whom value is produced.

- All models have a solid "through line" such that one model informs another, producing a clear connection between strategy and results.

- That everyone in the management team has all the information needed to support a decision and the tools to rationalize the various perspectives. Synergy is created across the team.

- There exists a basis for comparing not just one project with another, but to the rest of the operating enterprise.

- That investments are consistent with priorities.

- That complete models answer questions and do so consistently.

- That there is involvement in the initiation. Planning and execution of work is consistent with organizational mandates.

- That applicable resources are coherently organized to achieve the desired outcomes.

- An understanding of the capabilities needed to achieve objectives.

- That there exists a base for measuring and comparing enterprise performance.

- The ability to understand what is required to undertake enterprise change.

While EBA in general and the GSRM in particular introduce a new set of formalism to business, the formalities associated with building an enterprise business architecture and integrating it with enabling and supporting technologies do not necessitate discarding current strategic planning results and methods. Similarly, there is no need for the business to throw away existing capabilities in such areas as business process analysis and its associated reengineering tools, techniques, and methods. EBA does however demand that the organization adopt a more disciplined and rigorous culture and practice to document essential connections between all components, parts and pieces, and over time create a picture of the entire system called "the enterprise" or "the business". As this occurs it will become another tool for understanding the enterprise, analyzing its opportunities, developing initiatives to sustain a competitive advantage, and bringing coherence to the use of all resources, most especially to IT.

References

Chandler, A. (1996) Structure follows Strategy. Beard Books.

Fettke, P., Loos, P. (eds.) (2007). Reference modeling for business systems analysis. Idea Group Inc.

Gartner Group (2002). Business Models: The Architecture That Pays For Itself. Gartner Research Note July 9th, 2002.

George, R. St. (2007). Winnipeg Paves the Way in Fleet Management. APWA Reporter American Public Works Association, August 2007.

Government of Canada (2004). GSRM Service Reference Patterns Version 1.3 June 10, 2004. TBS

Jaques, E. (2006). Requisite Organization. Cason Hall and Company.

Osterwalder, A. (2007). How to Describe and Improve your Business Model to Compete Better. Draft 0.8. http://tinyurl.com/2c7uzu.

Porter, M. E. (1996). What is strategy? Harvard Business Review, November-December, 61-78.

Stanford, N. (2007). Guide to Organization Design. Profile Book.

Zachman, J.A. (2001). The Zachman Framework For Enterprise Architecture: Primer for Enterprise Engineering and Manufacturing by John A. Zachman; Zachman International.

About the Author

Neil Kemp is a senior consultant with 25 years experience in the federal, municipal and private sectors. He has extensive experience in program and project management and in project process improvement. Neil has extensive experience in the analysis and design of complex systems and in aligning these to strategic business objectives. More recently he has been focusing his practice on the provision of strategic guidance in the areas of organizational capability analysis, and strategic transformation planning and design. Neil has an MBA from Queens University in Kingston, is certified as a Project Management Professional, in ITIL, as a Quality Manager by the American Society for Quality and as a TOGAF Architect.

Neil Kemp MBA PMP CQMgr
Swift Fox Strategies Inc
www.swiftfoxstrategies.ca
neil.kemp@swiftfoxstrategies.ca

Section III

ENVISIONING THE FUTURE: LEADERSHIP AND COHERENCY MANAGEMENT

Chapter 15

CHIEF INFORMATION OFFICERS, ENTERPRISE ARCHITECTURE AND COHERENCY MANAGEMENT

Jean-Pierre Auffret

Editors' Preface

The role of the CIO is evolving. This has been very well documented in the book "The New CIO Leader" by Broadbent & Kitzis. There is a growing acceptance that the CIO could play a very critical role in ensuring organizational coherence. Though the CIO is not the only potential candidate, given the CIO is emerging as a business leader, the CIO is a very promising candidate. We believe that from a practicality point of view, especially in the 'embedded' mode, the CIO may be the most likely 'delegate' to perform the task.

The author recognizes the critical role of the CIO in ensuring coherency; the chapter extends the thought by comparing various CXO roles and their suitability to be responsible for coherency management. We believe this is important as there are situational, cultural and organizational factors due to which certain roles may be more suitable for certain types of organizations to ensure coherency. The comparison acts as an input to such decision-making processes from the Governance perspective. The chapter presents brief case studies about the adoption of EA in US, Japan, Indonesia and Vietnam. Besides the fact that this provides a good contrast between developed and developing countries, differences due to cultural factors are clearly evident. Most current literature on EA comes from / are about EA in developed countries. This chapter provides a good balance in its coverage.

Introduction

With the increasing importance of information and information technology to organizational success, the last several years have seen a continuing discussion on the executive and strategic role of the CIO. Whether in the private sector, public sector, developed country or developing country, many view the CIO as an executive leader who plays an integral part in the development and execution of organization strategy (Broadbent and Kitzis, 2005). The rationale is that the CIO is uniquely positioned to connect organizational strategy to operational execution, and in the many cases where information technology is a key factor, organizational strategy and success, for example in the airline and telecommunication industries, the CIO's efforts are tied directly to firm success.

Oftentimes CIO's do not have this executive and strategic role however. At times, CIO play a role closer to that of an IT manager, and quite often CIO's have limited input to organizational strategy as a result of reporting hierarchies or as a result of a lack of CIO position stature. Indeed the Fairfax County, Virginia, U.S.A. government CIO role was elevated and broadened to Deputy County Administrator for Information in an effort to formalize its executive stature and importance given how critical the position is to county government success.

CIO's are the focal point for organizational Enterprise Architecture efforts and these are traditionally seen as solely the domain of information technology departments. Coherency Management is an evolution, outcome and extension of traditional Enterprise Architecture efforts (Doucet, Gøtze, Saha and Bernard, 2008) and provides CIO's the opportunity to reach their organizational potential as full strategic executive leaders in both private sector firms and in government organizations. Coherency Management has the objective of providing an overarching logical consistency in the relationships of organizational and department objectives, strategy and operations (Doucet, Gøtze, Saha and Bernard, 2008).

Coherency Management is also a logical extension of management strategy practice where organizations develop internally consistent strategy or variable maps comprised of variables representing goals and objectives, internal capabilities, organizational environmental factors, strategies and outcomes, with associated cause and effect relationships and then try to operationalize the resultant overall strategy in a consistent manner.

COHERENCY MANAGEMENT

The three fundamental outcomes of Coherency Management, alignment, agility, and assurance, (Doucet, Gøtze, Saha and Bernard, 2008) are integral for organizational strategy and are the basis for the enhanced importance of the CIO role. Alignment is the coordination and consistency between internal organizations, individuals and organizations and processes within an overall organization. As examples, alignment in government is a consistency in approach to providing security; and alignment in the private sector is Apple's coordination of the strategy and operations for the Mac, iPod and iPhone product lines. Agility is the organization's ability to respond to different environmental factors such as new or enhanced competition or changing economic conditions. As examples, agility in government is the ability to quickly provide new services to citizens or respond to new government regulations such as changing tax or pension schemes; and agility in the private sector is the ability of businesses to quickly develop and provision new products or services such as MCI's speed to market with the new "Friends and Family" product in the late 1980's. Assurance is an organization's capability to ensure quality and control. As examples, assurance in government is the ability to provide citizen services in a quality and cost effective manner; and assurance in the private sector is the compliance with national regulations such as Sarbanes-Oxley Act (SOX) and the Financial Instruments and Exchange Law of Japan (J-SOX).

Coherency Management is predicated on an evolution of the approach to Enterprise Architecture from Foundation Architecture to Extended Architecture to Embedded Architecture and then to a synthesis of the three in a Balanced Architecture (Doucet, Gøtze, Saha and Bernard, 2008). Figure 1 below shows the goals, governance responsibility, development method and associated artifacts for each of the three approach modes.

EA Mode	Goals	Governance	Development Method	Artifacts
Foundation Architecture	IT Systems	CIO	Architecture Methods	Business Requirements
Extended Architecture	Enterprise Design	CXO and Process Owners	Architecture Methods	Strategic Goals and Business Requirements
Embedded Architecture	Strategic Alignment	CXO	Outcome of Business Processes	Business Process Artifacts

Figure 1. Three Modes of Enterprise Architecture
(Doucet, Gøtze, Saha and Bernard, 2008)

The first mode, Foundation Architecture, is technology focused and most often is primarily the responsibility of the CIO and their organization. The second mode, Extended Architecture, is the broadening and extension of Enterprise Architecture to describe non information technology business activities such as program design and services design. The third mode, Embedded Architecture, utilizes Enterprise Architecture techniques, such as reference models, in the development of processes for business functions such as planning and budgeting and human resources management.

As Figure 1 shows, governance for Foundation Architecture is the responsibility of CIO's, but governance for Extended and Embedded Architectures is the responsibility of the entire executive team. Leadership for Extended and Embedded Architectures can be delegated to one executive though and as the traditional focal point of enterprise architecture efforts, CIO's are a natural starting point for organizational Coherency Management initiatives. When organizations strengthen their approaches to enterprise design and commitment to strategic alignment through the Enterprise Architecture modes of Extended Architecture and Embedded Architecture, CIO's can build upon their experience and expertise to provide enhanced leadership to their organizations. Figure 2, below, outlines some of the considerations for Coherency Management leadership by each of the CXO roles.

Executive	Adequate Position Breadth	Focus and Expertise	Consistency w/ Role	Sufficient Stature
CEO	Yes	Strategy and Business	No	Yes
COO	Yes	Business and Operations	Possibly	Yes
CIO	Possibly	IT, Enterprise Architecture and Business	Possibly	Possibly
CFO	Yes	Finance and Business	Possibly	Possibly

Figure 2. Comparison of considerations for Coherency Management Leadership

CIO's who have a business and cross-organizational focus are in a good position to lead Coherency Management efforts as they also have the Foundation Enterprise Architecture expertise. As a result, they are able to apply Enterprise Architecture approaches and models to building organizational alignment though Extended and Embedded Architecture.

This paper builds upon these ideas by reviewing how the idea of Coherency Management ties into the evolving role of the CIO, and then by exploring the ramifications for private sector and public sector CIO's and Enterprise Architecture efforts. The paper concludes with a discussion of specific considerations related to CIO's, Coherency Management and new product development and service delivery.

The Changing Role of the CIO

As noted in the introduction, the evolution, extension and outcome of Enterprise Architecture as Coherency Management mirrors and surpasses the evolution and elevation of the CIO position from a purely technical role to a broader cross-departmental strategic role. The changes to the U.S. Federal CIO Core Competencies provide a good basis for visualizing the changes in the CIO role. (The Federal CIO Core Competencies were originally developed to meet the requirements of the U.S. Information Technology Reform Act of 1996 (the Clinger-Cohen Act) and are updated every two years. Figure 3 shows a comparison of the original 1997 Core Competencies, 2007 updated Core Competencies and the further changes that would ensue for CIO's who are delegated the leadership responsibilities for Coherency Management.

Desktop Technology Knowledge and Technical skills have given way to broader eGovernment, Information Security, Enterprise Architecture and Technology Management and Assessment Core Competencies. In addition, there has been an enhancement of cross-boundary process analysis and collaboration knowledge areas as part of these competencies consistent with the evolution of Enterprise Architecture, itself a foundation for Coherency Management.

1997 U.S. Federal CIO Core Competencies	2007 U.S. Federal CIO Core Competencies	Additional CIO Core Competencies with Coherency Management Leadership
Policy and Organization	Policy and Organization	Alignment Assurance
Leadership and Managerial Skills	Leadership and Management	Reference Model Optimization
Process and Change Management	Process and Change Management	Service Design
Information Resources Strategy and Planning	Information Resources Strategy and Planning	Program Design
IT Performance Assessment	IT Performance Assessment: Models and Methods	
Project and Program Management	IT Project and Program Management	
Capital Planning and Investment Assessment	Capital Planning and Investment Control	
Acquisition	Acquisition	
Technical Skills	eGovernment	
Desktop Technology Knowledge	Information Security and Information Assurance	
	Enterprise Architecture	
	Assessment	

Figure 3. Comparison of Federal CIO Core Competencies (1997, 2007) and prospective changes for Coherency Management leadership.

The CIO's Unique Perspective of Enterprise Architecture

"Enterprise Architecture in many companies refers to a detailed blueprint of systems, data and technology" (Ross, Weill and Robertson, 2006) and is a fairly traditional view of Enterprise Architecture in many organizations. This architecture is Foundational with the goal of developing good, cost effective systems. The Enterprise Architecture is developed by CIO staff whose office has the associated Enterprise Architecture development expertise.

Enterprise Architecture in the Foundational mode often provides a path from "As Is" to "To Be" for organizational system efforts.

Interestingly, CIO's perspectives of Enterprise Architecture and its relative importance to the role of the CIO vary around the world.

Figure 3 below shows a comparison by Obi and Iwasaki (Obi and Iwasaki, 2006) of rankings of the importance of CIO Core Competencies developed from surveys of CIO's and IT executives in the U.S. and Japan. While the rank of Enterprise Architecture by Japanese CIO's is much lower than by U.S. CIO's, the Japanese CIO's rank competencies related to coherency management – Leadership and Management, Policy and Organization, and Process and Change Management very highly.

Rank	Ranking of Importance of CIO Core Competencies – U.S.	Ranking of Importance of CIO Core Competencies - Japan
1	Information Strategy and Planning	Leadership and Management
2	Enterprise Architecture	Policy and Organization
3	Policy and Organization	Process and Change Management
4	Information Security	IT Performance Assessment
5	Leadership and Management	Information Strategy and Planning
6	Process and Change Management	Investment Management
7	Project Management	Technology Management
8	Technology Management	Project Management
9	IT Performance Assessment	Information Security
10	Investment Planning	Enterprise Architecture
11	eGovernment and eCommerce	eProcurement
12	eProcurement	eGovernment and eCommerce

Figure 4. Comparison of Ranking of Importance of CIO Core Competencies - U.S. and Japan (Obi and Iwasaki, 2006)

As Enterprise Architecture evolves and begins to become more business driven, the CIO continues to be the focal point. A leading example is the U.S. Federal CIO Enterprise Architecture (FEA) effort – which while business driven continues to be a Foundational Architecture - "To transform the Federal Government to one that is citizen-centered, results-oriented, and market based, the Office of Management and Budget (OMB) is developing the Federal Enterprise Architecture, a business-based framework for government-wide improvement". The effort is strategic, cross-organizational and led by the Chair of the U.S. Federal CIO Council[26]. The OMB overview continues, "In contrast to the many failed architecture efforts in the past the FEA is entirely business driven".

The effort utilizes Enterprise Architecture tools and methodologies and extends their application to the business and strategic context.

---

[26] Office of Management and Budget: www.whitehouse.gov/omb

The resulting FEA artifacts are Service Component, Data, Performance and Business reference models.

The U.S. FEA effort and its transformational goals is an example of the type of world class Foundation Architecture that provides a baseline for broadening and extending the possibility of Enterprise Architecture to Coherency Management. U.S. FEA success will result in alignment - cross-organizational consistency; agility - results-orientation; and assurance – measurable and managed performance.

Coherency Management and CIO'S

CIO's, as the focal point of Foundational Architecture and having the methodological expertise of reference models and process analysis, are well placed to play the leadership role as Enterprise Architecture reaches its potential in Coherency Management. While CIO roles have many similarities in the private and public sectors and in developing countries and developed countries, the context of Enterprise Architecture and the benefits of Coherency Management can be quite different. The following sections explore some of the considerations for organizations and CIO's in regard to Enterprise Architecture and Coherency Management.

Coherency Management and CIO's in the Private Sector

Private sector success is increasingly dependent on the consistent and logical implementation of corporate strategy across multiple departments and operating units. In turn, private sector competitive advantage is increasingly driven by innovative and agile business services and application of information technology, as many of today's corporations are more global and more networked than in decades past.

Telecommunications companies, airlines and utilities in networked industries rely on information technology for most of their operations. The development and rollout of new products and services by these networked industry firms is dependent on the development and modification of IT and non IT aspects of services such as ordering, purchasing, provisioning, scheduling, billing and pricing. Success with new products and obtaining the associated competitive advantage results from corporate agility, alignment and assurance - the goals of Coherency Management.

Similarly for global manufacturing firms, such as Toyota - agility, alignment and assurance are key components of company success. Indeed part of Toyota's competitive advantage lies in its focus in each of these areas – in bringing new automobile models to market faster than competitors; in aligning objectives and processes of geographically distant organizations; and in assuring quality and reliability

As information technology is a key aspect of competitive success in these industries (and in others such as service industries – for example in banking), the role of the CIO has evolved towards the executive role as described by Broadbent and Kitzis in "The New CIO Leader" (Broadbent and Kitzis, 2005). Foundation Architecture provides an opportunity to strengthen company efforts in these industries by aligning company strategies and processes and information technology. Coherency management then provides a further opportunity by aligning company strategy, initiatives and processes across business units.

Elizabeth Hackenson, Senior Vice President and CIO, Alcatel-Lucent (Hackenson, 2007) at the "2007 Global CIO Leadership Conference - Creating Better Government and Society through Enhanced CIO Leadership" held at George Mason University highlighted several major current and future themes for CIO's and organizations:

- Agility is paramount in the global environment

- There is great internal and external pressure to deliver fast

- It is imperative for CIO's to speak in business terms and to communicate value to the business

While these are the themes for CIO's Enterprise Architecture efforts in the mode of Foundation Architecture, they are also important in relation to Coherency Management. Agility is the goal of Coherency Management, while CIO's, delegated as leaders of Coherency Management efforts, must not only communicate clearly about business value, but must also be business oriented as with their additional responsibilities only a part of their role will be IT focused.

Ms. Hackenson closed by saying that IT is fast becoming more and more at the forefront of corporate strategy. And by implication IT focused efforts such as Foundational Architecture are becoming more business and strategy focused through extension to Extended Architecture and then Embedded Architecture.

Coherency Management and CIO's in the Public Sector

While a somewhat different context and with somewhat different challenges than for the private sector, governments can equally benefit from the extension of Enterprise Architecture to Coherency Management. As for the private sector, government CIO's can and should play a focal role.

A major challenge in government in general, and especially in eGovernment, is cross-departmental coordination. Developed countries ranking higher in ICT Readiness and with more experience in eGovernment and applying information technology to better government have greater experience in aligning governmental organizations, but nevertheless the challenge exists in both developed and developing countries.

Nagy Hanna (Hanna, 2006) outlined five types of institutional models for cross-government coordination of information technology:

- Shared Responsibility Model – responsibility is shared by government ministries

- Policy Coordination Model – responsibility is coordinated by a central policy group comprised of representatives from different ministries such as the U.S. Federal CIO Council

- Lead Ministry Model – responsibility is undertaken by one ministry

- ICT Agency in Civil Service Model – responsibility is undertaken by a civilian agency

- ICT Agency in Public – Private Partnership Model – responsibility is undertaken by a public-private partnership

Each of these institutional models aims to achieve the coherence of strategy, process and information systems that is the objective of coherency management. And the coordinating organization in each of these models would be well placed to lead Coherency Management efforts for their governments.

The discussion of the development of the U.S. FEA earlier has shown the Policy Coordination Model in practice where the U.S. Federal CIO Council has responsibility for oversight of government wide architecture and information system initiatives. The objective of CIO Councils is cross-government information technology coherency, and extending Enterprise Architecture to the Coherency Management framework will help further the potential of the councils and assist agencies and ministries to achieve their goals.

CIO Councils aim to foster and facilitate cross-government information technology coherency for functions such as procurement, best practices and innovation, program management, security, budgeting, and enterprise architecture (Auffret, 2007). With Coherency Management, Enterprise Architecture becomes a method for achieving organizational alignment and agility in addition to information technology alignment and agility.

Coherency Management and CIO's in Developing Countries

The concept and objectives of coherency management are particularly relevant in developing countries and for their government reform and associated eGovernment efforts.

EGovernment has enabled government reform and reinvention (Yong, 2005). In turn e-Government success is predicated upon eLeadership, initially as informal e-Champions and then as more formalized CIO's (Hanna, 2006 – 2). Cross-coordinating institutions then provide the framework for overall government eGovernment success (Hanna, 2006-1), (Auffret, 2007). .

The challenge for many developing country governments is in fostering these cross-coordinating institutions and providing mechanisms to enable them to succeed. Coherency Management is directly relevant to these efforts, as its goal of alignment, agility, and assurance through the development of logical consistency in the relationships of organizational and departmental objectives, strategy and operations, holds the promise of formalizing and strengthening governance approaches undertaken by cross-coordinating institutions.

One of the advantages of Coherency Management in general, and in particular for developing country governments, is that it is not about technology. As developing country governments utilize the concepts of coherency management – developing consistent strategies and processes in building organizations and institutions, they'll then be better placed to benefit from the potential and promise of eGovernment.

The experiences of Indonesia and Vietnam show some of the goals, challenges and successes of eGovernment and the potential for CIO's and coherency management. For perspective, Indonesia is ranked 65th in the 2007 Economist ICT Readiness Rankings and Vietnam 67th. (The top five are: Denmark, U.S. Sweden, Hong Kong and Switzerland.) (Economist Intelligence Unit, 2007)

Both countries are between the eGovernment stages of Internal and Information on a scale comprised of: Internal (internal systems); Information (providing information to citizens); Interaction (interacting with citizens); Transaction (conducting transactions with citizens); and Transformation (Transforming government). Both countries are also working to formalize the position of CIO and are beginning to try to develop information technology institutional frameworks and cross-agency coordination.

Indonesia

Indonesia has had many eGovernment and IT successes over the last several years including greatly expanding telecommunications infrastructure and formalizing the role of the CIO in government. Several of the challenges for the Indonesian government are in the areas addressed by coherency management. These include (Suhono, 2007):

- Government organizations have many strategies and plans but ineffective execution

- There is an absence of consistent ICT planning amongst government bodies and an absence of centralized ICT organization amongst government bodies

- Government organizations oftentimes have an unwillingness to share data

- Lack of capabilities and willingness of users

- Projects are sometimes duplicated in different parts of government.

An additional challenge, insufficient budgets (Suhono, 2007), can also be helped by the greater effectiveness provided by a successful Coherency Management program.

As part of Indonesia's efforts to strengthen their approach to cross-departmental cooperation, Indonesia government CIO's issued the 2007 Jakarta Statements calling for good corporate governance, collaboration of all stakeholders, improvement of human resource capability and overcoming the digital divide – the first two of which are aspects of Coherency Management.

Vietnam

Vietnam has also made much progress in its eGovernment efforts over the last several years. Currently they are in the process of undertaking efforts to both formalize the role of the CIO and to develop a national government Enterprise Architecture. Many of the challenges are similar to Indonesia's – differing organizational models and jurisdictions and inconsistent scope of responsibilities that hinder cross-organizational collaboration and sometimes result in turf battles (Tien, 2007). As with Indonesia's efforts, Coherency Management would supplement Vietnam's efforts in fostering and facilitating cross-organizational strategy and process consistency as well as cross-organizational collaboration. Coherency Management would also strengthen the new role of the CIO in cases where they are delegated as leaders of Coherency Management as the efforts would broaden CIO's focus beyond technology issues to those of organizational alignment, agility and development of consistent strategy and processes.

Coherency Management, New Product Development and Service Delivery

Alignment, agility and assurance, which are the result of a coherency of strategy and process, are the three goals of coherency management and are three factors in new product development and service delivery success.

Harrah's Total Rewards Customer Loyalty Cards program, which was a key component in Harrah's revenue and profit growth, is a case in point. The initial challenge in developing the program was alignment – aligning the strategies of the different casinos so that customers would be rewarded by loyalty to Harrah's overall instead of to a specific Harrah's casino. The second challenge was agility – agility in developing and rolling out the program successfully. And the third was assurance – assuring that the program runs in an efficient, reliable, high quality manner.

In contrast are the many unsuccessful (at least partially) cases of product development and service delivery for emergency communications. In these, Coherency Management would provide a great opportunity for success as there is usually no alignment – jurisdictions have different strategies and processes and lack of agility – projects have long time frames and limited assurance – resulting services can be unreliable. Undertaking Coherency Management can provide a benefit in these cases by helping to build collaboration and cross-organizational consistency.

From Foundational Architecture to Extended Architecture with IT Governance

IT Governance provides organizations and CIO's with a pathway for initiating and leading Coherency Management efforts and indeed some organizations are focused on Coherency Management without calling it as such.

An example is the government of Fairfax County, Virginia. In Fairfax County Government, "Strategic direction determines all government investment, including eGovernment and IT investments" (Molchaney, 2006). The strategic direction itself is the result of discussions with constituents, elected officials and the county senior leadership team. The strategic planning efforts and the associated artifacts are consistent with the Extended Architecture of Coherency Management in that Enterprise Architecture approaches are used to describe non information technology business efforts. In addition, Fairfax County has incorporated Enterprise Architecture approaches in non information technology business functions, including budgeting, in a manner consistent with Embedded Architecture of Coherency Management.

The Deputy County Executive for Information, working with the Senior IT Steering Committee, comprised of county government executives, then develops funding priorities consistent with Fairfax

County Government strategy. These funding priorities are in the areas of mandated requirements; leveraging prior investments, enhancing county security, improving service and quality efficiency and ensuring a current and supportable infrastructure. Proposed investments are considered in light of the Fairfax County Government Enterprise Architecture which is the Foundational Architecture of the Coherency Management model. Fairfax County Government's synthesis of Foundational, Extended and Embedded is then a balanced architecture.

Conclusion

Coherency Management is a new way of thinking that is directed towards the development of consistent strategies and processes across organizations. Coherency Management is an extension and outcome of Enterprise Architecture and provides CIO's with an opportunity to strengthen their role as a key executive leader.

CIO's are well placed to be leaders and facilitators of Coherency Management efforts due to their experience and responsibility for Foundational Architecture and as a result of their cross-organizational leadership experiences. As part of that experience, CIO's have the expertise in Enterprise Architecture tools such as reference models which are often used in moving from Foundational Architecture to Extended Architecture. At its heart though, Coherency Management leadership is business leadership, CIO's will need a business focus in those cases where they are appointed leaders of Coherency Management efforts.

Coherency Management can provide a benefit for both developing countries where cross-organizational collaboration efforts are often at beginning stages, and developed countries which are aiming for greater alignment, agility and assurance in the planning and provisioning of services (as are developing countries). Coherency Management can also provide a benefit for private sector companies, especially those in networked and service industries or those with geographically distant operations. Two areas where the benefits for private sector firms can be explicitly seen are in new product development and management and in service delivery.

References

Auffret, J.P. (2007). CIO's, ICT and Transition Economies. Presented at 2007 Hanoi Forum on ICT, Hanoi, Vietnam.

Barnes, J. and Hobbs, I. (2006). 2006 Clinger-Cohen Core Competencies, Letter to Federal CIO Council Members, U.S. Federal Chief Information Officers Council.

Broadbent, M. and Kitzis, E. (2005). The New CIO Leader: Setting the Agenda and Delivering Results. Harvard Business School Press, Boston, Massachusetts.

Doucet, G., Gøtze, J., Saha, P., and Bernard, S. (2008). "Coherency Management: Using Enterprise Architecture for Alignment, Agility and Assurance", *Journal of Enterprise Architecture*, May 2008, pp. 1 – 12.

Economist Intelligence Unit (2007). 2007 ICT Readiness Rankings. Economist, London, England.

Hackenson, E. (2007). CIO's of Today and the Future. Presented at the 2007 Global CIO Leadership Roundtable – Creating Better Government and Society through Enhanced CIO Leadership, George Mason University, Fairfax, Virginia.

Hanna, N. (2006). Institutional Leadership for Transformation. Presented at World Bank InfoDev Learning Program, Washington, D.C.

Hanna, N. (2006). From Envisioning to Designing e-Development: The Experience of Sri Lanka (Directions in Development). World Bank Publications, Washington, D.C.

Molchaney, D. (2006). Aligning IT to Organizational Goals Creating a Knowledge Based Economy In Fairfax County, Virginia. Presented at the CIO's and CIO Councils: Good Government, Good Business Global CIO Conference, George Mason University, Fairfax, Virginia.

Obi, T. and Iwasaki, N. (2006). New Trends of Core Competencies for CIO's in the Private Sector in U.S. and Japan. Presented at the CIO's and CIO Councils: Good Government, Good Business Global CIO Conference, George Mason University, Fairfax, Virginia.

Ross, J., Weill, P., Robertson, D. (2006). Enterprise Architecture as Strategy. Harvard Business School Press, Boston, Massachusetts.

Schofield, J. (2004). Casino Rewards Total Loyalty, *The Guardian*, January 15th 2004.

Supanghat, S. (2007) CIO Innovation and Leadership in Indonesia. Presented at the 2007 Global CIO Leadership Roundtable – Creating Better Government and Society through Enhanced CIO Leadership, George Mason University, Fairfax, Virginia.

Tien, T. (2007) IT Leadership in Vietnam. Presented at the 2007 Global CIO Leadership Roundtable – Creating Better Government and Society through Enhanced CIO Leadership, George Mason University, Fairfax, Virginia.

Yong, J. (ed) (2005). Egovernment in Asia: Enabling Public Service Innovation in the 21st Century. Marshall Cavendish Business, Singapore.

About the Author

J.P. Auffret is co-founder and director of the Center for Advanced Technology Strategy, and co-founder and vice president of the International Academy of CIO. He is also recent director of the Technology Management Program at George Mason University and has been a member of the business school faculty at Mason, the University of Maryland and American University; and physicist-in-residence at American University. He has 25 years of technology, industry and academic experience, including management and executive positions, with MCI and its joint venture with British Telecom, Concert. J.P. earned a B.S. degree from Duke University, an M.B.A. from the University of Virginia and a Ph.D. in Physics from American University.

Director, Center for Advanced Technology Strategy
Professor, George Mason University, USA
jauffret@gmu.edu

Chapter 16

A PRAGMATIC APPROACH TO ENLISTING THE SUPPORT OF CEOS FOR ENTERPRISE ARCHITECTURE

Larry R. DeBoever, George S. Paras & Tim Westbrock

Editors' Preface

According to recent surveys, most EA programs globally are still largely done within the context of IT. This is not necessarily undesirable and many times, given their unique knowledge about all key aspects of the organization, IT departments may actually be at advantage to trigger and drive the EA. However, this does create acceptance challenges as the IT departments attempt to convince the executive leadership about the benefits of EA to all parts of the organization. If EA is just used to derive a list of technology initiatives, then this is a recipe for disaster, as getting the CEO's attention, buy-in and active involvement becomes an uphill task.

This chapter elaborates on the organizational situations and conditions that favor and work better for adopting an EA based approach. Such favorable situations include: (a) inducting a new CIO who comes from the 'business-side'; (b) existence of near term business threat; and (c) a clearly defined need for an IT-enabled business transformation. These, of course, represent different situations that provide numerous leverage points for organizations to plan, design and implement their EA. These conditions could further be used to derive the reasons for doing EA. However, it is to be noted, in some sense all of these are not the typical 'business-as-usual' situations.

The chapter presents an approach to assess organizational receptivity to EA. We think this is important because many a times while the right conditions may exist, EA may still not take off as the receptivity is low. The chapter combines the favorable situations with the receptivity level to craft strategies and tactics that organizations can use to enhance engagement levels with the CEO and Executive Leadership. Current EA literature focuses a lot on the frameworks, artifacts and models to be developed as part of the EA program. This chapter presents the often neglected area of getting the CEO and Executive Leadership buy-in.

Introduction

Most CEOs of complex organizations quickly acknowledge that the rate of change in their business, markets and industry is accelerating and creating profound challenges. These CEOs recognize that to effectively respond to these challenges, their organizations must significantly increase their overall agility, as well as accelerate the coordination, and integration of business processes, systems and information across the breadth of their business, as well as those of their business partners, and, more broadly, their company's extended value chain. All of which must be done in a coherent manner to be successful.

Coherency Management postulates that the coherence needed by complex organizations to achieve the requisite degree of agility, coordination and integration (i.e. enterprise coherence) can best be achieved by the broad adoption of Enterprise Architecture (EA) across the breadth of the organization; most importantly by the CEO and the executive leadership team. A mediocre EA that is supported by the CEO and executive leadership, and is broadly understood and implemented across the breadth of the enterprise, has much greater value and quantifiable ROI than a brilliantly designed EA which is neither supported by executive leadership nor consistently implemented across the enterprise.

A major challenge confronting EA teams who aspire to have EA broadly embraced by the CEO and the leadership team, is that few CEOs understand the role and fundamental concepts of Enterprise Architecture; fewer have grasped the potential value of EA, and even fewer have embraced and operationalized EA. In addition, the lack of understanding of EA by CEOs results in the EA function being viewed as an IT responsibility and not a comprehensive enterprise-wide strategy. This organizational placement of EA responsibility further inhibits EA's ability to get the needed attention of the CEO and leadership team. Until these challenges are adequately addressed, the potential value of EA will not be attained and Coherency Management will not be achieved.

In this chapter we draw upon our experiences mentoring the EA teams and the IT leadership of hundreds of complex organizations (including the public sector) to effectively position Enterprise Architecture with CEOs and executive teams so that they understand the potential of EA to help them address the demands for agility, coordination, integration, and coherence across the organization and the extended value chain. In our experience, only a handful of organizations have achieved a largely Embedded Architecture, however, many have begun to evolve their Extended Architecture toward Embedded Architecture.

There is no single approach that will ensure that an Embedded Architecture (aka "EA Nirvana") is achieved. Organizations have very diverse cultures, operations, activities and goals. CEOs have broadly varying knowledge, competencies, experiences, and biases, as well as very different tactical and strategic objectives. The executive leadership teams that support CEOs create even more diversity, as does the perception and role of the information technology (IT) function in the organization. Some organizations have had no exposure to Enterprise Architecture. Other organizations have had one or more, highly visible, failed EA efforts.

While there is no single approach to obtaining the support of the CEO and executive leadership for Embedded Architecture, there is a very common event that often determines the near-term fate of EA. That event is the initial presentation to the CEO of the role and value of Enterprise Architecture. Almost always, this presentation is made to the CEO and executive leadership as a topic in their regularly scheduled meetings. If this presentation fails to garner CEO support for further EA efforts, it is likely that EA will not, for the immediate future, have executive attention or support.

Because of the importance of this presentation, we are often asked to lead the presentation or otherwise participate. In our absence, we recommend the CIO, whom we often mentor regarding this presentation, be the primary presenter. We recommend that the Chief Architect be present but not have a significant role.

This chapter is intended to make the reader much more effective in preparing an EA strategy that will gain the full support of the CEO and leadership, and evolve EA from a largely IT-centric function to an enterprise-wide strategy (from Extended Architecture to Embedded Architecture). The preparation of an effective EA strategy includes:

- A in-depth understanding of the current business situation, current objectives and long term strategy (although there are several ways to address the lack of a long term strategy)

- An understanding of the organizational conditions which facilitate the adoption of EA and leveraging them

- Assessing the CEO and leadership team's potential receptivity to EA and adjusting the presentation, approach and strategy as appropriate

- Identifying and leveraging potential centers of influence, particularly executives (this does not mean that the person advocates the adoption of EA but rather that they advocate a project, direction or strategy that favors the adoption of EA)

- Communicating the value of EA in a manner that is consumable by the CEO and the leadership team (which may even result in avoiding the use of the phrase "Enterprise Architecture")

- Educating the CEO and the leadership team on their roles and responsibilities in supporting Enterprise Architecture and Coherency Management to achieve full value from these strategies

In addition, until the EA function is relocated out of the IT organization, the EA team must demonstrate business and IT alignment in a manner that is easily understood by the CEO and leadership team.

Enterprise-Wide Commitment to Holistic Optimization

We have consistently found that complex organizations which are committed to optimizing their business processes and capital investment holistically, at an enterprise level, are much more likely to embrace Enterprise Architecture and achieve Coherency Management. Holistic optimization often requires that some business processes and capital investments be sub-optimized to achieve maximum, overall benefit. For example, a manufacturer might decide that it will only sell the quantity of goods that can be produced in a single shift as there is not enough demand to justify a second shift, and the marginal impact of trying to meet the additional demand through overtime is not attractive. In this example, the manufacturer has deliberately decided to maximize the gross margin while sub-optimizing revenues and asset utilization. (Similarly, a CIO might decide to migrate to a LAMP environment using low cost Intel platforms and horizontal scaling. While this significantly reduces hardware and software costs, it leads to some increase in support costs.)

It is the CEO, supported by executive leadership, who envisions and drives an enterprise-wide commitment to holistic optimization. To achieve this, mid-level management, staff supervisors and working staff must understand the goal of holistic optimization *and behave in a manner that will ensure that this goal is achieved*. In addition, customers and business partners often must be educated. The need for continuing and consistent communication that reinforces the stated vision, and effective metrics, is essential (e.g. "One GE").

The introduction of Enterprise Architecture to CEOs does not require that an enterprise-wide commitment to holistic optimization be fully developed as there are certain organization conditions which will often lead to this commitment.

Organizational Conditions which Favor the Adoption of Holistic Optimization and Enterprise Architecture

In working with hundreds of organizations to increase the awareness and adoption of EA by CEOs and executive teams, we have identified four organizational conditions which often lead to an enterprise-wide commitment to holistic optimization and significantly facilitate meaningful EA-related conversations with CEOs. In our experience, the existence of one or more of these conditions considerably improves the opportunity for the successful introduction of EA, or the evolution of EA from Extended Architecture to Embedded Architecture.

Hiring of a New CEO

New CEOs almost always want to "make their mark" on the organization. They usually establish a new vision for the organization and strive to significantly improve the organization's performance. This is especially true where the CEO is hired from the outside to replace an underperforming or ineffective CEO, or to succeed a CEO who held the position for a lengthy period but introduced little change in the later years. Today's newly hired CEOs consistently drive initiatives focused on globalization, integrated view of customers, process and systems integration with business partners, innovation and reinvention, margin improvement, etc. Generally speaking, the goal of all of these types of initiatives is enterprise-wide optimization. Often the newly hired CEO has discussed these types of initiatives with the Board as part of the hiring process and for a period of at least a few quarters; the CEO will enjoy the Board's full support.

The establishment of a new vision for the organization by a newly hired CEO, and the resulting initiatives, create a significant opportunity to introduce EA.

Hiring a New CIO from Outside IT

When a new CIO is hired and they come from outside the organization, or from leading a line of business (LOB) within the organization, they almost always have been asked to be a change agent. (In contrast, when a new CIO is appointed from within the IT organization this most often indicates that the CEO is satisfied with the state of IT, which could mean that IT has little influence and respect, and will remain that way.)

Typically, the mission of CIO's hired as change agents is to significantly improve the effectiveness of IT in supporting the business. One of the first manifestations of the new CIO's mission and the support of the CEO is the appointment of the newly hired CIO to the executive committee or equivalent leadership group. Within the first few months of hiring, the CIO-as-change-agent typically engages directly with executive leadership regarding their strategies and operational objectives, begins to develop an IT strategy focused on achieving business/IT alignment, and launches several highly visible initiatives in support of the business which provide "quick wins" such as:

- Significantly enhancing corporate portals (e.g. functionality, self-service)

- Externalizing existing systems for real-time integration with business partners

- Expanding business intelligence capabilities and real-time reporting

- Real-time integration of core systems

In addition, the CIO-as-change-agent launches a set of projects to improve the efficiency and effectiveness of IT while also signaling a significant change in IT strategy. Enterprise Architecture is often one of these efforts. Other examples include:

- Developing an enterprise strategy for service-oriented architecture (SOA)

- Moving toward continuous operations and zero-downtime

- Virtualization of infrastructure

- Establishing/expanding LAMP infrastructure stack

- Embracing open source

- Outsourcing selected IT functions

- Selectively adopting ITIL

Clearly, each of the potential projects outlined above, whether focused on supporting specific business requirements or driving IT effectiveness, has significant implications for EA.

We have found that the hiring of a CIO-as-change-agent is the best organizational condition for establishing, expanding or re-starting EA activities. This is particularly true during the new hire's first six months as they are likely to have the full and unconditional support of the CEO.

Recognition of a Clear and Present Threat To the Business

The recognition by the CEO and executive leadership of a clear and present threat to the on-going business often drives a fundamental, holistic evaluation of the organization, its strategies, objectives and processes. Examples include: fundamental shifts in markets; major innovations by competitors; technology discontinuities; significant losses; etc.

The holistic evaluation of the business that results is an ideal opportunity for the introduction of EA to the CEO and executive team regardless of whether the CEO has developed a strategy for responding to the threat. EA can play a significant role in the evaluation process as well as ensuring the effective execution of the resulting strategy.

Commitment to Significant Business Transformation

The recognition of a major threat to the business (as described above) will drive business transformation. At the same time, CEOs will drive significant business transformation, without the existence of an immediate threat to the business, to achieve competitive advantage and improve margins. Examples include:

- Corporate restructuring
- Fully integrating and leveraging a major acquisition
- Introducing new products and/or services
- Streamlining business processes
- Enterprise-wide quality initiatives

The commitment of the organization to a significant business transformation is an excellent opportunity to introduce EA to the CEO and executive team.

It is not unusual for the four organizational conditions discussed above to occur in combination: a new CEO hires a CIO from the outside; the recognition of a clear and present threat to the business drives business transformation efforts; a current CEO sees the opportunity to acquire a major competitor and wants to leverage the acquisition to drive comprehensive transformation of the combined firm, and hires a new CIO to help accomplish this, etc.

None of these four conditions or any combination thereof ensures the successful adoption of Enterprise Architecture; however, they are very positive indicators to the EA team that the organization will be taking an increasingly holistic, enterprise-wide approach in its strategies and there will likely be a number of supporting projects which will benefit from EA-related activities. The absence of these conditions does not mean that the introduction of EA to the CEO and executive leadership will be unsuccessful, only that it will likely be more difficult.

Assessing An Organization's Receptivity To Enterprise Architecture

The four organizational conditions just described increase the likelihood that the CEO will make a commitment to holistic optimization of the organization. While this creates an environment that is conducive to the successful introduction of EA to the CEO and executive team, it does not, in any way, guarantee it.

A comprehensive assessment of the CEO and the organization's potential receptivity to Enterprise Architecture significantly assists in developing effective strategies for introducing EA concepts. When the EA function is part of IT and the organization has not achieved an Embedded Architecture, we work with the CIO, IT leadership and EA team to perform this assessment. The tools we use:

- Analyze the extent of holistic optimization in the enterprise

- Analyze the attitudes of the CEO and the leadership team to holistic optimization

- Analyze the perception by the CEO and the leadership team of IT's effectiveness

When an organization is evolving toward an Embedded Architecture and we have the opportunity to work as part of that process, we use one or more of these same tools to facilitate discussion with the CEO and leadership team.

Analyzing the Extent of Holistic Optimization in the Enterprise

The purpose of this tool is to analyze the extent of holistic optimization in the enterprise by looking at four specific organizational behaviors. Each of these behaviors is a strong indicator because there often is considerable disagreement between the CEO and executive leadership on the extent to which each of these four behaviors ought to be optimized at the enterprise level versus optimized within each line of business (LOB) or country market operation.

For each behavior, we want to determine the degree to which the current behavior is optimized on an enterprise-wide basis. We also want to determine the stated direction of optimization for the same behavior. These two assessments can be presented as two axes. The organizational behaviors we evaluate are:

- *Customer Ownership* – Is there a single, enterprise-wide view of all customers? Or, is a customer 'owned' by a specific line of business or sales channel? (In the public sector, this would be a citizen.)

- *Executive Bonus Structure* – Is a significant portion of each executive's bonus (i.e. 40% or more) tied to the overall performance of the enterprise? Or, are executive bonuses primarily tied to the achievement of LOB and/or personal objectives?

- *Globalization of Processes* – Are corporate processes defined globally (e.g. finance, human resources, logistics)? Or, do corporate processes vary by country market or region?

- *Corporate Planning/Strategy* – Is there a strong, corporate planning or corporate strategy function (not in title but in function)?

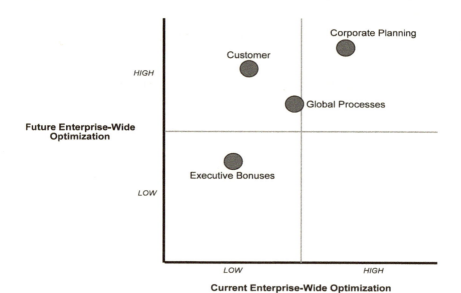

Figure 1. Example Diagram for Analyzing the Extent of Holistic Optimization.

COHERENCY MANAGEMENT

After evaluating each of these four behaviors they are plotted on the diagram presented earlier. What follows is an example of how this tool is applied.

In the above example, the Corporate Planning function is well established and currently focused on enterprise-wide efforts and that focus is expected to increase. Global Processes are being established but currently are not quite enterprise-wide in nature but the clear direction is to implement consistent processes across all country market operations. Customers today are owned by the LOBs but the vision is that Customers will be owned by the enterprise. This likely is a very politically contentious issue, as there probably are a wide range of views on how Customer centralization should be accomplished and governed, and the technical migration issues are typically significant. The current Executive Bonus structure incents leadership to optimize the performance of their LOB even if it is to the detriment of the enterprise as a whole and there is no indication that this will significantly change. (In our experience, it is not necessary that the Executive Bonus structure be dramatically revised as long as the CEO and leadership team openly acknowledge the need to "do the right thing" despite the possible impact on their bonuses.)

Analyzing the Attitudes of the CEO and Leadership Team to Holistic Optimization

The purpose of this tool is to analyze the attitudes of the CEO and each member of the leadership team to holistic optimization. Our goal is to identify those members of the executive team most likely to be open to Enterprise Architecture and Coherency Management as well as to identify executives who are most likely to ignore or actively resist these concepts.

For each executive we assess the degree to which they think the organization is currently optimized on an enterprise-wide basis, and the degree of holistic optimization they desire for the organization. Following these assessments we plot the results as shown in the example below:

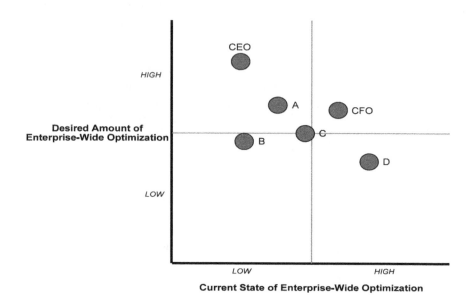

Figure 2. Analyzing CEO & Leadership Team Attitudes Towards Holistic Optimization

In the above example, the CEO has the lowest opinion of the current degree of enterprise-wide optimization (along with 'A') and the highest aspirations. This is somewhat typical for a CEO who is driving broad, fundamental business transformation. The CFO can be described as "steady state" as the CFO has the opinion that the organization is somewhat optimized today and does not need any significant change.

'A' is most aligned with the CEO in desiring increased enterprise-wide optimization but 'A' views the current organization as more optimized than the CEO and does not see the need for the breadth of enterprise optimization envisioned by the CEO. 'B' sees the need for some increased optimization while 'C' sees the need for only minimal increased enterprise-wide optimization. 'D' on the other hand, believes that the current organization is excessively optimized and that this should be reversed. It is likely that the CEO and 'D' disagree on a number of issues beyond the degree of enterprise-wide optimization.

This analysis suggests that the CEO, 'A' and, to a lesser extent, 'B' will be the most open to discussions of the potential role of Enterprise Architecture.

COHERENCY MANAGEMENT

It also suggests that the CEO needs to convince the CFO of the need for increased optimization so that the CFO will support the necessary investments for the transformation during discussions with the Board. Demonstrating the ROI and EPS contribution of enterprise-wide optimization is most likely required to achieve this. Finally, 'D' presents a significant point of resistance that the CEO must address. (When mentoring an EA team we would typically advise them to avoid 'D' until 'D's' position on optimization changes.)

This tool is also effective when used as the basis for a dynamic exercise done with the CEO and the leadership team in which each person is asked to plot themselves using the diagram presented above. The plotted data is then used to discuss (usually in a facilitated manner):

- Reasons for the differing views on the current state of enterprise optimization
- Reasons for differing views on the desired end state
- Strategies to resolve those differences and get to consensus

Analyzing the Perception by the CEO and Leadership Team of IT's Effectiveness

The purpose of this tool is to analyze the perception by the CEO and leadership team of IT's overall effectiveness in achieving the organization's current objectives and long-term strategies. If IT is broadly perceived by the CEO and leadership team as being ineffective, this will significantly inhibit obtaining support for EA even where there is broad, enterprise-wide commitment to holistic optimization, and there are one or more organizational conditions and behaviors which favor EA.

In these situations, it is important to position EA as an approach that will significantly strengthen IT's effectiveness with the derivative consequence being considerably improved IT capacity to enable enterprise-wide optimization.

For each executive we assess their perception of IT's current effectiveness in achieving the organization's objectives and strategies, and the level of IT effectiveness needed to achieve the organization's objectives and strategies.

'Change', Enterprise Architecture & The CEO

As discussed earlier, there is no single approach that will ensure that *EA Nirvana* is achieved due to the enormous diversity among organizations, their objectives and strategies, their leadership teams, etc. Despite this diversity, there are five interrelated themes that consistently resonate with CEOs and their leadership teams. These five themes facilitate discussions related to holistic optimization, Coherency Management and Enterprise Architecture:

- Business value is created through change

- The range of change in business is increasing

- Complexity inhibits changes in business models and processes

- Because complexity inhibits business change, complexity inhibits increasing business value

- Successful organizations enable rapid business change rather than inhibit it

When we present to CEOs regarding the value of Enterprise Architecture we touch on all five themes using examples taken directly from their business or industry. We develop these themes very quickly (10-15 minutes) so that we can move directly into the application of EA to address these issues. When possible, we present these themes drawing on the whiteboard rather than using prepared slides. We strive to covey these foundational themes without patronizing.

If the client wishes that the initial EA presentation to the CEO and executive team be done by internal staff, we recommend that the newly hired CIO-as-change-agent be the presenter. In our experience, internal EA teams that deliver these themes are usually not effective as executives are less inattentive or lose patience.

Business Value is Created through Change

Additional business value is only created through change. (As used herein, change refers to any alteration in function, process or cost; including quality efforts, product development, acquisitions, divestitures, business partnerships, changes in suppliers, introduction of self-service, etc.)

If nothing changes, internally or externally, then business value is steady state. Business value can be maintained but not improved. *If nothing changes internally but there are external changes (e.g. competition, markets), then it is highly likely that business value is eroding.*

Most CEOs, private or public sector, are tasked with increasing stakeholder value. CEOs believe that organizations that introduce new products and services, modify existing processes, and generally innovate faster than their competition, will gain significant advantage.

At the end of this discussion, we want the CEO and leadership team to agree that business value is only created through change.

The Rate of Change in Business Is Increasing

Most CEOs agree that the rate of change in business is increasing but, in many cases, CEOs are unaware of the accelerating rate of change and the potential consequences if the organization is not prepared to absorb and/or respond in a timely manner to these changes. This challenge goes to the heart of Coherency Management and the characteristics of an Embedded Architecture. In our experience, CEOs and their leadership teams often do not recognize the degree of enterprise design, enterprise agility, organizational alignment, decision capability, etc. that may be required to respond to future changes.

Care must be taken in discussing the rate of business change with CEOs and leadership teams to ensure that the presenter is earnest and is not perceived as sophomoric or condescending. Examples taken from the industry in which the client participates are essential in establishing relevance and credibility.

We begin by discussing changes in the client's industry from the late 1950s through the end of the 1980s, when most professionals believed that, generally speaking, core business processes had a 'lifecycle' on average of about every seven (7) years before a fundamental change to that business process was made as shown:

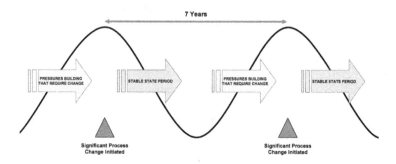

Figure 3. Rate of Change in Core Business Processes: 1950s to 1980s

During this period new information systems took 3 to 7 years to develop and implement. IT assets such as mainframes and COTS were often amortized over 5 to 7 years and even longer.

Today, if you ask the CEOs and Boards of many our clients how fast they would want a major change implemented in their core processes, a new partner relationship implemented, a recent acquisition's products and customers integrated, most will reply "yesterday". CEOs want major integration efforts to be measured in weeks not years and minor changes to be performed in days or even hours. This acceleration in the rate of change is illustrated below:

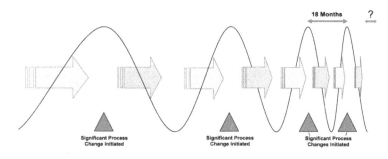

**Figure 4. Accelerating Rate of Change in
Core Business Processes: 2000 - ?**

Today, CEOs and executive teams expect that, for the foreseeable future, the rate of change is going to continue to accelerate.

At the end of this discussion, we want the CEO and the leadership team to agree that the rate of change in their industry is accelerating, illustrated with specific examples, and that change is going to continue.

Complexity Inhibits Changes in Business Models and Processes

It is self-evident to most CEOs and leadership teams that complexity in existing processes and in the underlying technology infrastructure, inhibits an organization's ability to change their business models and processes in an efficient and timely manner, regardless of whether that change is proactive or reactive.

At the same time, CEOs are often unaware of the underlying complexity in their current processes and systems. In preparation for this discussion, we work with the EA team to identify a handful of egregious examples of complexity within the client organization. We begin by asking, "What is the hardest change to implement that the business might request?" (The example might be as simple as increasing the length of product number in current systems.) Our goal is to make sure that the leadership team is fully aware of the number of distinct touch points involved in the scenarios presented.   When EA teams are trying to evolve from an Extended Architecture to an Embedded Architecture, are within the IT organization, and lack sufficient credibility with executive leadership, we recommend that they initially discuss the organization's complexity from an IT perspective. Examples of IT complexity we have identified in past clients and discussed with their executive teams include:

- Number of separate database tables or files that exist in the organization (as recent as April of 2008 we found 3,500 separate FoxPro databases on a single shared drive at one client)

- Number of separate database tables or files that contain customer name, vendor ID, etc.

- Number of changes of addresses required by a client who moved and had all the insurance/financial products offered by a firm (in one client we found 17 separate change of address requirements, one for each policy line)

- Number of different hardware server models, server OS releases, database product releases, etc. currently owned

- Number of distinct applications deployed across the enterprise

Most CEOs are surprised, and sometimes alarmed, at the depth of complexity of their underlying infrastructure (and many IT organizations believed they were providing a service by hiding the underlying complexity from management). Today it is common for a reasonably complex organization to have hundreds of thousands of discrete technology components.

Once the EA team has sufficient credibility in analyzing and describing IT complexity, it becomes much easier to credibly analyze the enterprise-wide complexity of business processes, decision making, organizational alignment, etc.

Complexity Inhibits Increasing Business Value

As a general rule, because complexity inhibits business change, complexity inhibits increasing business value. It is important to illustrate how complexity inhibits the organization's ability to make certain changes in a timely manner by using specific examples.

We are very careful to point out that not all complexity is bad. Complexity that provides unique, competitive differentiation and has quantifiable ROI is very valuable. (Enterprise architects should ensure that technical complexity is an exception and that, when it is proposed or exists, there is a valid business case.)

Enabling Rapid Business Change Rather Than Inhibiting It

We typically end this presentation by providing examples of successful organizations that are able to implement changes in their products and services, core business process, and overall business model faster than their competition. These same organizations typically have an enterprise-wide commitment to holistic optimization and a highly effective IT organization as technology is, increasingly, the core enabler of change.

At this point (10-15 minutes into the presentation) we often use potential business scenarios that are relevant to the client which may result from possible industry changes to explore the degree of enterprise design, enterprise agility, organizational alignment, decision capability, etc. that may be required for the client to effectively respond to these changes in a timely manner.

Enterprise Architecture & the Value Imperative

In this context, the goal of Enterprise Architecture is to enable the strategic objectives of the organization by:

- Understanding the core business processes of the organization

- The potential changes to those processes to increase value

- The potential for new technologies to improve or alter those processes (including cost)

- Understanding the complexity of the underlying information and technology infrastructure (in the broadest sense)

- Reducing the complexity of the information and technology infrastructure so as to enable business change as efficiently and rapidly as possible

When done correctly, Enterprise Architecture is a manifestation of an organization's mission, and the business and IT strategies that enable that mission. When this accomplished, we have achieved Coherency Management.

When a CEO asks us "So, what do you do for us?" we have a very short response (i.e. the "elevator pitch"). We simply say, "We focus on reducing the complexity of IT and business processes across the breadth of an enterprise so your business is much more agile." We do not try to define what Enterprise Architecture is or what it does. Instead, we have expressed the outcome of EA that is most important to the CEO which is enabling stakeholder value.

Often, we don't initially use the phrase "Enterprise Architecture" when talking with CEOs and their leadership teams as introducing the phrase leads to a conversation about the meaning and boundaries of EA which is not an efficient use of the limited time we have with the CEO and leadership team.

12 Additional Tactics for Increasing Effectiveness when Engaging CEO and Executive Leadership

There are a number of additional tactics from which we select when we are assisting EA teams in enlisting the support of CEOs and their leadership teams for Enterprise Architecture. In this section, we discuss the 12 tactics we most commonly use.

1. Develop an In-depth Knowledge of the Business, Competitors and Markets

The internet provides virtually unlimited access to information about a business, their competitors and their markets. We strongly recommend that Chief Architects, EA teams and consultants thoroughly immerse themselves in available information before beginning to engage the executive team. As consultants, we find that we are almost immediately challenged, directly or indirectly, by the CEO or other member of the leadership team regarding the depth of our knowledge about their firm and their industry. (Similarly, CIO's unfamiliar with our work will often do the same.)

We are no longer surprised when we meet an EA team for the first time and we know more than they know about the company's performance, the challenges presented by the company's competitors and current issues in the industry. Without an adequate depth of knowledge, it is not possible for an EA team or a consultant to establish adequate credibility with the CEO.

2. Analyze the CEO's Management Style, Interests and Biases

The more insight that you have into the style, interests and biases of the CEO the more effective you will be when enlisting their support. If the CEO has a bias towards a particular management approach or uses a particular jargon, then we incorporate that into our presentation materials and our conversations. For example, if the CEO is talking to the leadership team about Good to Great (Jim Collins), The 7 Habits of Highly Successful People (Stephen Covey), When Markets Collide (Mohamed El-Erian), The Tipping Point (Malcolm Gladwell), or another current business best seller, we incorporate it. If the CEO worked in another industry, we find a way to include examples from that industry as well. If the CEO is a fan of a particular sport, use examples from that sport as appropriate.

3. Partner with Corporate Strategy/Planning Function

As noted earlier, one of the organizational behaviors which considerably improves the opportunity for a successful introduction of EA is the existence of a strong corporate planning or corporate strategy function. Before meeting with the CEO you want to thoroughly educate the head of the planning/strategy function on the potential value of EA and enlist their support.

4. Understand and Leverage Other Centers of Influence

In addition to the corporate strategy/planning function, you should attempt to introduce EA to members of the executive team who are most closely aligned with CEO as identified in the tools discussed earlier. A newly appointed CIO-as-change-agent often can serve as an effective entry point to those executives.

In addition, identify rising stars in the organization and look for opportunities to meet with them (e.g. the executive who led the most recent acquisition integration team). We recommend proposing very short meetings to begin (e.g. "I only want 10 minutes of your time").

5. Develop & Retain the Trust of the CIO

EA teams who are successful in getting the support of the CEO and the opportunity to add significant value to the organization on an enterprise-wide basis, invariably have the support of the CIO. The CIO must be educated in basic EA concepts and methods, and trust that the EA team will act in a manner that is in the best interest of the CIO.

6. Communicate in a Manner that is Easily Consumable by the CEO

EA teams must develop EA artifacts that appeal to, and are easily consumed by, the CEO and executive leadership. We recommend that for maximum impact with CEOs:

- Artifacts should be abstracted to a single page
- Artifacts should be 'self-describing' (i.e. the artifact does not have to be explained by someone)

- Artifacts should be consistent and easily map from one to the next
- Artifacts should be easily comprehended
- Artifacts should have a high 'pass-along' quotient (as executives who see an effective document are very likely to pass it along to others)

7. Provide CEO and Executive Leadership with Informed Choices

In our experience, the most influential EA teams ensure that the CEO and the executive leadership are provided with a set of informed choices when significant process or technology decisions are to be made. For each choice, the strengths and weaknesses, and short-term as well as long term implications are provided. Too often, IT staff recommends a single solution to a business issue without fully evaluating and/or disclosing the implications of the recommendation or fully describing alternatives. Most significant IT decisions have meaningful business implications which should require that the decision be made by leadership.

8. Use Business Scenarios to Validate EA

EA teams should work with management to develop several potential future business scenarios such as a major acquisition, competitors merge, decision to launch a new product line, sharp economic downturn, major disaster affecting a data center or corporate headquarters, etc. The EA team should use these scenarios to validate and/or test aspects of the Embedded Architecture such as:

- Is enterprise agility fully enabled?
- Is the enterprise fully aligned?
- Is decision capability clearly communicated and correctly delegated?
- Do all needed services exist and are they readily accessible?

9. Create an Understanding of the Long-Term Trends in the Economics of Technology and Consequent Implications

One of the most significant forces driving business innovation is the continuing improvements in the price/performance of information technology. The significant improvements in storage price/performance enabled the explosion of business intelligence, data marts, operational data stores, and the development of comprehensive customer profiles. The significant improvements in network price/performance enabled data center consolidation, telecommuting, the explosion in customer self-service and, more generally, the internet. The significant improvements in processor and server price/performance enabled server consolidation, event streaming, predictive modeling, and real-time systems. The impact of open source on software licensing, as well as hardware commoditization cannot be understated.

Despite the extraordinary impact of these changes, few EA teams have educated themselves, let alone executive leadership, on the long-term economic trends in technology and the consequent implications (e.g. "How would our business change if bandwidth was free?").

10. Use EPS as A Key Metric

We have found that projecting the impact of proposed business innovation or IT projects in terms of earnings per share (EPS) is much more impactful in discussions with the CEO and the executive leadership of public companies than discussing return on investment (ROI). For example, describing the impact of an enterprise-wide initiative to increase overall organizational agility as "contributing $0.05 a share this year, $0.20 next year and $0.30 to $0.35 a share in year three" will typically get much more attention than saying "ROI over three years is $2,375,000".

One of the reasons is that using EPS as a key metric is more impactful than ROI in a public organization is that EPS is the primary metric by which a public company is measured and requires no translation. In our experience, it also appears that the executive leadership of some organizations generally view ROI projections for new projects as likely inflated to gain approval while EPS estimates are firmer promises.

11. Create Awareness of the Potential for Innovation

One of the ways in which an EA team can increase its value to the enterprise is to increase the general awareness among the CEO and executive leadership of the potential for innovating using new business models, new processes, and available or near-term technology (e.g. Wi-Fi, RFID, MDM, complex event processing, transaction data management). These discussions can be especially valuable when they include real-world applications that have provided significant competitive advantage.

12. Describe Enterprise Architecture as a Continuous Process

It is imperative that the CEO and the executive leadership understand that Enterprise Architecture is a continuous process and not a one-time project. As discussed earlier, business change is continuing to accelerate, and product and technology innovation will be never ending. Consequently, an organization must continually adapt to these changes. This adaptation must be coherent and enterprise-wide in scope. This can only be achieved by evolving EA to an Embedded Architecture.

Demonstrating Alignment of IT Objectives and Strategy with Business Objectives and Strategy

As discussed earlier, in our experience only a handful of organizations have achieved a largely Embedded Architecture, however, many have begun to evolve their Extended Architecture towards Embedded Architecture. In addition, the EA function is typically viewed as an IT responsibility and not a comprehensive enterprise-wide strategy.

In our experience, the support for EA teams by the executive leadership outside of IT is often (fairly or unfairly) tied to the IT leadership team's capacity to demonstrate to the CEO and the executive leadership that IT's near-term projects and long-term strategies, and supporting processes, fully support, and are aligned with, business objectives and business strategy in a manner that is easily consumed and embraced by leadership. Said differently, if the "IT house is not in order" the credibility of the EA team is directly impacted and the EA team will not find support for virtually any initiative that is needed to achieve an Embedded Architecture (e.g. Enterprise Business Architecture, Outcome Modeling, enabled agility, intrinsic architecture, enterprise-wide organizational alignment).

Consequently, in most organization's we believe it is in the EA team's best interest to ensure that business/IT alignment is effectively demonstrated to the CEO and the executive leadership in a manner that they can easily understand and consume. We have found that most IT organizations fail to do this. Most strategic IT plans are simply not consumable by executive leadership due to their length, technical jargon and project minutia.

In our experience a well designed simple matrix is often very effective in demonstrating business/IT alignment. (As discussed earlier, initial EA artifacts are most effective with a CEO and leadership team when they fit on a single page and are self-describing.) The sample matrix presented below demonstrates the alignment of current technology initiatives with core business objectives in a hypothetical company named 'Best Stuff Inc.'. In this example, Best Stuff has five core business objectives for the current year which are presented on the horizontal axis (the Executive Sponsor is in parentheses):

- Integrate all Customer data (Sales)
- Increase Customer self-service by 30% (Customer Service)
- Provide 7x24 Customer access (Customer Service)
- Real-time visibility into the inventory of Suppliers (Procurement)
- Provide Supplier's with on-line access to their performance evaluations (Procurement)

Six major IT technology initiatives in the current year are presented on the horizontal axis. The matrix shows which technology initiatives support which business objectives, as well as the degree to which the business objective is supported. In this example, each technology initiative supports two or more business objectives with the initiative to 'Achieve 7x24 Continuous Operations' supporting all five business objectives.

Best Stuff Inc.
CORE BUSINESS OBJECTIVES - 2008

TECHNOLOGY INITATIVES - 2008	SALES	CUSTOMER SERVICE		PROCUREMENT	
	Integrate all Customer data	Increase Customer self-service by 30%	Provide 7x24 Customer access	Real-time visibility into Supplier inventory	Provide Supplier performance reports on-line
▶ Achieve 7x24 Continuous Operations	○	●	●	○	●
• Open 2nd data center in Cinn; share workload					
▶ Major Network Upgrade		●	●	●	●
• Significant increase both domestic & international capacity					
▶ Implement Real-Time Customer Data Integration (CDI)	●	○	○	○	○
• Replace existing LOB solutions					
▶ Implement Transaction Data Management Solution	●	●	○		
• Enables both CDI and ContinuousOps initiatives					
▶ Upgrade Customer Portal (Release 3.0)	○	●	●		
• Improve scalability, cross-selling & personalization					
▶ Implement Supplier Performance Portal (Release 1.0)				●	●
• Initial release to top 9 suppliers (45% of revenues)					

Figure 5. Example of High-Level Business/IT Alignment Matrix

Preparing this type of information is outside the responsibilities of most EA functions. In an ideal situation, a CIO would have a full-time strategy and planning function that would prepare and maintain these types of artifacts. In the absence of an effective IT strategy function, EA is best positioned to take temporary stewardship of this responsibility as EA has, more than any other function within IT, an enterprise-wide focus emphasizing holistic commitment. However, to achieve an Embedded Architecture, IT must develop a strong IT strategy function and EA must evolve outside of IT and assume enterprise-wide responsibilities.

We have used matrices for a broad range of high-level EA artifacts in addition to business/IT alignment. We have used them for:

- Enterprise Business Architecture (EBA) - including mapping organizational structure to a functional hierarchy

- Enterprise Application Architecture (EAA) – including mapping application systems to a functional hierarchy

- Enterprise Information Architecture (EIA) – including mapping information artifacts to a functional hierarchy and mapping information artifacts to application systems

- Enterprise Technical Architecture (ETA) – including creating an ETA Reference Model and mapping the ETA to application systems.

We have also used matrices for service-oriented architectures (e.g. mapping services to EBA), security architectures (e.g. mapping security capabilities to the ETA). Finally, we have used matrices to demonstrate the logical consistency and decomposition, between and among, distinct artifacts (e.g. EAA to EIA).

The bottom line is that simple but well conceived and thoughtful matrices can be very effective in demonstrating business/IT alignment and this significantly increases the credibility of the EA team with the CEO and the executive leadership.

Educating the CEO and the Leadership Team on their Potential to Influence Adoption of Enterprise Architecture

When the CEO and the leadership team embrace an enterprise-wide commitment to holistic optimization and the potential value of Enterprise Architecture, it is imperative that we educate them on their potential to influence EA adoption and, in turn, the accelerated achievement of business goals and objectives. In our experience, CEOs are willing to invest time and effort to promote EA-related themes when they believe that their efforts will facilitate adoption. On the other hand, we find that EA teams are often reluctant to ask the CIO to approach the CEO.

When approaching the CEO it is essential to be very clear about what actions you want the CEO to take and to give them all the collateral they need to take those actions (e.g. text, slides, and schedules). We recommend that the CEO be tasked with, at a minimum:

- Broadly communicating the need for holistic optimization and EA-related activities to all staff (in the form on a voicemail to all employees, during a corporate-wide town meeting, employee email or other communication) and continuously reinforcing this message whenever possible

- Establish objectives, milestones and metrics to measure the organization's progress towards an Embedded Architecture

- Incorporate 1-2 slides on the companies enterprise-wide strategy for achieving Coherency Management into their standard corporate presentation to staff, shareholders and financial analysts

- Provide introductory comments at selected EA working sessions

- Communicate to staff about the need to reduce complexity and to achieve Coherency Management.

When the CEO is fully engaged in supporting EA, it becomes much easier to develop similar strategies for each executive that are adapted to the specific objectives and challenges of their organizations.

The active support of the CEO and the leadership team significantly increases the likelihood that the entire organization will fully examine holistic considerations before making strategic or tactical decisions. When this change in behavior among working staff is achieved, the EA team will have accomplished its objective, Coherency Management is well underway, and, most importantly, value to stakeholders is increasing.

About the Authors

Larry R. DeBoever is recognized as one of the pioneers of Enterprise Architecture having founded DeBoever Architectures (DAI) in 1990. Mr. DeBoever conceived the concept of Adaptive Architecture and published one of the first EA process methodologies in the early 1990s. DAI was acquired by the META Group in October 1996 where Mr. DeBoever started the Enterprise Architecture Strategies (EAS) practice, the first EA research service (now Gartner). In 1997, he started the Enterprise Architectures Conference (EAC) and chaired the event in its early years. He sits on several Boards and has Masters Degrees from Purdue and the USC. Larry can be reached at ldeboever@eadirections.com.

George S. Paras is a widely recognized speaker, writer, coach and thought leader in Enterprise Architecture (EA), Strategy and Planning, and IT Governance with more than 26 years of information technology and business experience. He has coached hundreds of IT leaders in the practical aspects of creating effective EA programs. He serves as Chairman for the Enterprise Architectures Conferences (EAC) and Editor-in-Chief of Architecture and Governance Magazine. Mr. Paras has held positions as VP of the Enterprise Planning and Architecture Strategies service at META Group, Troux Technologies, as well as senior architect at a major airline. George can be reached at gparas@eadirections.com.

Tim Westbrock is a leading authority on enterprise architecture (EA), enterprise portfolio management, governance, and enterprise-wide planning. He has worked with 300+ companies in various industries and the public sector to mentor them in EA. He has advanced the state of the art of EA processes and was the driving force behind META Group's EA research agenda and METAmethod – a best-practice transformation method for EA development. A frequent lecturer at industry events, Mr. Westbrock has over 18 years experience as an analyst, consultant and architect. Before joining META Group, he was the chief architect for Anthem, Inc., responsible for driving its enterprise architecture strategy. Tim can be reached at twestbrock@eadirections.com.

Chapter 17

THE FUTURE OF ENTERPRISE ENGINEERING

Peter Bernus

Editors' Preface

A lot of current EA efforts have been expended to build frameworks, refer-ence models, languages, notations, tools and maturity models. Almost all of the current literature views EA in the 'foundation' mode. While this is acceptable as a starting point in organizations, over time, we believe that organizations must add elements and characteristics of 'extended' and eventually 'embedded' modes. In reality, it is almost impossible for a small team of 'enterprise architects' to develop the complete architecture. We believe that moving forward into the future the onus of developing the ar-chitecture will be equally shared between the dedicated team of architects and the line managers themselves. Coherency will be achieved through use of the common meta-models, frameworks, structures, procedures etc. by both these groups.

The chapter looks at EA as a way to manage change and in general as a way to enable the development of enterprises (not just IT / IS). It is a well-known paradigm that every architecture artifact must address one or more stakeholder concerns. If it doesn't then it is not needed. By nature stakeholders and their concerns are very different in the three modes of EA. The chapter identifies a representative set of such concerns across the three modes and presents / discusses the artifacts that could be utilized to ad-dress such concerns. We view this as an important contribution to the EA literature as such 'concern-artifacts-processes' combinations could be cap-tured as architecture patterns. Furthermore, the chapter strongly makes the case for the need of enterprise to be 'designed'. This envisions the evolving role of the enterprise architect. Though not mentioned explicitly, the complex and organic nature of enterprises calls for a more hybrid approach to enterprise architecting.

Introduction

This chapter is organized around two significant problems that the enterprise engineering / enterprise architecting (EE/EA) community needs to address in the future in order to foster the trust in the discipline's ability to contribute to the management of change, and in general to the development and management of enterprises.

The first problem is: how to ensure that the artifacts created in the EE/EA process adequately address real stakeholder concerns, support good communication and mutual understanding, and help achieve co-coordinated action – both on the level of individuals and organizations, to go from strategy making to implementation and operation. The roots of present difficulties are exposed and future solutions predicted, based on presently available research results in Enterprise Architecture.

This chapter demonstrates how enterprise modeling frameworks can be used in practice to consider the potential scope and type of models (artifacts), and then how strategic objectives and stakeholder concerns dictate the selection of the actual scope, type and depth of modeling, i.e. what is practically needed.

The second problem is: EE/EA proposes that the architecture of the enterprise should be (able to be) designed. However, enterprises are not like a car or a television set, they are complex socio technical systems that are known to grow and evolve organically, therefore if enterprises can be engineered then it must be a special kind of engineering, not just following the template of engineering methodologies that worked for cars and television sets, in the hope they will also work for enterprises. Since this author has been a proponent of enterprise engineering for some time (thirty-two years to be precise) the above comment is not intended to be taken as a counter argument against EE, rather it is a caution to those who are new to the area who try to quickly extrapolate engineering methodologies from other areas to enterprise engineering. Both the complexity and the organic nature of enterprises has consequences to what works and what does not, and a special problem of this homeostatic evolution is how the enterprise can ensure that its information content increases (its entropy decreases) – which is a rather abstract way of stating the problem of information management in EE/EA (treated in the second half of this writing).

Addressing the problems discussed in this chapter is a prerequisite of a successful future for enterprise engineering. A very large proportion of enterprise engineering / enterprise architecture (EE/EA) efforts of the past 10-15 years have addressed the proverbial 'business - IT alignment', therefore the majority of stakeholders were either IT people or business managers who were directly engaged in the effort to help IT provide better solutions for business. As a consequence, the terminology, the methods and the scope of EE/EA projects has *seemingly* been restricted to IT-related problems, while other business stakeholders had limited engagement with EE/EA practice.

In contrast, more and more EE/EA projects started to work on other business transformation problems, such as a) the creation of enterprise networks, virtual organizations, and supporting professional networks, b) the introduction of Service Orientation (SOA) on the level of the organization to create lean and agile organizational structures (rather than using SOA as a way to optimize IT applications for reuse), c) the introduction of process improvement methods, such as Six Sigma, Software Process Improvement, d) the transformation of the enterprise into a 'process based organization', and a range of other initiatives that require enterprise level change but are not IT focused, even if IT plays a role in their implementation.

To make the stance of the author clear: in reality, the chief architect of an enterprise is (supposed to be) the CEO, supported by the Board, and Enterprise Architecture as a discipline (together with its methods, tools, concepts and frameworks) has developed to satisfy this. In turn the mandate of an Enterprise Architecture Program in the enterprise is (supposed to be) to oversee and co-ordinate various Projects that address one or several strategic transformation objectives (with appropriate governance that ensures participation of High level management and of Business Unit managers). The very nature of EA dictates that Strategic Projects that transform manufacturing, logistics, communication, product development, customer relationships, management and organization (such as mergers or acquisitions), and IT support should be co-coordinated rather than pursued in isolation. It is easy to understand that there are necessary links among the various transformation objectives if we realize that EA is only a new (and perhaps better) name for what used to be called Enterprise Integration (EI) (NB not to be confused with

Enterprise Application Integration!), whereupon the goal of EI is to ensure that 'all material, resources and information should be available whenever and wherever needed, in the quality and quantity needed and that they are being utilized as needed' — thus EA is practiced to achieve and maintain EI.

A major tool of EA/EE practice is Enterprise Modeling, whereupon explicit representations are built and perused by various stakeholders (either to create better designs of the organization, technology, processes and information, or simply to understand these designs and make informed decisions about them). Thus enterprise modeling significantly contributes to the self-information of the enterprise, which intimately links enterprise modeling with the second problem, that of information management.

The Role of Enterprise Models in EE/EA

The introduction of Enterprise Architecture practice, and in particular the use of enterprise modeling, hinges on the organization's readiness to do so. This condition of 'readiness' includes a number of factors, including the organizational type (Mintzberg, 1979), the organization's history, and the availability of a number of capabilities that together form the prerequisite of successfully using enterprise modeling in EA practice (Hysom, 2003).

The international standard ISO 15704:2000 (ISO, 2000) defines a scope that enterprise modeling should be able to cover, but the modeling frameworks that help practitioners define the scope of modeling only identify areas, which are 'a holding place for a host of possible models'. According to previous work of the author on GERAM and ISO15704:2000: "the enterprise engineering process needs models for some pragmatic purpose. For example, models can be used to a) express a design choice; b) simulate a process in order to find out some process characteristics, such as cost or duration; c) analyze an existing process for finding inconsistencies or other problems in the information or material flow; d) analyze decision functions and find missing decisional roles", etc. (Section 2.3.1.5.2, IFIP-IFAC, 2003).

Both the scoping problem (what needs to be modeled and to what level of detail) and the model selection problem (which modeling language to use) are significant, as discussed in the sections below.

The Scoping Problem – Selecting which Enterprise Entity is the 'System of Interest'

Enterprise Architecture has too often been interpreted as enterprise ICT architecture and therefore a significant part of the potential of EA has not been discovered by many. Some projects, in which the author participated, were exceptions to this trend. For example, in early enterprise architecture projects within the Globeman 21 (GM21) and Globemen (GMN) consortia, the business problems solved using EA principles and methodologies were the creation of a) various Enterprise Networks and Virtual Enterprises / Virtual Organizations (Tølle and Bernus, 2003) , which had the preparedness to allow the quick creation of competitive and predictable bidding projects (GM21), and b) Enterprise Networks to allow virtual service enterprises to be created on demand. These projects were concentrated on the creation of new business models, determining their policies, principles, contracts, processes, and organization, whereupon in these projects information technology played an important but subordinate role (given that the IT needs could mostly be satisfied by using existing software products and supporting IT services).

Thus, the first scoping question is: where are the boundaries of the System from which the change or transformation can be attacked using EA practice? In other words, is the System of Interest the entire supply chain, or the entire company, or perhaps a subset of entities within the enterprise for the change we need to address?

The answer to this question seems trivial at first: any of these can be the 'System of Interest'. However, when looking into the practicality of the problem, we have to realize that a complete enterprise is so complex that our present capabilities are not satisfactory to cover the potential scope of enterprise modeling. Therefore, while the standards can be used to define a complete potential scope of enterprise modeling, all we can do in practice is to define a complete actual scope in which EA practice will be operating at any given moment in time.

The scoping exercise determines what part of the System of Interest we shall consider, and what part will remain hidden (with perhaps some boundary conditions representing what is hidden). This works, as long as we did not cut our System of Interest in the 'wrong place', leaving us with too many boundary conditions to consider.

Since complexity cannot be completely done away with, it is wise to construct our system of interest in a way that it is 'relatively independent' from other systems in its environment. By relative independence we mean that the interface through which the system of interest (the enterprise entity in question) interacts with its environment (other enterprise entities) is simple, i.e., the number of connections and number of interfaces is low. Companies tend to (or are at least trying to) cut down on their own complexity in this way. For example, the establishment of customer relationship management services (to cut down the complexity of the company-to-customer interface), and the application of Service Oriented Architecture (to cut down the complexity of the relationship between IT Application Services and Business Units) are manifestations of this trend.

Any entity can be the target (or host) of EA practice, but for the practice to be successful; the entity needs to be defined in a way that allows the simplification of the interface between the entity and its environment (notice that this service orientation principle can be applied recursively). Some companies (e.g. JetStar, a wholly owned subsidiary of Qantas) (Haverty, 2006) applied this principle very successfully, leading to a Business Model that allows dynamic re-configuration because a well defined service (with a simple interface) is much easier to be replaced by another equivalent service entity, than would be the case if this service were intrinsically interconnected with a large number of internal components of the system that uses the service. Naturally, this principle is applicable to IT / Application Services, but the principle is not limited to that area.

The above discussion hopefully clarifies that a particularly bad way of cutting the enterprise into constituent systems is to separate IT from non-IT, because IT systems and the rest of the enterprise they service are so much interconnected that the cut does not simplify the problem, but instead, makes it even worse. If the service orientation principle is applied consequentially, then every 'relatively independent' entity would (at least potentially) include both human and automated elements, and should have its own well-defined service, as well as its own management (both consisting of human and automated components, such as a combination of IT, logistics and manufacturing technology). The front face of GERAM's modeling framework (IFIP-IFAC, 2003) shows this in a graphical form (see Fig.1.).

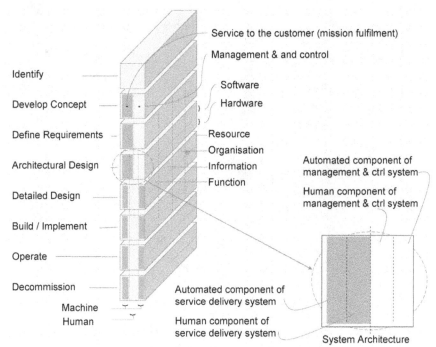

Figure 1. Scope of Enterprise Entities

A (special type of) Business Model can be drawn according to the application of the service orientation principle to the structure of a business (see Figure 2).

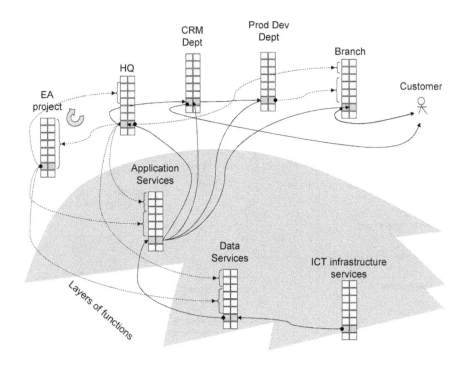

Figure 2. Service Oriented Business Model
(Legend: solid arrows show operational interactions, e.g. entity A operationally supports entity B's operation; dotted arrows show generative interactions, whereupon entity A covers life cycle activities of entity B.)

In Figure 2 each entity has its own service that it provides either to customers, or to other Enterprise Entities, as well as a management & control component that manages the entity's service. Note that some entities are either entirely or partially 'virtual' in the sense that an entity may have a defined and complete end-to-end process (defined and maintained by the management of that entity), but in fact all or most of the activities in that process are performed by another (supporting) entity by way of operational interactions. While Projects are typically virtual entities, the concept is not limited to Projects; e.g. the GMS consortium developed Virtual Service Enterprises that continuously provide after sales service to factories (services, such as chemical factory optimization, production turnaround, troubleshooting, etc).

In Figure 2 the symbols representing Enterprise Entities describe these entities together with their life cycles, whereupon 'life cycle' has no temporal connotation (in the spirit of GERAM/ISO

15704:2000). Strictly speaking this life cycle representation would not be necessary to illustrate the concept of service orientation in the business model (a simple box, split into service and management of service, further subdivided into human and automated components would be sufficient). However, further in this chapter the same figure will be used to illustrate another important architecture principle: the recursive generation of entities by one another (or by themselves).

Some Architecture Frameworks (e.g., PERA, GERAM, Zachman) are explicit about the inclusion of the human / organizational component into EA, while others (e.g., DoDAF) are not, and a suitable extension would most likely benefit the users of the latter type frameworks –according to the ISO15704:2000 architecture framework requirements.

In summary, the Scope of EE/EA practice can be a suitably selected Enterprise (Business) Entity ('System of Interest'), which may be a company, a factory, an office, even a complete supply chain, etc. However, scoping will only help reduce complexity if the entity is defined to be 'relatively independent'; otherwise too many boundary conditions need to be considered.

The scoping Problem – Selecting Enterprise Models to Support EE

Provided we settled for an Enterprise Business Entity (EBE), of which the change or transformation is to be supported by EA/EE, the next question is: what are the models or descriptions of the EBE that need to be created and maintained?

EE/EA practitioners can become frustrated when in the process of EE/EA they develop various models, which are subsequently misunderstood, misinterpreted, disregarded in decision making, not appreciated, or not used and maintained by other stakeholders as intended. Whose fault is this and what is the remedy?

Notice that the problem does not exist (or only to a lesser extent) in traditional engineering. For example, every VLSI designer knows which models of the product must be created and why, as well as how and for what purpose to use them, including their use for decisions in engineering and engineering management. In fact almost every field of engineering has such a standardized set of artifacts.

In contrast, EE/EA can only standardize a set of mandatory (and optional) models if it restricts that standard to a type of application area and type (or class) of problems that the EE process, project or program needs to solve.

Models respond to Stakeholder Concerns; While EA methodologies might define a general list of models that are 'compulsory' to develop, it has to be taken into account that the role of enterprise models is to support the explicit representation of aspects of the EBE that some stakeholders need, and based on which representation their questions can be answered, common understanding can be attained, and mutual agreement can be reached. A rigid list of models would clearly not be sufficient: the list would have to be determined in the knowledge of stakeholders, their concerns, and their assumed knowledge (to read, analyze, understand, or otherwise interact with the model) (Bernus and Kalpic, 2006). Typically the same model can be expressed using different formalisms, or 'externalizations' (textual, tabular, graphical, static or dynamic) and the ability of the stakeholder to interact with the model may significantly be improved if the means of presentation are selected according to their abilities and preferences. This property could be called the *usability* of the model.

Even if the above determinations have been made, the right level of detail needs to be provided to these stakeholders, representing that part of the model that responds to their needs, and hiding the rest to avoid unnecessary complexity and to increase the chances of good communication.

Therefore, enterprise architects need a good understanding of who are the stakeholders, what are their concerns, as well as the ability of various modeling languages to express models which can respond to stakeholder concerns – and of course a good knowledge of stakeholder capabilities (regarding their ability to peruse these models). While IEEE 1471 (2000), the standards that elaborate on stakeholders, stakeholder concerns and architecture descriptions, and ISO 15704 (2000) can already be used as guiding standards, IEEE 1471's future revised release of the ISO standard version (ISO/IEC 42010:2007), together with the future release of an updated ISO15704 standard (both work- in-progress at the time of this writing), will further harmonize the terminology surrounding enterprise models, and are expected to provide even better guidance for scoping and model selection.

Note that the names of these standards are somewhat misleading. ISO15704:2000's title 'Industrial automation systems -- Requirements for enterprise-reference architectures and methodologies' suggests that the standard is only applicable to industrial automation systems, whereupon in reality the standard's content applies to any Enterprise Architecture Framework. Similarly, the title of IEEE 1471 and ISO/IEC 42010 'Systems and Software Engineering -- Recommended practice for architectural description of software-intensive systems' suggests that the standard applies to predominantly software systems, whereupon in reality there is nothing in the standard that is specific to software systems or software intensive systems; the standard's requirements apply to any architecture description, including the descriptions of socio-technical systems, such as enterprises.

Buckl *et al* (2008) developed a catalogue of typical stakeholder concerns, what management methods are typically addressing these concerns, and accordingly, what stakeholder views are to be created from which underlying enterprise model(s). While version 1 of this catalogue is listing only IT related business concerns, the method of developing a standard set of questions and best practices to address them is generalizable to the entire scope of EA. The concept of 'stakeholder concern' in IEEE 1471 is exactly the same as the concept of 'competency questions' developed by Grüninger and Fox (1995), and it is important to look at stakeholder concerns in the light of this. Competency questions are statements about the kind of questions a formal ontological theory should be able to answer, thus guiding the design of enterprise modeling languages to be used to develop models – the analysis of which models can in turn answer questions that stakeholders have. NB questions can be asked both about models and model instances, such as a workflow (process) type or a set of workflow (process) instances.

Models have a *Status* in EA processes; An often-disregarded aspect of enterprise models is their role in the identification, concept development, analysis, design, decision-making and implementation process, as well as in the operation of enterprise entities. Each model can have a *status* in the processes surrounding enterprise architecture practice. The usual division is simple: 'AS-IS' and 'TO-BE' models. However, models have a number of other attributes that are crucial for them to be interpreted correctly. Who created the model? For what purpose? What is the status of agreement on this model? What is the version history of this model? These and a number of other model-attributes (qualified with a value statement, explaining risk, cost, effort, and feasibility, to name a few) have been studied in detail by Hysom (Hysom, 2003). The relevance of keeping these model attributes clear is that contrary to popular belief even the most formal models have *many* meanings (Bernus, 2003), and EA practitioners must make sure that all expected interpretations by all stakeholders are consistent. A significant part of model interpretation is their situated meaning (Barewise and Perry, 1983) and this fact calls for the above mentioned (and other) contextual attributes to be reckoned with when determining the form and content of models to be produced and maintained. Without these attributes the risks of misinterpretation and unnoticed disagreement are too high.

Consequences for multidisciplinary and geographically and culturally distributed EE/EA programs, projects and teams; The use of enterprise modeling in EE/EA offers the hope that due to the formal and exact nature of models it will be easier to communicate proposals, discuss problems and to agree on solutions than it would be using traditional methods (meetings, verbal discussions, text-only documents and informal figures). Indeed, under conditions where mutual understanding cannot be taken for granted (due to the lack of shared educational, cultural or work backgrounds) the expression of one's ideas using formal and explicit models can be of great help. However, it is a false hope that formal models alone are a guarantee of success in communication.

Formal models can be used to great effect if the stakeholders involved in creating / reading or otherwise perusing these models have the motivation to do so, and have the necessary set of skills (expertise). As part of this skill-set, agreed ontological models of enterprise engineering (at least on the metamodel level, which embodies the terminological component of the ontology) are of great importance, because they define the languages of modeling, and also importantly the language of communication in general.

Part of the experience that natural language (free text) is inadequate for achieving common understanding and for communicating unambiguously is due to the lack of a clear and agreed terminology. Therefore, even those stakeholders whose roles do not necessitate the perusal of formal enterprise models would reap the benefits of using exact terminology. ISO 15704:2000 argues that the concepts used in communication should be able to be expressed in multiple forms – including *exact* natural language descriptions (such as glossaries), meta-models, and ontological theories (*c.f.* 'Generic Enterprise Modelling Concepts' of ISO 15704:2000), which are mutually consistent.

To emphasize this point: the author has experienced a situation where the presenter declared that 'Information Architecture' has been developed for an enterprise entity. The artifact *actually* developed was only a large Entity Relationship schema, without reference to how the information modeled was planned to be aggregated and embodied in technical and human implemented parts / components of the entity in question. The difference went unnoticed and the audience believed that the architectural design of the entity had been finished, while in reality it had not even started, the misunderstanding having an effect on budgeting and planning the given EA program.

Furthermore, many types of models are formal in the sense that they represent formal structures, but the 'terminal symbols' in the model must be assumed to be understood as intended – otherwise communication using the model cannot be guaranteed. It is the underlying situated interpretation of enterprise models (Bernus, 2003) that makes communication efficient, rather than just effective – this is because the size and complexity of formal models that stakeholders can interpret in a situated manner is far less than that of a computer executable model.

As a consequence of the above, teams from different backgrounds must be trained and become competent in the use of formal models before the true benefits of formal enterprise models can be used to the full extent. The level of training does not have to be uniform across all teams, because *views* of the same set of models can be presented in a form and to a level of detail that is appropriate for the roles of the stakeholders – some may have to be able to create, maintain and analyze these models using these model views, while others only need to be able to understand, read, critiqué, or simply use some aspect of the same models by viewing a partial representation that is relevant for them.

Many Enterprise Modeling Tools exist today that can provide model views customized to the user's needs, revealing or hiding model details as necessary, and offering several possible representations (graphical, tabular) as well as offering various media of presentation (interactive, web-based publication and print). Where further developments would be desirable is a) the usability of the graphical user interfaces of these tools, b) the integration of the tools' model databases with systems that support the operation of the enterprise. An important development in this (second) regard is the appearance of process modeling tools that allow business users to create processes on their own and publish them as executable workflows. It can be predicted that such direct involvement of business users (process owners) in modeling will soon result in a cultural change and make enterprise modeling and model-based control a much more ingrained practice in businesses than it is today.

Many management, design and other creative processes are not procedural; therefore behavioral modeling languages are not adequate for modeling them. However, activity models can still be used to model such processes. Further future developments are needed in the ability of process modeling tools to not only model non-procedural processes but to also create corresponding 'workflows' – a full support for such processes by 'workflow engines' is in R&D stage today.

Information Management in Enterprise Engineering

The vision of enterprises maintaining their own representation as models certainly appeals to engineers: it is unconceivable to an automotive engineer not to have a detailed drawing for every aspect of a car model; indeed it would not be possible to agree on the design of the model, or on how cars of that model will be produced. Similar examples can be described for all engineering fields, perhaps with the exception of software engineering. Before software engineers protest: consider the number of large and complex software systems of which the specification, and design documentation is a complete and up to date set of formal models, ready to be retrieved from a central repository. Software engineers intuitively know that these models would be desirable, but the complexity of the task usually makes this prohibitive. At the same time, complex software systems are a fact of life.

Given that complex software and hardware (manufacturing, communication, computer & control) systems are part of today's enterprises, not surprisingly, enterprise engineering faces an even greater challenge. Therefore the idea that a small group of enterprise architects will create and maintain such a complex repository of descriptions and models of the entire enterprise certainly poses some questions.

While we recognize what a daunting task it is to create such reflexive description of the complete enterprise, one cannot escape the lure of such a future: if the enterprise has such a description then the enterprise as an entity has made a great step towards becoming self-aware. The aware enterprise, or the intelligent enterprise, is an entity that is in control of its own destiny, because the objectives of the enterprise as a whole and the actions of the enterprise as a whole can be connected through planning and continuous monitoring – if the plan does not work, change the plan or change the objective (an ability which is the essence of intelligence, at least according to the accepted definitions of intelligent agents in the artificial intelligence community).

Consider the enterprise as an organized system of systems, where the component systems are humans (individuals) extended with technology. Humans cannot be a priori considered to be intelligent agents, because given the agent's objectives, human capabilities might not be sufficient to decide and act within the limits of time to perform complex planning, or to perform some task that is beyond human physical abilities. Therefore the elementary building block of the enterprise is best considered a hybrid agent (a human / individual together with some technology that extends the individual's capabilities so as to be able to act as an intelligent agent).

As a consequence, there are two questions: 1. what support technology does a human need to remain an intelligent agent in complex situations in which he/she needs to act, and in addition to technology that extends physical capabilities, what information technology is needed for the human to be a reflective agent? 2. What are the rules of co-ordination and interaction between and among such hybrid agents which can ensure that a group of agents forms an emergent agent, with properties similar to the individual hybrid agent? The problem has been studied in a limited way under the name of holonics (Voth, 2004) and fractal factory (Warnecke, 1993), however, these studies concentrated on the co-ordination aspects, and not on the reflexive capability (self-knowledge and self-awareness) of the constituents. The area of multi-agent systems research (Wooldridge, 2002) has concentrated on the design and implementation of completely automated agents (and multi-agent systems), but this research should in the future be extended to hybrid agents.

Whenever a complex system is architected, a good principle to reduce the complexity of the problem is to consider the complex system to be a system of systems, and the principle can be recursively applied. For such complexity reduction to work, the system of interest needs to be cut into pieces which enjoy relative independence, down to the level of (potentially hybrid) individual agents. Perhaps surprisingly, we arrived at the same principle that is expressed as service orientation and which has been discussed in the previous section – it is only that we have an additional condition: when defining component systems (and subsystems, etc), the intelligent enterprise needs to be (recursively) constructed out of intelligent subsystems, until we reach the individual hybrid agent.

Looking at so-called generative life cycle relationships (e.g. in Fig.2., Headquarters (HQ) identifies, develops the concept of, and defines the requirements of Application Services) it is clear that there needs to be feedback loops established for the enterprise to 'design itself'. E.g. HQ identifies an EA program, the program establishes an enterprise engineering project, which in turn makes changes to HQ. However, if these large feedback loops are constructed out of many small feedback loops, then in fact every enterprise engineering activity can eventually be reduced to small self-improvement cycles. Under these circumstances hybrid agents engage in precisely two activities: a) improve the self, thus create, analyze, change and maintain the information about themselves, and b) improve the system of which they are an immediate part, thus create, analyze, change and maintain the information of their immediate community.

Notice that the roles of individual agents in such a community of agents are heterogeneous; every participant has potentially different activities to perform in the group's process(es), which includes the group's management process. The group's management process has the task of coordinating local improvement cycles, and needs to rely on the models maintained by the individual constituents of the group. Applying this principle recursively up the chain of aggregation, the enterprise can maintain its self-image in a distributed manner. Every individual is responsible for the maintenance of the enterprise model of his / her immediate interest (and which is consistent with the negotiated objectives of the role taken by that individual).

The establishment of such a distributed enterprise engineering / information management removes the bottleneck from EE, because there is no separation of designer and actor. At the same time the tools necessary for such a distributed enterprise model repository can be provided to individuals as an infrastructure service.

The cultural and educational implications of this idea are significant, however, the author believes that the bottlenecks of centralized design need to be addressed, and therefore future research is needed to overcome the cultural and educational barriers.

Conclusion

The future of enterprise engineering seems to be bright, but practitioners must ensure that they judiciously consider the implications of the theory of enterprise models, and in particular the conditions under which enterprise modeling is seen as a relevant and useful activity by all stakeholders. A longer term objective for enterprise engineering is to make the practice a distributed activity, whereupon enterprise models become the everyday tool for all actors in the enterprise, from workers to the CEO. The chapter proposed a high level design to achieve this.

References

Bernus, P. (2003). Enterprise Models for Enterprise Architecture and ISO9000:2000. Annual Reviews in Control 27(2) 2pp211-220

Barewise, J. and Perry, J. (1983). Situations and Attitudes. MIT Press, Cambridge, MA.

Buckl, S., Ernst, A.M., Lankes, J,. Matthes, F. (2008). Enterprise Architecture Management Pattern Catalog. V1. TB 0801. Software Engineering for Business Information Systems (Sebis). TU München, München.

Grüninger, M., Fox, M.S. (1995). The Role of Competency Questions in Enterprise Engineering. In A.Rolstadås (Ed) IFIP WG5.7 Workshop on Benchmarking - Theory and Practice, (Trondheim, Norway, 1994). Chapman & Hall, London. pp2-31.

Haverty, B. (2006). Jetstar: Stephen Tame, CIO. Interview in ZDNet Australia (19 September 2006)

Hysom, R. (2003). Enterprise Modelling. In Handbook on Enterprise Architecture. P.Bernus, G.Schmidt and K.Mertins (Eds). Springer, Berlin. pp.373-416.

IEEE (2000). ANSI/IEEE 1471-2000, Recommended Practice for Architecture Description of Software-Intensive Systems". IEEE Computer Society, New York, NY.

IFIP-IFAC Task Force. (2003). GERAM: The Generalised Enterprise Reference Architecture and Methodology. In Handbook on Enterprise Architecture. P.Bernus, G.Schmidt and K.Mertins (Eds). Springer, Berlin. pp.22-64

ISO (2000). ISO 15704:2000. Industrial automation systems. Requirements for enterprise-reference architectures and methodologies. International Standards Organization, Geneva.

Kalpic,B., Bernus,P. (2006). Business Process Modelling Through the Knowledge Management Perspective. 10(3) International Journal of Knowledge Management. pp40-56

Mintzberg, H. (1979). The Structuring of Organizations. Prentice Hall, Englewood Cliffs, NJ.

Tølle,M., Bernus,P. (2003). Reference models supporting enterprise networks and virtual enterprises. Int. J. Networking and Virtual Organisations. 2(1) pp2-15

Voth, D. (2004). Holonics in Manufacturing: Bringing Intelligence Closer to the Machine" IEEE Intelligent Systems. pp4-6

Warnecke, H. J. (1993). The Fractal Company. Springer-Verlag, Berlin.

Wooldridge, M. (2002). An Introduction to Multiagent Systems. John Wiley & Sons, Chichester, UK.

About the Author

Since 1976 **Dr Peter Bernus** has worked internationally on various aspects of enterprise integration as a researcher, consultant, project leader and trainer for industry (for a wide range of organizations internationally), for government and for defense (ADF). Dr Bernus is also series editor for Springer Verlag, managing editor of the Handbook on Enterprise Architecture and the Handbook on Architectures of Information Systems, and is a member of the editorial boards of several international journals. He is past chair of the IFIP-IFAC Task Force for Architectures for Enterprise Integration, which developed GERAM, a generalization of architecture framework requirements (ISO 15704:2000), foundation chair of Working Group 5.12 on Enterprise Integration of IFIP. He is currently an Associate Professor at Griffith University teaching in the Masters of Enterprise Architecture program.

Associate Professor Peter Bernus
School of Information and Communication Technology, Enterprise Integration Group
Faculty of Science, Environment, Engineering and Technology
Griffith University
Nathan (Brisbane) Queensland 4111 Australia
P.Bernus@griffith.edu.au
http://www.cit.gu.edu.au/~bernus

Chapter 18

MARKETING COMMUNICATIONS FOR COHERENCY MANAGEMENT

Thom Kearney

Editors' Preface

The following chapter delivers a key message for all EA Practitioners around the world. It is quite often said that a critical success factor for Enterprise Architecture is a Communications Plan. This is only part of the solution. In these days of competing sound bites and information overload it is absolutely essential to also consider marketing.

In this chapter Thom Kearney introduces us to the key aspects of marketing and follows up with an applied true example.

Introduction

Marketing and communications are key enablers for the practice of Enterprise Architecture and for helping an organization progress towards maturity in Coherency Management. To mature, an organization must change and this chapter provides a concise overview of some marketing concepts and techniques that have proven effective in promoting change within organizations.

Key concepts

Marketing communications is a fairly broad topic that draws on the body of knowledge around business, social sciences, education, physiology, learning theory and social behavior. It is informed by research into social and consumer behavior and it is practiced in one form or another by companies, non-profits and political organizations around the world.

This section explores five key ideas from the rich body of knowledge that has developed around marketing and communications over the last century, namely:

- Marketing is about meeting needs
- Personal selling is about meeting needs
- The communications model
- The change process
- AIDA – Attention, Interest, Desire and Action

Marketing is about meeting needs

Marketing is a term that is widely used with an almost infinite number of interpretations. Some see it as the root of all evil, being responsible for promoting an unsustainable consumer state and destroying our planet. There is no doubt that marketing techniques can be used to influence behavior and accelerate change. Whether that change is a positive or negative thing, depends on the goals of the marketer. For the purposes of this discussion the marketing concept is defined as:

> *"Meeting the needs of a target group in a way that also meets the objectives of the organization."*

Many people view marketing as the process of selling stuff. The concept of personal selling is often an important part of a broader marketing mix. In fact, in situations when the idea to be sold is complex or the target audience is relatively small, it can be the dominant element. Given that many Coherency Management programs involve both a complex message and a relatively small audience, Personal Selling is discussed next.

Personal Selling is about meeting needs

Personal selling is the use of interpersonal communications skills to persuade an individual to take a particular action. In commercial applications this usually means an exchange of money for a product or service. Within organizations it is used to sell an idea or project where the objective is to get commitment from others to behave in a particular way. For instance, using a consistent approach to defining Enterprise Architecture artifacts.

One of the more powerful methods for selling an idea or product is that of Need Satisfaction Selling. Basically the idea is to show how your proposition satisfies a need that the prospect is both aware of and cares about. Need Satisfaction Selling is a discipline unto itself that can be explored in detail on the internet or through professional development courses.

The idea of Relationship Selling extends the basic concept of needs-satisfaction over time and is focused on building trust between individuals and organizations.

Objections are good
When a client offers an objection to your proposition it is an opportunity to learn more about their needs. Objections and the motives for those objections should be well understood before they are addressed.

Note: objections should not always be seen as logical arguments to be aggressively attacked as this can frequently weaken the relationship. Take the time to thoroughly understand the objection prior to responding. And when you do respond be certain to respect the other party's point of view.

Listening is more important than talking

Personal Selling requires interpersonal communications. Listening skills are an essential part of successful relationships and are frequently one of the biggest opportunities for improvement in an organization. An internet search will reveal hundreds of sources for information. Some of the more pertinent ideas for improving listening skills are:

- **Listen for ideas and central themes.** Don't get lost in details or delivery errors. Be careful not to jump to conclusions. Get the whole message before responding.

- **Assume the position.** Just like speaking, your body language counts when listening. Look at the speaker, assume an active posture, take notes, nod occasionally, encourage the speaker to continue.

- **Beware of emotion.** Certain words, phrases or non-verbal cues can set us up for an emotional response. Be aware of this in yourself and work to confirm your understanding rather than reacting emotionally.

- **Use your brain**. Our brains can process information much faster than we can speak. This excess capacity can lead to distractions and get you thinking about something other than what is being said. Use the moments between words to try and put yourself in the other's shoes, to understand their perspective and where they are coming from.

- **Respond appropriately.** Jumping in with a counter argument is not listening. You should be trying to understand the other party's point of view so you can ultimately appeal to their needs. Be candid and open in your response. Be sure to clarify with paraphrasing and ask questions that encourage the speaker to continue. Always respect the other party.

- **Listening is hard work.** Active listening takes effort and concentration. You have to block out distractions, process many potential meanings for each word, make comparisons to your own experience and try and determine what the speaker is really saying.

The communications model
With so much riding on the ability to effectively communicate, it is important to have a good understanding of what is going on. The diagram below illustrates a simplified view of the process between two parties:

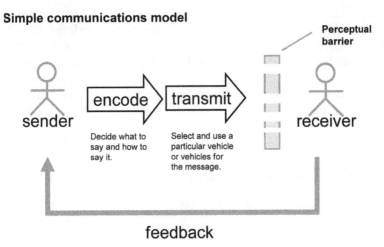

Simple communications model

Perceptual
barrier

encode
Decide what to
say and how to
say it.

transmit
Select and use a
particular vehicle
or vehicles for
the message.

sender

receiver

feedback

Figure 1. The communications model

The process starts with the Sender who has to decide what to say and then how to say it. Effective messages are simple, meaningful and credible. Sometimes how you decide to say something is as important as what you decide to say. Crafting the right message depends on understanding the receiver and is more art than science.

The second thing the Sender does is decide how to deliver the message. This might be a phone call, email, presentation or corporate newsletter. The way the message is transmitted carries meaning as does the non-verbal elements of a conversation. In fact some studies have shown that non-verbal elements can carry more meaning in a conversation than the words.

The perceptual barrier is a self-defense mechanism. The average North American is bombarded by hundreds if not thousands of demands for their attention every day. We automatically block most of these. The openings in the barrier are dynamic and represent the individual interests of the receiver at a point in time. For instance, an executive may be far more receptive to a message about achieving alignment if they have recently attempted to integrate a process from another division only to discover that the documentation used an entirely different standard.

To complicate matters, we tend to interpret messages in a way that is consistent with our existing beliefs. For example, some people believe that change is good, while many find any change at all threatening. The glass is half full or half empty is another example of a predisposition that affects perception and understanding. If a prospect believes that Enterprise Architecture is an academic process with little practical value, you have an additional challenge.

The feedback loop is the same process in reverse. Listening to feedback is the only way you can determine if the message has been understood.

Implications of the communications model

- The effectiveness of the message (encode), depends on how well it relates to the receiver's interests. So when you develop your messages, focus on things that the audience cares about – not what you think is important.

- The effectiveness of the vehicle used, (transmit) depends upon its ability to reach the receiver. Choose vehicles that the sender is likely to consider credible and will be exposed to.

- Together the vehicle and the message must get through the receiver's filters before it can even be processed much less understood.

- Communication is an iterative, two-way process. The steps may have to be repeated, feedback listened to, and the message modified many times before understanding takes place.

The adoption of change process

The success of Coherency Management and Enterprise Architecture depends upon the organization (people) modifying the way that they currently operate. It may be a big change or a small change, but the process is likely to follow a similar pattern.

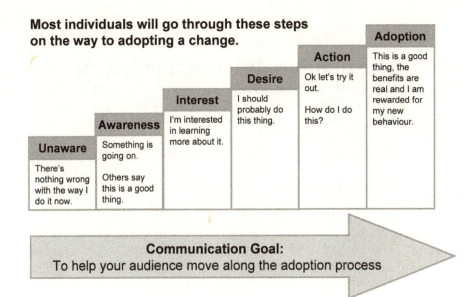

Most individuals will go through these steps on the way to adopting a change.

Unaware	Awareness	Interest	Desire	Action	Adoption
There's nothing wrong with the way I do it now.	Something is going on. Others say this is a good thing.	I'm interested in learning more about it.	I should probably do this thing.	Ok let's try it out. How do I do this?	This is a good thing, the benefits are real and I am rewarded for my new behaviour.

Communication Goal:
To help your audience move along the adoption process

Figure 2. The adoption of change process

This cycle repeats itself to varying degrees every time an individual makes a change in their behavior. Sometimes the process takes weeks or months, other times it takes seconds, e.g. an impulse purchase of some gum versus quitting smoking. For a large organization to change many individuals need to change and that can take years or decades.

It is important to recognize that for most things, a single communication event will not be enough to move someone through the complete cycle. This means that you need to plan for a series of communication encounters designed to progressively move your prospect through the stages of adoption over time.

AIDA – Attention, Interest, Desire, Action

The AIDA method has been a staple of advertising for decades and it succinctly encapsulates basic consumer behavior and communications knowledge into a checklist for developing or evaluating communications from the point of view of user behavior. It also fairly closely maps to the change model described earlier. It goes like this:

Attention

Before you can communicate with someone you have to get their attention. We are presented with thousands of requests for our attention. This background clutter of competing messages presents the first challenge. One of the most effective ways of cutting through the clutter is to use contrast. Understand what most of the clutter looks or sounds like and consciously be creative and different. If something does not readily fall into a category that can be easily ignored, our brain kicks it up for further processing, because it might be important.

Interest

Getting attention is one thing, but if the message is not relevant in some way our internal spam filters trash it pretty quick. To receive further consideration a message needs to be relevant to something that the recipient cares about. The underlying need might relate to business, (funding, people, efficiency, effectiveness) or it might be personal (safety, social, esteem, etc) . The point is that the message needs to appeal to a current need the individual is facing and recognizes. To get interest you have to appeal to a need and make a promise that the audience can believe.

Desire

Desire is the motivation to take action. Once an individual is interested in what you have to say they will be looking for proof that the proposition is real and they will want to know what it is they have to do to get the promised benefit.

Action

COHERENCY MANAGEMENT

Astute marketers know that motivation to take action can be fleeting and they strive to make it easy for their customers to purchase their product or service. In the consumer world we see this in the location of retail outlets, one click shopping online, drive through food service and a multitude of other ways. In the business world, a single point of contact, simple tools and well-formed processes play the same role. Making it easy for organizations (people), to take the action you need is essential to close the loop and achieve the support you need.

Applying the concepts

Coherency Management strives to ensure that the different parts of the organization have a logical and consistent relationship to each other. In most organizations this will require some changes to how the parts describe themselves and may even require changes to the parts themselves. In either case this means that individuals will have to buy in to the change and ultimately modify their behavior in some way. Planning for this might follow a process similar to this one:

- Define your objectives
- Understand your target groups
- Practice good communications
- Listen and adapt accordingly

Define your objectives

Communication objectives are typically about some change in behavior or attitude. The adoption of change process introduced earlier provides a framework for planning communication objectives. The idea is that if you have a sense of where your audience is on the adoption staircase, you can focus your efforts on moving them to the next stage.

For instance the communications objective might be to move the prospect from unaware to interested, or from interested to action. Figure 3 shows how related activities might change depending upon the objective.

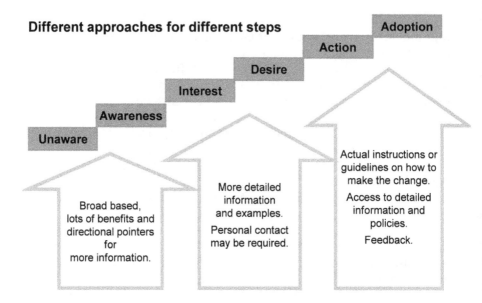

Figure 3. Implications of the adoption process

In the context of coherency, marketing communications is both a lever for enabling the operationalization of the coherency dimensions as well as a tool for accomplishing broad behavioral change objectives.

As a lever, communications can:

- Create awareness of the need for Enterprise Architecture and Coherency

- Promote specific activities and help generate support for work in key focus areas

- Promulgate decisions around key focus areas

In the broader context, communications can:

- Generate awareness of the concept of Coherency Management or of specific components

- Promote the benefits of Coherency Management (stimulate interest)

- Educate targeted groups on specific components and how to take action

COHERENCY MANAGEMENT

Coherency maturity and communication

Your precise objectives will depend upon the target group and their state of awareness but here are some typical objectives you might consider given the coherency maturity level you are working on developing.

Coherency Management State	Typical objectives
0. Absent (Level 0)	Recognition of the importance and role of coherence Create awareness of the need and value proposition Generate inquiries about what the EA practice can do
1. Introduced	Understanding of the steps required to achieve the value proposition Promote isolated application of CM to encourage adoption elsewhere in the organization
2. Encouraged	Reinforce value perception Promote existing practices Introduce idea of formality
3. Instituted	Broaden the application of Coherency Management Reinforce best practices and procedures
4. Optimized	Communicate results of ongoing assessments Communicate organizational improvements in CM Reinforce the value perception – communicate results achieved
5. Innovating	Reinforce the value perception Promote new processes, activities and mechanisms to be institutionalized Recognize innovation and engage sustained interest in continuous improvement

Table 1. Coherency maturity and communications objectives

Whatever objectives you decide upon it is important to have some idea of how you will measure success. It may be worthwhile to conduct a survey before and after your communications program. In the case of a small group, this survey can be a short (1-3 questions) poll at the end of a presentation. It is also a good idea to have a structured way to capture anecdotal evidence as you move forward, for example through short testimonials or mini-case studies, (short means that it comfortably fits on a single presentation slide).

Understand your target groups

There is nothing more fundamental than understanding the perspectives of your target audiences. In fact getting through the perceptual barrier illustrated in the Communications Model (Figure 1) depends upon appealing to the interest and needs of the Receiver. Defining the target groups for your communications is essential. This section discusses three essential aspects of this important activity:

- Don't assume your target group cares about the same things as you

- Segment by role and perspective

- The integrated target group reference model

Don't assume your target group cares about the same things as you

It is natural to assume that your target audience shares your knowledge, attitudes or motivation, but chances are they don't. Making the assumption they do, can easily lead to misunderstanding and dissatisfaction on all sides. Step out of yourself and if you can, get feedback from members of the audience on your trial messages before using them.

In almost every communication situation, with the exception of face-to-face conversations, there is more than one relevant segment. Each segment or target group may care about different things; they play different roles in an organization and have needs that reflect those roles.

Defining and reaching those segments with appropriate messages is what marketing communications is all about.

Segmenting by role and perspective

One way to view target segments for Coherency Management might be to identify key target groups; such as Core Enterprise Architects, Implicit Enterprise Architects and the Applied Architects described elsewhere in this book. Only the first two groups can be expected to have any advance knowledge of Enterprise Architecture, and all three groups will likely have different perspectives and needs that reflect their roles.

Another way is to consider the business perspective of the individuals. For instance policy people and business line people are likely to have different views on the relevance and importance of some policy guidelines. To the policy wonk they are everything, to the service delivery people policies may be viewed as unnecessary interference.

Segmenting by working level

Every situation is different and you need to take the time to understand the relevant groups in your organization. One easily identifiable characteristic that can sometimes be useful is that of working level. For example it may be possible to make some generalizations like the following:

- Senior Executives care about management performance indicators, departmental plans and metrics, relationships with other senior executives, government priorities, personal reputation and that of their organization

- Executives care about departmental and branch plans and priorities, personal advancement and reputation

- Managers care about branch and divisional plans and priorities, people management, project support and metrics

- Line managers care about personal achievement, personal advancement and reputation

Segmentation is an exercise in generalization, there will often be exceptions and every organization will be different.

The integrated target group reference model

Coherency Management demands an understanding of your target groups, so if you have a target group reference model use it, if you don't, then you will need to create one. An effective target segment description might look like the following:

Segment name	
Segment Description:	
Describe the segment using characteristics like: Demographics: age, gender, language, cultural background, Psychographics: opinions, activities, interests	
Product Usage (user behavior), Working level: senior executive, executives, managers, line, etc, Estimated size and importance, Level of awareness or state in the innovation process	
Media preference: (what's the best way to reach them)	
Motivators: why will they act?	
Other defining characteristics	
What you want from them	**What they might want from you**
Define your objective for this segment. What is the action you need from them in order to be successful. Remember to be realistic given their likely position in the adoption process.	This is a critical bit; if you can answer this question accurately you will know precisely where to focus your efforts.

Table 2. Integrated target group reference model

Having a description like the above for each relevant target group segment will be an extremely useful reference as you move forward in your communications efforts. As you begin to collect feedback, the reference models should be constantly updated.

Practice good communications

Interpersonal communications, presentation, listening and persuasion are all key skills that should be developed by the Coherency Management marketing team. This section presents some tips to get you started.

- Speak directly
- Keep it simple & bold
- Think visually
- The rule of seven
- The rule of three

Speak directly whenever you can

Peter Drucker, the management sage, once observed that every time a management directive flowed from one person to the next up to 50% of the content of that message was either lost or modified. That means that after a message has been passed through 2—3 layers of a hierarchy there is a pretty good chance the message that is being delivered is not the same as that which was intended. There are two strategies for combating this:

1. Speak directly to your target audience and do not rely on intermediaries and,

2. Keep the message as simple as possible

Speaking directly to your target audience obviously keeps the communications channel simple and reduces the opportunity for error. However that is not always possible so to ensure that the message received is similar to that you intend, the key is keep the message simple.

The importance of simplicity

Enterprise Architecture is a fascinating field with endless levels of detail. However it is important that your message be tailored to the audience in question. Too much detail will result in most audiences dismissing the communication and missing the point.

Your introductory presentations should be high level and focus on simple benefits. You can and should plan for providing escalating levels of detail, but keep the initial message simple and bold. Remember the perceptual barrier will simply block out messages that are seen as irrelevant. Sell the sizzle, not the steak is the old advertising saying. The sizzle is the benefit, or what a particular person might receive of value from your proposition. You must be prepared to support that benefit as you move up the ladder of adoption but it is not usually a good idea to try and tell the whole story at once.

Keep your initial contact short, simple and full of impact if you can. More detailed content can be provided in follow-up presentations or via web sites and white papers, but care should be taken to ensure that the first contact with the subject is at an appropriate level of detail. It is almost always far better to err on the side of simplicity.

Relentlessly pushing mind-numbing detail at a business target audience does not result in a better understanding and enhanced credibility, but rather ends up confusing and frustrating the audience. On the other hand, an over simplified business message may not seem credible or complete to a more scientific audience.

Finding the right level of detail for a given communication is part of the art of communication. Providing an escalation path for increasing detail and depth is a key part of the overall communications plan.

Think visual

Advertisers have long known about the power of pictures. Even when the visual aspect is not available as in radio, good advertising paints a word picture to get the message across. For many people visual metaphors seem to communicate more directly than words alone. Also, visual elements tend to communicate on an emotive level whereas words are sometimes better at conveying the logical message. The point is, words alone are not as powerful as a combination of words and pictures.

The rule of seven

Most people can only hold seven ideas in their head at any one time. One story is that 7 is the average number of people in a human family over the centuries – resulting in a genetic predisposition for the number. Whatever the reason, the evidence is fairly clear that if you ask a person to process too many things at once, nothing will be remembered. Here are some examples of how to apply the rule of seven:

- Limit the number of bullets in a list to less than seven

- Have no more than seven arguments in your sales pitch

- Don't present more than seven architectural concepts at one time

The rule of three

Just like the rule of seven except that the maximum number is reduced to three. This rule applies when the target audience is attention challenged such as is the case with many executives who have to make decisions quickly. If your time is limited and the audience senior the rule of three can often become the rule of one.

Listen and adapt accordingly

Communication and marketing are complex dynamic processes, and although consistency is important for eventual understanding, blindly repeating the same message over and over is a waste of time if it is not being received or processed. You need to spend some time periodically evaluating the success of your efforts.

Having SMART (Specific, Measurable, Attainable, relevant and Time limited) objectives can really help. It is equally important to have some kind of understanding of the baseline that existed prior to your efforts. For instance what percentage of your audience was aware, interested or have adopted Enterprise Architecture. With that benchmark in hand you can then periodically check to see if numbers are improving.

Coherency Management is generally practiced within an enterprise and it may not be practical to spend large amounts of money on research, however even small scale informal research can help. For example:

- Conduct telephone interviews with key individuals to determine their level of understanding and adoption
- Look for examples of leaders repeating your messages in speeches or in policy documents
- Measure the number of artifacts created that follow a standard
- Ask for, (and listen carefully to) feedback every time you present
- Record what you hear and see against your objectives

Adjust your communications; if at first you don't succeed, try a different approach.

Case study: So what's with the duck?

Problem: How to communicate the benefits of Enterprise Architecture

In the summer of 2007 the Enterprise Architecture and Standards Division, of CIOB TBS GC, faced a dilemma. Over the previous three years they had invested heavily in creating a robust and comprehensive approach to business transformation. Called BTEP for Business Transformation Enablement Program, this approach integrated business architecture and project management concepts into a disciplined methodology for horizontal change. After several successful implementations it had begun to attract attention and communications with potential adopters became important.

Unfortunately, the brilliant scientists that created the methodology responded to this interest using the sometimes arcane language of the discipline and simply overwhelmed business people with detailed descriptions of what they had done. A few like-minded individuals got the message and were enthusiastic, however, most business people simply didn't get it.

The division knew it had important knowledge and useful tools that could help. But they also had learned that selling Enterprise Architecture using the language of the discipline only worked with other architects. Strategically they understood that they needed to change their approach to communications and had hired a senior communications person, (the author), the year previously. This individual was a recent convert to the idea of Enterprise Architecture and was not steeped in the language of the discipline. Knowing the power of images and metaphor he searched the web, and the shared drives and presentations throughout the enterprise looking for images that might help communicate the benefits of Enterprise Architecture. He stumbled upon the idea of ducks in a row and added it to the spider web, gear images, and railroad metaphors as things to try out.

Importantly, at the same time as this search for images was taking place, the leaders of the division had been exploring their vision and mission, recently they had settled on the grand vision of coherent government by design.

In early 2008 the most senior levels of management in the Public Service began to ask questions around alignment. They wanted to know if projects they were being asked to fund were aligned, that is did they follow strategy, use compatible technology, comply with policy, and not duplicate one another? Alignment is a key goal for Enterprise Architecture and the division had been working on ways to measure (and create) alignment as part of its efforts to stimulate coherence. What interests our bosses, fascinates us, so naturally the division wanted to bring its alignment work to the forefront.

Having previously worked in advertising, the communications specialist sought to obtain a visual to go along with the words coherent government by design. In order to cut through the visual clutter and get noticed the image had to be different than what people were used to seeing. The concept of ducks in a row seemed to resonate and a search for a suitable royalty free image ensured. Using istockphoto.com, an image of four different colored ducks in a row was acquired and tested in a power point presentation. The brightly colored ducks were nothing like the complex diagrams and charts that populated most of the decks in the division. There was no question they got attention.

We added the slide to an executive presentation the CIO was giving and while talking to the slide he associated the different color of each duck with the unique personalities of the departments in the federation that makes up the Government of Canada. The argument being that they did not have to give up their autonomy to move in the same direction. This additional message moved departmental audiences from attention to interest as they saw their needs recognized.

So now we had messages that covered the first two steps in the AIDA method. The ducks got attention in a relevant way and the allowance for diversity resonated with the audience, creating interest. Desire came from another source entirely. In Canada, project funding is dependent on the approval of a Deputy Minister committee, the same people that were asking questions about alignment. Therefore departments that were interested in improving their chances of getting funding approval wanted to show they were aligned. They were no longer just interested in alignment; they wanted to prove they had it.

The division facilitated action by making available alignment assessment services that would provide an objective assessment of the level of alignment to the stakeholder. The assessments were then used to either prove alignment existed or to make adjustments to the project to improve alignment.

This completed the AIDA method—the ducks get attention; appealing to need generates interest, the need for funding creates desire and the availability of assessment services makes action simple.

A further innovation in the division's marketing mix should be noted here. To coordinate requests of all types the division had established a service desk with a generic email address. The mail box is monitored by a rotating team of employees who ensure that all requests are dealt with in a timely manner. To get an alignment assessment all a client needed to do was send an email. The idea was to make it easy for prospects to take action.

The ducks turned out to be an excellent metaphor, not only because they communicate the central message of alignment, but because they are well suited to an extension into the physical world. The division has taken to giving out rubber ducks as instant achievement awards. These ducks sit on desks and bookcases, as a means of drawing attention. The question always arises... What's with the duck?

Where to go from here?

The field of marketing communications has been around for as long as people have been selling things and ideas. There is a broad and deep body of knowledge to explore and this chapter has tried to provide an introduction to some of the concepts most applicable to selling Coherency Management.

We have reviewed a basic communications model that illustrates the complexity of communication and the importance of listening and relating to the audience's needs and interests. The AIDA (attention, interest, desire and action) model provides a useful check list for planning how to move your audience through the adoption process. Some ideas for understanding your various target groups and identifying what they care about are summarized in the target group reference model while the good communications tips will help you get you started on your journey of change.

Hopefully your interest is aroused and you are ready to move towards adopting marketing communications in your efforts to make Coherency Management a success. There are many excellent resources available on the internet and in print and video for those that are interested.

References

Shenk, D. (1997). Data Smog Surviving the Information Glut. Harper Edge.

Patterson, K., Grenny, J., Maxfield, D., McMillan, R., Switzler, A. (2008). Influencer, the power to change anything. McGraw-Hill.

Selnow, G.W., Crano, W.D. (1987). Planning, Implementing, and Evaluating Targeted Communication Programs: A Manual for Business Communicators. Greenwood Publishing Group

Maister, D.H., Green, C.H., Galford, R.M. (2000). The Trusted Advisor. The Free Press, New York

About the author

Thom Kearney has more than 25 years experience in marketing, communications, education, enterprise architecture and change. He can be contacted at thomk@rogers.com.

Chapter 19

PROFILE OF GOVERNMENT OF CANADA'S INTERNAL SERVICES

Richard Bryson & Bruce Stacey

Editors' Preface

In this chapter Richard Bryson and Bruce Stacey present an operational work product from the Government of Canada. What is most important about this chapter is how little it looks like an EA project. This is intentional and best represents what happens when EA actually becomes embedded within the existing operational processes of the enterprise.

As is usually the case in the public service, the government of Canada reports its budget expenditures and results (planned and/or actual). It has done this for years but the way this is done varies from government to government and quite often the model morphs within the governments to deal with pressures and interests of the day. Most recently, the office Results-Based Management Division in the Expenditure Management Sector of the Treasury Board Secretariat steers this annual process.

The profile presented in this chapter is remarkable because it is a normative model penned by the Enterprise Architecture Division of the Treasury Board Secretariat in close collaboration with many people across the government.

The Profile of GC Internal Services is a primary example of the Embedded Architecture, as described in chapter 1. As noted in chapter 1, the only difference between Foundation and Extended is the purpose and utility of the Enterprise Business Architecture (EBA). Whereas, Foundation's EBA was used by the CIO to understand requirements, the Extended's EBA is done by business managers wanting to (design or) redesign their business. The Profile of GC Internal Services, as presented, amplifies an example of Embedded Architecture, particularly since it is applied enterprise-wide for:

- Annual planning artifacts that employ architecturally aligned rules for how annual plans are expressed. That is, they follow the normative models (e.g. Reference models) for expressing what the business is about, their clients, goals, objectives, etc.

- Strategic planning that uses the methods and a common language to ensure a holistic plan which aligns to all other key players in the planning arena. (e.g., strategic plan uses outcome logic model which every division leader / functional head can link in to); and

- Public reporting that uses terms and language which is consistent throughout the enterprise.

The internal services all have something in common, they have an underlying structure and descriptive rules based on a common vocabulary informed and aligned with GC TBS / Central Agency policy instruments (the business), reference models like GSRM (Government of Canada's Strategic Reference Model), an emerging pan-Canadian model for describing government services; and other community of practice standards like COBIT – Control Objectives for Information.

As this profile gets rolled into the budget processes this will become the way these are described by all employees. Eventually, other process owners will reference the profile and Canada will talk about internal services consistently. This sounds small but it will enable the Government to:

- Understand the cost of each internal service (e.g. Human Resources Management Services, Financial Management Services, Information Management Services, etc).

- Plan for changes with correct information about the current state.

- Transform internal services to be common, shared, and/or interoperable which will lower costs and become employee centric.

- Study effectiveness and efficiency across departments on a fair basis.

- Use the same underlying architecture for services whether designing web apps or in preparing a report to parliament.

- Model Services and Processes from an enterprise perspective, across the 100+ departments and thousands of employees.

This is just a small part of the budget but as the normative models prove themselves useful then other parts of the budget can start to adopt EA based models in other services areas (not just internal). The budget has always been filed, it is not new, but this year part of the budget will be in accordance with the standards of EA. Embedded EA is exactly this. It is about getting existing process owners to recognize that they are contributing to the design, plan and 'architecture' of the enterprise. If we do it together, supported by the standards, models and techniques of EA (while also being active with the foundation and extended modes of EA) then we can become coherent.

Introduction and Purpose

Introduction

As part of the Government of Canada's (GC) Expenditure Management System (EMS), the GC's Program Activity Architecture (PAA), led by GC's Treasury Board Secretariat (TBS), represents a common government-wide approach to the collection, management and reporting of performance information.

The GC PAA provides detailed information on all government programs; establishes the same structure for both internal decision-making and external accountability; links resources to results for each program – planned and actual; and is being implemented across government. A program is a group of related resource inputs and activities that are managed to address (a) specific need(s) and to achieve intended results, and that are treated as a planning and budgetary unit.

Internal services are an integral component of the GC's PAA and a department's Management, Resources and Results Structure (MRRS). GC Internal Services are groups of related activities and resources that are administered to support the needs of programs and other corporate obligations of an organization.

Purpose

This document presents the Profile of GC Internal Services, developed in partnership with Chief Information Officer Branch (CIOB) and TBS's Results-Based Management Division (RMD), as a basis for structuring and describing a department's internal services within the GC PAA.

The Profile of GC Internal Services outlines a common vocabulary and taxonomy of the GC's internal services and forms the basis for a common government-wide approach to planning, designing, budgeting, reporting and communicating all internal services.

The Profile of GC Internal Services has been adopted for the GC PAA as the basis for defining consistent plans and budgets prepared by GC departments / agencies, government-wide.

Approach

The Profile of GC Internal Services is the culmination of significant efforts of an interdepartmental "Internal Services Working Group", which was composed of representatives of the GC's Senior Financial Officers (SFO) community representing departments / agencies and chaired by TBS. The co-chairs of the working group were the senior executives leading TBS's MRRS and CIOB (Enterprise Architecture).

The approach used in developing the Profile of GC Internal Services followed a series of iterations, steps and activities, including:

- Researching and analyzing common GC internal service planning and policy support references, such as the Expenditure Reviews on Corporate and Administration Services (ERC 2004), common service design initiatives (e.g. CPSA HR Design, CIOB Profile of IT Services), multi-jurisdictional reference models (e.g. Governments of Canada Strategic Reference Models, CIOB), and the Multi-Institutional Disposition Authorities, Common Administrative Records (Library and Archives Canada);

- Developing an early draft set of normative definitions of Internal Services as part of MRRS Policy Instructions to Departments for Developing a Management, Resources, and Result Structure, in preparation for the PAA update process for 2008-09;

- Scanning external best practices on common terms, vocabularies and models for internal services;

- Developing a controlled vocabulary and normative model of Internal Services, informed and aligned with affinity analysis across GC internal service policy domains and consultations with Offices of Primary Interest (OPIs);

- Presenting an early draft of Profile of Internal Services at Quarterly Senior Financial Officers (SFOs) meeting;

- Forming the Internal Services SFO working group representing an authoritative cross-section of departments / agencies; completing authoritative reviews, refinements and recommendations for GC Internal Services during April to October 2007;

- Completing working sessions, building in refinements from feedback; completing an analysis and alignment of relevant GC / TBS policies as a basis in forming a controlled vocabulary;

- Presenting completed results and recommendations completed by Internal Services SFO working group during October 31/2007;

- Presenting draft Profile of GC Internal Services for final endorsement by various TBS governance committees during March 2008; and

- Adoption of the final draft Profile of GC Internal Services as part of GC PAA (see instructions to departments / agencies for fiscal year 2009-10 - Revised Profile of the Government of Canada's Internal Services, Assistant Secretary, Expenditure Management Sector, July 2008).

Context – PAA Programs and Internal Services

GC PAA and Management, Resources and Results Structure (MRRS)

The Management, Resources and Results Structure (MRRS) is the foundation of the renewed GC Expenditure Management System (EMS) and represents a common approach to the collection, management and reporting of performance information. It provides detailed information on all government programs; establishes the same structure for both internal decision-making and external accountability; links resources to results for each program – planned and actual; and is being implemented across government.

The GC PAA provides detailed information on all government programs; establishes the same structure for both internal decision-making and external accountability; links resources to results for each program – planned and actual; and is being implemented across government.

A program is a group of related resource inputs and activities that are managed to address (a) specific need(s) and to achieve intended results, and that are treated as a planning and budgetary unit.

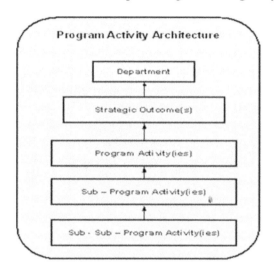

Figure 1. GC Program Activity Architecture

The GC PAA:

- Groups related program activities and links them logically to the Strategic Outcomes they support;

- Provides the framework by which planned resource allocations are linked to each activity at all levels and against which financial results are reported;

- Provides the framework by which expected results and performance measures are linked to each activity at all levels and against which actual results are reported;

- Establishes the structure for Estimates display, Public Accounts, and parliamentary reporting;

- Serves as the basis for resource allocation by Parliament, the Treasury Board, and departmental management; and

- Forms the foundation for constructing any horizontal program activity architectures involving more than one department.

In short, the PAA serves to create an overview of how a department's programs and activities are linked and how their expected results are organized to contribute to achieving the department's Strategic Outcome and mandate. It provides a skeleton structure with which financial and non-financial performance information will be associated.

For more detailed information on the PAA, refer to The Management, Resources, and Results Structure Policy: Instructions to Departments for Developing a Management, Resources, and Result Structures at the TBS website[27].

GC Internal Services – Definition

Internal services are an integral component of the GC's Program Activity Architecture (PAA) and a department's Management, Resources and Results Structure (MRRS). GC Internal Services are groups of related activities and resources that are administered to support the needs of programs and other corporate obligations of an organization.

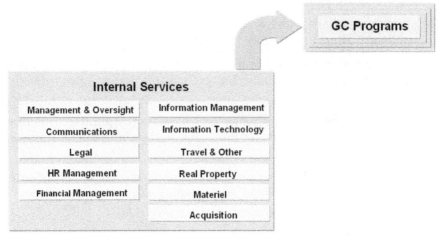

Figure 2. Context of GC Internal Services

---

[27] http://tinyurl.com/c94nzl

These groups are: Management and Oversight Services; Communications Services; Legal Services; Human Resources Management Services; Financial Management Services; Information Management Services; Information Technology Services; Real Property Services; Materiel Services; Acquisition Services; and Travel and Other Administrative Services. Internal Services includes only those activities and resources that apply across an organization and not to those provided specifically to a program.

Profile of GC Internal Services – Described

Overview

The Profile of GC Internal Services outlines a common vocabulary and taxonomy of the GC's internal services and forms the basis for a common government-wide approach to planning, designing, budgeting, reporting and communicating all GC internal services.

In concert with the GC PAA, the goals of the Profile of GC Internal Services as a common reference model are to:

- Establish a common vocabulary and taxonomy for describing and communicating internal services, government-wide;

- Enable a collaborative and consistent approach to guide the design and alignment of internal services;

- Ensure a standardized approach to the collection, management and reporting of planning, budgeting and reporting of information;

- Provide a common language to situate performance measures, proposed investments and more detailed costing of GC services; and

- Provide a useful context for decision-making and helping develop future capabilities of internal services.

Internal Service Groupings

The following portrays the Profile of GC Internal Services and associated levels of the PAA supported with three main categories of the 11 internal service groupings. As shown in table 1, the Profile establishes a separate GC Program Activity and structure for Internal Service within all departmental PAAs. Along with the Internal Services Program Activity, the Profile also establishes a structure of three Sub Activity categories and 11 Sub-Sub Activity categories for Internal Services.

The Governance and Management Support Services include three sub-sub activity levels of internal service groupings:

- Management & Oversight,
- Communications, and
- Legal.

The Resources Management Services include five sub-sub activity levels of internal service groupings:

- Human Resource Management,
- Financial Resource Management,
- Information Management,
- Information Technology, and
- Travel and Other Administrative Services.

The Asset Management Services include three sub-sub activity levels of internal service groupings:

- Real Property,
- Materiel, and
- Acquisition.

PAA Levels	Internal Services Groupings
Program Activity	**Internal Services**
Sub-Activity	**Governance & Management Support**
Sub-Sub Activity	Management & Oversight
Sub-Sub Activity	Communications
Sub-Sub Activity	Legal
Sub-Activity	**Resource Management Services**
Sub-Sub Activity	Human Resource Management
Sub-Sub Activity	Financial Management
Sub-Sub Activity	Information Management
Sub-Sub Activity	Information Technology
Sub-Sub Activity	Travel and Other Administrative Services
Sub-Activity	**Asset Management Services**
Sub-Sub Activity	Real Property
Sub-Sub Activity	Materiel
Sub-Sub Activity	Acquisition

Table 1. Summary of GC Internal Services and PAA Levels

Descriptive Definitions of GC Internal Services

The Profile of GC Internal Services consists of 11 major groupings:

- Management and Oversight Services;
- Communications Services; Legal Services;
- Human Resources Management Services;
- Financial Management Services;
- Information Management Services;
- Information Technology Services;
- Real Property Services;
- Materiel Services;
- Acquisition Services; and
- Travel and Other Administrative Services.

The following presents descriptive definitions for each of these 11 groups of internal services, informed and in alignment with associated GC / TBS policy instruments which help to assure a common and controlled vocabulary for GC internal services.

Profile of GC Internal Services – Described

Management and Oversight Services

Management and Oversight Services involve activities undertaken for determining strategic direction, and allocating resources among services and processes, as well as those activities related to analyzing exposure to risk and determining appropriate countermeasures. They ensure that the service operations and programs of the federal government comply with applicable laws, regulations, policies, and/or plans. Service Groupings for Management and Oversight Services include: Strategic Policy and Planning and Government Relations (incl. Federal / Provincial / Territorial / International); Executive Services; Corporate Policy, Standards, Guidelines; Program / Service Management; Investment Planning; Project Management; Risk Management; Performance and Reporting; Internal Audit; Evaluation.

Communications Services

Communications Services involve activities undertaken to ensure that Government of Canada communications are effectively managed, well coordinated and responsive to the diverse information needs of the public. The communications management function ensures that the public – internal or external – receives government information, and that the views and concerns of the public are taken into account in the planning, management and evaluation of policies, programs, services and initiatives. Service Groupings for Communications Services include: Public Opinion Research; Corporate Identity; Consultations; Media Relations; Advertising, Fairs, Exhibits; In-Person Service, Telephone, Facsimile, Mail, Internet; Translation; Publications.

Legal Services

Legal Services involve activities undertaken to enable government departments and agencies to pursue policy, program and service delivery priorities and objectives within a legally sound framework. Services include the provision of: policy and program advice, direction in the development and drafting of the legal content of bills, regulations, and guidelines; assistance in the identification, mitigation and management of legal risks; legal support in ensuring compliance and enforcement of standards, regulations and guidelines; and representing the Crown's interests in litigation. Service Groupings for Legal Services include: Legal Advice; Preparation of Legal Documents; Litigation Services; Legislative Drafting; Legal Oversight.

Human Resources Management Services

Human Resources Management Services involve activities undertaken for determining strategic direction, allocating resources among services and processes, as well as activities relating to analyzing exposure to risk and determining appropriate countermeasures. They ensure that the service operations and programs of the federal government comply with applicable laws, regulations, policies, and/or plans. Service Groupings for Human Resources Management Services include: HR Planning, Work, Organization Design and Reporting; Job and Position Management; Employee Acquisition and Orientation; Total Compensation; Employee Performance, Learning, Development and Recognition; Permanent and Temporary Separations; Workplace Management.

Financial Management Services

Financial Management Services involve activities undertaken to ensure the prudent use of public resources, including planning, budgeting, accounting, reporting, control and oversight, analysis, decision support and advice, and financial systems. Service Groupings for Financial Management Services include: Financial Planning & Budgeting; Accounting Management; Expenditure Control; Payments Service; Collections and Receivables Service; Asset and Liability Management Service.

Information Management Services

Information Management Services involve activities undertaken to achieve efficient and effective information management to support program and service delivery; foster informed decision making; facilitate accountability, transparency, and collaboration; and preserve and ensure access to information and records for the benefit of present and future generations. Information management is the discipline that directs and supports effective and efficient management of information in an organization, from planning and systems development to disposal or long-term preservation. Service Groupings for Information Management Services include: Information Needs Management; Information Structure Design and Maintenance; Information Acquisition; Information Organization; Information Provisioning; Information Protection, Preservation and Disposition.

Information Technology Services

Information Technology Services involve activities undertaken to achieve efficient and effective use of information technology to support government priorities and program delivery, to increase productivity, and to enhance services to the public. The management of information technology includes planning, building (or procuring), operating and measuring performance. Service Groupings for Information Technology Services include: Distributed Computing; Application/Database Development & Maintenance; Production and Operations Computing; Telecommunications Network – (Data and Voice); IT Security.

Real Property Services

Real Property Services involve activities undertaken to ensure real property is managed in a sustainable and financially responsible manner, throughout its life cycle, to support the cost-effective and efficient delivery of government programs. Real property is defined as any right, interest or benefit in land, which includes mines, minerals and improvements on, above or below the surface of the land. Service Groupings for Real Property Services include: Acquisition; Operations and Management; Disposal.

Materiel Services

Materiel Services involve activities undertaken to ensure that materiel can be managed by departments in a sustainable and financially responsible manner that supports the cost-effective and efficient delivery of government programs. Materiel is defined as all movable assets, excluding money and records, acquired by Her Majesty in right of Canada. Materiel management entails all activities necessary to acquire, hold, use and dispose of materiel, including the notion of achieving the greatest possible efficiency throughout the life cycle of materiel assets. Service Groupings for Materiel Services include: Acquisition; Operations and Management; Disposal.

Acquisition Services (formerly Procurement Services)

Acquisition Services involve activities undertaken to acquire a good or service to fulfill a properly completed request (including a complete and accurate definition of requirements and certification that funds are available) until entering into or amending a contract. Service Groupings for Acquisition Services include: Goods Acquisitions; Services Acquisitions; Construction Acquisitions; Other Acquisitions (acquisitions that fall outside the definitions of goods or services).

Travel and Other Administrative Services. Travel and Other Administrative Services include GC travel services, as well as those other internal services that do not smoothly fit with any of the internal services categories. Service Groupings for Travel and Other Administrative Services include: Travel; Other Administrative Services.

Management and Oversight Services	Human Resources Management Services	Information Technology Services
Strategic Policy & Planning and Government Relations	HR Planning, Work, Organization Design and Reporting	Distributed Computing Application/Database Development & Maintenance
Executive Services	Job and Position Management	
Corporate Policy, Standards, Guidelines	Employee Acquisition and Orientation	Production and Operations Computing
Program / Service Management	Total Compensation	Telecommunications Network (Data and Voice)
Investment Planning	Employee Performance, Learning, Development and Recognition	IT Security
Project Management		
Risk Management		**Real Property Services**
Performance and Reporting	Permanent and Temporary Separations	Acquisition
Internal Audit	Workplace Management	Operations and Management
Evaluation		Disposal
	Financial Management Services	
Communications Services		**Materiel Services**
Public Opinion Research	Financial Planning & Budgeting	Acquisition
Corporate Identity		Operations and Management
Consultations	Accounting Management	
Media Relations	Expenditure Control	Disposal
Advertising, Fairs, Exhibits	Payments Service	
In-Person Service, Telephone, Facsimile, Mail, Internet	Collections and Receivables Service	**Acquisition Services**
		Goods Acquisitions
	Asset and Liability Management Service	Services Acquisitions
Translation		Construction Acquisitions
Publications		Other Acquisitions
	Information Management Services	
Legal Services		**Travel and Other Administrative Services**
Legal Advice	Information Needs Management	Travel
Preparation of Legal Documents	Information Structure Design and Maintenance	Other Administrative Services
Litigation Services	Information Acquisition	
Legislative Drafting	Information Organization	
Legal Oversight	Information Provisioning	
	Information Protection, Preservation and Disposition	

Table 2. Summary of GC Internal Services

COHERENCY MANAGEMENT

Conclusion

Internal services are an integral component of the GC's Program Activity Architecture (PAA) and a department's Management, Resources and Results Structure (MRRS). GC Internal Services are groups of related activities and resources that are administered to support the needs of programs and other corporate obligations of an organization.

The Profile of GC Internal Services outlines a common vocabulary and taxonomy of the GC's internal services and forms the basis for a common government-wide approach to planning, designing, budgeting, reporting and communicating all internal services.

As departments / agencies implement MRRS and develop their PAAs, work will continue in the following areas:

- Incorporation of the Profile of GC Internal Services as part of the authoritative PAAs for 2009-10.
- Starting in fiscal year 2009-10, Main Estimates will report on Internal Services as a distinct Program Activity for each department.
- Departments to work on more accurate attribution of internal services to programs to develop accurate program costs.

The next phase of work on the Profile of GC Internal Services will include efforts to engage functional communities (e.g. human resources management, IM/IT) to develop government-wide service standards, which would serve the basis of measuring "Internal Service" performance as part of overall efforts to engender a culture of performance management across Government.

More and more, central agencies will be asking departments to situate new proposed investment proposals within existing GC PAA structures in memoranda to Cabinet and Treasury Board submissions. The departmental PAA will become the authoritative basis on which departments and central agencies will conduct reviews and analyses to assess whether programs are consistent with federal priorities and focused on results and value for money.

References

American Productivity & Quality Center (2008). APQC Process Classification Framework.

Corporate Administrative Services Review. Chief Information Officer Branch.

Library and Archives Canada (2006a). Business Activity Classification Sub-system (BASC), Organizing Business Information to Meet Government Objectives.

Library and Archives Canada (2006b). Multi-Institutional Disposition Authorities, Common Administrative Records – Administration, Modern Comptrollership, Human Resources, Real Property.

Natural Resources Canada (2003). Support Services Process Framework.

Office of Management and Budget (2005). Federated Enterprise Architecture (FEA) Consolidated Reference Model Document. OMB.

Public Service Commission (2006). Initial Target Human Resources (HR) Business Design. PSC.

Public Service Human Resource Management Agency of Canada (2006). End-to-end HR Story. Draft. PSHRMAC.

Treasury Board Secretariat (2003). Defining Corporate Services Components – Senior Financial Officer (SFO) Working Group

Treasury Board Secretariat (2004a). Corporate Administrative Services (CAS) Survey. Government of Canada (GC) Expenditure Review Committee (ERC).

Treasury Board Secretariat (2004b). Governments of Canada Strategic Reference Model (GSRM) - Business Transformation Enablement Program - Executive Overview, Methodology, Service Patterns, Handbook.

Treasury Board Secretariat (2005a). Government of Canada (GC)

Treasury Board Secretariat (2005b). Government of Canada (GC) Expenditure Review Committee – Final Report.

Treasury Board Secretariat (2006a). Information Management (IM) Program Vision. Draft. Chief Information Officer Branch, Information Management Strategies Division.

Treasury Board Secretariat (2006b). Information Management

Program and Services Alignment Model (PSAM). Chief Information Officer Branch, Information Management Strategies Division.

Treasury Board Secretariat (2006c). Profile of GC Information Technology (IT) Services. Chief Information Officer Branch, Enterprise Architecture.

Treasury Board Secretariat (2006d). TBS Management Accountability Framework (MAF).

Treasury Board Secretariat (2007). TBS Management, Resources and Results Structure (MRRS) Program Activity Architecture (PAA) Instructions – 2007-08.

Treasury Board Secretariat (2008). TBS Policy Suite Renewal (PSR). Various documents.

Treasury Board Secretariat (2009). TBS Policies (various): MRRS, Internal Audit, Information Management, Management of Information Technology, HR related policies, Finance related policies, Real Property, Materiel, Procurement, Project Management, Investment Planning, Risk Management, Communications; and associated Policy Frameworks.

About the Authors

Richard Bryson and Bruce Stacey co-lead the GC's Profile of GC Internal Services.

Richard Bryson is Acting Executive, Alignment and Interoperability Division, Chief Information Officer Branch, Treasury Board Secretariat, Government of Canada. He leads the development of a GC framework of architecture standards, guidelines, tools and reference models enabling collaborative enterprise-wide approaches for consistent design and alignment.

Bruce Stacey is Executive Director, Results-Based Management Division, Expenditure Management Sector (EMS), Treasury Board Secretariat, Government of Canada. He leads the Management Resources and Results Structure policy, directives, and guidelines, and the GC's Program Activity Architecture.

Acknowledgements

Several groups of individuals are gratefully acknowledged for their considerable contributions, commitment, and efforts in supporting the development and realization of this guideline. These groups include: The partnered project team of individuals of the Treasury Board Secretariat (TBS), notably the Alignment and Interoperability Division (AID), Chief Information Officer Branch (CIOB) and the Results-Based Management Division (RMD), Expenditure Management Sector (EMS); The Internal Services Senior Financial Officer (SFO) working group representing a cross-section of departments / agencies; and various TBS/Central Agency Policy Centres.

Richard Bryson
Acting Executive Director
Alignment and Interoperability Division
Chief Information Officer Branch, Treasury Board Secretariat
bryson.richard@tbs-sct.gc.ca

Bruce Stacey
Executive Director
Results-Based Management Division
Expenditure Management Sector, Treasury Board Secretariat
Bruce.Stacey@tbs-sct.gc.ca

Chapter 20

COMMENCING THE JOURNEY: REALIZING COHERENCY MANAGEMENT

Gary Doucet, John Gøtze, Pallab Saha & Scott Bernard

Editors' Preface

This final chapter discusses how to implement Coherency Management in the context of an enterprise-wide architecture to improve strategic alignment, business agility, and risk assurance for that enterprise. Prior chapters defined the concept of Coherency Management, the need for coherency in an organization, and the role of enterprise architecture (EA) in enabling coherency. This chapter amplifies and extends a number of those concepts, including the critical roles that the CEO and Chief Enterprise Architect play, the role of other architecture positions in creating coherency, the introduction of a general framework for coherency management, and a proposed assessment approach.

Introduction

The opening chapter of this book introduced the idea of managing coherency in an enterprise and its importance in improving agility, alignment, and assurance. The first chapter also discussed how Enterprise Architecture (EA) and its three modes are critical to an enterprise being able to successfully deal with the coherency challenge. Chapters 2 through 19 provided the thoughts of contributing authors on Coherency Management and examples of how EA is used in various ways to improve enterprise design, function and effectiveness. Some chapters discussed and demonstrated best practices in the "Foundation EA" mode, where approaches to system design are enterprise-wide and based on a strong and structured business understanding. Others discussed concepts from the "Extended EA" mode where the science of EA was being used to drive business transformation and where services, programs, lines of business, and policy were being designed to achieve the enterprise's intended outcome. Some chapters revealed the power of common language and design capability being rolled into the existing processes of the enterprise to ensure the artifacts (reports, information, plans, etc.) that they created would advance the cause of enterprise alignment with little additional resources. Such is the case with the "Embedded EA" mode. Many chapters presented concepts covering more than one mode of EA, which reflects the reality that multiple modes are often in play in an enterprise.

Up until now in the book, the focus has been on EA and its role in improving coherence in the enterprise. In this chapter, we move coherency to the center of the conversation.

Introducing a concept such as Coherency Management is exciting, but we (the editors) recognize that this "inspiration" now requires "perspiration". Plenty of hard work will be needed by writers and practitioners to evolve this idea into a mature discipline that is based on the successes and lessons-learned that will come with implementation across a variety of public and private sector enterprises. We also believe that all types of enterprises face challenges associated with increasing complexity and therefore need to become more coherent to be successful. Coherency management can reach across all elements of an enterprise so that these elements are described and designed consistently. Coherency should be actively assessed so that misalignment is discovered and corrected as it occurs, even through periods of change. Some organizations may be quite coherent today by design or accident, but in the future enterprises will be able to systematically plan for and assess coherency, not only with indirect measurement or anecdotal evidence. However, that point in time is years away.

As Lao Tzu, the founder of Taoism said: "A journey of a thousand miles must begin with a single step." So it is with the concepts presented in this book that we take our first step towards understanding what coherency is and being able to manage it in an enterprise. In this final chapter of the book, the editors propose a path to reach that vision. These ideas will form the basis of an evolution in the emerging discipline of Coherency Management. As such, we expect the ideas to be reviewed, revised, extended, transformed, and applied by theorists in various areas of inquiry and by practitioners across a wide variety of enterprises. Value will be achieved incrementally as enterprises benefit from each change that is made in support of increasing coherency. In this way, the journey brings value soon after it is started and one can think of this chapter as that beginning.

This chapter continues with a discussion on the role of the CEO and the Chief Enterprise Architect in the practice of Coherency Management. These two roles have been carefully chosen, as we believe that both have a critical role to play in realizing enterprise-wide coherency. The roles played by the CEO and the Chief Enterprise Architect are presented as key action items (imperatives) that must be accomplished in order for enterprises to become coherent. As part of this discussion the editors introduce a structured Coherency Management Operational Framework (CoMOF) and a Coherency Management Assessment Framework (CoMAF). The intent of the CoMOF and CoMAF is to allow an enterprise to better prepare for the implementation and maintenance of Coherency Management concepts. The CoMOF is a combination of organization structures, practices, policies, resources, artifacts, key focus areas and feedback activities. CoMOF can be viewed as a metamodel that organizations adopt to suit their specific needs. The chapter articulates the comprehensive yet generic CoMOF in detail.

Coherency Management Imperatives

Bringing coherency to large, complex organizations might seem like a daunting task, and it would be if an enterprise tried to do it all at once. Coherency Management is largely about embracing ongoing and continuous small changes in the context of a larger enterprise vision and strategy. Coherency Management is hence a balancing act between innovation and efficiency:

Innovation (Explore new knowledge)	Coherency (Architecting knowledge)	Efficiency (Exploit existing knowledge)
Need for variation of knowledge domains, integration and continuous challenge of different knowledge domains (diversity).	Knowledge domain management through alignment, agility and assurance.	Need for specialization (fewer domains) and broad acceptance of the dominating organizational domain (homogeneity).
Breaking with the past	Balance and fruition	Reproducing the past, e.g., what we know worked well.
Results later	Continuous results	Results now

Table 1. Positioning Organizational Coherency

The CEO (or any equivalent leader in public and private sector enterprises) should be the champion (sponsor) of Coherency Management. If not the CEO, it is important that the champion have senior executive status. The Chief Enterprise Architect position is that by name or can be a near equivalent existing position. But if no one comes close to fulfilling that role in your enterprise and you believe in this message, then you must sell the idea to the CEO and the executive management team to create the Chief Enterprise Architect position and fill it with a qualified candidate. Chapter 15 (Aufret) has additional information on doing this. The following are imperatives for the CEO to follow when implementing Coherency Management.

Imperatives for the Chief Executive Officer	
1.	**Believe** that coherency management is critical and creates a shared organization vision
2.	Develop a high-performing Coherency Management Group and **delegate**
3.	**Commit** organizational resources
4.	Derive and demonstrate **benefits**
5.	Institutionalize the feedback channels and **verify**

Table 2. Coherency Management Imperatives for the CEO

1. **Believe:** *Believe this is critical and must be done and be willing to lead the Board and senior managers in this effort.*

   This action requires the CEO to become the champion for this effort. It sounds easy and self-evident but it will be difficult at times as there will be days when the CEO will be the only one moving the yardsticks. The leadership of the CEO is vital for this to be as effective as possible and done in the shortest time possible. The CEO must be encouraged to pose questions, look for examples and be certain. This is not a case where half-hearted support will suffice because at various times each part of the enterprise will rebel against the effort as it forces a change in their area with little or no apparent benefit to them. This is a question of whole system optimization and as W. Edwards Deming once said: "To optimize the whole, we must sub-optimize the parts".

2. **Delegate:** *Get a Chief Enterprise Architect and direct this person to:*

   - Establish an EA program that includes strategy, business, and technology.
   - Establish a Coherency Management practice within the EA program.
   - Institute coherency assessment as an integral part of key functions and processes.
   - Demonstrate organizational coherency and produce an annual coherency report.

   Finding a good Chief Enterprise Architect can be difficult because the discipline has only recently evolved to include all dimensions (strategy, business, and technology) across all of the enterprise's lines of business. The Chief Enterprise Architects of the past were often technology focused and EA has moved well beyond that. The most important attributes to look for are:

- Whole of business knowledge and experience.
- Scientific thinker, logical, ordered, and systematic.
- Excellent communicator with a sales flare.
- Excellent facilitator, flexible, but NOT spineless.
- Knowledge of Enterprise Architecture frameworks, tools and methods.
- Extensive experience in influence roles (not power roles).
- Project management and control experience.

The first order of business is to establish an EA program (if one does not already exist) that will continually provide authoritative information in three areas: the current state (as-is) architecture, the future state (to-be) architecture, and a transition plan. The EA program is an ongoing management practice, a key part of which is Coherency Management.

3. **Commit**: *Initiate activities to ensure executive pay-at-risk is tied (at least partially) to success with coherency management practices.*

This action is one which will cause some angst and which will probably be greeted with cynicism, but once it gets started the result will be a more robust approach since everyone will be taking a much closer look at what is being proposed / requested.

4. **Benefit**: *Make major decisions with the benefit of a Coherency Assessment.*

The most obvious benefit will come in the form of advice that indicates how much a particular investment that the enterprise is making in business or technology is aligned with strategic initiatives, within and between lines of business. A coherency assessment process will yield early benefits, even when only partially developed.

5. **Verify**: *Conduct a third-party review every several years to ensure that EA and Coherency Management are delivering on the investment.*

The idea of coherency management requires a leap of faith but some return should come within the first year or two. This could be in the form of gaps and/or overlaps that are spotted in annual budgets, architecture documentation of existing and planned business processes / technology solutions, or new project proposals. Whatever the case, the results need to be recorded (good or bad). This information can then be fed into independent reviews by the executive and management teams with the Chief Enterprise Architect.

The following are imperatives that the Chief Enterprise Architect should follow in assisting the CEO and executive leadership team in implementing Coherency Management.

Imperatives for the Chief Enterprise Architect
1. Transform the organizational EA practice
2. Prepare and shape expectations
3. Get senior executive management buy-in
4. Implement and realize coherency management
5. Iterate and continuously improve

Table 3. Coherency Management Imperatives
for the Chief Enterprise Architect

1. **Transform EA Practice:** The first thing a Chief Enterprise Architect must do is to transform any existing EA program to accommodate the concepts of a Coherency Management practice within its program. Refer to Chapter 1 for the three modes of EA and Chapter 8 (Bernard & Grasso) on EA Program Maturity for details. Additionally, Chapter 12 (Hungerford) discusses the evolving role of EA in the context of a specific organization.

2. **Prepare and Shape Expectations:** It is recommended that the Chief Enterprise Architect function manage the full scope of Coherency Management. Eventually, we might see this function, perhaps called Enterprise Coherency Management (ECM), growing beyond the scope of the Chief Enterprise Architect function (see Figure 1) but, for now, it is best to concentrate on building out the Coherency Management

function within the EA program and the way that the three modes of EA are being practiced.

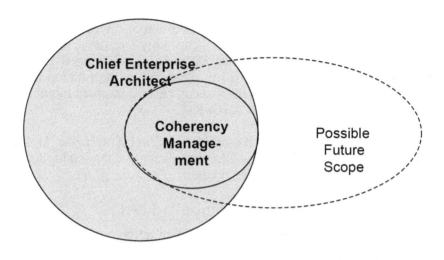

Figure 1. Role of Chief Enterprise Architect vis-à-vis Coherency Management

There are two main approaches for achieving coherency in the enterprise.

Design Based Coherency (Transformational): Usually project-based (or transformational change), this is where the traditional application of Enterprise Architecture provides the rigor necessary for well formed strategic designs. This can occur to drive out well-formed architecture for technical systems, as in Foundation EA, and for reaching well designed business policy/services/business lines/programs/processes which is the Extended Mode of EA. On top of the systems-oriented EA and business-oriented EA, the practice of coherency management introduces processes and capabilities to explicitly deal with the issue of coherency. In particular, such projects are harvested so that the second style of Coherency Management is enabled.

Assessment Based Coherency (Incremental): Gaps and overlaps in vision, strategies, designs, processes, and systems will be found as a matter of normal process and the enterprise can make mid-course corrections without necessarily embarking on major transformations. It is no secret that many chief executives, Boards of Directors, politicians and senior bureaucrats are weary and wary of 'big bang' style change, even more so, if there is a large IT component in the proposal. This will still occur, but with the assessment-based approach we enable Incremental Coherency, where the enterprise achieves major change in regard to coherency in small manageable steps. Coherency Management permeates the necessary processes by adding a rule, extending a method or defining a measurement. In this way, we allow business owners to see the enterprise more clearly and to make better decisions of design and operations.

3. **Get Senior Executive Management Buy-In**: At this point in your coherency journey, you've prepared for the broader roll-out of CoM by getting the traditional EA community engaged, developing your Coherency Management Assessment Framework (CoMAF) and mapping out the maturity against an agreed model. Now you are ready to launch a more broad-based effort with your community in full support. The two key activities in this phase include:
   * Assemble the Launch Team: Form a team to launch Coherency Management with the aim being to kick off the CoM effort in an effective manner within the EA program. The team will help build the storyboard, roadmap and sales message for your enterprise. The single most important task will be the creation of the governance structure.
   * Sell Coherency Management to the CEO: Once everything is set up and the meetings have been arranged, there is a special pitch to be built and delivered to the CEO (or equivalent) for expanding the role of EA into all significant process centers of the enterprise. Professional help at this juncture is critical and it should be of the marketing/communications type.

4. **Implement and Realize Coherency Management:** Once the CEO and executive management has bought into the idea, their first order of business is to establish the formal governance. The governance structure may be considered the enterprise's "Coherency Council" and they would:
   * Oversee major investment decisions.
   * Act as the governing body for coherency assessment process.

- Run an annual assessment process.
- Be comprised of managers for key design/describe processes.
- Agree on a maturity/measurement model.

To establish this governance mechanism with the right level people, there will need to be a concerted sales and marketing effort.
- Develop a pitch for expanding the role of EA into all significant process centers of the enterprise.
- Build a business case for a sustainable practice.
- Allow for an off-ramp with harvested results and restart capability.

5. **Iterate and Institute Continuous Improvement:** The Coherency Management initiative will be very modest in the beginning. Maybe there will be one or two standards deployed in a few processes but eventually these changes cascade in and of themselves. This last action is to ensure that the enterprise is, in fact, looping through a standard set of processes in a continuous improvement fashion. This includes, ensuring that:
   - The assessments are linked into transactional based planning.
   - That the annual planning is including considerations for Coherency Assessment.
   - The release of major designs, solutions, plans, etc triggers a coherency review.
   - The idea of collecting and aggregating assessment results on an annual basis to produce a publication with regard to the 'state of coherency'.

Coherency Management Guidelines

Understand Architecture

Almost everything that humans create and build requires some sort of architecture or a 'description' that can inform those that do the construction. Descriptions can be in various formats (e.g. text, graphics, spreadsheets) to describe how to build, maintain, and improve whatever is being looked at, be it a physical entity (e.g. building or bridge) or a virtual entity (an enterprise). The architecture and associated documentation explain the parts of the entity and how they fit together to form a coherent whole. If the entity is a birdhouse, it may be acceptable to hold the architecture in your head (i.e. implicit architecture) but once it gets a little more complex (e.g. a house), then a documented architecture (i.e. explicit architecture) is needed. If the house needs a change (e.g. new rooms), then the architecture will need to be adjusted. Hence, it is important to have an explicit, formally documented architecture that reflects the current state of the entity and the future envisioned state of the entity, as well as a transition plan. For complex virtual entities (enterprises), change is constant, so the architecture is dynamic and must be maintained as part of an ongoing EA program.

Understand Enterprise Architecture

To create a functioning organization (enterprise) the required descriptions (words and pictures) would have to include everything from a strategic mission statement to organizational design documents and technology solution descriptions. This includes business process models, system specifications, information and data models, network diagrams, security control descriptions, and the like. In the case of a franchise business, the 'architecture' for the enterprise would be all of the words and pictures, in sufficient detail, for local outlet owners to build their businesses in conformance with franchise standards and for headquarters to do the required higher level functions. Enterprises are constantly changing. Maybe it's the current business priority or crisis du jour, but every day something happens that, in essence, impacts the enterprise and therefore its architecture. This is why we've identified 'Embedded' Architecture as a key part of Coherency Management. Most business change is implemented through some sort of documentation but, because there is no pervasive standard for describing all things in an enterprise, one cannot clearly see the whole, the parts, or the numerous changes under way. So, improvements become less effective and our risk of making design errors increases. See Chapter 2 for EA Design Models (Saha) and their impact on the enterprise in general, and EA programs specifically.

The Enterprise Architects

The transformation of the EA practice requires appreciating and evolving the role of the EA program and the various types of architects that support EA at the enterprise, line of business, and system levels (e.g. business architects, data architects, network architects, and security architects). As organizations gain capability and maturity in the three modes of EA, the role of the various types of architects in the EA program will play a critical role in enabling this gradual evolution. We believe that, eventually, organizations would have three distinct groups of architects with differing, but closely complimentary, roles. The groups of architects would be:

Core Enterprise Architects – Experts in EA Theory and Practice
The 'core' architects lead the EA Practice and understand the various approaches for doing EA, such that they can choose the right approach for that enterprise. They are architecture subject matter experts in EA overall and in various supporting disciplines. They develop the standards, models, repositories, principles and the like. They are expected to be familiar with the numerous standards, conventions and communities involved in the EA discipline. (e.g., IEEE 1471, ISO 14258, ISO 15704, TOGAF, Zachman, DODAF and EA[3]). They also form an EA team that is capable of conducting business requirements analyses at various levels of the enterprise, identifying viable alternatives and creating designs on behalf of the business owner(s) from the alternative that is selected. If this EA team already exists, then delineating their responsibilities as 'core' within the overall context of EA is all that needs to be done.

Implicit Enterprise Architects – Those Who Support EA Work
Since business plans, organization designs, job descriptions, process models, workflows, project plans, system specifications, information models, and the like, comprise the enterprise's architecture, we realize that the people that create such artifacts are, in a very real way, architects. They, however, do not normally consider themselves to be 'Architects'. The idea behind Embedded EA is that we can provide these people certain tools so that the 'architecture' they create can be standardized and their designs can be well constructed. Then, the Enterprise Architect can use the 'as found' documentation more readily. That is, the Enterprise Architect can use the documents as they were created for other prior purposes instead of reformatting them, re-creating them, modifying them, or entering them into a different tool. One of the great benefits of doing this is that the EA stays more current because it is being done by the various process owners (implicit architects) as a part of their job, not as some extra task. These people have the potential to create and maintain much of the architecture, and are an important part of the EA team. There could be hundreds or thousands of implicit enterprise architects in medium and large size enterprises. Implicit enterprise architects can, and should, continue to function

under their normal job titles, unless it is beneficial to give them a formal title that describes a specific architecture function. Therefore, the term 'implicit' enterprise architect is a concept, not a job title or label that should be given to an individual.

Applied Enterprise Architects – Those Who Define EA Requirements

Bridging the world of 'core' and 'implicit' enterprise architects is a group that we call the 'applied' enterprise architects'. They have the task of figuring out which EA capabilities are needed, in what form, and where. They conduct the assessments and they help to promote something that we call 'opportunistic architecture.' This is where they take advantage of projects with certain characteristics to advance the goal of Coherency. For example, they might, from previous assessments, know that the enterprise needs to standardize the way they describe clients throughout all the processes. If they see a project with a strong element of customer relationship management, they would support that project with an aim towards developing that standard. They would, as they start, ensure that major process owners from across the enterprise know that the standard for describing 'client' is going to be established during the course of the project and then they would leverage those process owners in the development of the standard. The 'applied' enterprise architects are usually a subset of the core EA team but we have logically separated them here to draw attention to the idea that, from a pragmatic point of view, they might make compromises and prioritizations that the core architects should not need to consider.

It is certain that there are 'implicit' enterprise architects in all enterprises since these are the people designing and describing the various parts of the enterprise on a regular basis. Furthermore, in any medium to large enterprise, there is also a good chance of finding 'core' and 'applied' architects. All of them need to be brought together to accomplish the three modes of EA and to achieve coherency across the enterprise. The relationship of these types of architects is shown in Figure 2.

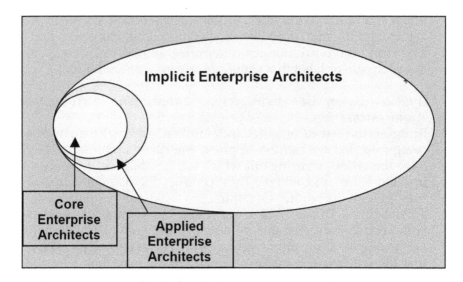

Figure 2. Types of Enterprise Architects

Enterprise architecture is, in many ways, the art of creating coherency among many knowledge domains. A knowledge domain represents a unique set of perspectives (i.e. ways of understanding a particular situation or problem), and heuristics (i.e. ways of making decisions in a particular situation or solving a particular problem), and these perspectives and heuristics form our identities. Through our identities as enterprise architects, coherency is always our perspective on things, and we always aim to apply coherent heuristics when approaching an architecture challenge.

Core EA Community of Practice

Chapter 17 (Bernus) discusses how EA is likely to evolve in the future (synopsize the changes). Such a move will obviously impact the role of the Enterprise Architect. The 'core' Enterprise Architects will need to modify their efforts to deal with the coherency mandate. This means expanding their efforts beyond the foundation mode engagement to also deliver tools, methods and support to processes not traditionally part of their mandate. For example, the core architects will need to work with the Human Resources Department to identify and describe new types of jobs throughout the enterprise as coherency drives changes at the enterprise, line-of-business, and program/system levels. They will also (for example) need to ensure that the budget and technology teams talk about results in the same way that service delivery teams do.

The EA program and core architects are often located in the central management office of an enterprise, but elements of the EA program can also be found in departments and divisions and working for internal process owners. The EA program needs to harmonize and integrate EA practices at the enterprise, line-of-business, and program/system levels in a way that brings together the core, implicit, and applied architects and the internal process owners. The EA program should also serve to advance the core standards, methods, tools, reference models, and frameworks for describing the enterprise in all dimensions. There are several holistic EA approaches that are suitable for doing this, including the TOGAF, MODAF, DODAF, FEAF, and EA3. There are also several EA analysis and reporting models - called 'reference' models' – that augment holistic EA approaches, including the U.S Federal Enterprise Architecture (FEA) Reference Models and Canada's Governments of Canada Strategic Reference Model - GSRM.

Participants in the EA program should become a Community of Practice (CoP) that provides a formal governance structure over the models, tools, etc, which can become mandatory or best practice within the EA program. A CoP can be characterized as a group of professionals embodying a store of knowledge or a shared knowledge domain. In order for practice to generate coherence within a community, we know that mutual engagement, shared repertoire, and joint enterprise must be present[28]. This will enable the community of practice to act as a locally negotiated regime of competence. Within such a regime, knowledge is no longer undefined, but can be defined as what would be recognized as competent participation in the practice. This explains what happens when the core, implicit, and applied architects manage to bring their practices together.

The EA CoP and architecture project teams have tremendous design capability and are critical for providing the proper EA context for major projects throughout the enterprise. The Chief Enterprise Architect and the core architects will also need to keep current on where global EA theory and practice are headed. In this book, we have presented several chapters from contributing authors who provide thoughts on where EA is heading. The EA CoP needs to knit together these advances with evolving coherency management practices on a continuing basis. CoP members can also help to validate the ability of the enterprise to adopt the EA standards that are being proposed.

---

[28] With reference to the work of Etienne Wenger.

The role of Applied Enterprise Architect (as defined in this book) is one that can easily reside within the same management structure as the core EA team. The applied architecture operationalizes the theory and promise of EA. This is not where precise standards and models are developed, tested and declared, but where those rigorous tools are implemented in the functioning enterprise. Some examples of how this is done include:

- Interpreting business needs to prioritize the work of Core Architects. (e.g. which architecture artifacts need to be done first).
- Developing the corresponding plan for which process owners to involve and when.
- Guiding the work of the Coherency Assessment process and tools.
- Populating the knowledge base with investments and project data to support future assessment and sharing.
- Managing the repository of assessments and tracking the variances and bring forward items.
- Supporting key projects, on demand, or as an embedded architect.

Highlighting the division of duties between the Core Architect and the Applied Architect roles allows us to have each function performed without hindering the other. Core EA practitioners can sometimes be accused of being too precise or inflexible, but that is the nature of their job. The Applied Architect can make educated compromises in the interest of 'good enough' because they understand the science (i.e. models, standards and tools) and also understand the realities of operational business imperatives. In this way, the application of EA can be 'good enough' so as to be tailored without compromising the core EA standards for models and methods. Several chapters in this book discuss instances of how EA is actually embraced in real organizations. These include: Chapter 5 (Aitken), Chapter 9 (Mo & Nemes), Chapter 10 (Anthopoulos), Chapter 11 (Marx Gómez & Biskup), Chapter 12 (Hungerford), and Chapter 14 (Kemp).

For example, if an EA standard is changed to implement a unique budget office requirement, then there are impacts to consider. The downstream problems could set back the coherency objective by morphing the standard into something that might be rejected by others. In this case, the core architects compromised core models in the interest of enterprise optimization. A better model would have had the Core Architect defending the quality of the standard (assuming it is correct) against the business need of the Applied Architect (who represents the Budget Office). The Applied Architect would eventually have to create a construct that keeps the core standard pure but satisfies the business need (e.g. maybe by creating an extension to the core standard). Then, the next user of the standard will see an unspoiled standard. The idea of tailoring EA tools and applying extensions to core concepts is a real strength of applied EA. Both core architects and the business community can realize value.

Assess and Plan

Once the core and applied communities are on board with the concepts of Coherency Management and the supportive role that the EA program plays, a plan for broader adoption can be developed. To help assess the EA community and their ability to take the next step, we have developed a set of questions for the EA CoP, which is shown in Table 4.

Is your EA Community Ready for Coherency Management?
Does the EA Community of Practice believe: • That most of the EA already exists (implicit and explicitly)? • That EA, even when unstructured or malformed, is still EA? • That Implicit Architects write most of the EA and need to be supported in the creation of their process artifacts? • That business architecture can be done as part of foundation EA? • That EA still provides a valuable design and design facilitation service within the context of Coherency Management?

**Table 4. Checklist to Assess Readiness for
Formalized Coherency Management**

For the EA CoP to be ready to implement Coherency Management, the answers to all of these questions should be "yes." If the opinion is that this is not the case, then do not start the next step. Instead, revisit the principles of Coherency Management and work on the Core and Applied EA communities until there is concurrence on the way forward. Once there is confidence that the EA CoP is ready, it is time to plan the rollout. EA has three distinctive modes that should be recognized as this plan is developed. Using the Coherency Planning element of the Coherency Management Operation

Framework (presented in Figure 3) an enterprise can determine what needs to be done to advance each mode of EA. The assessment will be repeated on a regular basis (perhaps annually) as part of a continuous improvement process. Please remember, the three modes are not maturity models. You do not do one mode and then the other; you do all three simultaneously, in a way that best fits the maturity level of each mode. The plan should have loosely coupled dependencies between the activities in each of the modes.

Select an EA Framework

The objective of Coherency Management is to extend the nature and scope of EA; therefore, there is some latitude in how an enterprise implements the EA practice. Chapter 8 (Bernard and Grasso) presents an EA Audit Model and one possible way to establish your program. Other chapters within this book also provide possible guidance on setting up an EA practice. Most EA approaches and frameworks can be fit within the Coherency Management model. Important criteria for selecting an EA approach and framework are (1) completeness – that the EA approach includes integrated elements for governance, methodology, framework, artifacts, repository, and best practices; and (2) if the approach provides guidance in terms of estimating the scope and effort that will be required for an EA program. Chapter 4 (Janssen) presents a meta-framework for analyzing architectural efforts.

Develop and Adopt a Coherency Management Operation Framework

The Coherency Management Operation Framework presented in the following pages is 'generic'. It is meant to be tailored to meet the needs of each organization and business unit. This is not a replacement for the EA framework, as it works within the meta"umbrella" of the EA framework and related program activities. It is a view of how EA gets utilized with other practices, techniques and processes to assess and action coherency objectives. Figure 3 depicts the Generic Coherency Management Operation Framework, while the following sections elaborate the various components and how they interact to positively influence organizational coherency.

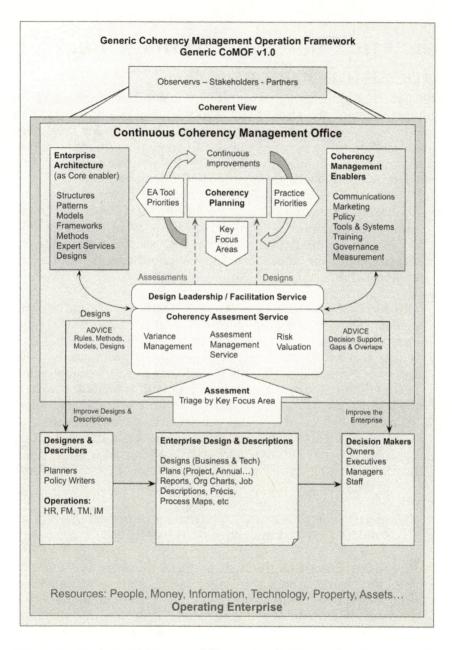

Figure 3. Generic Coherency Management Operation Framework
Generic CoMOF v1.0

Generic Coherency Management Operation Framework

The *Generic Coherency Management Operation Framework* (CoMOF) unifies the major concepts of Coherency Management. It is labeled generic because each enterprise is encouraged to tailor their own view based on the generic model and to take into account local language, governance models, and existing EA practice among others. Here is a brief explanation of the CoMOF's elements.

- **Operating Enterprise**: This is the full organization in all dimensions. The key thing is to recognize the way in which EA and CoM practices are deployed within the existing view of the enterprise. They are not external to the enterprise (e.g. not as an audit function).

- **Observer – Stakeholders – Partners**: Those people and organizations that deal with the enterprise will (as a result of Coherency Management) see a 'Coherent' view. For an external customer, that might mean unified services or programs without gaps or overlaps in intended outcomes. As a stakeholder, (shareholder, voter, parliamentarian, and potential investor) precisely what is going on inside the enterprise and in aggregate form is visible. Total investments towards particular outcomes or client group are visible and correct. Partners will benefit with the coherent view because there will be a reduced chance of getting to the wrong service or getting conflicting instructions from within the same unit.

- **Coherent View**: Coherency Management improves the way all stakeholders view and interact with the enterprise.

- **Resources**: Resources (human, financial, information, relationship) are clearly a part of the functioning enterprise, and since processes act on resources supported by documentation, there is a strong role in coherency management. Processes describe (and design) resources (or their use) and these are a critical part of the Coherency Management plan, especially in the area of Embedded EA mode.

- **Describers / Designers**: There are many people that will describe parts of the enterprise. It might be a document detailing the current processes, future plans or organizational details. In any case, these are the 'Implicit Enterprise Architects' and they play a vital role in the advancement of the coherency objective.

- **Enterprise Designs & Descriptions**: This includes designs and descriptions of everything within the enterprise. This is what the Designers/Describers produce. They can be process owners (e.g. budget office) or they can be the classic Enterprise Architect producing strategic designs of a newly transformed business. The graphic has a background grid to represent the idea that these artifacts will (over time) become more structured and help support enterprise perspectives more fully. This happens as a result of Embedding EA as discussed in Chapter One.

- **Decision Makers**: One of the key benefits of Coherency Management practiced within the context of the EA is how it improves the quality of information and design advice for any decision. Whether you are the CEO wondering about what service lines best fulfill a long-term corporate objective or an analyst trying to get processes to work well together, your decisions will benefit from the coordinated activities of Coherency Management and Enterprise Architecture.

- **Coherency Planning**: The all-important coordinating aspect of Enterprise Architecture sits at the heart of Coherency Management planning, because continuous improvement requires a real-time, integrated approach to planning across the enterprise. This should be done on a regular, timed basis, as well as, transactionally. The timed planning can be based on the EA, budget, and other planning cycles (e.g. annual) but Coherency Management needs a hook into them so that major decisions, assessments, designs, etc have a feedback loop into CoM Planning to allow for reprioritization or in-year adjustments. Along with planning, the capability to sense and respond is critical when dealing with special (and perhaps unpredictable) events. For instance, a coherent response to a crisis is an imperative. Chapter 10 (Anthopoulos) discusses how this is accomplished in case of the Hellenic Ministry of Foreign Affairs.

Using coherency concepts within a robust EA program might seem like an overwhelming challenge and it will be, if you attempt to fix everything all at once. In order for you to achieve success with this, we recommend that management performance pay be somehow tied to the adoption and implementation of coherency management. The EA/CoM dividend may not be experienced locally for a time, so senior executive leadership is an important success factor. Continuous improvement is the key to success. The gradual improvement we refer to is, specifically, the transformation towards greater coherency. We fully expect other transformations (e.g. changing product lines, sourcing changes, SOA implementation, regulatory changes, mergers and acquisitions) to occur at a pace dictated by the market. To plan Coherency Management activities within the EA program, we recommend three major planning outputs:

I. **EA Tool Priorities:** There can be literally hundreds of standards, reference models, and patterns waiting to be developed. In this part of the planning process we prioritize what tools to work on based on feedback from assessments, the planning process, design efforts, and others. A tool might be a standard for describing clients or a pattern for multi-channel service delivery. As these tools (or rules) are developed, there should be a cross-reference of which rules go with which processes which can then be married up to the prioritizations established in the Key Focus Areas.

II. **Practice Priorities:** Coherency Management is a new way to look at solving an old problem. It relies on existing fields of study (e.g. EA, Change Management, etc) which can lead people to an incorrect understanding of its worth and their role. Therefore, there needs to be a plan for a series of enablers:

- *Communications* – The communications plan must be developed to help plot the course for who gets told what and when. It is pretty standard fare but gets complicated when you start to take in to account that every piece of the enterprise might need its own communications approach.

- *Marketing* – Perhaps more important than communications is the Marketing plan. The idea that you have to sell the idea and the on-going commitment to employees and managers might seem odd but it is critical.

- *Policy* – Depending on the nature of your organization, you may need to implement Coherency Management policy, standards, procedures, etc.

- *Tools & Systems* – Coherency Management will need some degree of automation and systems support within the EA program. There is a need for a tie-in to the EA Registry/Repositories for Assessment Results, Variance Management, Impact Tracking, Assessment Inputs, Enterprise Artefacts (EA Tool based or unstructured), planning tools, etc.

- *Training* – Success with Coherency Management will require training on many fronts. There will need to be training for Enterprise Architects (Core and Applied), Internal Management Process Owners, Executives, Business Analysts, Auditors, Evaluators, etc. This will have to be developed and delivered in accordance with the Key Focus Areas (discussed next).

- *Governance* – Another critical requirement is to understand the role of governance (and the different types) and plan for these, also in accordance with the key focus areas. There needs to be governance over:
  - The EA Practice and the Models developed.
  - The prioritization of Coherency Targets and Goals.
  - Key Focus Areas.
  - Tools and Systems.

- *Measurement* – The setting of goals, and measuring against those targets, is a critical part of all continuous improvement models. With Coherency Management, goals are set for:
  - The Coherency Management Capability and Capacity.
  - The EA Capability and Capacity.
  - The level of coherency in the operating enterprise (by target areas).

III. **Key Focus Areas:** With EA tool and practice priorities in place, we enable the enterprise to become coherent gradually and ultimately to become more effective, efficient and knowledgeable. The coherent enterprise will have rules and processes, which allow descriptions to be compared for coherency and refined. Agility (responsiveness) is achieved because the designs are coherent, which includes a developed understanding and a practice of loose coupling by design instead of tight coupling by accident. Assurance is gained through an ability to not only have the required information but also, through coherency, to have the information provide real knowledge. The embedded processes are well architected and project-based architecture efforts in Foundation and Extended are incrementally better because of the better sources of information. The list of Key Focus Areas will be those parts of the enterprise that need attention first, in order to support the broad enterprise alignment approach. These can be:

- Business units (e.g. HR Management, Sales Unit, Health Department, etc).

- Horizontal Files (e.g. Climate Change).

- Descriptive or Design Processes which could implement the new EA Tools.

There must be a structured approach to getting these done. The best place to start is by looking at the planning processes so that enterprise Visions, Strategies, and Designs can be aligned first. This allows the context for the evolution of the coherent enterprise to be set (e.g. customers are now classified consistently in web applications, budget documents, annual reports, across divisions, and across regions). However, the question of which business units, horizontal files or descriptive techniques to prioritize can be a daunting task. Refer to the Coherency Management Assessment Framework and Metamodel for understanding how to know your enterprise and where the priorities need to be placed to maximize the return for the investment made in Coherency Management.

For each planning target, you must decide the development priorities within the context of the EA (future architecture plans). This is not necessarily a complicated affair, it can simply be a prioritized list of Rules, Description Processes and functional areas of the enterprise that are in most need of alignment. We recommend that Coherency Management is, at times, practiced opportunistically, which means that you will not necessarily do the first thing first but, generally speaking, you should end up doing the important things early. When first starting, this will seem like a guessing game, but once assessments start happening, this list gets modified rather quickly. For example, if you attempt to assess the alignment of two major projects, you will quickly realize that the way they are described requires some rules.

- **Enterprise Architecture:** According to IEEE 1471-2000, architecture is *"the fundamental organization of a system, embodied in its components, their relationships to each other and the environment, and principles governing its design and evolution"*. The Enterprise Architecture element of the framework is the core enabler of Coherency Management. EA provides the science to make better decisions, descriptions and designs by way of reference models, principles, standards, and methods. There are certain characteristics that Coherency Management needs to be successful but these are not exclusive to any one style of EA:

  - Strong business orientation – Reference models and tools can be utilized by business community to do design and to prepare descriptions of the enterprise.

  - Preferable for the framework to have strong BPM capability.

  - Most beneficial to support program and service modeling.

  - Allows 'as found' artifacts to be incorporated into the view of the enterprise architecture.

  If you are attempting to establish a Coherency Management activity within the EA program, you must ensure that the EA function is doing the three modes of EA and maturing as quickly as possible. The EA function is also responsible for developing new EA Tools (or 'rules') based on priorities determined in the Coherency Planning function. One way to do this is to develop the models (usually based on authoritative sources) independently and then prototype or pilot them to prove their validity. The second way this occurs is by harvesting the work of projects to build the models. This is why project support is so critical. Some projects are better for developing or validating certain models (e.g. CRM projects might be great for developing or validating a target group reference model, whereas a project to develop a common internal service offering is ideal for developing or validating an Internal Service Reference Model.). EA tools have been prioritized and work is done according to the plan to develop/evolve these tools.

- **Design Leadership / Facilitation Service:** The EA team can (upon request) produce strategic designs based on business priorities, especially when the current state of architecture does not allow 'as found' documentation to be used for designs very easily. The ability for EA to do design or lead a cross-disciplinary team in the creation of an agreed way forward has always been a strength. This is still the case but now the design will be based on steadily improving 'as found' artifacts. In addition, the design function will provide advice to Implicit Architects as to how to improve their artifacts in support of the CoM Objective.

- **Coherency Assessment Service:** One of the most strategic elements of CoM will be the Coherency Assessment process, again done within the context of the EA and related activities. This process allows for the review of project documentation, annual budget, reports, designs, etc. These reviews are done on the documentation that is being created in the enterprise descriptions to, as much as possible, reduce the amount of EA specific documentation. The assessments will indicate how an investment is aligned to other investments, broad policy, and local priorities. It should be stressed, at this point, that the Coherency Assessment function only ever provides advice and it does so strictly from an enterprise perspective. There are many cases where local business imperatives will require a variance (permanent or temporary). As such, there can be debates for the accuracy of the assessment but the office running the assessment function does not make assertions as to the operational priorities dictating when (and if) misalignment might be corrected. The process is completely transparent, so reasons for not correcting misalignment will need to stand public and managerial scrutiny. This is normal, but now we'll see, plan, and measure such cases so they can be properly managed. Three major elements of the Assessment function are:

  - Assessment Management Service with a repository for capturing all assessment results, as well as information gathered for assessments. This data is to be leveraged in subsequent assessments.

  - Variance Management process to allow issues to be carried forward, tracked, and measured.

  - Risk Valuation process to provide the predicted affect of found misalignment. This is a priority area of development for CoM but it is envisioned that misalignment be tracked over time as well as losses (e.g. project failures, public embarrassment). Correlation analysis can eventually allow this process to provide a risk statement on current misalignment based on historical data. This is a long term effort given the amount of historical data needed to perform the correlation analysis.

Decision Support: Coherency Assessment provides advice to 'Decision Makers' in two ways. First, anyone submitting artifacts for assessment is advised of gaps and overlaps of their design/description (e.g. Policy, Solution Design, Organization Chart, and Business Strategy) when compared to similar artifacts from others. This is sometimes called horizontal alignment assessment. Second, there will be an assessment against the organizational priorities, strategies, and mandates. This is sometimes called a vertical alignment assessment. This advice is provided to executive managers as well as business analysts. Anyone making a decision can benefit from better knowledge.

New Rules, Methods, Models and Designs: This is the point at which rules and designs are fed into the processes according to prioritization (discussed in the next section). Once a rule has been developed and tested by the EA team it should be rolled out into key processes. For example, the target Group Reference Model developed on the CRM project should likely be embedded into the budget process (so we can attribute investment to target group need), the services directory (for clients and partners), the corporate planning process (so we can plan changes to targets groups), and perhaps corporate reporting (so stakeholders can see what we are doing for who). By embedding these 'rules' into the processes that create the 'as found', they are well formed the next time around. This is where the Continuous Coherency Improvement is made continuous. The feedback is this:

1) Experiences in core science, designs and assessments to help create better design/description capability.

2) Improved design/description capability helps create better design/descriptions.

3) Better designs (and descriptions):
   i. Improves coherency in the enterprise.(e.g. Better aligned policy).

ii. Improves our ability to assess.

4) Better Assessments give us:
   i. Better advice for Deciders. (Adding coherency to the enterprise).
   ii. Better design/description advice for Designers/-Describers.

Coherency Management Assessment Framework and Meta-model

The CoMOF discussed earlier presents an approach for organizations to embrace Coherency Management as a practice. Even so, planning for Coherency Management can be quite a challenge. If Coherency Management is to become a professional management discipline, it is essential to have a reliable and objective approach to evaluating organizational coherence.

It is against this background that we see the need for an approach which:

* Allows a holistic assessment of organizational coherency management covering all key aspects and influencing factors,

* Allows derivation of suitable steps for organizations to benchmark and improve their coherency related activities,

* Is an embodiment of systematic and structured mechanisms that ensures transparency and predictability,

* Is comprehensible and allows cross-references to proven management concepts and models, and

* Facilitates the development of explicit action plans in response to assessments.

Figure 4 depicts the Coherency Management Assessment Framework (CoMAF) Meta-model. It is high level but does provide an idea of how organizations should assess and deal with coherency assessments. It is based on the following definitions of meta-model elements:

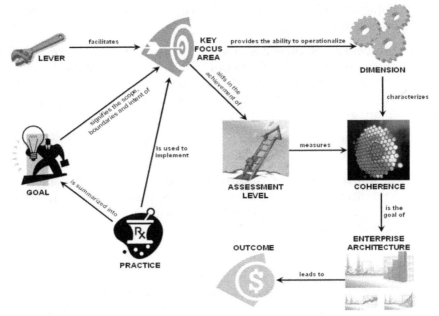

Figure 4. Coherency Management Assessment Framework Meta-model

Assessment Level: Represents the six successive levels of coherence - (1) Absent, (2) Introduced, (3) Encouraged, (4) Instituted, (5) Optimized, and (6) Innovating. Each assessment level is indicative of a level of coherence in the organization.

Key Focus Area: Represents the critical area that the organization needs to concentrate on in order to achieve a certain assessment level.

Goal: Is a cluster of related practices and ascertains whether a specific key focus area has been effectively dealt with.

Practice: Represents the activities that the organization needs to undertake to achieve a goal.

Enablers: Represent a factor that enables the operationalization of the coherency dimensions with the aim of enhancing organizational coherence. Levers include: (1) Awareness & Communication, (2) Policies, Plans and Procedures, (3) Tools and Systems, (4) Skills and Expertise, (5) Governance and Management, and (6) Goal Setting and Measurement.

Dimension: Characteristics that collectively embody the concept of coherence. For an organization to be assessed as coherent, it has to have a relatively high score on all of the five dimensions.

Outcome: Represents the conclusions that were reached through the development and implementation of the organization's EA. The three outcomes are: (1) Alignment, (2) Agility, and (3) Assurance. These are collectively termed as 'manageability'.

Coherence: Is the logical, orderly and consistent relation of different parts of the organization.

Enterprise Architecture: The fundamental organization of a system, embodied in its components, their relationships to each other and the environment, and principles governing its design and evolution (IEEE 1471-2000, 2000).

In addition to understanding, assessment allows organizations to design, implement and evaluate coherency in their respective situations. Towards this end, a formal *Coherency Management Assessment Framework* (CoMAF) is provided. Organizations have been using assessment / maturity models for several years and have reaped significant benefits. As of now, we see coherence and coherency management as an emerging management practice. The CoMAF, briefly presented in the next few sections, is a collection of best-practices that, in our experience, were found to be effective and are in actual use in organizations in different forms and intensities. It depicts the essential elements of organizational coherence.

As organizations grow, they become complex and unwieldy. In such situations, coherence is usually the casualty. Without formal coherency management activities the risks of incoherence are far too large to ignore. The CoMAF is a staged assessment approach that guides organizations to move to higher levels of coherency achievements. The CoMAF allows organizations to plan, design, analyze, implement and continuously innovate their coherency related activities, within the context of EA standards and activities. Collectively, the questions that CoMAF addresses include:

1. Can/are we able to know what the various levels of achievement organizations can reach are?

2. Do we have key focus areas for each of the assessment levels? What must we focus on?

3. How do focus areas facilitate organizational coherence?

4. What are the goals of each of the focus areas?

5. What EA outcomes do the focus areas support?

6. What activities need to be undertaken to achieve a goal?

Based on the questions above, the CoMAF has been structured as a collection of logically linked components to support different stakeholders and their needs.

Table 5 summarizes the complete CoMAF, and contains the *assessment levels, their brief descriptions* and *associated key focus areas*:

	Description	Key Focus Areas
Level 0 (ABSENT)	Characterized by absence of formal coherency mechanisms; while coherency may be assessed, there are no formal ways of doing it; the organization is completely reliant on individual contributors	0. None
Level 1 (INTRODUCED)	Organization recognizes the role of coherence and establishes ways and means to manage coherence; there is general willingness and consensus; formally practiced in some functions or departments of the organization, but not organization-wide.	1. Business Unit Facilitation and Commitment 2. Business Unit Product and Process Integration 3. Business Unit Process and Product Assurance 4. Qualitative Business Unit Assessment 5. Enterprise Architecture Program Tie-In
Level 2 (ENCOURAGED)	Value of coherency management is recognized; the organizational culture encourages activities pertaining to improving coherence; initial organization-wide practices and mechanisms are put in place.	6. Enterprise Perspective 7. Enterprise Competency Management 8. Enterprise Resource Management 9. Enterprise Configuration Management 10. Enterprise Policy, Rule and Procedure Management 11. Enterprise Architecture Activity Coordination
Level 3 (INSTITUTED)	Formal management of organizational coherence is practiced; mechanisms to share best practices are provided; centralized and shared repositories are established; leadership and management oversight is brought into the picture to formalize coherency and its management.	12. Enterprise Governance and Leadership 13. Enterprise Product and Process Integration 14. Enterprise Alignment Assessment 15. Enterprise Coherence Entities' Taxonomy 16. Enterprise Common Asset Management 17. Enterprise Architecture Repository Integration
Level 4 (OPTIMIZED)	Coherence and its impact on the organization is systematically assessed; the effectiveness is evaluated establish predictable outcomes.	18. Quantitative Capability and Performance Management 19. Risk Assessment and Management 20. Future Architecture Focus
Level 5 (INNOVATING)	Organization's processes on management of coherence are continuously reviewed' new process, activities and mechanisms are discovered and institutionalized in an ongoing basis.	21. Innovation Planning and Coordination 22. Planned Innovations 23. Opportunistic Innovations 24. Enterprise Innovation Adoption and Deployment

Table 5. Assessment Levels of Coherency Management

Figure 5 depicts the five dimensions of organizational coherency. For an organization to be considered coherent, it has to score well in all the five areas that collectively represent the extent of coherency. These dimensions are mutually exclusive and collectively exhaustive.

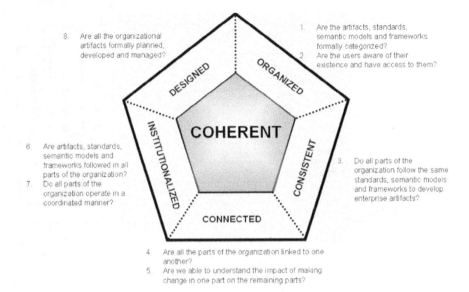

Figure 5. Dimensions of Organizational Coherence

To be able to successfully realize the assessment of coherency management, the next step is to associate the assessment levels (and their constituent key focus areas) to the coherency dimensions. Such an association addresses the issue of how the various key focus areas influence and impact the various areas of organizational coherency. This forms the very basis of coherency management as it allows organizations to design and execute their coherency management practices. Table 6 shows the linkages between the key focus areas and the dimensions of organizational coherency. For finer granularity the linkages have been categorised into 'primary' and 'secondary'.

Levels	Key Focus Areas Legend: P → Primary Enabler S → Secondary Enabler	Coherency Dimensions				
		Connected	Consistent	Organized	Designed	Institutionalized
Level 1	Business Unit Facilitation and Commitment	S	S	S	S	S
	Business Unit Product and Process Integration		S	S	S	
	Business Unit Product and Process Assurance	S		S		
	Qualitative Business Unit Assessment		S			S
	Enterprise Architecture Program Tie-In					P
Level 2	Enterprise-Wide Perspective	S	S			P
	Enterprise Competency Management		S		S	P
	Enterprise Resource Management		P	S	S	P
	Enterprise Configuration Management	S	P			S
	Enterprise Policy, Rule and Procedure Management		P	P	P	S
	Enterprise Architecture Activity Coordination	S	P	P		P
Level 3	Enterprise Governance and Leadership		S			P
	Enterprise Product and Process Integration	P	P	S		
	Enterprise Alignment Assessment	S	P			P
	Enterprise Taxonomy	P	S		S	P
	Enterprise Common Asset Management	S	S	S	S	P
	Enterprise Architecture Repository Integration	S	S	S	S	S
Level 4	Quantitative Capability and Performance Management	S	S	S	S	P
	Organization Risk Assessment and Management					S
	Future Architecture Focus		S		S	
Level 5	Organization Innovation Planning and Coordination			S	S	P
	Planned Innovations			S	S	P
	Opportunistic Innovations			S	S	P
	Enterprise Innovation Adoption and Deployment	P	P			P

Table 6. Mapping of Assessment Key Focus Areas to Coherency Dimensions

Maturity	Key Focus Areas		Arch. Outcomes Alignment	Agility	Assurance	Goals
Level 1	1	Business Unit Facilitation and Commitment	P			Effort is estimated. Commitments and agreements are approved Plans are documented and consistent.
	2	Business Unit Product and Process Integration		S	P	Activities and tasks are standardized. Results and outcomes are objectively evaluated. Non-conformances are resolved.
	3	Business Unit Product and Process Assurance	P		S	Linkages between work products are identified. Commonalities and standards are utilized. Work products are rationalized.
	4	Qualitative Business Unit Assessment	S	S	P	Coherence is evaluated qualitatively Evaluations are utilized as feedback
	5	Enterprise Architecture Program Tie-In	P		S	EA program is formalized EA program is established as a means to achieve coherency
Level 2	6	Enterprise-Wide Perspective	S	S	S	Active Participation and involvement. Participation and involvement is sustained.
	7	Enterprise Competency Management	S	S	S	Competency requirements are planned and developed. Competency requirements are fulfilled. Competency is evaluated.
	8	Enterprise Resource Management	S	S	S	Resources are identified and assigned to coherency practice. Resources are managed with capacity plans. Performance and results are linked to competency and assessed.
	9	Enterprise Configuration Management			P	Configurable items are identified Configurable items are controlled. Configurable items are reported.
	10	Enterprise Policy and Procedure Management	P	S	P	Processes, policies and procedures are identified and documented. Processes, policies and procedures are implemented. Processes, policies and procedures are integrated.
	11	Enterprise Architecture Activity Coordination	S	S	S	Enterprise architecture activities are formalized Enterprise architecture activities are coordinated
Level 3	12	Enterprise Governance and Leadership	P			Coherency is recognized as a critical business success factor. Top management attention and involvement is obtained. Governance modes and practices are designed. Governance models and practices are adopted.
	13	Enterprise Product and Process Integration	P	S	S	Assets are integrated. Commonalities and standards are utilized.
	14	Enterprise Alignment Assessment	P			Alignment viewpoints are identified Alignment is assessed. Alignment is reported.
	15	Enterprise Taxonomy	P			Coherency objects are identified. Coherency objects are categorized. Coherency objects are associated to processes, policies and procedures.
	16	Enterprise Common Asset Management		P	S	Common assets are developed. Common assets are utilized. Common assets are updated.
	17	Enterprise Architecture Repository Integration			S	Assets are integrated to the Enterprise Architecture repository
Level 4	18	Quantitative Capability and Performance Management	S	S	S	Performance indicators and metrics are established. Performance indicators and metrics are quantified. Baselines / benchmarks are established. Capability and performance is quantitatively assessed. Capability and performance is reported and acted upon.
	19	Enterprise Risk Assessment and Management			P	Risk factors are identified. Risks are quantified. Risks are reported. Root causes are determined and addressed.
	20	Future Architecture Focus	P		S	Future architecture is established and realized Future architecture is kept relevant Future architecture is used as a way to drive change
Level 5	21	Enterprise Innovation Planning and Coordination		P		Innovation strategies and practices are defined. Innovation framework and needs are established. Innovation is aligned with organizational objectives.
	22	Planned Innovations		P		Innovations are developed. Innovation deployments are planned.
	23	Opportunistic Innovations		P		Opportunities are monitored. Innovations are developed. Innovation deployments are planned.
	24	Enterprise Innovation Adoption and Deployment		P		Innovations are deployed. Innovation impacts are observed. Innovations are refined.

Table 7. Mapping of Assessment Key Focus Areas to Architecture Goals and Outcomes
[Legend: P → Primary Enabler | S → Secondary Enabler]

Chapter 1 presented and discussed the core theme of this book, i.e. using Enterprise Architecture as the means to achieve organizational coherency. We believe that EA has three primary outcomes: alignment, agility and assurance. As we see the role and impact of EA programmes extended beyond their use to build better IT systems to being a truly enterprise-wide organization design and transformation approach, the completion of coherency management assessment needs to factor in the primary outcomes of architecture programmes and the goals of each of CoMAF focus areas. Table 7 above is a mapping of the key focus areas to the EA outcomes and associated goals for the key focus areas.

As part of the CoMAF, Figure 5 and Table 5 represents the 'what' of the assessment framework, while Figures 6 and 7 depict 'how' the assessment framework could be used by organizations to design their coherency management practices. Between Tables 6 and 7, the CoMAF addresses the following key concerns:

1. In what way do the coherency key focus areas enable the coherency dimensions?

2. In what way do the coherency key focus areas influence and contribute to the achievement of architecture outcomes?

3. What are the goals of the coherency key focus areas?

A full and detailed description of the CoMAF is outside the scope of this chapter, so the practices and levers are not depicted here. We foresee the above described CoMAF being used in one or more of the following ways:

- As a guide for coherency improvement programs: This is expected to be its most frequent reason for extensive usage as it provides a structured and formal body of knowledge for organizations to adapt and adopt.

- Assessing the risk of lack of coherence (or incoherence): Most organizations understand the need for coherence, but generally lack the tools and techniques to assess and do something about it. 'Do-nothing' is not recommended for organizational coherency issues, and the risk of incoherence can be an effective trigger to get management on-board.

- Benchmarking: Management may use it to evaluate and compare where the organization stands relative to its key competitors and industry segment partners.

Conclusion

The ideas presented in this chapter are not representative of a single existing enterprise. They are a composite of the various ways in which EA is being applied today, brought together in a single practice (Coherency Management) under the broader discipline of Enterprise Architecture. We expect no enterprise to immediately implement the exact framework and models as shown. We would hope that the body of knowledge started today and carried forward allows enterprises to gradually introduce change to their organizations and begin to harvest the benefits of a more coherent business, sooner rather than later.

Given the substantive impact that coherency can have on an enterprise and the need for coherency in the discipline, this work needs to be collaborative in the broadest terms, therefore, we invite all readers to join www.coherencymanagement.org where we will continue the journey as a community.

EPILOGUE

Everything new and exciting becomes commonplace and less exciting over time. We are sure that fire was pretty big, electricity was probably exciting, and in-door plumbing might not have been 'exciting', but surely there was a time when it wasn't taken for granted. Ask anyone in a third world nation, where some of these things are still new and exciting prospects.

If an innovation survives the test of time, it will lead to others and eventually, what was 'new' sinks from our vision to become foundation. This is obvious in technology, as every new computer incorporates the latest advancements from around the world. This is not purely a technical reality. Our knowledge in medicine, the pure sciences, the universe, and our knowledge of ourselves as a species constantly evolves.

It is our contention that Enterprise Architecture is an innovation of the enduring sort. It will still be new for years and decades to come. But if it is to evolve, what does it become the foundation for? Before you answer that question, let's look at what we brought to you in this book.

We introduced a way to look at three distinct modes of EA in chapter one. The exact names and categorizations aren't the critical idea here. But we hope we made the case that things are moving in the exciting field of Enterprise Architecture.

We then saw several chapters on the EA discipline itself. We had the Four Design Models of Enterprise Architecture in chapter two, and the Business Engineering Navigator in chapter three which gave us a very interesting look at Enterprise Architecture Management. In chapter four we saw how to use EA as A Meta-Framework for Analyzing Architectural Efforts in Organizations. Chapter five tied together three interrelated fields, namely Enterprise Architecture, Strategic Management and Information Management. Keeping with the strategic theme, we presented the 'The Strategic Dimension of Enterprise Architecture' in chapter six. Finally, EA can't simply happen, it needs some rigor and course correction, which we gave it in chapter eight with Enterprise Architecture Formalization and Auditing.

Then we looked at several ways that EA is applied. We tackled very complex issues like Engineering the Sustainable Business in chapter seven, Mergers and Acquisitions as discussed in chapter nine, and crisis management as we saw it in chapter ten. We also saw how to bridge EA Goals and Technology Requirements with Conceptual Programming (chapter eleven). We then saw how it is evolving within a single company in chapter twelve.

Almost all chapters focused on the business value of the EA initiative, but some chapters moved us more into the business side of the conversation, such as chapter thirteen, which showed us how to realize the Business Value of Enterprise Architecture through Architecture Building Blocks. The reference models being developed for all orders of government in Canada are profoundly business oriented, as we saw in chapter fourteen. Interestingly, the case presented there has more business speak than technology speak.

As things evolve, we need to look closely at who does what, and the first stop has to be the Chief Information Officers and their relationship to Enterprise Architecture and Coherency Management which we presented in chapter fifteen. But we don't get anywhere without CEO support, so we presented that point of view in chapter sixteen. These people will need to support and believe in this expanded role for EA, especially when you look at the possibility of Enterprise Engineering as presented in chapter seventeen. All of this will be for naught, if you can't really solve the communication challenge. Chapter eighteen explained the world of Marketing Communications, which we need for EA and Coherency Management to be successful.

Then, we looked at the role of non-EA leaders and their part in coherency management. The organization responsible for reporting results within the Government of Canada is rolling out a modest change to its requirements this year. The standard by which you describe your internal or corporate services was developed in conjunction with the EA team. In chapter nineteen we looked at the standard and began to glimpse the future of coherency management. This is a future where everyone talks about the same things in the same manner.

Finally, in chapter twenty, we pulled all of these together and asked ourselves 'what if'. What if EA was really the overarching meta-discipline? What if it really broke through to the business side of the house? How would you use it? What would it do? And what would be the result?

This is not the building of a bridge. There is not a day in the future where we will put down our tools, remove the barricades and then redirect the traffic. This is continuous improvement! However, some day in the future a business decision will be more correct, an operation will be more efficient, knowledge will be more complete and someone will not remember that EA enabled it or that the coherency management practice was in the mix. These things will have become the ferment of future innovations.

Until that day, we have much to do, many steps to climb, mistakes to correct, innovations to discover and invent. It will take some time and some will get to coherency quicker than others, the same way that in-door plumbing has yet to reach everyone. Then someday we'll be chasing some other challenge because there is no more optimization to do, correction to find or waste to fix within our organization. We won't even remember the days where left hand and right hand were oblivious to each other. Yet, no one would fully appreciate the effort started when Zachman drew his first EA table and the thousands that would toil from that day forward. It would be taken for granted.

Imagine … a day when enterprises were coherent and nobody noticed.

INDEX

O

Object Management Group, 155, 292

Office of Personnel Management, 345

Offices of Primary Interest, 480

Operating Enterprise, 514

Organization Design, 382, 488

Outcome, 370, 389, 428, 483, 524

P

Personal Selling, 457

Policy Coordination Model, 396, 397

Powercor Australia, 257, 258, 259, 263

Profile, 9, 218, 382, 477, 479, 480, 481, 484, 486, 487, 491, 494

Program Activity Architecture, 479, 482, 483, 491, 494

Program Audit, 229, 230

Program Service Accountability Model, 373

Provincial Strategic Reference Model, 362

R

Reference Architecture, 46, 190, 211, 348, 452

Restructuring, 159

Risk Assessment, 152, 378, 526, 528, 529

S

Sarbanes-Oxley Act, 228, 389

Semantic Model, 368, 373

Semantics, 367

Senior Financial Officers, 480

Service Integration and Alignment Model, 373, 374, 376

Service Orientation, 437

Service-Oriented Architecture, 105

Shared Infrastructure, 112

Shared Responsibility Model, 396

Shared Services, 377

Small and Medium Enterprise, 285

Software Engineering Institute, 99, 222, 232

Software Product Lines, 296, 307

Solution Architecture Guidance, 351

Solutions Reference Model, 61

Standard CMMI Appraisal Method for Process Improvement, 222

Standard Operating Environment, 58

Standardization, 56, 59, 144

Standardized Construction Language, 83

Strategic Analysis, 162, 168

Strategic Capability Networks, 339

Strategic CBM Map, 341

Strategic Enterprise Architecture Framework, 159, 161, 173, 174

Strategic Gap Analysis, 339

Strategic Governance, 163, 169, 222

Strategic Planning, 123, 127, 129, 145, 179, 180, 260

Strategic Projects, 321, 327, 437

Strategy Execution, 163, 172, 177

Strategy Formulation, 162, 168, 172, 177

Structured Repository, 195

Sustainability Reporting Framework, 187

SWOT Analysis, 142, 152

Syngenta, 8, 311-30

System of Interest, 439, 443

Systematic Construction, 84

T

Target Group, 370, 373, 374
Target Group State
  Transition Model, 373
Technology Differentiation
  Model, 56, 59, 60, 61, 67, 70, 73
Technology Reference Model,
  58
Technology Standardization
  Model, 56, 57, 58, 59, 62, 67, 70,
  73
The Open Group Architecture
  Framework, 55, 74, 125, 146, 153,
  156, 328, 335
To-Be Architecture, 166
Toolkit, 77
Toyota Production System,
  251, 265
Transformation, 7, 25, 39, 159,
  233, 322, 335, 356, 398, 412
Transition Plan, 166, 167, 169,
  171, 176
Treasury Board Secretariat,
  47, 269, 477, 479, 494
Triple Bottom Line, 182, 212

U

US Federal Government, 52, 62,
  334
User Groups, 350

V

Value Chain, 344, 345
Value Imperative, 423
Value Proposition, 56
Variance Management, 517, 520
Vietnam, 387, 398, 399
View Model, 304
Viewpoints, 91
Virtual Enterprise, 265, 439
Virtual Organizations, 439

W

Winnipeg Fleet Management
  Agency, 360

Z

Zachman Framework, 13, 29, 54, 136,
  140, 146, 153, 156, 365, 382